BRACHYTHERAPY FROM RADIUM
TO OPTIMIZATION

DR FRANCES L W WONG

Brachytherapy from Radium to Optimization

Edited by

R.F. Mould
J.J. Battermann
A.A. Martinez
&
B.L. Speiser

COPYRIGHT STATEMENT

© 1994

ISBN 90-5353-035-5

Published by:

Nucletron International B.V., Waardgelder 1, 3905 TH Veenendaal, The Netherlands, Tel. (31) 8385-33133, Fax (31) 8385-50485.

Subsidiaries

Australia
Nucletron Pty. Limited
Suite 3, 2nd Floor
79-85 Oxford Street
Bondi Junction, Sydney
NSW. 2022
Tel.   (61) 2 369-1990
Fax   (61) 2 369-1994

Belgium
S.A. Nucletron N.V.
Jos Ratinckxstraat 3
2600 Antwerpen
Tel.   (32) 3 4481525
Fax   (32) 3 4481846

Federal Republic of Germany
Theranostic Medizintechnik GmbH
Huestrasse 109
D-45309 Essen
Tel.   (49) 201-21815
Fax   (49) 201-297911

France
Nucletron S.A.R.L.
182/184 Avenue du Maréchal
de Lattre de Tassigny
94134 Fontenay-Sous-Bois Cedex
Tel.   (33) 1-48778599
Fax   (33) 1-48777439

Hong Kong
Nucletron Far East (HK) Ltd.
4F/406, Tsimshatsui Center
66 Mody Road
Tsimshatsui East, Kowloon
Tel.   (852) 311-
         2683/2684/3025
Fax   (852) 311-3672
Telex 43979 nucle hx

India
Nucletron Trading PVT Ltd.
No.2, D'Silva Road
Mylapore
Madras - 600 004
Tel.   (91) 44-4991871
         44 -4992877
Fax   (91) 44-4991967
Telex 41-8010 nucle in

Italy
Nuclital S.R.L.
Via Monte Cervino 21
20052 Monza (Milan)
Tel.   (39) 39-745156/745937
Fax   (39) 39-735037

People's Republic of China
Nucletron Far East (HK) Ltd.
Beijing Liaison Office
12D Citic Building
Jianguo Men Wei
Beijing, 100004
Tel.   (86) 5002255-1264
Fax   (86) 5002255-1264

Spain
Nucletron S.A.
C/Montera 33
28013 Madrid
Tel.   (34) 1 523-4454
Fax   (34) 1 521-0838

United Kingdom
Nucletron UK Limited
Nucletron House
Chowley Oak
Tattenhall
Chester CH3 9EX
Tel.   (44) 829-71111
Fax   (44) 829-70979

USA
Nucletron Corporation
Sales/Service
7080 Columbia
Gateway Drive
Columbia MD 21046-2133
Tel.   (1) 410-312-4100
Fax   (1) 410-312-4199

Printed and bound by Veenman Drukkers, Wageningen, The Netherlands.

Contents

Head & Neck Brachytherapy

Brain Tumours & Stereotactic Radiosurgery

Intralumenal Brachytherapy

Interstitial Brachytherapy

Pulsed Brachytherapy

Safety & Quality Assurance

Optimization & 3-Dimensional Treatment Planning

Brachytherapy for the Future

Editorial Note

Brachytherapy From Radium to Optimization is the latest in a series of brachytherapy reference books published by Nucletron. The majority of the chapters are updated work from that presented at the International Brachytherapy Working Conference held in Baltimore, MD, USA in September 1992. Following a historical introduction there are major sections on:

Radiobiology
Gynaecological Brachytherapy
Head & Neck Brachytherapy
Brain Tumours & Stereotactic Radiosurgery
Intralumenal Brachytherapy
Interstitial Brachytherapy
Pulsed Brachytherapy
Safety & Quality Assurance
Optimisation & 3-Dimensional Treatment Planning
Brachytherapy for the Future

These chapters represent a useful compendium of current brachytherapy practice which together with a comprehensive Subject Index gives the reader easy access to all topics.

I would like to take this opportunity to express my thanks to my editorial colleagues, Prof. Jan Battermann, Dr Burton Speiser and Dr Alvaro Martinez, for their considerable help. In addition, I am most grateful to Ms. Jacqueline van Zetten for her valuable secretarial assistance and to Mr. Reggy Schreuders for his expertise with the desk top publishing work necessary for the production of the book. Finally, the helpful encouragement and advice of Mr. Eric van 't Hooft and Mr. Miles Mount is gratefully acknowledged.

Richard F. Mould
February 1994

1

Radium Brachytherapy: Historical Review

R.F. Mould

2, Elmfield Way,
South Croydon,
Surrey CR2 0ED,
United Kingdom.

Introduction

Radium was discovered in Paris in 1898 by Marie and Pierre Curie and within five years the first successful brachytherapy treatment for cancer had been histologically proven (two cases of basal cell carcinoma of the face: in St. Petersburg 1903), the principle of afterloading had been proposed in the medical literature (Munich 1903) and surface moulds, intracavitary and interstitial techniques had been applied.

The beginnings of dosimetry occured around 1904 with a proposal for a gamma-ray unit of strength/intensity/activity. Terminology varied but this first unit was typically defined by the following statement. 'Radium when pure, has about 2,000,000 times the activity of an equal weight of uranium. Its activity is therefore said to be 2,000,000'. This was followed by the units milligram-hour (1909), curie (1910) and millicurie-destroyed (1914). Units based on biological effects were also proposed and the Quimby & Failla (1933) defined threshold erythema dose (TED) was equated by Quimby in 1944 in her publication *'Dosage tables for linear radium sources'* as being equivalent to 1000 gamma-röntgens.

However, until the general acceptance of the röntgen as a unit for both X-rays and gamma rays, following the ICRU 1937 recommendation, the milligram-hour remained by far the most popular radium unit, with the millicuri-destroyed per sq.cm the most popular unit for radon applications.

Radium sources, generally tubes and needles but also small capsules (as with the Heyman radium packing technique for cancer of the endometrium) remained in widespread clinical use well into the 1960s and even today in some non-industrialised countries they are still occasionally used.

However, the biggest problem today with radium is the disposal of the obsolete sources since currently there is great resistance from governments to provide disposal sites for such a long-lived radioactive material. Many hospitals worldwide are therefore forced to retain their old radium stock, although unused for several years. One such example of historical interest is in the Maria Sklodowska-Curie Memorial Cancer Center & Institute of Oncology (formerly named the Radium Institute) in Warsaw, where the stored but no longer used radium stock is that actually given by Marie Curie to the Institute. The engraved initials MSC (for Maria Sklodowska-Curie) can still be deciphered: although in some cases because of long usage only the letter M can be visualised.

The words *quality control* are now a feature of importance in brachytherapy, but they really only entered into fashion in the 1980s. Previously with radium there were in fact some quality control procedures but they fell into the classification of radiation protection procedures. These included wipe tests and autoradiographs to determine whether a source was fractured (the frequency of these tests depended on the number of staff available for the task) and counting 'out' and counting 'in' the number of sources moved from a radium stock room to operating theatre to ward, back to operating theatre and back to the radium stock room. There were in practice plenty of opportunities for loss of radium sources in the 1930s and earlier and many 'horror stories' of monitoring sewers, incinerators, pigs and garbage disposal dumps exist from this time.

That these searches were not always successful was due in part to the then technology of survey monitors: a gold leaf electroscope was not good enough, for instance, if the source was lodged 10 cm beneath a drain cover in the drain wall mud (as the writer found in 1963!). The era of the Geiger counter had to appear before adequate technology was available.

The single most important dosimetry proposal in the radium era was the Manchester system of Paterson & Parker, which was devised in the 1930s. This stood the test of time for more than 30 years and was a standard worldwide. It is only now with the technological advances in computer treatment planning and systems such as that of Paris for iridium-192 wire and ribbon sources, that have made the Manchester system largely redundant, both for point A doses for cancer of the cervix as the sole dosimetric requirement, and also for the interstitial geometrical and activity rules for single plane, double plane and volume implants. Surface mould dosimetry was equivalent to single plane interstitial implants.

This brief review, with several illustrations which evoke the early treatments far better than mere words, will now continue with surface moulds, intracavitary, interstitial and intralumenal techniques. These provide a great contrast with the brachytherapy techniques leading up to the end of the 20th. century, which are described in the remaining chapters of *Brachytherapy from Radium to Optimization*.

Surface Mould Brachytherapy

Many of the early radium techniques were those involving a surface application. Radium tubes and needles could be mounted on wax, leather, plaster of Paris or other suitable material, with this 'base' being moulded to the shape of the area for treatment such as face or neck. The advantage of the method was that the radium was easy to apply: just position the mould, plaque or applicator (three terms for the same device) in the correct position and leave it in position for a fixed number of hours, which could be spread over a given number of fractions.

Figure 1 shows the Skin Department of St. Vincent's Hospital, Melbourne, Australia in 1905 with five patients all sitting in line holding their applicators in position: radiation protection was obviously not considered a problem. Figure 2

Figure 1. Surface applicator treatment in a Skin Department.

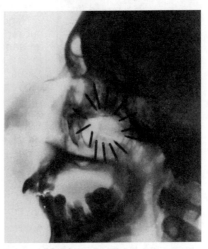

Figure 2. Surface applicator for which a uniform distribution of radium sources was used and it was incorrectly thought that this would provide a uniform dose distribution at the treating distance. This fallacy was corrected with the Manchester system of Paterson & Parker.

Figure 3. Treatment of a rodent ulcer in the temporal region using 14 radium needles.

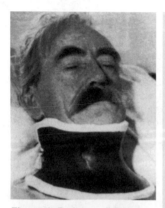

Figure 4. Radium collar.

Figure 5. Oropharyngeal radium applicator holding apparatus.

Figure 6. Paris technique cork applicators.

is from the late-1920s/early-1930s, prior to the Manchester system papers. It dates from the period when it was often assumed that a uniform distribution of radium sources would produce at a treatment depth below the applicator, usually 0.5 cm or 1.0 cm, a uniform radiation dose distribution. It was not realised that this assumption was incorrect.

Figure 2 uses radium tubes for the applicator but radium needles could equally well be used, as seen from Figure 3 for the treatment of a rodent ulcer of the temporal region in the mid-1920s. The eyelets in some of these needles can be clearly seen. Radium collars were a special type of surface applicator, of which Figure 4 is an example from the 1920s. This is a Columbia paste collar for the treatment of the cervical area and is 15 mm thick. The radium sources are beneath the adhesive plaster strip and in this manner fixed in position to the paste collar.

Intracavitary Brachytherapy

From the inception of brachytherapy, the site most often treated using intracavitary methods was the cervix uteri, although there were other sites amenable to intracavitary techniques, such as endometrium (for which the standard technique was Heyman packing with radium capsules), vagina, rectum and nasopharynx. The oropharynx could also be described as a 'cavity' and Figure 5 shows a rather unusual technique as advertised in a 1935 issue of Acta Radiologica, for an apparatus for holding radium sources in the treatment position.

Table 1
Summary of treatment schedules for Paris, Stockholm and Manchester techniques
for the intracavitary treatment of cancer of the cervix uteri.

System	Schedule
Paris	Continuous treatment for 120 hours Uterine tube of 33.3 mg radium Two vaginal cylindrical corks: 13.3 mg radium each
Stockholm	Three insertions each of 22 hours: separated by 1-2 weeks Uterine tube of 50 mg radium Two vaginal silver boxes containing a total of 60-80 mg radium
Manchester	Two insertions each of 72 hours delivered over 10 days Three uterine sources were available and the choice depended on the length of the uterine cavity. Source activities were 35, 25 and 20 mg radium for uterine lengths of 6, 4 and 2 cm. Large, medium and small vaginal ovoids were available with activities of respectively 22.5, 20 and 17.5 mg radium.

However, to return to cancer of the cervix, Table 1 gives the treatment schedules for the three major techniques of the radium era. The Paris system with its cork applicators, Figure 6, was the first of these techniques and the Manchester system with the black rubber vaginal ovoids was an improvement on the original cork applicator design, Figure 7. Examples of Stockholm box applicators are also shown in this figure. There were, though, many other designs of applicator, including the forerunner of the modern ring applicator: Figure 8 is from Munich in 1920. The total number of gynaecological applicator designs during the 20th century probably totals in excess of 300 when one considers pre-loaded radium designs, those for manual and remote afterloading, those with and without shielding and afterloading design modifications relating to the fixation methods for the vaginal and uterine portions of the applicator.

Although the role of intracavitary brachytherapy for cancer of the cervix is now well accepted, this was not always the situation and the physicians who espoused the use of radium in the 1920s and earlier were engaged in 'warlike verbal exchanges' with the gynaecological surgeons who stuck to the view that

Figure 7. Manchester technique vaginal
ovoids and Stockholm technique boxes.   **Figure 8.** 1920 design of a ring applicator.

only surgery was worthwhile considering. It is therefore interesting to view the radium *versus* surgery figures of the mid-1920s which were used as 'ammunition' by those promoting the use of radium in a generally hostile medical environment, Table 2.

Table 2
Comparison between surgery and radium
in terms of five-year survival rates.

Radium

Five-year rates after radium as quoted by
Regaud of Paris at the International Society
of Surgery in Rome, 1926. Results have
been combined from several centres.

Grade	Definition	5-year rate (%)
I	Early cases	40-60
II	Operable	30-40
III + IV	Inoperable	5-15
I-IV	All cases	15-20

Surgery

Five-year rates after surgery as quoted by
Heyman of Stockholm in Acta Radiologica,
1927. Results for 'permanent cures' for the
Wertheim operation.

Series	5-year rate (%)
Bonney	41
Franz: two series	45 & later 54
24 of the best series	
for a total of 3659 operations	35

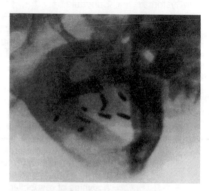

Figure 9. Radon seeds in platinum used to treat the tongue and floor of mouth.

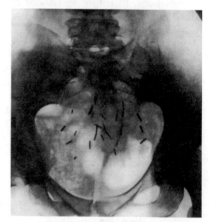

Figure 10. Radon seed treatment for cancer of the rectum.

Interstitial Brachytherapy

Interstitial brachytherapy was first suggested in the USA by Alexander Graham Bell (1903), the inventor of the telephone, but was independently being used in France and Germany at about the same time and therefore it is difficult to give priority to any one person. However, the first interstitial brachytherapy case illustrated in the medical literature was from Dublin, Ireland in 1914. Two cases were reported on, one was for treatment of an inoperable parotid sarcoma and the second was for the treatment of a non-malignancy: a fibrous scar. The radioactive sources were radon within glass capillary tubes placed 'within ordinary steel serum needles as supplied by any medical instrument maker'.

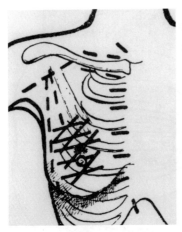

Figure 11. Interstitial brachytherapy plan for the treatment of cancer of the breast.

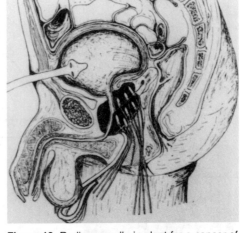

Figure 12. Radium needle implant for a cancer of the prostate.

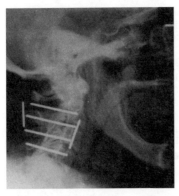

Figure 13. Radium needle implant to the neck according to the Manchester system of Paterson & Parker.

Radon seeds were indeed very popular for interstitial work which was by no means limited to radium needles. Figure 9 shows a radiograph (then called a skiagram) circa. 1920 of '10 removeable platinum seeds in the tongue and floor of mouth' and Figure 10 from 1929 shows a radiograph of a radon seed treatment of a cancer of the rectum.

Figure 11 shows the arrangement in 1929 of radium needles to treat a carcinoma of the breast where a total of 32 sources can be identified. A total dose of 16,000-21,000 milligram-hours was not unusual. Prostatic cancer was also treated by interstitial radium needling from the early 1920s. Figure 12 shows an open perineal approach for a technique where the needles were left in position 18-21 days for an average dose of some 7,000 milligram-hours.

Figure 13 ends this interstitial group of illustrations with a more readily recognisable technique than those of Figures 9-12. It is from a later period, the 1960s, and is a Paterson & Parker radium implant to the neck, using a 1 cm separation between needles with both implant ends crossed.

Intralumenal Brachytherapy

The only intralumenal techniques applied using radon seeds or radium needles were for cancers of the oesophagus and to a much lesser extent cancers

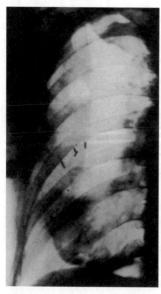

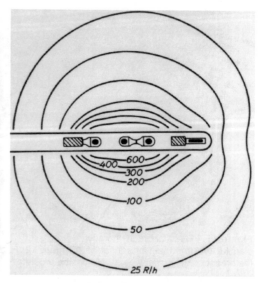

Figure 14. Radon treatment of bronchial carcinoma.

Figure 15. Isodose distribution for the Walstam remote afterloading machine which just preceded the Henschke remote afterloader with its cycling source.

of the lung. Figure 14 shows a radon seed treatment for a technique which was first attempted in New York in 1921, following which it was observed that 'the implantation of radon in the lower respiratory tract for bronchial carcinoma is an advance in the treatment of what has been a hopeless condition. Even this, however, is probably not the last word in the treatment of bronchial carcinoma'. A very prophetic comment when one now considers the possibilities with HDR remote afterloading brachytherapy using an iridium-192 stepping source and the great improvement in quality of life which can be achieved.

Afterloading

With a book devoted to modern brachytherapy techniques of afterloading and of dosimetry optimisation, it is appropriate to end this review with a diagram relating to the first remote afterloading machine described in the literature (1962). This was designed by Rune Walstam at the Radiumhemmet in Stockholm with a three-linked source system of three 50 mg and one 9 mg radium tubes. Figure 15 shows the distribution in röntgen/hour.

Reference Source

The material for this chapter has been obtained during historical research for the 1993 Mould R.F. book *'A History of X-Rays & Radioactivity in Medicine with Emphasis on Photographic Records of the Early Years'* published by the Institute of Physics, Bristol & Philadelphia.

2

Dose Rate Considerations

E.J. Hall

Center for Radiological Research,
College of Physicians & Surgeons,
Columbia University,
New York,
NY 10032,
USA.

Introduction

Implanting radioactive sources directly into a tumour was a strategy first suggested by Alexander Graham Bell (1903) soon after the turn of the century. Various groups in different countries coined different names for this type of therapy, using the prefix *brachy* from the Greek for *'short-range'*, or *endo* from the Greek for *'within'*.

This chapter reviews the rationale for the use of low dose rate (LDR) brachytherapy and its alternatives, high dose rate (HDR) brachytherapy and the recently developed pulsed brachytherapy (PDR). Low dose rate continuous irradiation has similar biological advantages to hyperfractionation. In many instances the ability to place radioactive sources by topical mould, intracavitary or interstitial placement in close proximity to, or within a tumour, represents the optimal conformal dose delivery system for targeting high doses of radiation to target tissues and minimising radiation damage to normal adjacent tissues.

Rationale for Low Dose Rate

LDR brachytherapy is characterised by three factors, [1] to [3] overleaf, all of which contribute to its efficacy.

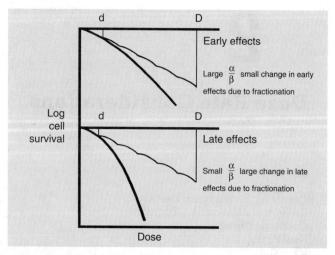

Figure 1. Comparing the effect of fractionation (and dose rate) on early and late responding tissues. The dose response relationship for late responding tissues is more 'curvy' for late than for early responding tissues, ie. α/β is smaller for late than early. Consequently, the effect of fractionation is more pronounced in late responding tissue. There is also a larger dose rate effect since continuous low dose rate is effectively an infinite number of infinitely small doses.

[1] Since the dose is delivered by radioactive sources in or near the tumour, good dose distributions can usually be achieved. This is a physical advantage and will not be discussed further here.

[2] Since the radiation is delivered continuously over a period of time, repair of sublethal damage can take place during the treatment maximising the differential between early and late responding tissues.

[3] LDR is usually delivered over a much shorter overall treatment time than conventional external beam radiotherapy: accelerated treatment par excellence.

In the early 1980s Withers et al (1982) made the key observation that early and late responding tissues respond in a very different way to the effects of fractionation and, by implication, dose rate. To understand their insight, consider the dose response curves in Figure 1. Since the dose response curve for late responding tissues is more *curvy* than for early responding tissues, an increase in the number of fractions (or a decrease in dose rate) causes a relatively bigger change for late than for early responding tissues.

To put it another way, for a given dose, increasing the dose rate will increase late effects much more than it will increase tumour control. Conversely, decreasing the dose rate will decrease late effects much more than it will decrease tumour control. Thus, the therapeutic ratio (ratio of tumour control to complications) will increase as the dose rate decreases.

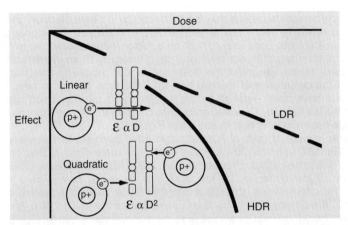

Figure 2. Illustration of the production of two double strand breaks, which interact to form lethal lesions that kill the cell. At low doses both breaks are likely to be caused by a single electron: the probability of an interaction is proportional to dose. At high doses in an acute exposure the two chromosome breaks are likely to result from different electrons: the probability of interaction is proportional to (dose)^2. In protracted exposures at low dose rate, the dose response curve is simply an extension of the initial slope.

This differential between early and late effects for LDR, as well as in itself improving the therapeutic ratio, allows the delivery of a complete treatment in a short time, allowing the effects of tumour repopulation to be minimised.

These then are the primary rationales for LDR radiotherapy & three *golden rules* follow: see below.

[1] In general, decreasing the dose rate increases the therapeutic ratio, limited only by tumour cell repopulation.

[2] The relative efficacy of LDR will depend on the tumour cell repopulation rate.

[3] Alternative protraction schemes involving smaller numbers of fractions or higher dose rates should, in general, be designed based on equi effect considerations for late complications, not tumour control.

In parallel with the development of a clear radiobiological rationale for LDR has been the development of biophysical models for predicting responses to alternative fractionation schemes based on the linear quadratic formulation.

Laboratory Dose Rate Studies

The rate at which radiation is delivered is one of the most important factors which determines the biological consequences of a given total dose. The dose rate effect is best understood in terms of the production and repair of the basic radiation lesion, namely the interaction between two double strand chromosome breaks.

Two chromosome breaks may be produced by a single electron; the probability of a resulting interaction is proportional to dose and since only a single electron is involved, dose rate cannot be a factor. Alternatively, the two breaks may result from two different electrons; the probability of an interaction is then proportional to the **square** of the dose and is also related to the time interval between the occurrence of the two breaks. If the time interval is long, the first break may have been repaired before the second occurs, in which case there can be no interaction. Consequently, this component of radiation damage is dose rate dependent. This is illustrated in Figure 2.

A wide variety of cells of human origin have been studied *in vitro*, normal and malignant, exposed to high and low dose rates (Hall & Bedford 1964, Bedford & Mitchell 1973, Brenner & Hall 1991, Kelland & Steel 1986, 1988). The survival curves fan out at low dose rate because, as well as a range of intrinsic radiosensitivities, there is a range of repair times of sublethal damage, Figure 3. Frequency distributions are available of the values of α and β (the constants from the linear quadratic fit to the survival data) and for $T_{1/2}$ (the half-time of repair of sublethal damage) (Brenner & Hall 1991a). There are limited quantitative data for the *in vivo* situation (Ang et al 1987).

Brachytherapy Dose Rate Variation: Clinical Significance

Interstitial implants usually involve the range of dose rates where the variation of biological effect with dose rate is substantial and important, at least as

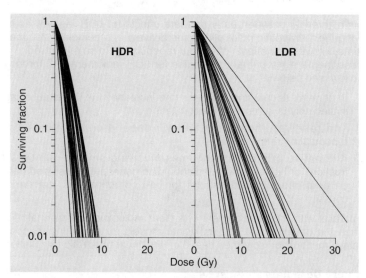

Figure 3. Survival curves for 40 cell lines of human origin cultured *in vitro* and irradiated at high dose rate (HDR), shown in the left hand panel, or at low dose rate (LDR) shown in the right hand panel. The data analysis is described in detail in Brenner & Hall (1991a). Note how the survival curves fan out at low dose rate because of the variation of repair times of sublethal damage as well as the variation of intrinsic radiosensitivity.

observed for cells in culture where precise measurements are possible. In the case of interstitial implants with radium needles it was pointed out by Paterson (1963) that the limiting factor is the normal tissue tolerance, which should be used fully to maximise the possibility of tumour control.

The maximum dose that can be delivered without unacceptable damage to surrounding normal tissue depends critically on the dose rate as well as on the volume of tissue irradiated. In the 1960s, Paterson (1963) and Ellis (1968) independently proposed equi-effect doses based on limiting late effects, for treatments given at different dose rates. With 60 Gy in seven days as the standard, they proposed that an implant of shorter duration should use a slightly lower dose, and an implant of longer duration an augmented dose, Figure 4.

The introduction of iridium-192 wire as a substitute for radium needles in interstitial brachytherapy, resulted in a considerably larger variation of dose rates associated with implants. Two factors are involved.

[1] The relative short half-life of iridium-192, of 74 days means that during the period of several months that the material is clinically useful there will be a range of linear activities.

[2] The Paris system of dosimetry, using the same linear activity for all sources and varying the separation of the radioactive wires for different lengths also results in dose rate variations. Larger volumes contain more activity and are associated with higher dose rates.

These two factors result in a threefold variation in the total irradiation time for delivery of a given tumour dose, (Pierquin et al 1973). Nevertheless,

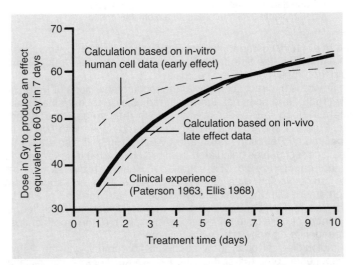

Figure 4. Dose equivalent to 60 Gy in 7 days calculated in different ways. (a) Based on clinical experience of normal tissue tolerance. (b) Calculated from α/β and $T_{1/2}$ values related to late effects. (c) Calculated from the average from a/ß and $T_{1/2}$ values for cells of human origin cultured in vitro, ie. early effects.

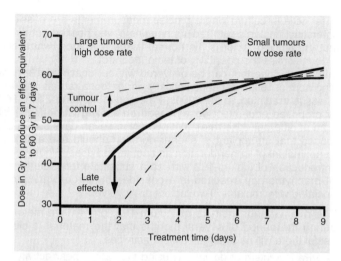

Figure 5. Solid lines: Calculated iso-effect curves for *in vitro* data representing tumours and *in vivo* data corresponding to late responding normal tissue. Dotted lines: These illustrate qualitatively the way in which the iso-effect curves change owing to the bias of higher dose rates being associated with larger tumours. Larger tumours require a larger dose for a given level of local control. This tends to flatten the iso-effect curve for tumour control. By contrast, the iso-effect curve for late effects in normal tissues is steeper since larger implanted volumes can tolerate smaller doses.

Pierquin et al (1973) came to the conclusion that, over an overall time range of three to eight days, the time factor (and therefore the dose rate) was unimportant, both for tumour control and necrosis.

This advice is in direct conflict with the recommendations of Paterson (1963) and Ellis (1968), and does not agree with radiobiological data that would predict a substantial dose rate effect over the dose rate range used in iridium-192 implants. Figure 4 shows the variation in tolerance dose with overall treatment time proposed by Paterson (1963) and by Ellis (1968). It also shows the corresponding isoeffect curves calculated from radiobiological data for cells in culture and for late effects *in vivo*. The variation in dose with overall time calculated from the radiobiological data relating to late effects *in vivo* shows remarkably close agreement with the clinical experience of Paterson and of Ellis based on tissue tolerance. The isoeffect curve for any early responding tissue, including tumour control or cells cultured *in vitro*, is shallower ie. the isoeffect dose shows **less** dependence on dose rate or overall time.

The radiobiological data, then, seems in agreement with the Paterson and Ellis recommendations, rather than the Paris predictions. A complication in the interpretation of clinical data relating dose to produce an equivalent effect to implant time (and therefore to dose rate) is the fact that, for interstitial implants, the dose rate tends to increase as the size of the implant increases. This correlation is particularly strong for implants using iridium-192 wires, as used in the

Paris system, which are all of the same linear activity, but less so when there is a variation in linear activity, as in the Paterson & Parker system (Meredith 1967). The bias of larger tumours and larger volumes associated with high dose rates, while smaller tumours and smaller treatment volumes are associated with lower dose rates, was pointed out by Pierquin et al (1973). Larger tumours require a larger dose for a given level of local control, while the maximum dose that can be tolerated by normal tissues decreases as the volume implanted increases.

This volume/dose rate bias has an interesting effect on the isoeffect curves. At the one extreme, higher dose rates are associated with large tumours and large implanted volumes. This will **increase** the dose required to result in a given level of tumour control and **decrease** the dose that can be tolerated to produce a given level of necrosis ie. the tumour control isoeffect curve is made shallower, and the normal tissue isoeffect curve is made steeper by the bias of high dose rate being associated with larger tumours and vice-versa. This is illustrated in Figure 5.

Based on these considerations, and with the benefit of hindsight, it is clear why the Paris school and the Paterson/Ellis school differed so radically in their prescriptions for dealing with dose rate changes. The correlation between tumour size and dose rate flattens the isoeffect curve for tumour control, but does not remove the dependence on dose rate. We conclude, therefore, that in general, dose rate is an important factor in determining the outcome of interstitial, and presumably intracavitary brachytherapy.

Two recent papers from the Paris school would seem to confirm this conclusion. The first describes the analysis of local tumour control and incidence of necrosis in a large cohort of patients with T1 and T2 squamous cell carcinoma of the mobile tongue and the floor of the mouth, who were treated with interstitial iridium-192 (Mazeron 1991b). Patients were grouped according to dose rate, either more or less than 0.5 Gy/hour. There is a substantially higher incidence of necrosis in patients treated at the higher dose rate. By contrast, dose rate makes little or no difference to local control provided the total dose is high enough, namely 65-70 Gy, but there is a clear separation at lower doses (60 Gy), with the lower dose rate being less effective. These results are in good accord with the radiobiological predictions, where the isoeffect curve is steep for late effects (necrosis) but shallow for early effects, including tumour control.

The second paper analyses data from a large group of patients with carcinoma of the breast who received an iridium-192 implant as a boost to external beam radiotherapy (Mazeron 1991a). These results allow an assessment of the effect of dose rate on tumour control, but provide no information on the effect of dose rate on late effects, since there was only one case that involved necrosis. The interstitial implant comprised only part of the radiotherapy and a fixed standard dose was used, so only limited conclusions can be drawn from these data. However, the results show a correlation between the proportion of recurrent tumours and the dose rate. For a given total dose, there were markedly fewer recurrences when the radiation was delivered at a higher dose rate rather than a lower dose rate. The authors concluded that the higher dose rates should be used. This is a reasonable conclusion in view of the virtual absence of significant late effects. However, an alternative conclusion would be to use a lower dose rate and increase the total dose with a view to maximising the therapeutic differential.

Rationale for Fractionated HDR versus LDR for Cancer of the Cervix

Based largely on patient convenience, cost and machine availability, there is a strong move towards the use of HDR intracavitary brachytherapy for treating carcinoma of the uterine cervix. In general, a move from LDR to HDR involves a greater probability of late effects for a given level of tumour control.

There is, however, an exception to this rule pointed out by Dale (1990) and Brenner & Hall (1991,b). This is for intracavitary brachytherapy of the uterine cervix. What makes this situation different from almost all others is that the radiation dose that produces unwanted late sequelae is significantly less than the treatment dose. This is because the dose limiting organs at risk, rectum & bladder are some distance away from the brachytherapy sources. An additional factor to consider is that the short treatment time characteristic of HDR allows packing and retraction of the sensitive organs, estimated by Orton (1992) to result in a 20% further decrease in rectal/bladder dose. This is a physical **advantage** that more than cancels out the radiobiological **disadvantages**.

The radiobiological principles summarised above lead to clear guidelines as to the use of HDR brachytherapy of cancer of the cervix.

[1]   When the dose to the dose limiting critical normal tissues, bladder & rectum is less than about 75% of the prescribed dose, for equal early responses, HDR results in comparable (or less) late effects than LDR.

[2]   For those patients where the dose to the bladder/rectum is comparable to the prescribed dose, HDR is contraindicated.

[3]   When HDR is indicated, HDR protocols comparable to those at LDR should be designed based on matching **early** rather than late effects.

[4]   For other sites of interest for HDR (eg. endometrium), unless the dose limiting organs receive a significantly smaller dose than the treatment dose, HDR might be expected to result in some loss in therapeutic efficacy.

Pulsed Brachytherapy

The general idea here, as illustrated in Figure 6, is to replace a continuous LDR interstitial treatment lasting several days with a series of short, ~10 minute, HDR irradiations say, every hour. This technique has come to be known as pulsed brachytherapy (PDR). During each pulse, a single, high activity source would be stepped through all the catheters of the implant, with computer controlled dwell times in each position reflecting the required dose distribution. There are obvious practical advantages for the patient, as well as the potential of improved dose optimisation. These include the use of a single source, which removes the need to maintain an inventory of different sources.

The radiobiological problem is to determine what pulse, and what repetition frequency, would yield equivalence between PDR and continuous LDR. Based on α/β data and repair times of sublethal damage for more than 40 sets of sur-

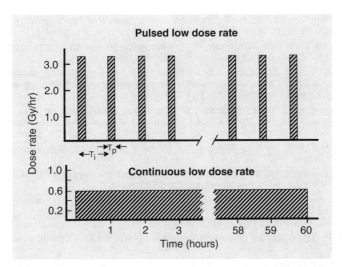

Figure 6. Illustration of the principle of pulsed brachytherapy. Continuous low dose rate irradiation at (say) 60 cGy/hr is replaced by a 10 minute pulse repeated every hour in which a dose of 60 cGy is given. As the iridium-192 source decays the pulse length is increased to compensate and maintain the average dose rate.

vival curves for cells of human origin cultured *in vitro*, Brenner & Hall (1991a) concluded that a 10 minute pulse, repeated at hourly intervals, would produce a biological effect that was essentially indistinguishable from continuous irradiation at 0.5 Gy per hour.

In addition, to the advantages mentioned above, PDR allows the overall treatment time and the average dose rate to be maintained as the activity of the source decays by simply increasing the pulse length. The problems of a changing dose rate discussed in the previous section, are thus avoided.

References

Ang KK, Thames HD, van der Kogel AJ & van der Schueren E, *Is the rate of repair of radiation induced sub-lethal damage in rat spinal cord dependent on the size of dose per fraction?*, Int. J. Radiation Oncology Biology & Physics, **13**, 557-562, 1987.

Bell AG, *The uses of radium*, American Medicine, **6**, 261, 1903.

Brenner DJ & Hall EJ, *Conditions for the equivalence of continuous to pulsed low dose rate brachytherapy*, Int. J. Radiation Oncology Biology & Physics, **20**, 181-190, 1991a.

Brenner DJ & Hall EJ, *Fractionated high dose rate versus low dose rate regimens for intracavitary brachytherapy of the cervix. 1. General considerations based on radiobiology*, Brit. J. Radiobiology, **64**, 133-144, 1991b.

Dale RG, *The use of small fraction numbers in high dose rate gynaecological afterloading: some radiobiological considerations*, Brit. J. Radiology, 63, 290-294, 1990.

Ellis F, *Dose time and fractionation in radiotherapy, in:Current topics in radiation research*, Ebert M & Howard A (Eds), 359-397, North Holland Publishing Company:Amsterdam, 1968.

Hall EJ & Bedford JS, *Dose rate: its effect on the survival of HeLa cells irradiated with gamma-rays*, Radiation Research, **22**, 305-315, 1964.

Kelland LR & Steel GG, *Differences in radiation response among human cervix carcinoma cell lines*, Radiotherapy & Oncology, 7, 259-268, 1988.

Mazeron JJ, Simon JM & Crook J et al, *Influence of dose rate on local control of breast carcinoma treated by external beam irradiation plus iridium-192 implant*, Int. J. Radiation Oncology Biology & Physics, **21**, 1173-1177, 1991a.

Mazeron JJ, Simon JM & Le Pechoux C et al, *Effect of dose rate on local control and complications in definitive irradiation of T squamous cell carcinomas of mobile tongue and floor of mouth with interstitial iridium-192*, Radiotherapy & Oncology, **21**, 39-41, 1991b.

Meredith WJ (Ed), *Radium dosage: the Manchester system*, 2nd. edn, Williams & Wilkins:Baltimore, 1967.

Mitchell JB, Bedford JS & Baily SM, *Dose rate effects in plateau-phase cultures of S3 HeLa and V79 cells*, Radiation Research, **79**, 520-536, 1979.

Orton CG, Seyedsadr M & Somnay A, *Comparison of high and low dose rate remote afterloading for cervix cancer and the importance of fractionation*, Int. J. Radiation Oncology Biology & Physics, **21**, 1425-1434, 1992.

Paterson R, *The treatment of malignant disease of radiotherapy*, Edward Arnold:London, 1963.

Pierquin B, Chassagne D, Baillet F & Paine CH, *Clinical observations on the time factor in interstitial radiotherapy using iridium-192*, Clinical Radiology, **24**, 506-509, 1973.

Withers HR, Thames HD & Peters LJ, *Differences in the fractionation response of acute and late responding tissues*, in:*Progress in radio-oncology II*, Karcher KH, Kogelnik HD & Rheinartz G (Eds), 287-296, Raven Press:New York, 1982.

3

Biological Equivalence of LDR and HDR Brachytherapy

C. Deehan[1] & J.A. O'Donoghue[2]

[1]Beatson Oncology Centre &
Dept. of Clinical Physics & Bioengineering,
Belvidere Hospital,
London Road,
Glasgow G31 4PG,
Scotland.
[2]Department of Radiation Oncology,
Glasgow University.

Introduction

Over the last decade there have been rapid developments in intracavitary radiotherapy with the introduction of remote afterloading, a system which has many advantages over older manual loading techniques. These advantages include low exposure to theatre and nursing staff and greater flexibility of source geometry, as well as improved reproducibility of treatment and shorter treatment times.

When changing to remote afterloading many radiotherapy centres have also changed from treating with low dose rate (LDR) to treating with high dose rate (HDR). Increasing the dose rate is known to produce increased biological effects on a dose for dose basis. Additionally the effectiveness of HDR is different for tumours and acute or late responding normal tissues. It is therefore important to know the number of fractions and total dose that should be given at HDR to produce the same effects on tumour and normal tissue as the LDR treatment. These quantities can only be determined if a reliable method exists which allows comparison of the biological effects produced by treatments using different dose rates. The experience of HDR users and randomised clinical trials will ultimately determine the optimal HDR fraction number and total dose required. Experience so far has varied and has not produced a clear result, but recent publications have begun to yield definitive clinical patterns for HDR use, (Joslin 1990, Orton 1991).

The field of radiobiology has provided us with isoeffect models which attempt to predict the effects of radiotherapy treatments on tumour and normal tissue. Predictions are typically based on effect calculations performed at specific points of interest surrounding the insertion and this method has been used to investigate biological equivalence between LDR and HDR treatments. The linear quadratic (LQ) model is used here to show that as well as point calculations, effect curves or surfaces can be calculated around an insertion and that these can be of value in assessing the biological equivalence of LDR and HDR.

Dose Rate Effects

The useful range of dose rates in radiotherapy extends from about 0.1 Gy/hour to a few Gy/min (Hall & Brenner 1991). Early intracavitary insertions of the type used in the Manchester system delivered dose rates in the lower part of this range, around 0.5 Gy/hr (to points A), and over many years a great deal of clinical experience was invested in treating in this dose rate region. The availability of radionuclides with high specific activity, combined with remote controlled afterloading systems has made it possible to achieve much higher treatment dose rates. Dose rate ranges have been broadly classified into three groups, low, medium and high (Corbett 1990), these are shown in Table 1.

Table 1
Dose rate definitions after Corbett (1990).

Low dose rate (LDR)	0.4 to 2 Gy/hr
Medium dose rate (MDR)	2 to 12 Gy/hr
High dose rate (HDR)	>12 Gy/hr but usually in the region of 150 Gy/hr

It is known from results obtained by irradiating cells in tissue culture that the fraction of cells killed by a given dose increases with dose rate and also that this effect differs for different cell lines. In addition, *in vivo*, acute and late responding normal tissues are affected in different ways when the dose rate is increased, late responding tissues being the more sensitive to changes in dose rate. Most tumours seem to respond to changes in dose rate in a way similar to that of acute responding tissues and it is this differential response to dose rate that lies at the heart of the debate concerning biological equivalence between LDR and HDR. In other words if the treatment dose rate increases how can an acceptable level of tumour control be maintained without exceeding normal late responding tissue tolerance?

Fractionation of HDR intracavitary brachytherapy appears to offset the differences between tissue responses and it seems obvious from clinical results that three or more fractions of HDR must be given to achieve results comparable to LDR, (Fowler 1990). In practice most centres use between three and six fractions but some use as many as 10, (Joslin 1990, Fowler 1990) and it is thus not clear what the optimum number of fractions and dose per fraction should be at HDR. Differences in insertion geometry and technique as well as the use of external beam radiotherapy all serve to complicate matters and make a valid comparison of clinical results difficult. However some LDR and HDR schedules have been reported recently in the literature which seem to give comparable clinical results.

In 1990 Joslin compared the clinical results of using an LDR and an HDR schedule. These were 40 Gy in 48 hours (LDR) and six fractions of 5 Gy/fraction over two weeks (HDR), both of which appear to produce similar effects on normal tissues with no distinguishable differences in tumour response. The most comprehensive comparison to date was that conducted by Orton (1991) in his survey of some 56 institutions who had experience of both LDR and HDR. He reports fraction numbers between four and six with the dose/fraction in the region of 7.5 Gy at HDR compared with LDR treatments of about 78 hours delivered at 0.85 Gy/hr. Analysis of these results suggested that the survival at HDR was at least as good as LDR and perhaps a little better and that HDR produced significantly less radiation toxicity. This clinical evidence strongly suggests that provided a suitable dose/fraction is chosen and the HDR is given in 4-6 fractions then results can be obtained which are biologically comparable to LDR.

Radiobiology

In parallel with the technical developments in intracavitary brachytherapy, advances have been made in the understanding of how tissues respond when radiotherapy treatments are altered. Work in the field of radiobiology has produced mathematical models which attempt to predict the response of tissues to changes in treatment. Early isoeffect models such as the NSD, TDF or CRE, which did not distinguish between acute and late reactions, have given way to more sophisticated formulae, for example the linear quadratic (LQ) model. These new models reflect the fact that different tissues react in different ways to changes in treatment schedules. The LQ model has proved to be a reliable means of comparing different schedules in both fractionated and continuous radiotherapy. This LQ model is used here to examine biological equivalence between LDR and HDR intracavitary brachytherapy.

Dale (1985) extended the LQ model for use in continuous radiotherapy treatments. For a given level of effect on a specific tissue a value known as the extrapolated response dose (ERD) can be calculated from equation [1].

$$ERD = NRT(1 + 2R/((\alpha/\beta)\mu(1-(1/\mu T) (1-exp(-\mu T)))) \qquad [1]$$

This is the general formula for long-lived radionuclides where R=dose rate (Gy/hr) and is regarded as constant during the intracavitary insertion time, N=fraction number, T=treatment time (hr). The α/β ratio and μ are tissue specific parameters so that the ERD which is calculated represents an effect associated with a specific tissue.

Here the two main considerations are the effects on tumour and late responding tissues. This is because it is desirable to maximise tumour control and at the same time minimise normal late responding tissue complications. It is important therefore to find representative values of α/β and μ which correspond to tumour and late responding tissue. Most tumours have an α/β ratio which is in the range 10-30 Gy, (Fowler 1989), while late responding tissues usually have lower values of around 3 Gy. The α/β ratio is inversely proportional to repair capacity so that tumour has less capacity for repair than late responding tissues and tumour is also less sensitive to changes in dose rate, (Fowler 1989). The values of the α/β ratio used here are shown in Table 2.

Table 2
Tissue parameters.

	Tumour	Late responding tissues	Reference
α/β (Gy)	10	3	Fowler (1990)
μ (hr^{-1})	1.4	46	Orton (1990)

The second tissue parameter μ which is known as the sublethal damage repair time constant is inversely proportional to the half-time for repair of sublethal damage and is a measure of the rate at which damage is repaired, (Dale 1985). Values of μ are not as well documented as those of the α/β ratio and here values of μ are taken as 1.4 hr^{-1} for tumour and 0.46 hr^{-1} for late responding tissues, (Orton 1990).

Biological Equivalence

If we do not look for improvements and confine our attention to the task of devising an HDR treatment which only produces the same results as a given LDR treatment, this would result in biological equivalence. Absolute or general biological equivalence would be achieved between an LDR and an HDR treatment if the various levels of biological effect produced by both on different normal tissues and tumour were equal. In terms of the LQ model this would mean that the ERD values at corresponding positions around the two sets, HDR and LDR, of brachytherapy intracavitary sources, would be identical. It can be shown that general equivalence defined in this way is impossible to achieve where different values of μ are involved, (Fowler 1989, Deehan & O'Donoghue 1991) and at best only near equivalence is possible.

To understand this, it is useful to consider how the LQ model has been used to devise isoeffective HDR schedules starting from a given LDR treatment. Three examples are given below using the tissue parameters shown in Table 2 together with an LDR reference schedule. Values of the ERD for tumour and late effects are calculated at the two points A assuming a Manchester type insertion.

Example 1

In this example, Table 3, two HDR schedules are shown each with a fraction number N = 4 and different doses/fraction (D). HDR(a) matches the LDR for tumour effects but overdoses for the late effects while HDR(b) matches for late effects but underdoses for tumour effects. This method is often used to arrive at suitable HDR treatment parameters. Although this process seems to be based on the arbitrary selection of an HDR fraction number and a dose/fraction, it has proved useful.

Table 3
ERD values for LDR and HDR schedules.

ERD	LDR N = 1:R = 0.5 Gy/hr T = 60 hrs	HDR (a) N = 4 D = 5.27 Gy/fr	HDR (b) N = 4 D = 4.90 Gy/fr
ERD Tumour	32	32	29
ERD Late	51	58	5

N = fraction number R = dose-rate T = treatment time D = dose per fraction

Example 2

This example, Table 4, is derived from a method suggested by Orton (1987) which can be used to match both tumour and late effects simultaneously and this was explored by Warmelink et al (1989). Equation **[1]** is solved to obtain values of N and T for schedule HDR(a) which simultaneously match tumour and late effect ERDs at point A for a given LDR schedule.

Warmelink et al (1989) also show that it is possible to find solutions for a given tumour ERD at the point A and another ERD at some point representative of late effects, HDR(b). This is perhaps a more realistic situation than solving for both tumour and late effects at point A. Although matching of effects is achieved at specific points, and in general there is still a mismatch at others, this is probably a better approach than that used in Example 1.

Table 4
ERD values for LDR and HDR schedules after Warmelink et al (1989).

ERD		LDR N = 1:R = 0.5 Gy/hr T = 60 hrs	HDR (a) N = 7.2 D = 3.34 Gy/fr	HDR (b) N = 3 D = 4.90 Gy/fr
"A" point ERD	Tumour	32	32	32
	Late	51	51	61
Late reference point ERD	Tumour	24	21	20
	Late	34	30	4

N = fraction number R = dose-rate T = treatment time D = dose per fraction

Example 3

This third example uses results derived by Liversage (1969), equation **[2]**. This determines the number of fractions (N) that must be given at HDR to match the effects of a given LDR treatment for a specific value μ. Table 5 shows the result obtained for tumour and late responding tissues.

$$N = \mu T/2(1-(1/\mu T)(1-\exp(-\mu T))) \qquad \textbf{[2]}$$

Table 5
ERD values for LDR and HDR schedules after Liversage (1969).

ERD	LDR N = 1:R = 0.5 Gy/hr T = 60 hrs	HDR (a) N = 42.5 D = 0.71 Gy/fr	HDR (b) N = 14.3 D = 2.09 Gy/fr
ERD Tumour	32	32	36
ERD Late	51	37	51

N = fraction number R = dose-rate T= treatment time D = dose per fraction

Matching for tumour effects requires 42.5 HDR fractions, whereas late effects are matched with 14.3 HDR fractions. The dose/fraction in each case is obtained by dividing the LDR total dose (30 Gy) by the HDR fraction number since the total dose remains constant in this case. Although an HDR schedule with 14.3 fractions (late matching) would not fall too far beyond practical limits, one with 42.5 fractions (acute matching) definitely would. Few people would suggest the use of such high fraction numbers and this example is given here only to illustrate two limiting cases of matching.

These three examples illustrate two points associated with the search for biological equivalence using isoeffect models. Firstly the values of N and D derived for the HDR schedules appear to vary over a wide range. Secondly they are restricted to point calculations and do not show a good overall comparison of the HDR and LDR treatments. Matching may be exact at a reference point but what about other positions? A better overview can be obtained by considering curves or three-dimensional surfaces of equal effects around the intracavitary insertions. These are called isoeffect surfaces.

Isoeffect Surfaces

Surfaces of equal dose (isodose surfaces) can be plotted around a distribution of radioactive sources and these are now in routine use in many centres

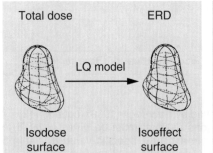

Figure 1. Isosurfaces.

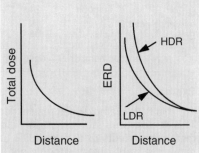

Figure 2. Total dose and ERD variation with distance.

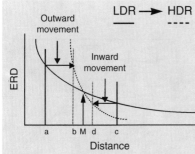

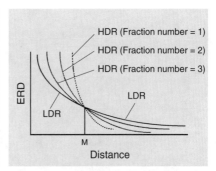

Figure 3. Movement of Isoeffect surfaces for tumour.

Figure 4. Movement of ERD plot for tumour with fraction number for HDR .

that plan gynaecological brachytherapy with the aid of computers. Using the LQ model it is possible to plot surfaces of equal effect, called isoeffect surfaces, in a similar way, see Figure 1.

Isoeffect lines or surfaces have been used in the past to display biological effects. These were calculated using the CRE model for fractionated (Kirk et al 1976) as well as for combined fractionated and continuous treatments (Joslin et al 1972). If a point at a specific distance from the insertion is considered, say point A, then for LDR an ERD can be calculated at that point for specific values of a/ß and μ. All points around the insertion which lie on the same isodose surface as point A will have the same ERD value and these points will form an isoeffect surface which will have the same shape as the isodose surface that passes through point A.

Now if we consider HDR, the dose rate at point A will increase and the ERD value it had at LDR will generally occur at a different position. The same will be true of all points which lie on the LDR isoeffect surface so that the isoeffect surface will have moved to a different position. As will be shown, the movement can be either inwards towards the insertion, or outwards away from the insertion.

Knowing the ERD at LDR and the HDR treatment time, equation [1] can be solved for dose rate. The point where this dose rate occurs corresponds to the new position of the isoeffect surface at HDR. Movement of isoeffect surfaces may help to answer some important questions about the biological equivalence of LDR and HDR. The magnitude of the movement may reveal how well matched are the insertions. The smaller the movement the better the match. The direction of the movement may make it possible to judge, relative to the LDR treatment, how more or less effective the HDR treatment is in terms of tumour control and also how much more or less damaging it is to late responding tissues.

Movement of Isoeffect Surfaces

To understand how isoeffect surfaces move in changing from LDR to HDR it is useful to consider first of all how the ERD changes with distance around a

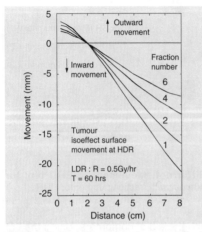
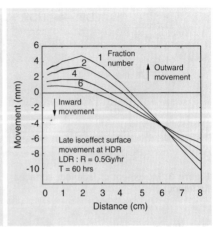

Figure 5. Variation of tumour isoeffect surface movement at HDR with fraction number: tumour ERDs matched at 2 cm.

Figure 6. Variation of late isoeffect surface movement at HDR with fraction number: tumour ERDs matched at 2 cm.

distribution of radioactive sources. If the variation in total dose is known along a line, for example that running outwards from the insertion from point P through point A, then using the LQ model the corresponding variation in ERD along that line can be plotted. An example is shown in Figure 2. The slope of the curve is steeper for HDR than LDR. This is a result of the increase in dose rate at all points around the insertion.

Although the movement of isoeffect surfaces takes place in three dimensions, it is useful to consider ERD variation along a single line. Figure 3 shows curves of ERD (tumour) versus distance for an LDR and an HDR insertion along the same line as in Figure 2. Displaying the effect curves in this manner shows some typical features.

[1] The two curves cross at some point M where the effects are matched.

[2] At distances smaller than M a level of effect expected at 'a' for LDR would now appear at a greater distance 'b' for HDR. This corresponds to the outward movement of the HDR isoeffect surface.

[3] At distances greater than M a level of effect expected at 'c' for LDR would now be expected at the shorter distance of 'd' for HDR. This corresponds to an inward movement of the HDR isoeffect surface.

Isoeffect surfaces occurring before the match point move outwards when changing to HDR and those occurring beyond the match point move inwards. This arises because of the relative steepness of the ERD curves and the fact that they cross at some point. When late effects are plotted a similar pattern emerges with the match point at a different position. This effect has been described by Brenner & Hall (1991).

Figure 4 illustrates the effect of varying the fraction number on the movement of isoeffect surfaces. It shows a number of HDR effect curves corresponding to schedules with different values of fraction number, N. As the fraction number increases the HDR curves move towards the LDR curve resulting in a smaller movement of the isoeffect surface in each case. Thus as expected, increasing the number of fractions reduces the movement of the surface when going from LDR to HDR. Notice that in this diagram all curves are for convenience matched at the same point M. This is achieved by choosing a suitable value of the dose/fraction D in each case.

A series of curves are displayed in Figures 5 and 6 showing the movement that takes place in tumour and late isoeffect surfaces respectively, for different fraction numbers at HDR, compared to a reference schedule at LDR. Once again this has been achieved by plotting the movement of isoeffect surfaces along a line going outwards from the insertion from point P and passing through point A.

The trend referred to above is seen in these figures, ie. outward movement at distances smaller than the match point and inward movement at greater distances. Both sets of data show a similar pattern, ie. if the fraction number increases then the movement decreases. In general, tumour and late isoeffect surfaces are displaced by different amounts at a given distance. This means that tumour and late iso-surfaces separate in going from LDR to HDR. For tumour, Figure 5, the movement varies between +2.5 mm at 1 cm distance and -21 mm at 8 cm if the HDR treatment is given in one fraction and matching occurs at 2 cm. As the fraction number increases to six, these movements reduce to +1.3 mm and -8.8 mm respectively assuming that the match point occurs in the same place. Similar displacements can be seen for late isoeffect surfaces in Figure 6.

How far do the isoeffect surfaces have to move in going from LDR to HDR before any significant clinical difference can be detected? The answer to this could be useful in determining the fraction number at HDR. It will also be obvious that the movement of isoeffect will be affected by differences in physical geometry of the insertions. As the HDR fraction number increases a point may be reached where the movement resulting from radiobiological considerations becomes small compared to that caused by changes in geometry. At this point, continuing to increase the fraction number in an effort to achieve better matching may not result in any significant improvement.

It is useful to examine the earlier results of matching effects at single points shown in Examples 1-3 by looking at isoeffect surface movements. As before, the movement of surfaces is plotted along a line going outwards from the insertions, from point P, passing through point A and the results are shown in Figures 7-12.

Figure 7 shows graphs of surface movement for both tumour and late responses corresponding to schedule **HDR(a)** in Table 1. Tumour effects are matched at 2 cm (zero movement) and late effects are matched at about 3.3 cm. At distances smaller than 2 cm the HDR treatment should be more effective than the LDR schedule with regard to tumour (outward movement of isoeffect surfaces) but less effective at greater distances (inward movement). Also from Figure 7, late effects ought to be greater than at LDR before 3.3 cms and progressively less thereafter.

The result if the late effects are matched at 2 cm, **HDR(b)** in Table 3, is shown in Figure 8. This time the tumour match point occurs at about 1.5 cm and

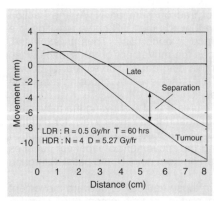

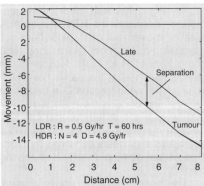

Figure 7. Isoeffect surface movement for schedule **HDR (a)** in Table 3.

Figure 8. Isoeffect surface movement for schedule **HDR (b)** in Table 3.

once again the pattern of inward and outward movement of surfaces is seen. Figures 7 and 8 suggest that **HDR(a)** would produce overall better tumour control than **HDR(b)** at distances shorter than 2 cm, but that **HDR(b)** would result in less overall late effects at distances greater than 2 cm. As to which of the two schedules is a better substitute for the LDR schedule greatly depends on the position of both the tumour and late responding tissue in relation to the insertion. Tumour at distances of between 1.5 cm and 2 cm would appear to be less effectively treated by schedule **HDR(b)** and late responding tissues lying between 2 cm and 3.25 cm would appear to be at greater risk with **HDR(a)**.

Movement obtained using the matching technique suggested by Warmelink et al (1989), example 2, is shown in Figures 9 and 10. Schedule **HDR(a)** in Table 4, where equivalent effects are achieved at point A is shown in Figure 9. Here, for both tumour and late responding tissues the zero displacement occurs

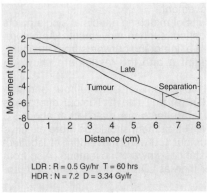

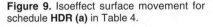

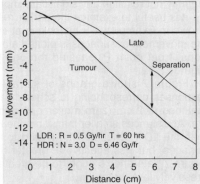

Figure 9. Isoeffect surface movement for schedule **HDR (a)** in Table 4.

Figure 10. Isoeffect surface movement for schedule **HDR (b)** in Table 4.

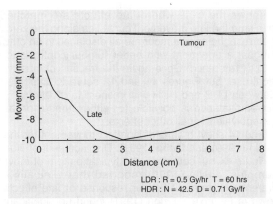

Figure 11. Isoeffect surface movement for schedule **HDR (a)** in Table 5.

at 2 cm corresponding to the position of point A. All the features seen in the previous examples appear again but this time the overall surface movement is less and so is the separation between tumour and late surfaces. This is due to a larger fraction number used to achieve matching.

Figure 10 shows the result when tumour responses are matched at point A and late responses are matched at some other reference point (effectively 65% of the point A dose rate), **HDR(a)** in Table 4. The results are similar to those in Figures 7 and 8 with the late response curve showing a match at around 3.5 cm. Figures 9 and 10 would suggest that **HDR(b)** should produce a greater level of late effects than **HDR(a)** at distances shorter than 3.5 cm with no real improvement in tumour response.

Results obtained using the Liversage (1969) equation [2], Example 3, are shown in Figures 11 and 12. These indicate a change to the pattern seen previously. **HDR(a)** in Table 5 produces an exact match for tumour effects with the entire late response movement curve falling below the zero displacement line (all movement inwards). This HDR schedule should produce identical tumour effects. The fraction number however falls far outside the range which could be used in practice.

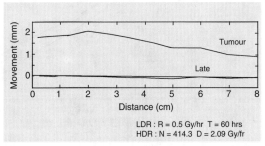

Figure 12. Isoeffect surface movement for schedule **HDR (b)** in Table 5.

Figure 12 shows the case where late effects are matched, **HDR(b)** in Table 5, and this time the late movement curve lies along the zero displacement line. Surfaces corresponding to tumour are all displaced in an outward direction. This would suggest a treatment with better tumour control and identical late effects as the LDR reference. Once again the fraction number is probably too high for practical use, but Figures 11 and 12 serve to illustrate that absolute equivalence between LDR and HDR with respect to all effects is not possible. Although exact equivalence is possible for either tumour or late effects, the treatment is not equivalent for all other effects.

Figures 13 and 14 show graphs of isoeffect movement for the comparisons reported by Joslin (1990) and Orton (1991). Displacement of isoeffect surfaces are greater in Figure 14 but both show the typical pattern of movement seen in the other examples. Joslin (1990) reported that clinically there was no detectable difference in terms of tumour response or late effects between the schedules shown in Figure 13. Orton (1991) found no significant difference in five-year survival between the schedules in Figure 14, but concluded from his survey that in general HDR produced less radiation morbidity compared to LDR.

Discussion

Absolute equivalence between LDR and HDR treatments with respect to all biological effects seems to be impossible on the basis of radiobiological theory. Fractionation of the HDR brachytherapy intracavitary insertion appears to offset differences in tumour and normal tissue responses caused by increases in dose rate. Clinical results seem to suggest that fewer fractions of HDR are required for acceptable tumour control and levels of morbidity than would be predicted by isoeffect models.

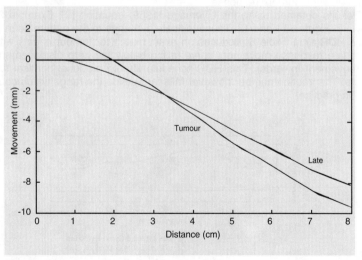

Figure 13. Isoeffect surface movement. LDR: R = 0.83 Gy/hr T = 48 hrs HDR: N = 6 D = 5 Gy/fr: after Joslin (1990).

The LQ model has been used in this chapter to investigate biological equivalence by calculating effects at specific points and by considering the movement of isoeffect surfaces. Studying the movements of surfaces may make it possible to determine how well effects are matched in going from LDR to HDR, since smaller movements mean better matching. The direction of the movement may also reveal how more or less effective an HDR insertion is compared to LDR.

Movement has been plotted against distance along a line running out from the insertion from point P and passing through point A. As the dose rate increases the general trend is for isoeffect surfaces to move outwards at short range (less than about 1-3 cm) and to move inwards beyond this point. Although only two-dimensional plots of movement have been shown, this type of analysis could be incorporated into a treatment planning computer.

Three-dimensional plots of isodose surfaces surrounding distributions of radioactive sources are now routinely available in computerised planning systems. These could be easily converted into isoeffect surfaces for LDR and then their new positions displayed at HDR. Some new planning systems have the facility to merge anatomical structures such as the rectum or bladder with a three-dimensional reconstruction of the insertion. Such a display would allow direct comparison of radiobiological effects of LDR and HDR to take place as the new positions of the isoeffect surfaces could also be superimposed.

As clinical experience grows, fractionation patterns for HDR ought to become well defined but as long as the need exists to refer back to an LDR *gold standard* then some means of comparing effects will be necessary. Point calculations of effect can be helpful but the use of isoeffect surfaces seems to provide a more complete picture of the changing effects. It must be emphasised

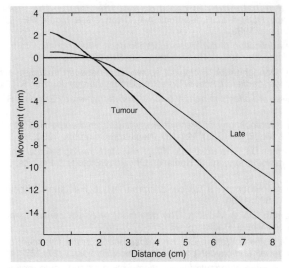

Figure 14. Isoeffect surface movement. LDR: R = 0.87 Gy/hr:
T = 75.4 hrs HDR: N = 5.3 D = 7.6 Gy/fr: after Orton (1991)
for stage I disease.

that the results obtained here using the LQ model are only as good as our knowledge of the tissue parameters α/β and μ. However if the values in Table 2 are representative of tumour and late responding tissue then the results in this chapter indicate the trends in biological effects which are involved in going from LDR to HDR.

If movement of isoeffect surfaces is large they could help understanding of trends seen in treatment, because if tumour effect surfaces move outwards (ie. are more effective) at short range and late effect surfaces move inwards (ie. less damaging) at longer range when going to HDR, this might mean that some HDR treatments have advantages over earlier LDR treatment. If movement is small, then this may indicate why satisfactory clinical results can be obtained with modest numbers of HDR fractions when radiobiological theory predicts that many more fractions should be necessary for an exact biological match.

Acknowledgments

The authors wish to acknowledge the helpful comments of Dr T.E. Wheldon and Dr R.G. Dale in this work and also the assistance of Dr W.A. Sandham for the generous provision of computer facilities.

References

Brenner DJ & Hall EJ, *Fractionated high dose rate versus low dose rate regimes for intra-cavitary brachytherapy of the cervix. 1 General considerations based on radiobiology*, Brit. J. Radiology, **64**, 133-144, 1991.

Corbett PJ, *Brachytherapy in carcinoma of the cervix: The state of the art*, in:*Brachytherapy HDR & LDR*, Martinez AA, Orton CG & Mould RF (Eds), 100-109, Nucletron:Columbia, 1990.

Dale RG, *The application of the linear-quadratic dose effect equation to fractionated and protracted radiotherapy*, Brit. J. Radiotherapy, **58**, 515-528, 1985.

Deehan C & O'Donoghue JA, *Biological equivalence between treatment schedules con-taning continuous irradiation*, Activity Selectron Brachytherapy Journal, 5, 131-134, 1991.

Fowler JF, *Dose-rate effects in normal tissues*, in:*Brachytherapy 2*, Mould RF (Ed), 26-40, Nucletron:Leersum, 1989.

Fowler JF, *The radiobiology of brachytherapy*, in:*Brachytherapy HDR & LDR*, Martinez AA, Orton CG & Mould RF (Eds), 121-137, Nucletron:Columbia, 1990.

Hall EJ & Brenner DJ, *The dose-rate effect revisited: radiobiological considerations of importance in radiotherapy*, Int. J. Radiation Oncology Biology & Physics, 21, 1043-1414, 1991.

Joslin CAF, *Brachytherapy: a clinical dilemma*, Int. J. Radiation Oncology Biology & Physics, **19**, 801-802, 1990.

Joslin CAF, Smith CW & Mallik A, *The treatment of cervix cancer using high activity cobalt-60 sources*, Brit. J. Radiology, **45**, 257-270, 1972.

Kirk J, Wingate GWH & Watson ER, *High dose effects in the treatment of carcinoma of the bladder under air and oxygen conditions*, Clinical Radiology, **27**, 137-144, 1976.

Liversage WE, *A general formula for equating protracted and acute regimes of radiation*, Brit. J. Radiology, **42**, 432-440, 1969.

Orton CG, Seyedsadr M & Somnay A, *Comparison of high and low dose rate remote afterloading for cervix cancer and the importance of fractionation*, Int. J. Radiation Oncology Biology & Physics, **21**, 1425-1434, 1991.

Orton CG, *Biological treatment planning*, in:*Brachytherapy HDR & LDR*, Martinez AA, Orton CG & Mould RF (Eds), 205-215, Nucletron:Columbia, 1990.

Orton CG, *What minimum number of fractions is required with high dose-rate afterloading*, Brit. J. Radiology, **60**, 300-302, 1987.

Warmelink C, Ezzell G & Orton CG, *Use of a time-dose-fractionated model to design high dose-rate fractionated schemes*, in:*Brachytherapy 2*, Mould RF (Ed), 41-48, Nucletron:Leersum, 1989.

4

Mathematical Models

C.G. Orton

Gerhenson Radiation Oncology Center,
Harper Hospital & Wayne State University,
Detroit,
MI 48201,
USA.

Introduction

Mathematical models used to estimate the biological effectiveness of a course of radiotherapy have been especially useful for brachytherapy in recent years with the advent of several new techniques such as remote afterloading with high dose rate (HDR), intermediate dose rate, pulsed low dose rate, HDR treatments with multiple fractions per day, new isotopes with different half-lives for permanent implants or systemic radiotherapy (eg. palladium-103, strontium-89) and a variety of single fraction HDR techniques, such as intraoperative, perioperative and stereotactic treatments.

Over the years several mathematical models have proven useful, such as NSD, CRE, TDF and linear quadratic (LQ). The first three of these are empirical models which are based upon the premise that there is a power law relationship between isoeffective dose and fractionation (for HDR) or dose rate (for LDR). On the other hand the LQ model is mechanistic and is derived from microdosimetric analysis of cell survival (Orton 1991).

Recent sophisticated statistical analysis has demonstrated that all these models provide only approximate fits to experimental isoeffect data. Furthermore, despite being based upon fundamental mechanisms of cellular interaction of radiation, the LQ model provides no better fit to the data than the empirical models, (Herbert 1989). Nevertheless, it is the LQ model that has become the most popular in the past few years, especially for brachytherapy.

The main reason for this is its versatility, especially with respect to the development of new, previously untested forms of therapy, such as most of those listed above, where there is little or no clinical data to which to fit the empirical models. Of course, this is also a danger which must be realised: the LQ model is just an approximation and in some situations, especially extrapolations into the unknown, it may even be quite wrong. Notwithstanding this reservation, however, this chapter will concentrate exclusively on the LQ model due both to its current popularity and to its ability to address bioeffect doses with 'the new brachytherapy' techniques.

Linear Quadratic Model

Bioeffect dose in the LQ model is the extrapolated response dose (ERD) for which the general equation is given below, (Barendsen 1982, Dale 1985, Fowler 1990).

$$ERD = Nd \left[1 + G \frac{d}{(\alpha/\beta)} \right] - kT \qquad \textbf{[1]}$$

where N is the number of fractions (either HDR or LDR), d is the dose/fraction (in Gy) and T is the overall time available for repopulation (usually in days). At constant dose rate, d=Rt, where R is the dose rate (in Gy.h^{-1}) and t is the time for each fraction (in hours). The other terms in equation, G, α/β and k are all tissue-specific parameters. At the cellular level, G relates to the rate of repair of sublethal damage, α/β (in Gy) represents the shape of the cell survival curve and k (usually in Gy.day^{-1}) refers to the rate of repopulation.

Typical values used for α/β are of the order of 2-3 Gy for late responding normal tissues, 5-50 Gy for early responding normal tissues, and 10-20 Gy for tumours. Values of k vary from 0-0.1 Gy.day^{-1} for late reactions, 0-0.3 Gy.day^{-1} for early reactions and 0-0.6 Gy.day^{-1} for tumours. However, sometimes a biphasic repopulation is assumed, where repopulation is slow initially up until a certain time T_0 typically 2-4 weeks, after which it accelerates. Hence, for $T<T_0$, k is small (or zero) and for $T>T_0$, k is large. The value of G is highly dependent upon the irradiation conditions, especially with respect to dose rate and time, (Orton 1991). The following are equations for G for a variety of applications.

Conventional LDR Treatments

For LDR therapy where the time for each application and the time between fractions are both long compared to the half-time for repair, (Barendsen 1982, Dale 1985), equation [2] applies.

$$G = \frac{2}{\mu t} \left[1 - \frac{(1 - e^{-\mu t})}{\mu t} \right] \qquad \textbf{[2]}$$

where μ is the repair-rate constant (in h^{-1}), ie. $0.693/\mu$ is the half-time for repair. Typical values used for μ are 0.46 h^{-1} for late-reacting normal tissues, corresponding to a half-time for repair of 1.5 h, and between 0.46 and 1.4 h^{-1} for early responding tissues and tumours, corresponding to half-times in the range 1.5-0.5 h, (Orton 1991).

Convential HDR Treatments

For HDR treatments where the duration of each fraction is short and the time between each fraction is long compared to the half-time for repair, the value of G is determined from eqation [2] by allowing t to approach zero. Mathematically, expansion of $e^{-\mu t}$ as a binomial series yields G=1.

Short Half-life Radionuclides

For LDR treatments where the isotope decays appreciably during the treatment time, the dose/fraction d in equation [1] is given by equation [3].

$$d = \frac{R_0}{A\lambda} \qquad [3]$$

where R_0 is the dose rate at the beginning of each fraction (in $Gy.h^{-1}$), λ is the decay constant of the radionuclide (in h^{-1}) and $A = 1/(1-\exp(-\lambda t))$, ie. 1/A is the fraction of the nuclei which have decayed in time t. For this situation the value of G is given by (Dale 1985), equation [4].

$$G = \frac{2A\lambda^2}{(\mu - \lambda)} \{A(B - C)\} \qquad [4]$$

where $B = (1 - e^{-2\lambda t})/2\lambda$

and $C = [1 - e^{-(\mu+\lambda)t}]/(\mu + \lambda)$

For short-lived radionuclide therapy one further factor needs to be considered if the treatment time is long enough for the dose rate to fall so low that the rate of increase of the ERD is less than the rate of decrease due to repopulation i.e. $\frac{d(ERD)}{dT} < k$.

This occurs at an effective irradiation time, T_{eff}, when cell survival reaches its miminum value, after which the rate of cellular repopulation exceeds the rate of radiation induced cell lethality. Hence, for tumours, if there are any tumour cells surviving at time T_{eff} the ERD will never reach tumouricidal levels. Conversely, for normal tissues, if their ERD has not reached tolerance by this time, then the treatment will be tolerated by that issue.

This critical ERD value is calculated using equation [1] but with kT replaced by kT_{eff}. However, calculation of T_{eff} is not too simple although it can be shown (Orton 1991) that it is a good approximation to use the time at which the dose rate (in Gy.day^{-1}) falls to a value equal to k, see equation [5], where in this case, R_0 is in Gy.day^{-1} and λ in day^{-1}. A method to accurately calculate T_{eff} is given elsewhere (Orton 1991).

$$T_{eff} \approx - [\, log(k/R_0)]/\lambda \qquad \textbf{[5]}$$

Permanent Implants or Systemic Radiotherapy

For permanent implants of short-lived radionuclides equation [3] for d and equation [4] for G can be used by allowing t to approach infinity. Hence: A= 1, B=1/2λ, C=1/(μ+λ). Then: d=R_0/λ and G=λ/(μ+λ).

For systemic radionuclides the effective decay constant is used instead of λ in these equations, ie. the sum of the physical and biological decay constants.

For both the above applications, however, it must be remembered that if repopulation is occurring during treatment the maximum ERD will not be reached in time t=infinity but at the effective irradiation time given by equation [5]. Use of this time in equations [3] and [4] will yield the maximum ERD value.

Incomplete Repair Between Fractions: HDR

When the time x(h) between fractions is not long compared to the half-time for repair then, for HDR treatments where each fraction is delivered in negligible time, G is given by equation [6], (Dale 1986), where K=exp($^{-\mu x}$)

$$G = \frac{N(1 - K^2) - 2K(1 - K^N)}{N(1 - K)^2} \qquad \textbf{[6]}$$

Pulsed LDR Treatments

With the pulsed LDR system there is as above, incomplete repair between fractions, but in this situation the dose rate is not quite as high as for convential HDR so the time for each fraction is not negligible compared to the half-time for repair. Repair during each fraction needs to be taken into account and equation [7] for G becomes a complex combination of the LDR equation, equation [2], and that for incomplete repair, equation [6], (Dale et al 1988).

$$G = \frac{2}{\mu t} [1 - \frac{(NY - SY^2)}{N\mu t}\,] \qquad \textbf{[7]}$$

where $Y = (1 - e^{-\mu t})$ and where $S = \dfrac{NK - K - NK^2e^{-\mu t} + K^{n+1}e^{-\mu Nt}}{(1 - Ke^{-\mu t})^2}$

Conclusions

The LQ model is useful for the calculation of bioeffect doses for a variety of situations encountered in modern radionuclide therapy. However, as with all time/dose models, it must be realised that it provides only approximate solutions, especially when pushed to the limits of potential validity, such as single fraction treatments and pulsed LDR. It is always prudent to keep this in mind when using the LQ model to design new treatment techniques. It is just a useful guide and must not be allowed to replace careful clinical judgement and observation.

References

Barendsen GW, *Dose fractionation, dose rate and iso-effect relationships for normal tissue responses*, Int. J. Radiation Oncology Biology & Physics, **8**, 1981-1997, 1982.

Dale RG, *The application of the linear-quadratic dose-effect equation to fractionated and protracted radiotherapy*, Brit. J. Radiology, **58**, 515-528, 1985.

Dale RG, *The application of the linear-quadratic model to fractionated radiotherapy when there is incomplete normal tissue recovery between fractions and possible implications for treatments involving multiple fractions per day*, Brit. J. Radiology, **59**, 919-927, 1986.

Dale RG, Huczkowski J & Trott KR, *Possible dose rate dependence of recovery kinetics as deduced from a preliminary analysis of the effects of fractionated irradiations at varying dose rates*, Brit. J. Radiology, **61**, 153-157, 1988.

Fowler JF, *The radiobiology of radiotherapy*, in:*Brachytherapy HDR and LDR*, Martinez AA, Orton CG & Mould RF (Eds), 121-137, Nucletron:Columbia, 1990.

Herbert DE, *Reflections on the L-Q model. Does it "fit"? (Does it matter)*, in:*Predictions of response in radiation therapy: analytical models and modelling, Part 2*, Paliwal B, Fowler JF, Herbert DE, Kinsella T & Orton CG (Eds), 400-516, AIP:New York, 1989.

Orton CG, *Recent developments in time-dose modelling*, Australasian Physics & Engineering, **14**, 57-64, 1991.

5

Mathematical Model for the Time Interval Between External Beam Radiotherapy & Brachytherapy

C. Bleasdale & B. Jones

Clatterbridge Centre for Oncology,
Clatterbridge Hospital,
Bebington,
Wirral,
Merseyside L63 4JY,
United Kingdom.

This work was awarded the **1992 Nucletron Brachytherapy Award** for the most innovative poster presentation at the 7th International Brachytherapy Working Conference, held in Baltimore/Washington, USA, 6-8 September 1992.

Introduction

There is considerable variation in the time interval used between initial external beam radiotherapy and subsequent brachytherapy and intervals of 1-2 weeks are commonly used. Some clinical authors have reported reduced tumour control if the overall treatment times are prolonged, (Fyles et al 1993, Pernot et al 1992). Even when brachytherapy is used alone, an increase in the time interval between two treatments has been shown to adversely influence the tumouricidal effect of treatment, (Murayama et al 1990). In other situations, probably because of slower regression rates and cellular proliferation rates, excellent tumour control is achieved after longer time intervals. For example, the method recommended by Papillon et al (1989) for the treatment of anal and rectal cancers involves a time gap of eight weeks. In terms of radiobiology there is a dynamic situation of increasing dose rates and cell kill as tumour regression occurs towards a brachytherapy source position. This effect will be opposed by continuous tumour clonogen proliferation. The model is applied to the situation of a line source inserted through the centre of a spherical tumour, Figure 1.

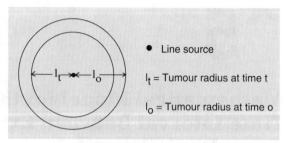

Figure 1. Schematic cross-section through a spherical tumour which defines the change in tumour radius with time. Tumour radius is measured from the mid-point of a line source placed at the tumour centre.

Mathematical Assumptions

In terms of the linear quadratic formula the log$_e$ cell kill for continuous low dose rate treatment is given by equation **[1]**, (Dale 1985). An explanation for the notation used in this and other equations is given in Table 1.

Table 1
Explanation for the notation used in equations.

D	= total dose (Gy) delivered to the tumour periphery by brachytherapy
d	= dose per fraction delivered by external beam therapy
n	= number of fractions of external beam therapy
α	= 0.35 Gy^{-1}
β	= 0.035 Gy^{-2}
μ	= 1.42 hr^{-1}
S	= duration of brachytherapy (hours)
$f(\mu S)$	= $\dfrac{2}{\mu S}$ for S > 10 hours (Dale 1985)
R_{max}	= maximum dose rate at surface of line source, a value of 4 Gy hr^{-1} was used
l_o	is the tumour radius on completion of external beam at time t_o (1.5 cm used)
l_t	is the tumour radius at the onset of brachytherapy
k	is an attenuation constant, measured as 0.7 cm^{-1} for a 6 cm 137-caesium line source on a low dose rate Selectron unit at Clatterbridge
T	is the overall treatment time from onset of external beam therapy to the day when brachytherapy is given
t	is the time interval between completion of external beam treatment and brachytherapy
T_p	is the tumour clonogen doubling time (values of 2.5, 7.5 and 15 days are used)
λ	is the tumour regression rate constant (values of 0.025, 0.05 and 0.075 week^{-1} used

1x10^9 tumour clonogens used in calculations involving tumour cure probabilities

$$E = \alpha D + \beta D^2 f \, (\mu S) \qquad \text{[1]}$$

To take into account tumour clonogen proliferation in the interval of time, t, between external beam radiotherapy and brachytherapy, equation [1] can be modified as described for fractionated radiotherapy by Fowler (1989) to equation [2].

$$E = \alpha D + \beta D^2 f \, (\mu S) - \frac{0.693 \, t}{T_p} \qquad \text{[2]}$$

For a combination of external beam radiotherapy and brachytherapy given in an overall time, T, the equation is further modified (Fowler 1990) to [3].

$$E = n(\alpha d + \beta d^2) + \alpha D + \beta D^2 f(\mu S) - \frac{0.693 \, T}{T_p} \qquad \text{[3]}$$

The limiting factor which will determine tumour control will be the minimum dose which is received at the tumour periphery due to brachytherapy. At the tumour surface the dose D will be RxS. For a single line source the fall-off in radiation dose rate can be described by equation [4].

$$R = R_{max} \, e^{-kl} \qquad \text{[4]}$$

where l is the distance from the line source and is also the tumour radius, which will diminish during regression. Tumour volume regression is known to be an exponential function of time (Thomlinson 1982) and tumour radius will clearly follow a similar function. This relationship is assumed to be that in equation [5].

$$l_t = l_0 \, e^{-\lambda t} \qquad \text{[5]}$$

which simplifies to equation [6]

$$l_t = l_0 \, (l - \lambda t) \qquad \text{[6]}$$

when λ is small and $t < 1/\lambda$. Thus the log cell kill can be calculated when reasonable assumptions for radiosensitivity and other constants are made, Table 1. The resultant equations for E are given in the *Mathematical Appendix*.

Values of E were calculated for variable values of T_p and λ for a tumour which measured 3 cm in diameter on completion of external beam treatment. Brachytherapy was assumed to be given at a dose rate of 1.0 Gy.hr^{-1} at a distance of 2 cm from the line source to a total dose of 24 Gy at intervals of 0-10 weeks following external beam treatment.

The occurrence of a minimum cell kill can be found by application of differential calculus but it is emphasised that λ is constant for any given tumour but varies between tumours. Consequently λ is regarded as a constant for the purpose of differentiation. The numerical value of the λ constant was varied independently in order to demonstrate the importance of regression rate. The current study uses values for λ for 0.025, 0.05 and 0.075 to demonstrate that changes of λ in this range cause major effects in log cell kill. When the value for λ is above 0.1 regression dominates even the most rapid clonogen proliferation rates.

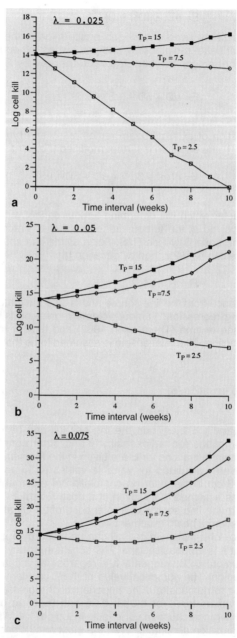

Figures 2a, 2b & 2c. The relationship of log cell kill with time interval between external beam treatment and brachytherapy when T_p and λ vary as shown.

In the absence of definite information regarding clonogen doubling times a further study of a hypothetical population of tumours was performed. This population was assumed to contain equal proportions of tumours with clonogen doubling times of 3.5, 5, 7.5, 10, 15 and 25 days. Poisson statistics were used to estimate tumour cure probabilities for a volume element of tumour exposed to the full external beam dose and the minimum brachytherapy dose as considered by Steel (1991), who estimated tumour cure probabilities with distance from a point source of radiation.

Table 2
External beam radiotherapy regimes.

Regime	Dose	No.of fractions	Total no.of days
A	50 Gy	25	35
B	45 Gy	20	28
C	37.5 Gy	15	21

Three different external beam regimes were studied, Table 2, which were followed at variable time intervals by brachytherapy of 20 Gy at 2 cm at 1 Gy.hr^{-1}. Tumour diameters between 2 cm and 6 cm at the onset of brachytherapy were considered.

Results & Discussion

When all other variables are kept constant, tumour cell kill due to brachytherapy will depend on the values of λ and T_p, Figures 2a-c. If sufficiently large, λ can dominate even short values of T_p, but only during the first few weeks following external beam treatment (Figure 2c, $\lambda = 0.075$, $T_p = 2.5$). Where T_p is long and λ is small (Figure 2a, $\lambda = 0.025$, $T_p = 15$) then delayed brachytherapy is advantageous. In one example, (Figure 2c, $\lambda = 0.075$, $T_p = 2.5$) there is a well defined minimum level of log cell kill capable of causing poor clinical results. This critical time is found to be 3.9 weeks using differential calculus; this value corresponds well to the graphical display.

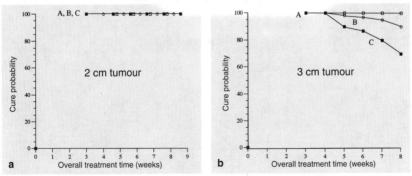

Figure 3a & 3b. The relationship between tumour cure probability and tumour diameter measured at the time of brachytherapy: at variable intervals of overall time.

For a heterogenous population of tumours with different T_p values, the dose schedule given by external beam influences the level of tumour control probabilities for tumours above 3 cm in diameter. The results are presented in Figures 3a-e which show that the extension of overall time (T) appears to result in a progressive loss of local control for any given size of tumour.

The predicted tumour control rates are highly dependant on tumour size at the time of brachytherapy. For small tumours, Figures 3a-b, the model predicts that brachytherapy is not followed by a reduction in tumour control when overall time is prolonged. The problem of reduced tumour control rates in the case of larger tumours is consistent with the clinical experience of Horiot et al (1988).

The importance of regression rate can be seen by careful inspection of Figure 4. For example, for regime A, a reduction in tumour diameter from 5 cm to 4 cm over weeks 5-7 produces a 5% increase in tumour control, whereas a 5 cm to 4.5 cm change over the same period results in a 6% loss of control.

Fyles et al (1992) using mostly regime B for the initial treatment of cervical carcinomas, found a loss of tumour control of 1% per day of treatment prolongation beyond 30 days, which may be due to time gaps in the initial external beam treatment or in the interval before brachytherapy. The model is consistent with their findings. For example the loss in local control seen in Figure 4b is

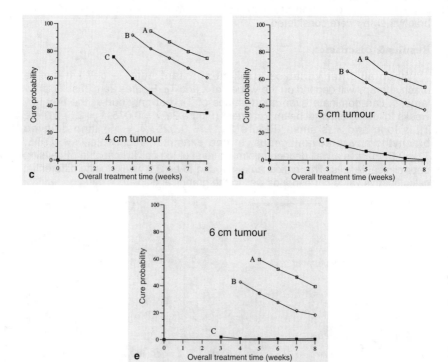

Figure 3c, 3d & 3e. The relationship between tumour cure probability and tumour diameter measured at the time of brachytherapy: at variable intervals of overall time.

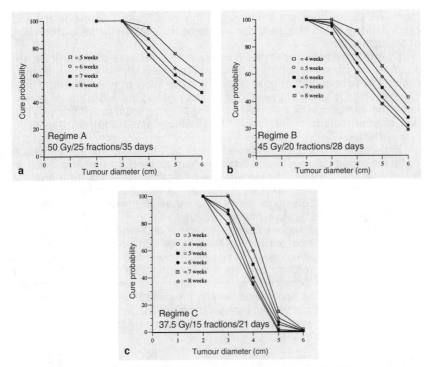

Figure 4a, b & c. The relationship between tumour cure probabilities for three external beam regimes, A, B and C, and tumour diameter at the time of brachytherapy.

approximately 0.8% per day between weeks 5 and 7. The effect of increasing overall time was noted to be most significant for larger tumours in the clinical study, which is consistent with the predictions of the model.

The local control of larger tumours could be improved by an increase in the total dose of brachytherapy given, but this is at the risk of causing increased normal tissue complications. There remains the possibility of increasing the tumour cell kill by the optimum use of brachytherapy at an appropriate calculated time interval. In this way the risk of late complications does not change, since the total dose has not changed and the treatment distance of normal tissues remains constant.

In addition, for tumours which are large following external beam therapy, there exists the possibility of using cytotoxic chemotherapy to prevent tumour clonogen repopulation in the interval of time prior to brachytherapy. For example, consider a tumour which measured 6 cm in diameter two weeks following a four week course of external beam therapy but continues to regress to 3 cm in diameter during a course of pulsed cytotoxic chemotherapy.

If the cell kill due to cytotoxic chemotherapy is assumed to be equal to tumour cell repopulation during the duration of chemotherapy, then the term T in equation **[3]** after Fowler (1990), continues to be 6 weeks. In the case of regime B, for the purposes of calculation the overall time T of teletherapy and brachytherapy would effectively continue to be six weeks regardless of duration of chemotherapy.

By inspection of Figure 4b, the 6 week overall time curve shows an improvement in local control from 30% to 97% for a reduction in diameter from 6 cm to 3 cm. Thus the potential gain from the integration of chemotherapy with brachytherapy is large. We are currently investigating this approach for persistent bulky carcinomas of the cervix following external beam radiotherapy by the use of short pulses of Bleomycin, Cisplatinum and Mitomycin C prior to brachytherapy.

Knowledge of clonogen proliferation rates and evaluation of the regression constant during external irradiation may help to predict whether a delay in brachytherapy would be advantageous or disadvantageous for individual patients. Tumour regression rates can easily be estimated by serial MR scan tumour volume measurements during external beam therapy. Flow cytometry techniques could be used to estimate T_p values.

The model described has used an example of a high dose rate gradient from a single line source, but such techniques are commonly used in intracavitary and intralumenal treatments. More uniform dose rate distributions occur in planar and volume implants and the reduction in dose rate with distance is smaller, but even in these circumstances similar considerations for regression and proliferation rates apply especially in the case of larger tumours where regression to a minimum volume is required before implantation is practical. For high dose rate brachytherapy treatments the model may be modified as shown in the *Mathematical Appendix*.

The model may also be used with negative values of t. This means the use of brachytherapy during or even prior to external beam treatment. Such integrated regimens have been used in clinical practice (Rotte 1978, Joslin 1989, Stannard 1992). For rapidly proliferating tumours an increase in cell kill is found, for example a value of E = 17.1 at t = -2 weeks (λ = 0.025, T_p = 2.5 days).

This exceeds the value of E = 14.1 at t = 0 and all values diminish as t increases (Figure 2a). In contrast, slowly proliferating and slowly regressing tumours have reduced cell kill at negative t values. For example, a value of E = 13.9 at t = -2 weeks (λ = 0.025, T_p 15) and higher values exists at all positive values of t.

It is apparent that if the rate of regression and the clonogen doubling time of a tumour are known, the optimum time for brachytherapy to be performed in an individual patient could be predicted from the model. Prospective clinical studies, in which these parameters are measured, need to be performed in order to test the validity of the model.

Mathematical Appendix

[1] **Continuous LDR Brachytherapy** when used after a course of external beam radiotherapy.

From the previous text, by substitution in equation [2], after Fowler (1989), we have the following expressions.

$$E = \alpha S R_{max} e^{-k(I_0 - I_0 \lambda t)} + \frac{2 \beta S (R_{max})^2 e^{-2k(I_0 - I_0 \lambda t)}}{\mu} - \frac{0.693t}{T_p}$$

$$\frac{dE}{dt} = kI_0 \lambda \alpha S R_{max} e^{-k(I_0 - I_0 \lambda t)} + \frac{4kI_0 \lambda \beta S (R_{max})^2 e^{-2k(I_0 - I_0 \lambda t)}}{\mu} - \frac{0.693}{T_p}$$

$$\frac{d^2E}{dt^2} = (kI_0 \lambda)^2 \alpha S R_{max} e^{-k(I_0 - I_0 \lambda t)} + \frac{8(kI_0 \lambda)2 \beta S (R_{max})^2 e^{-2k(I_0 - I_0 \lambda t)}}{\mu}$$

Since $\frac{d^2E}{dt^2}$ will always be positive, then if $\frac{dE}{dt} = 0$ we will have the solution for t yielding the time at which a minimum cell kill is achieved.

[2] **HDR Brachytherapy** is considered when integrated with external beam radiotherapy, as in the clinical regimes of Rotte (1978) and Joslin (1989) we have the following expressions.

$$E = n(\alpha d + \beta d^2) + \sum_{f=1}^{f=m} (\alpha D + \beta D2) - \frac{0.693 \, T}{T_p}$$

$$E = n(\alpha d + \beta d^2) + \sum_{f=1}^{f=m} (\alpha D_{max} e^{-kI} + \beta (D_{max})^2 e^{-2kI}) - \frac{0.693 \, T}{T_p}$$

$$E = n(\alpha d + \beta d^2) + \sum_{f=1}^{f=m} (\alpha D_{max} e^{-kI_0(1-\lambda \tau)} + \beta (D_{max})^2 e^{-2kI_0(1-f\lambda \tau)}) - \frac{0.693 \, T}{T_p}$$

In these expressions, m is the number of fractions of brachytherapy and τ is the time after onset of external beam therapy and the first brachytherapy fraction so that $(T/\tau) = m$. The brachytherapy fractions are assumed to be evenly spaced at intervals of time where f denotes the ordinal fraction number.

Acknowledgements

The authors wish to express their thanks to Dr J.E. Shaw for physics advice, to Mrs W. Fiander for secretarial assistance and to Dr T.J. Keane of Toronto and Dr S. Tucker of Houston for their helpful discussions.

References

Dale RG, *The application of the linear-quadratic dose effect equation to fractionated and protracted radiotherapy*, Brit. J. Radiology, **58**, 515-528, 1985.

Fowler JF, *The linear-quadratic formula and progress in fractionated radiotherapy*, Brit. J. Radiology, **62**, 679-694, 1989.

Fowler JF, *How worthwhile are short schedules in radiotherapy? A series of exploratory calculations*, Radiotherapy & Oncology, **18**, 165-181, 1990.

Fyles A, Keane TJ, Barton M & Simm J, *The effect of treatment duration in the local control of cervix cancer*, Radiotherapy & Oncology, In press, 1993.

Hawnaur JM, Johnson RJ, Hunter RD, Jenkins JPR & Isherwood I, *The value of magnetic resonance imaging in assessment of carcinoma of the cervix and its response to radiotherapy*, Clinical Oncology, **4**, 11-17, 1992.

Horiot JC, Pourquier H, Schraub S, Pigneux J, Brosens M & Loiseau D, *Current status of the management of cancer of the cervix in daily practice and in clinical research*, in:*Brachytherapy 2*, Mould RF (Ed), 199-214. Nucletron:Leersum, 1988.

Joslin CAF, *High activity source afterloading in gynaecological cancer and its future prospects*, Endocurietherapy/Hyperthermia Oncology, **5**, 69-82, 1989.

Muraya Y, Wierzbicki, Feola J & Urano M, *Regeneration in cervix cancer after 252Cf neutron brachytherapy*, Int. J. Radiation Oncology Biology & Physics, **19**, 61-67, 1990.

Papillon J, Montbaton JF, Gerard JP, Chassard JL & Ardiet JM, *Interstitial curietherapy in the conservative treatment of anal and rectal cancers*, Int. J. Radiation Oncology Biology & Physics, **17**, 1161-1169, 1989.

Pernot M, *General communication*, GEC-ESTRO Annual Brachytherapy Meeting, Nancy, 1992.

Rotte K, *A randomized clinical trial comparing a high dose rate with a conventional dose rate technique*, in:*High dose afterloading in the treatment of cancer of the uterus*, Bates TD & Berry RJ (Eds), Brit. J. Radiology Special Report **17**, 75-79, 1978.

Stannard C, Sealy R, Hering E, Hough J & Pereira S, *The treatment of carcinoma of the oropharynx with iridium-192 and iodine-125 interstitial implants*, GEC-ESTRO Annual Brachytherapy Meeting, **54**, Nancy 1992.

Steel GG, *Cellular sensitivity to low dose rate irradiation focuses the problem of tumour radioresistance*, Radiotherapy & Oncology, **20**, 71-83, 1991.

Thomlinson RH, *Measurement and management of carcinoma of the breast*, Clinical Radiology, **33**, 481-493, 1982.

6

Results of an International Review on Patterns of Care in Cancer of the Cervix

C.G. Orton & A. Somnay

Gershenson Radiation Oncology Center,
Harper Hospital & Wayne State University,
3900 John R,
Detroit,
MI 48201,
USA.

Introduction

A survey conducted on HDR remote afterloading fractionation practices and outcomes for cervical cancer treatments yielded data from 56 facilities treating a total in excess of 17,000 patients with HDR, (Orton et al 1991). Data on prior experience with LDR techniques was also requested for comparison with HDR results and with other LDR data recently published, such as in the latest FIGO Report, Volume 21, (1991), and from the French Cooperative Group of nine institutions, (Horiot et al 1988). This consortium of French centres, which about 20 years ago initiated a cooperative study of cancer of the cervix LDR therapy based on the 'Fletcher system' now has mature data for more than 1300 patients. Survival results from this study published by Horiot et al (1988) are amongst the best ever achieved.

Fractionation Results

As far as fractionation is concerned, the survey showed that there is clearly no consensus as to the appropriate number of fractions or dose per fraction. The number of fractions varies from as low as one to as high as 16. The dose per fraction to point A varied from 3 Gy to about 17 Gy.

However, many of these fractionation schemes were used only 'experimentally' in search of 'optimal' techniques. Early results quickly led to abandonment of the high dose per fraction regimes, and most clinicians have gradually settled on fractionation schemes which are close to the mean values obtained from our survey data, Table 1.

Table 1
Mean values for fractionation
schemes, Orton et al (1991).

Parameter	Mean value
No. of fractions	4.82 ± 0.21
Dose per fraction (Gy)	7.45 ± 0.20

Also requested in the survey were typical 'hot-spot' doses to rectal and bladder tissues (relevant to point A), for both HDR and LDR treatments. The results showed that these relative doses were reduced when converting from LDR to HDR by an average of $13\% \pm 4\%$.

Outcome Results

With regard to outcomes, crude five-year survival for all stages were slightly better for the HDR survey data than for LDR, but stage-for-stage only for stage III was the survival statistically significant in terms of improvement, Table 2.

Table 2
Five-year survival results.

Patient group	5-year survival rate (%)		P-value
	HDR	LDR	
All patients	60.8	59.0	0.045
Stage III	47.2	42.6	0.005

These survival figures were considerably better than the latest LDR data from FIGO on more than 20,000 patients treated with radiation alone or radiation combined with surgery from 1982-1986. However, they were not as favourable as the data of the French Cooperative Group, Table 3. However, the FIGO and the French data are actuarial survival rates and not crude survival rates and the stage III French data are not strictly comparable since they used the M.D. Anderson Hospital staging classification. Whereas the data for the survey (Orton et al 1991) and from FIGO are based on the FIGO staging classification where stage III is defined somewhat differently.

Table 3
Five-year survival results.

Reference	5-year survival rate (%)	
	Overall	Stage III
FIGO (1991)	52.7	37.4
Horiot et al (1988)	69.0	51.1

In order to compare the overall data, conversion ratios of actuarial-to-crude five-year survival rates were obtained by reference to data published in FIGO Volumes 19 (1988) and 20 (1991). Conversion of the survey crude data to actuarial data using these conversion factors yielded the data in Table 4.

Table 4
Overall five-year actuarial survival rates for the survey data of Orton et al (1991), for FIGO (1991) and for the French Cooperative Group (Horiot et al 1988).

Statistic survey	HDR survey	LDR Group	FIGO	French
No.of patients	7468	4738	21508	1383
5-year rate (%)	68.1	66.1	52.7	69.0

Although the HDR survival figures are not significantly different from those reported by Horiot et al (1988) this is not the case as far as morbidity is concerned as shown in Table 5. The data on complications for the French Cooperative Group was reported by Crook et al (1987).

Table 5
Severe (grade III) and moderate plus severe (grades II and III) morbidity for the HDR and LDR survey data compared with that reported for the French Cooperative Group.

Complications	Incidence (%)		
	HDR survey	LDR survey	French Group
Severe	2.23	5.34	9.77
Moderate + severe	9.05	20.66	27.59

The effect of fractionation on the HDR complication rates was also studied and the results are summarised in Table 6.

Table 6
Incidence of complications relating to point A doses
per fraction for HDR brachytherapy.

Complications	Incidence (%)	
	Point A dose/fraction ≤ 7 Gy	Point A dose/fraction > 7 Gy
Severe	1.28	3.44
Moderate + severe	7.58	10.51

Discussion

The results presented in this chapter show that HDR brachytherapy for cervical cancer is being successfully applied worldwide at an average dose/fraction to Point A of about 7.5 Gy. Since the linear-quadratic (LQ) model (Dale 1985) is being widely used to convert LDR to HDR regimes, it would be interesting to see if this 7.5 Gy/fraction clinical experience is supported by L-Q model calculations.

In Figure 1 we review the Point A dose/fraction (d) needed for HDR and LDR equivalence for a variety of "conditions". The following parameters have been assumed.

- An LDR rate to Point A of 0.8 Gy.h-1, which is about the mean value for the LDR data in our survey (Orton et al 1991).
- α/β values for late reacting normal tissue (l) and tumour (t) of 2.5 Gy and 10Gy respectively.
- A repair rate constant (μ) for late reacting normal tissue cells of 0.46 h-1,corresponding to a 1.5 hour half-time for repair and for tumour cells of either 0.46 h-1 or 1.4 h-1. This latter value corresponding to a 0.5 hour half-time.
- Values of the ratio of doses to normal tissues and tumour (Point A) of either 1 or 0.72 for LDR and 1, 0.72 or 0.63 for tumour. These latter two dose ratios are the mean values in our survey (Orton et al 1991).

Several interesting results are demonstrated in Figure 1.

[1] The equivalent dose per fraction for HDR is highly dependent upon the relative repair rate constant μ.

[2] If equal μ values are assumed, the Point A dose per fraction required for equivalence is much lower (approximately 3.5 Gy) than that typically used for HDR cervix cancer treatments (approximately 7 Gy), except when HDR provides extra protection to the normal tissues.

[3] If $\mu l < \mu t$, the equivalent HDR dose per fraction agrees well with that used clinically except when extra normal tissue protection is assumed as well, then the equivalent dose per fraction of 23 Gy is unrealistically high.

[4] Whether Dl is equal to or less than Dt seems to make little difference to the dose per fraction required for equivalence.

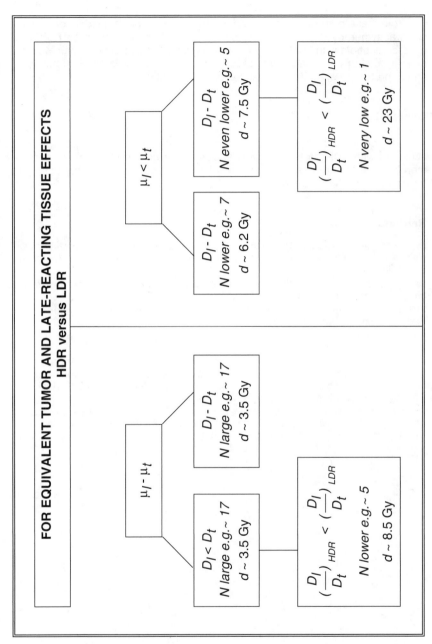

Figure 1. Summary chart for equivalent tumour and late-reacting tissue effects: HDR versus LDR.

From these considerations, therefore, the observation that HDR cervix cancer brachytherapy seems to be effective at a dose/fraction of about 7.5 Gy is quite compatible with LQ model calculations provided that either repair is more rapid in tumour cells than in late reacting normal tissue cells, or HDR provides added protection of normal tissues compared with LDR.

Conclusions

HDR cervical cancer brachytherapy can be as successful as the best achieved with LDR as far as five-year survival is concerned. With respect to morbidity, HDR can be significantly better than LDR, especially if the dose per fraction to point A is kept low.

References

Crook JM, Esche BA, Chaplain G, Insturiz J, Sentenac I & Horiot J-C, *Dose volume analysis and the prevention of radiation sequelae in cervical cancer*, Radiotherapy & Oncology, **8**, 321-332, 1987.

Dale RG, *The application of the linear-quadratic dose effect equation to fractionated and protracted radiotherapy*, Brit. J. Radiology, **58**, 515-528, 1985.

FIGO, *Annual report on the results of treatment in gyneacological cancer*, **20**, Radiumhemmet: Stockholm, 1988.

FIGO, *Annual report on the results of treatment in gyneacological cancer*, **21**, Radiumhemmet: Stockholm 1991.

Horiot J-C, Pigneux J, Pourquier H, Schraub S, Achille E, Keiling R, Combes P, Rozan R, Vrousos C & Daly N, *Radiotherapy alone in carcinoma of the intact uterine cervix according to G.H. Guidelines: a French cooperative study of 1383 cases*, Int. J. Radiation Oncology Biology & Physics, **14**, 605-611, 1988.

Orton CG, Seyedsadr M & Somnay A, *Comparison of high and low dose rate remote afterloading for cervix cancer and the importance of fractionation*, Int. J. Radiation Oncology Biology & Physics, **21**, 1425-1434, 1991.

7

Dose Rate Correction in LDR Intracavitary Therapy

R.D. Hunter

on behalf of
The Department of Clinical Oncology (Radiotherapy),
Christie Hospital,
Wilmslow Road,
Manchester M20 9BX,
United Kingdom.

Introduction

The Manchester Radium system for intracavitary therapy in carcinoma of the cervix was developed at the Christie Hospital between 1932 and 1952 and was then used without a change until 1978. During the mid-1970s the hospital became aware that new Ionising Radiation Regulations were being prepared which would require a very significant reduction in staff exposure levels and a decision was made to move from the preloaded radium system to a remote afterloading technique. An essential requirement of the new system was that applicators of identical dimensions to those of the classical system were to be employed and standard dose distributions were to be reproduced. The only deviation that was allowed from the original system was that the normal dose rate, (53cGy/hr to Point A) would be allowed to rise by a factor of up to 3.5. This change was allowed because of a consensus that the safe retention of remote afterloading applicators over periods of time greater than 24 hours in patients who were isolated in a radiation protected environment would be difficult and from a desire to offer both the patient and the hospital an efficient service.

The Department took delivery of the first equipment available to meet the specification, a Selectron-LDR/MDR, in 1978 and opted for the maximum possible pellet strength of 40 mCi caesium-137. This gave an initial dose rate of 180 cGy to Manchester Point A. Due to natural decay the dose rate has varied in patients being treated for carcinoma of the cervix throughout the last 14 years

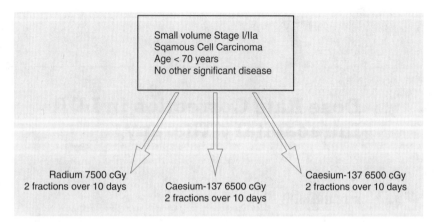

Figure 1. Treatment methods in the Christie Hospital ICTS study of 1983-1985.

and fell as low as 140 cGy/hr during the late 1980s. All of the treatments under-taken in that time have therefore utilised dose rates between 2.6 and 3.4 times those of the radium system.

In our contributions to previous conference proceedings in this series which have been reported in *Brachytherapy 1984* and *Brachytherapy 2*, (Hunter 1985, Stout & Hunter 1989), my colleagues and I have described the results of the ini-tial pilot study (1978-1980) and the first phases of the internal departmental studies (1980-1982) undertaken sequentially since 1980. This chapter concen-trates on a group of patients treated from 1982-1985 with intracavitary therapy alone for small volume stage 1b and 2a squamous cell carcinoma of the cervix whose follow-up is now complete at five years and then brings those results together with the results of the earlier group of patients treated from 1980-1982 in an examination of the dose response relationships that have emerged.

Between 1982 and 1985 a total of 232 consecutive patients referred by gynaecologists for radiation therapy were treated in one of three methods, Figure 1. All patients were treated using standard intrauterine and vaginal appli-cators of identical dimensions to those of the radium system. No patient had external beam radiation, surgical or chemotherapeutic treatment as part of their initial management. The group has been continuously monitored for relapse including particularly evidence of central pelvic failure and information has been sought on any possible radiotherapy related morbidity. This latter data is expressed as major or minor morbidity because of the way the database was set up in the early 1980s but it has been made consistent with G3/4 (major) and G2 (minor) categories of the Franco-Italian morbidity glossary. All patients have been monitored to death or to five years and detailed information on any possi-ble significant illness has been sought from other specialists involved. Application of patients to the treatment groups was carried out sequentially and randomly unless the clinical judgement of the treating consultant was that one particular technique was in the patient's interest. No stratification for age or stage was undertaken.

Results

Survival

The overall survival (corrected for intercurrent deaths) of the three groups is presented in Figure 2. There is no significant difference in the survival of any of the groups (P=O.46). The five-year survival rate of approximately 75% reflects the mixed stage groupings of the patients.

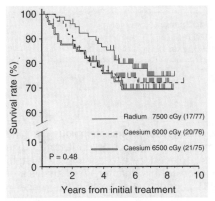
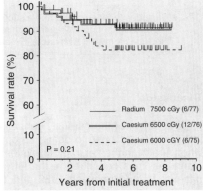

Years from initial treatment   Years from initial treatment

Figure 2. Overall survival results for the three treatment groups, corrected for inter-current deaths: November 1982 to November 1985.

Figure 3. Central pelvic control results for the three treatment groups: November 1982 to November 1985.

Central Pelvic Control

An interim analysis in 1988 had suggested that a significant difference in central pelvic control was emerging. This has not been sustained, Figure 3 (P=0.21), but there is a trend towards increased central failure in the caesium-137 6000 cGy group (12/76) compared with 6/77 for radium and 6/75 caesium-137 6500cGy, although with no effect on survival. A further analysis of the place of other known prognostic factors will form part of the final report.

Morbidity

The morbidity analysis in Table 1 reveals small insignificant differences in morbidity levels between the three groups. The number of complications in each group is too small to allow meaningful analysis of complications by site.

An unexpected difficulty in this part of the analysis was that some of the younger patients treated at this time and placed on hormone replacement therapy had dysfunctional symptoms that led to subsequent successful hysterectomies. These patients are included among the G2 complications although technically they might be excluded completely. Any patient who had a hysterectomy for a radiation reaction is recorded as G3.

Table 1
Morbidity analysis.

5 years died of disease	Primary failure	Number of patients	Complications G2	G3
17	6 Ra(7500)	77	6	3
20	6 Cs(6500)	75	9*	4
21	12 Cs(6000)	76	6#	2

* Includes 3 patients who had a successful hysterectomy for a non-malignant non-X-ray therapy related reason.
# Includes 1 patient who had a hysterectomy for benign disease.

Discussion

The object of the carefully controlled introduction of this technique over the last decade has been to define an optimum dose rate correction factor for use when the Manchester radium system is replaced by a caesium-137 system along the lines described in the introduction to this chapter. This analysis of patients treated between 1982 and 1985 suggests that no true difference in overall result has been seen when the prescribed dose to Point A was reduced by 12.5% and 19% in the caesium-137 group.

There is a trend towards increased primary failure when a 19% correction factor was employed but it does not reach significance (P=0.21) and does not influence overall survival (P=0.46). One conclusion of the 1988 paper in *Brachytherapy 2*, that the optimum dose rate correction factor appeared to lie between 9% and 19% has not been challenged. The final choice of dose rate correction factor for use in an individual patient may be influenced by tumour volume, dosimetry problems related to anatomy or coexistent general medical conditions but will normally lie in the range 9%-19%.

An interesting fact that has emerged from the fuller analysis possible in this type of prospectively monitored study is that the classical radium system has been associated with a higher level of significant radiation related morbidity than had been described in retrospective analyses. Among the 114 patients treated radically by radium alone in the studies from 1980-1985 17 (15%) experienced mild or major morbidity with eight patients (7%) associated with G3/4 levels. Some of this morbidity was undoubtedly due to local distribution problems associated with the use of preloaded applicators which are not attached to each other and to the extremes of ante and retroversion of the uterus sometimes seen among a group of patients. These are not regular features or contributors to morbidity in the remote afterloading situation when high quality applicators, whose relationship to each other is fixed, are utilised.

The previously reported change of applicator positioning seen with the move from soft preloaded to rigid remote afterloaded applicators (Jones et al 1987) means that some changes of dose distribution inadvertently may have obscured the answer to what was hoped originally to be a straightforward radiobiological question. In spite of all the measures taken to isolate the dose rate change as the only variable, unavoidable dose distribution changes have undoubtedly taken place.

The results reported in this chapter are achieved by treating patients using the complete Manchester system in a very selected group with early carcinoma of the cervix. It cannot be assumed that they can be applied directly to other treatment situations where external beam therapy of variable volume and dose is being mixed with intracavitary therapy using different applicators and/or different loading patterns. There is no reason, however, to doubt the principle that dose rate correction factors must be employed when moving from classical dose rates to dose rates 2.6 to 3.4 times the original. It also seems probable that if the original technique being utilised works at similar levels of tolerance to those described here then a dose rate correction factor between 10% and 20% would appear to be most suitable clinically.

Brachytherapy systems operating at up to 200 cGy/hr are defined as low dose rate and those immediately above as medium dose rate (ICRU 1985). It is a potential source of confusion to have the division between LDR and MDR as an arbitrary point, particularly since evidence is now emerging of applicability of dose rate correction factors in interstitial therapy at dose rates under 100 cGy/hr (Mazeron 1993). If "low dose rate" is used to describe dose rates of the classical system and "medium dose rate" situations where a dose rate correction factor must be applied then a separation at 100 cGy/hr might be more appropriate than at 200 cGy/hr.

The emerging information about dose rate correction factors suggest that such a pragmatic approach is probably wrong and it might be best to separate the elements of dose rate into low dose rates and high dose rates only and to accept that within low dose rates there is a range of dose rates and that dose rate correction factors have to be employed if significant changes are being utilised.

References

Hunter RD, *Clinical studies of changing dose rate in intracavitary low dose rate therapy*, in: *Brachytherapy 1984*, Mould RF (Ed), 1-5, 1985.

ICRU, *Dose and volume specification for reporting intracavitary therapy in gynaecology*, ICRU Report No.38, ICRU:Bethesda, 1985

Jones D, Notley M, Hunter RD (Eds), *A comparative study of the geometry adopted by Manchester radium applicators and Selectron afterloading applicators in intracavitary treatment for carcinoma of cervix uteri*, Brit. J. Radiology, **60**, 481-486, 1987.

Mazeron JJ, Boisserie G & Baillet F, *Pulsed LDR brachytherapy:current clinical status*, in: *Brachytherapy 3*, Mould RF, Battermann JJ, Martinez AA & Speiser BL (Eds), Chp.11, Nucletron:Veenendaal, 1993.

Stout R & Hunter RD, *Clinical trials of changing dose rate in intracavitary low dose rate therapy,* in: *Brachytherapy 2*, Mould RF (Ed), 219-222, 1989.

Chapter

8

Comparison of HDR versus LDR Regimes for Intracavitary Brachytherapy of Cervical Cancer: Japanese Experience

T. Okawa[1], S. Sakata[2], M. Kita-Okawa[1], Y. Kaneyasu[1],
T. Inoue[3], H. Ikeda[3], Y. Takekawa[4], T. Nakano[5], S. Wada[6],
M. Fishiki[7], T. Dokiya[8], K. Akuta[9], N. Miyaji[10],
Y. Hishikawa[11], Y. Ogawa[12], M. Miyoshi[13] &
M. Hareyama[14].

[1]Tokyo Women's Medical College,
8-1 Kawada-cho,
Shinjuku-ku, Tokyo 162,
Japan.

[2]Chiba Prefectureal Cancer Center,
[3]Osaka University,
[4]Tokushima University,
[5]National Institute of Radiological Science,
[6]Kyushu Cancer Center,
[7]Shiga University, of Medical Science,
[8]National Tokyo Second Hospital,
[9]Kyoto University,
[10]Kagoshima University,
[11]Hyogo College of Medicine,
[12]Tohoku University,
[13]Kyusyu University,
[14]Sapporo Medical College.

Introduction

Low dose rate intracavitary brachytherapy, usually in conjunction with external radiotherapy, was a commonly used treatment for carcinoma of the uterine cervix. Recently, however, there has been an increasing trend in Japan towards the use of high dose rate brachytherapy.

An optimal standard LDR brachytherapy dose in Japan, depending on the disease stage, involves a total dose of 20-50 Gy delivered in two to four fractions at a dose rate within the range 0.6 Gy/hour to 0.9 Gy/hour. External beam radiotherapy is also given, with or without a midline shield.

HDR brachytherapy has been used for over 25 years for the treatment of cervical cancer. The dose fractionation relationship for HDR and LDR for stages I and II cervical carcinoma have been examined by Arai et al (1980) for the period 1961-1972. These authors concluded that the dose rate factor was 1.72 for LDR/HDR or 0.58 for HDR/LDR. However, the recent dose fraction prescription at point A for HDR brachytherapy has been decreased compared to the practice of the earlier period 1961-1972. To compare the dose rate factor a questionnaire was circulated to 13 brachytherapy facilities in Japan with a request for data.

Material & Methods

The questionnaire provided information on the following patient characteristics.
- [1] Age.
- [2] Past history and complications.
- [3] Tumour stage (FIGO classification).
- [4] External beam irradiation.
  - Duration.
  - Dosage.
  - Central shielding.
  - Dose per fraction.
  - Total dose.
  - Number of fractions.
  - Number of days.
  - Area of irradiated field.
- [5] Intracavitary irradiation.
  - Regime (LDR/HDR).
  - Duration.
  - Dose per fraction at points A and B.
  - Total dose.
  - Number of fractions.
  - Dose to reference rectal point.
  - Dose to reference bladder point.
- [6] Tumour response on completion of radiotherapy.
- [7] Treatment failure.
  - Recurrence.
  - Metastasis.
  - Time & location of any recurrence &/or metastasis.
- [8] Late radiation complications.
  - Time, location, severity & treatment.
- [9] Survival data including date & cause of death.

The material for this study was all patients with squamous cell carcinoma of the uterine cervix who underwent radical radiotherapy during the 10 year period from January 1975 to December 1985 and who also satisfied the following criteria.

[1] Age less than 76 years.

[2] FIGO stages I-III.

[3] Follow-up for at least five years.

[4] External beam irradiation of the whole pelvis using central shielding throughout treatment for patients in stage I or II, restricted to 30 Gy for patients in stage III.

Survival rates were expressed in terms of cumulative survival and statistical analysis was performed using the chi-squared test, the Mantel-Haenzel test, the generalised Wilcoxon test and the Log rank test.

Data on 551 patients from 13 institutions were collected in this study. 300 patients were treated by HDR radiotherapy (forming the HDR group for analysis) and 251 patients were treated by LDR radiotherapy (forming the LDR

Table 1
Patient characteristics.

		HDR group	LDR group
No. of cases		300 (54.4%)	251 (45.6%)
Age (years)		34-84 (mean 63.2)	31-86 (mean 62.6)
FIGO stage	I	63	36
	II	123	109
	III	114	106
Medical status			
Undergone abdominal surgery		33	49
Obesity		8	4
Hypertension		39	49
Diabetes mellitus		21	19

Table 2a
Number of fractions and total dose in the HDR group.

No. of fractions	No. of cases	Point A dose/fraction (Gy)	Point A total dose (Gy)	Treatment duration (days)
3	20	7.23±1.04	21.7±3.11	15.8±2.11
4	129	6.74±0.71	27.0±2.82	23.9±4.95
5	73	5.42±0.55	27.1±2.74	29.1±8.29
6	57	5.04±0.42	30.2±2.51	35.0±7.44
7	14	5.00±0.19	35.0±1.35	44.3±16.11
8	5	4.85±0.73	38.8±5.88	42.4±7.767
9-10	2	4.07	39.2	57.0
Total	300	6.00±1.05	27.9±4.18	28.0±10.03

group for analysis). The patient characteristics and medical status of the two groups are given in Table 1. Obesity, hypertension and diabetes are considered as pre-brachytherapy complications. External irradiation was performed using 6-15 MV photons for 511 patients and using cobalt-60 gamma-rays for 40 patients. The regime used was 1.8-2.0 Gy/day with five fractions delivered per week. HDR intracavitaty irradiation was performed in 3-10 fractions, see Table 2a, and in the LDR group 1-5 fractions, see Table 2b.

Results

Tumour response was assessed one month after completion of radiotherapy and the results are givenin Table 3 for complete response. Overall this was 83% in the HDR group and 79% in the LDR group. No significant difference could be demonstrated between the two groups. The five-year survival rates for the two groups as a function of stage are given in Table 4 and Figure 1. No significant difference could be demonstrated.

Table 2b
Number of fractions and total dose in the LDR group.

No. of fractions	No. of cases	Point A dose/fraction (Gy)	Point A total dose (Gy)	Treatment duration (days)
1	2	22.9	22.9	1.0
2	51	24.9±4.82	49.8±9.65	11.8±10.01
3	162	15.8±1.61	47.4±4.83	22.6± 7.81
4	29	12.4±1.29	49.5±5.17	29.0± 7.40
5	7	9.8±1.96	48.7±9.78	46.5±17.71
Total	251	16.9±6.59	48.0±6.78	21.4±10.97

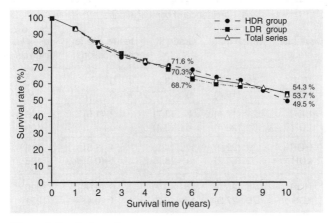

Figure 1. Survival results.

Table 3
Complete response (CR) as a function of stage.

Stage	CR in HDR group (%)	CR in LDR group (%)	CR in total series (%)
I	62/63 (98)	31/36 (86)	93/99 (94)
II	111/123 (90)	93/109 (85)	204/232 (88)
III	77/114 (68)	73/106 (69)	150/220 (68)
I-III	250/300 (83)	197/251 (79)	447/551 (81)

(No statistically significant differences were found)

Table 4
Five-year survival rate as a function of stage.

Stage	5-year survival rate (%)	
	HDR group	LDR group
I	87	80
II	76	73
III	58	59
I-III	72	68
All 551 cases	70	

(No statistically significant differences were found)

Table 5
Incidence of complications by dose rate group and stages.
(Figures in brackets are percentages)

Stage	Dose rate group	Incidence of complications			Total no. of cases for analysis	P-value (χ^2 test)
		Grade II-III	Grade III	Deaths due to complications		
I	HDR	15 (23.8)	2 (3.2)	0	63	NS
	LDR	7 (19.4)	0	0	36	
II	HDR	21 (17.1)	7 (5.7)	2 (1.6)	123	NS
	LDR	31 (28.4)	4 (3.4)	0	109	
III	HDR	39 (32.2)	17 (14.9)	4 (3.5)	114	NS
	LDR	32 (30.2)	9 (8.5)	1 (0.9)	106	
All stages	HDR	75 (25.0)	26 (8.7)	6 (2.0))	300	NS
	LDR	70 (27.9)	13 (5.2)	1 (0.4)	251	

(NS = Not significant)

Table 6a

Incidence of bladder complications by dose rate group and stage.

(Figures in brackets are percentages)

Stage	Dose rate group	Grade II-III	Grade III	Deaths due to complications	Total no. of cases for analysis	P-value (χ^2 test)
		Incidence of complications				
I	HDR	6 (9.5)	2 (5.6)	0	63	NS
	LDR	2 (5.6)	0	0	36	
II	HDR	7 (5.7)	1 (0.8)	0	123	NS
	LDR	10 (9.2)	0	0	109	
III	HDR	11 (9.6)	4 (3.5)	1 (0.9)	114	NS
	LDR	7 (6.6)	2 (1.9)	0	106	
All stages	HDR	24 (8.0)	7 (2.3)	1 (0.3)	300	NS
	LDR	19 (7.6)	2 (0.8)	0	251	

(NS = Not significant)

Table 6b

Incidence of rectal complications by dose rate group and stage.

(Figures in brackets are percentages)

Stage	Dose rate group	Grade II-III	Grade III	Deaths due to complications	Total no. of cases for analysis	P-value (χ^2 test)
		Incidence of complications				
I	HDR	6 (9.5)	0	0	63	NS
	LDR	5 (13.6)	0	0	36	
II	HDR	12 (9.8)	6 (4.9)	2 (1.6)	123	NS
	LDR	16 (14.7)	4 (3.7)	0	109	
III	HDR	25 (21.9)	11 (9.6)]*	3 (2.6)	114	*P<0.05
	LDR	18 (17.0)	3 (2.8)	0	106	
All stages	HDR	43 (14.3)	17 (5.7)	5 (1.7)]*	300	*P<0.05
	LDR	39 (15.5)	7 (2.8)	0	251	

(NS = Not significant)

A recurrence or metastases occurred after radiotherapy in 73 (25%) patients in the HDR group and in 68 (27%) patients of the LDR group. The failure rates for the respective groups were 13% (eight patients) and 8% (three patients) in stage I; 21% (25 patients) and 28% (30 patients) in stage II; and 36% (40 patients) and 34% (35 patients) in stage III. Thus the results for the two groups were again statistically similar for the incidence of recurrences/metastases as they were for complete response and survival rates.

Late radiation complications were classified by severity into grade I-III according to Kottmeir's classification. Grade II or III complications occurred in 75 (25%) patients in the HDR group and in 70 (27.9%) patients in the LDR group: results which were not significantly different. Grade III complications occurred in 26 (8.7%) patients in the HDR group and in 13 (5.2%) patients in the LDR group with 6 (2%) HDR patients and 1 (0.4%) LDR patient dying of complications related to the small intestine. Again, no significant differences were observed between the two groups, Table 5.

Bladder complications in the two groups, HDR and LDR, by stage and grade are shown in Table 6a and rectal complications are given in Table 6b. The overall incidence of grade II and III rectal complications was similar for HDR and LDR, but the incidence of grade III complications in patients with stage III disease was significantly higher in the HDR group than in the LDR group (P<0.05). A total of five (1.7%) HDR patients died of rectal complications, significantly higher than in the LDR group (P<0.05).

Summary

In summary, comparable therapeutic results have been obtained in the 300 HDR patients and in the 251 LDR patients because no significant differences between the two groups have been demonstrated for five-year survival rates, incidence of recurrences/metastases and incidence of radiation related complications. The dose rate effect factor of HDR relative to LDR was calculated to be 0.58 (ie. LDR/HDR=1.72) based on the mean total dose to point A. This HDR/LDR ratio was 0.58 for stage I disease, 0.57 stage II disease and 0.59 for stage III disease, Table 7.

Table 7
Mean values of dose/fraction and total dose to point A.

Stage	HDR group Dose/fraction (Gy)	HDR group Total dose (Gy)	LDR group Dose/fraction (Gy)	LDR group Total dose (Gy)	Ratio of total doses HDR/LDR (LDR/HDR)	
I	5.90±0.97	28.2±4.07	16.7±3.96	48.7±5.59	0.58	(1.73)
II	5.96±1.05	28.0±4.00	17.3±4.80	48.7±6.64	0.57	(1.74)
III	6.10±1.08	27.7±4.41	17.2±5.39	46.9±7.25	0.59	(1.69)
I-III	6.00±1.05	27.9±4.18	17.2±4.96	48.0±6.78	0.58	(1.72)

Reference

Arai T, Morita S, Kutsutani Y, Iinuma T, Masubuchi K, Tsuya A, Onai Y, Ito Y & Tazaki E, *Relationship between total iso-effect dose and number of fractions for the treatment of uterine cervical carcinoma by high dose rate intracavitary irradiation*, in:*High dose rate afterloading in the treatment of cancer of the uterus*, Bates TD & Berry RJ (Eds), 89-92, British Institute of Radiology Special Report 17, BIR:London, 1980.

9

Factors Influencing Treatment Strategies Using MDR Brachytherapy for Cervical Cancer

K.A. Dinshaw[1], S.K. Shrivastava[1], M.A. Muckaden[1], V. Sharma[1], S.M. Deore[2] & P.S. Viswanathan[2]

[1]Departments of Radiation Oncology & [2] Medical Physics,
Tata Memorial Hospital,
Bombay 400 012,
India.

Introduction

Cancer of the uterine cervix is the commonest malignancy in Indian women. It accounts for approximately 26% of all malignancies in females and 75% of all female genital cancers (Tata Memorial Hospital Cancer Registry 1991). Radical surgery and radiation therapy are equally effective treatments in the early stages, while radiation therapy is the treatment of choice in the more advanced lesions. Several factors have been identified, which influence the clinical outcome. These include: age of the patient, size of the lesion, clinical stage, pelvic lymph node involvement, histopathological type, treatment methods and intracavitary dose rates. The impact of these factors on the outcome of the treatment will be outlined, reflecting strategies and policies for future protocols.

Material & Methods

Our study comprises 2472 patients with carcinoma of the uterine cervix who were seen at the Tata Memorial Hospital between January 1983 and December 1985. All cases were evaluated jointly by the gynaecological and radiation oncologists and were staged according to the FIGO staging system. 11% patients were in FIGO stage Ib, 6% in IIa, 25% in IIb whereas a large group of 58% were staged as III and IV. Of these 1838 (Ia 238, IIa 120, IIb 462, III+IV 1018) patients completed the prescribed treatment and were available for evaluation, Table 1 and Figure 1.

Table 1
Treatment strategies by stage.

Stage	Total number of cases	WH	Preoperative ICBY + WH	Preoperative EXRT + WH	Radical radiotherapy	5-Year DFS rate (%)
IA	238	95	62	-	81	69
IIA	120	12	-	38	70	73
IIB	462	4	-	115	343	61
III+IV	1018	-	-	-	909	35

DFS = Disease free survival
WH   = Wertheim hysterectomy
ICBY = Intracavitary brachytherapy
EXRT = External beam radiotherapy

The peak age incidence was in the fourth to sixth decades with a mean age of 48 years. The youngest patient was 21 years and oldest 80 years. 18% of patients were below the age of 35 years. Histologically, 95% of patients were reported as epidermoid carcinoma, predominantly in the grade III (68%) sub-group. The patients were treated either with radical surgery (Wertheim hysterectomy), pre-operative irradiation followed by a Wertheim hysterectomy or by radical irradiation.

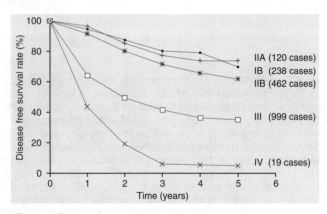

Figure 1. Disease free survival rates by stage.

During this period of time due to the nature of clinical presentation in the majority of cases with large volume disease, poorly differentiated subtypes and shortage of inpatient brachytherapy facilities, the radical radiation treatment relied essentially on external beam therapy followed only by a single intracavitary insertion. The external beam therapy was delivered to the pelvis using 14 cm x 14 cm or 15 cm x 15 cm anterrior-posterior portals with either cobalt-60 gamma rays or 6/10 MV photons from a linear accelerator. For stages I and II the mid-pelvic dose was 46 Gy in 23 fractions over 4.5 weeks duration. Treatment was given five times a week with daily fractions of 2 Gy. Few patients with stage IIb were given extended field irradiation, where the pelvic and para-aortic areas were radiated to a dose of 50 Gy in six weeks with 1.5 Gy per fraction. The single intracavitary insertion was given two to three weeks after completion of external irradiation. The intracavitary brachytherapy was carried out with either a manual afterloading Henschke applicator or with a remote afterloading Fletcher-Suit applicator. The ovoids were unshielded. The Henschke applicator used caesium-137 tubes delivering 3000 cGy to point A with a dose rate of 200 ± 50 cGy/hour.

Pre-operative radiotherapy was given either with an intracavitary insertion or with external radiation. In patients with stage Ib, the pre-operative radiation dose of 2000 cGy was given in the form of an intravaginal application. Whilst in stage IIa and IIb the pre-operative radiation was delivered with external radiation therapy to the pelvis with a dose of either 40 Gy in 20 fractions over four weeks or with 30 Gy in 10 fractions over a two week period. The pre-operative irradiation was combined with a Wertheim hysterectomy three to four weeks after radiation. This permitted adequate shrinkage of the primary tumour without inducing pelvic fibrosis to impede the surgical dissection. The Wertheim hysterectomy included removal of the uterus, the vaginal cuff, the parametrium, adenexae and the clearance of obturator and iliac nodes.

A total of 95 stage Ib patients were treated with a Wertheim hysterectomy and further 81 patients by radical radiotherapy. Additionally, 62 patients were treated with pre-operative intracavitary brachytherapy. 12 patients with stage IIa were treated with a Wertheim hysterectomy, 38 patients received pre-operative external irradiation followed by a Wertheim hysterectomy and 70 patients received radical irradiation. A total of 115 patients with FIGO stage IIb were treated with either pre-operative external irradiation followed by a Wertheim hysterectomy and a furthur 343 by radical irradiation.

A total of 1018 with stage III and IV disease were treated with radiation therapy alone. Of these, 909 patients were randomised to four different fractionation regimes with five fractions per week (200 cGy/fraction), three fractions per week (300 cGy/fraction), two fractions per week (400 cGy/fraction) and one fraction per week (540 cGy/fraction) to a total dose of 50 Gy, 45 Gy, 40 Gy and 37.8 Gy respectively, in an overall period of five to six weeks. The total doses for these fractionation regimes were matched with the daily fraction regime using the TDF model, (Orton & Ellis 1973, Orton 1974).

The follow-up records of these patients were reviewed. In the majority of the patients the follow-up information was obtained from the case papers maintained in the hospital records. For a few patients the information was obtained through correspondance. The minimum follow-up period after completion of treatment was six months and the maximum was 79 months.

Results

Disease Free Survival

The five-year disease free survival rate for stage Ib was 69% calculated using a life table method. This disease free survival data was further analysed with respect to the treatment modality, Table 2. Patients with FIGO stage IIb and treated with pre-operative radiotherapy and surgery had a five-year disease free survival rate of 78%, compared to 51% with radical radiotherapy. This is a significant difference (P<0.05). There was, however, no difference with pre-operative external irradiation doses of 40 Gy/20 fractions/4 weeks or 30 Gy/10 fractions/2 weeks. Probably, the shorter pre-operative external irradiation is as effective as the four weeks external radiation therapy schedule.

Table 2
Post-operative histopathological findings.

Stage	Treatment	Number of cases	Positive cervix	Positive cut margins	Positive nodes	5-year DFS rate (%)
IB	Surgery alone	95	95	9 (9%)	23 (24%)	66
	Preop.ICBY+ WH	62	52 (84%)	11 (18%)	11 (18%)	70
	RT alone	81	-	-	-	71
IIA	WH alone	12	12	4 (33%)	2(17%)	80
	Preop. EXRT + WH	38	25 (66%)	3 (8%)	5 (13%)	72
	RT alone	70	-	-	-	70
IIB	Preop. EXRT + WH	115	80 (70%)	6 (5%)	15 (13%)	7
	RT alone	343	-	-	-	51

DFS = Disease free survival
WH = Wertheim hysterectomy
ICBY = Intracavitary brachytherapy
EXRT = External beam radiotherapy
RT = External beam radiotherapy

Table 3
Correlation of nodal stages with disease free survival.

Nodal stage		No.of cases	5-year DFS rate (%)	P value
Stage IB	Positive node	34	38	< 0.001
	Negative node	123	76	
Stage IIA	Positive node	7	50	0.2
	Negative node	43	84	
Stage IIB	Positive node	15	55	< 0.05
	Negative node	100	80	

For stage III and IV, the five-year disease free survival rate was 35%, Table 1. This rate was analysed with respect to the treatment regime of external fractionation. A maximum five-year rate of 42% was observed with a conventional regime of daily 2 Gy/fraction and a minimum of 27% with a once a week hypo-fractionation regime of 5.4 Gy/fraction.

Lymph Node Involvement

Lymph node involvement was shown to have an adverse effect on the result of the treatment (Alcock & Toplis 1987, O'Brien & Carmichael 1988, Lee et al 1989, Kamura et al 1992). In our patients we have recorded a higher incidence of pelvic nodal disease than those in the literature, Tables 2 and 3. In stage Ib disease, 23/95 (24%) 95 patients who underwent a Wertheim hysterectomy had positive pelvic nodal disease, Table 2. The patients with negative pelvic lymph nodes did significantly better than those with positive nodal disease, P<0.001, Table 3.

The incidence of positive lymph nodes with stage IIb was expected to be higher than in stage 1b. However, due to the use of pre-operative external irradiation only 13% of patients were reported with positive pelvic nodes, Table 2. The disease free survival was 55% for the patients with positive nodes which is significantly lower than the 80% figure for those with negative lymph nodes, Table 3.

Tumour Volume

The volume of the primary lesion was also seen to be related to prognosis (Kovalic et al 1991, Mendenhall et al 1991). On clinical examination, tumours larger than 4 cm were assigned as having bulky disease. In stage Ib the five-year disease free survival rate was 51% for bulky tumours in comparison to 76% for patients with non-bulky disease. Similarly for other stages, bulky tumours have shown a significantly worse survival rate than those with non-bulky tumours, Table 4.

Table 4
Correlation of tumour size with disease free survival.

Stage	Disease size	No.of cases	5-year DFS (%)	P value
IB	Bulky	80	51	< 0.02
	Non-bulky	158	76	
IIA	Bulky	43	61	< 0.03
	Non-bulky	77	82	
IIB	Bulky	221	52	0.2
	Non-bulky	241	61	
III+IV	Bulky	470	27	< 0.04
	Non-bulky	439	39	

Age & Histology

The impact of age and histology has also been observed by some workers (Eifel et al 1990, Kamura et al 1992). Only 18% of our patients were below the age of 35 years. Stage by stage, the younger patients did not respond as well as the patients over 35 years of age. Patients with stage I and II, of less than 35 years of age had 53% five-year disease free survival rates compared to 66% for the patients aged above 35 years of age. The differences were statistically significant, P<0.01. The difference was also significant in stage III and IV. In our series of patients, adenocarcinoma cases have shown a worse survival compared to those with a squamous carcinoma histology, though this was not statistically significant, Table 5.

Table 5
Correlation of age and Histology with disease free survival.

Parameter	Stage I+II			Stage III+IV		
	No. of cases	5-year DFS rate (%)	P value	No. of cases	5-year DFS rate (%)	P value
Age						
< 35 years	183	50	< 0.01	153	26	< 0.02
> 35 years	637	66		865	33	
Histology						
Squamous carcinoma	768	64	0.1	986	34	0.2
Adenocarcinoma	44	47		26	27	

DFS = Disease Free Survival

Dose Rate & Dose/Fraction

During the past few years there has been renewed and increased interest on dose/fraction and dose rate in radiation therapy. The influence of dose/fraction of external irradiation on the clinical outcome appears to be well established, (Deore et al 1991,1992). However, the influence of brachytherapy dose rate on clinical outcome still remains unresolved, (Deore et al 1991, Kovalic et al 1991, Singh 1978, Turesson & Notter 1984). In the light of these prevailing uncertainties, a retrospective analysis was undertaken to study the influence of dose rate and dose/fraction on clinical outcome.

Of 1512 patients treated with radiation therapy alone, 832 patients were selected to evaluate the effect of dose rate in intracavitary brachytherapy and dose/fraction from external beam irradiation. All patients received external beam radiation therapy and single intracavitary brachytherapy using either Fletcher-Suit (464 patients) or Henschke (368 patients) applicators, Table 6.

The recurrence rate was analysed for different stages and different fractionation regimes. The crude recurrence rate was 22% for stage Ib and II (18% for Ib, 20% and 24% for stage IIa and IIb). The highest recurrence rate of 59% was observed in the subgroup of stages III and IV.

The majority of recurrences seen were within first two years after treatment. There was a marginal reduction of the recurrence rate with the Fletcher-Suit applicator compared to the the Henschke applicator. This was probably because of the better design of this applicator, Table 6.

Table 6
Recurrence rate and applicator types.
(Data for 1512 patients treated only by radiotherapy)

	Fletcher-Suit	Henschke	Intravaginal	Total
No. of cases	464	368	680	1512
Point A dose	24 Gy	30 Gy	2000 mghr	
Dose rate (cGy/hr)	200 ± 50	100 ± 10	-	
Stage I+II				
No. of cases	298	101	95	494
Response rate (%)	94	91	83	90
Recurrence rate (%)	19	23	34	22
Stage III+IV				
No.of cases	166	267	585	1018
Response rate (%)	80	81	60	78
Recurrence rate (%)	50	55	77	59

As the prescribed dose to point A was not adjusted according to the dose rate, its influence on recurrence rate was studied. The point A dose rate varied within the range 150-250 cGy/hour for the Fletcher-Suit applicator and within the range 90-110 cGy/hour for the Henschke applicator, for a prescribed dose of 24 Gy with Fletcher-Suit and 30 Gy with Henschke. As shown in Figure 2, the maximum recurrence rates were observed when the dose rate with the Fletcher-Suit applicator was 150-169 cGy/hour, whereas it was less with the higher dose rates (220-250 cGy/hour). Similarly, Figure 3, for the Henschke applicator, for dose rates lower than 100 cGy/hour there was seen to be a marginal increase in recurrence rates compared to dose rates higher than 100 cGy/hour. However, the differences are not statistically significant.

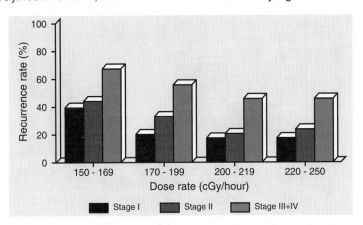

Figure 2. Crude recurrence rate variation with dose rate to point A in patients treated using a Fletcher-Suit applicator. The prescribed dose to point was 24 Gy: statistical significance P> 0.1.

Table 7
Correlation of crude recurrence rate with external beam radiotherapy
fractionation regime.

Fractionation regime	Stage I+II		Stage III+IV	
	Recurrence rate (%)	Complication rate (%)	Recurrence rate (%)	Complication rate (%)
46 Gy/23 fr/30 days (2 Gy/fr)	17	2.4	-	-
50 Gy/32 fr/44 days (1.5 Gy/fr)	26	4.5	-	-
50 Gy/25 fr/35 days (2 Gy/fr)	-	-	41	3.5
45 Gy/15 fr/35 days (3 Gy/fr)	-	-	44	6
40 Gy/10 fr/35 days (4 Gy/fr)	-	-	53	5.2
37.8 Gy/7 fr/42 days (5.4 Gy/fr)	-	-	59	19.7

Furthermore, the recurrence rate was analysed with respect to the fractionation regime of external irradiation. In stage Ib and II the external radiotherapy
regimes were either conventional fractionation of 46 Gy in 4.5 weeks with
2 Gy/fraction or an extended field technique with 50 Gy in six weeks
(1.5 Gy/fraction). The recurrence rates were higher in patients treated with
extended fields, obviously because of the increased overall period. In late
stages of III and IV among four fractionation regimes matched using the TDF

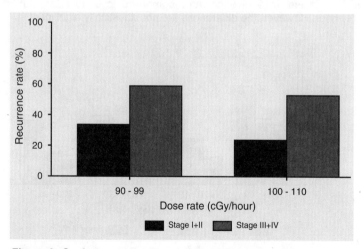

Figure 3. Crude recurrence rate variation with dose rate to point A in
patients treated using a Henschke applicator. The prescribed dose to point
A was 30 Gy: statistical significance P> 0.1.

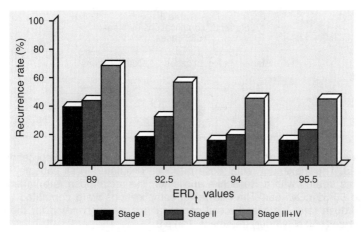

Figure 4. Recurrence rate correlated with extrapolated response dose (ERD$_t$) values, linear quadratic model: α/β and μ were taken as 10 Gy and 0.69/h: statistical significance P > 0.09.

model, the hypofractionation schedules showed higher recurrence rates than the conventional 2 Gy/fraction regime. The highest recurrence rate was seen with the once a week schedule of 5.4 Gy/fraction, Table 7.

Finally, the recurrence rate was analysed using the linear quadratic model (Barendsen 1982). The extrapolated response dose (ERDt) values or biological equivalent doses (BED) delivered to point A were calculated for all the patients, using an α/β value of 10 Gy. For brachytherapy ERD calculations the value of the repair constant (μ) was taken as 0.69h-1 (Dale 1985). The total ERDs delivered to point A were correlated with the recurrence rate.

As shown by the histograms in Figure 4, an increased recurrence rate was observed in patients who received smaller ERD values to point A. The ERDs showed a correlation with the recurrence rate for all the stages. As the ERD values of linear quadratic model accounted for different variables (such as, dose rate, dose/fraction, repair and proliferation), it is very interesting to note this correlation with the recurrence rate. However, the correlation was not statistically significant.

Late Complications

As well as tumour control or recurrence rate, another important clinical parameter is the incidence of late complications. A retrospective analysis of late rectal and recto-sigmoid complications was undertaken for 669 patients. There were 56 patients with stage 1b, 275 patients with stage II and the remaining 338 patients had stages III & IV. The incidence of late complications was observed to be increasing with the stage of the disease. A maximum incidence of late rectal complications of 8.3% was observed for stages III & IV and of about 4% for stage I and II, Table 8.

Table 8
Late rectal complications by stage:
669 cases.

Stage	No. of cases	Complications (%)
I	56	3.6
II	275	4
III+IV	338	8.3

The influence of dose rate on the incidence of late rectal complications was studied. The maximum rectal dose rate was estimated in all patients. For the patients treated with a Henschke applicator, the rectal dose rate varied in the range 50-69 cGy/hour. The late rectal complications were correlated with the rectal dose rate. Increased rectal complications were observed for the higher dose rate (>60 cGy/hour) treatment, Table 9.

Table 9
Late rectal complications related to rectal dose rate by stage and applicator type.

Applicator & maximum rectal dose rate (cGy/hour)	Late complications (%)		
	Stage I	Stage II	Stage III + Stage IV
Fletcher-Suit			
80-99	11	9	3
100-119	-	-	-
120-139	-	-	1.5
> 140	9	6	8
Henschke			
50-59	-	3	4.5
60-69	-	9	6

Similarly, for patients treated with a Fletcher-Suit applicator, a maximum rectal dose rate was estimated. The rectal dose rate varied in the range 80-140 cGy/hr. The late rectal complications were related to the rectal dose rate. Unexpectedly, a marginally increased incidence of late rectal complications was observed for the lower dose rate range of 80-99 cGy/hr, but the difference was not statistically significant, Table 9.

The incidence of late rectal complications was correlated with the fractionation regime or dose/fraction of external irradiation. For combined stages I and II the incidence of late rectal complications was higher with 2 Gy/fraction than with 1.5 Gy/fraction. For combined stages III and IV, the incidence of late rectal complications was significantly ($P<0.05$) higher with weekly hypofractionation than with daily 2 Gy/fraction, Table 7.

The late rectal complications were analysed using the linear quadratic model. The ERD values were calculated for all patients using an α/β value of 2.5 Gy, (Barendsen 1982). The ERDs for continuous irradiation were calculated

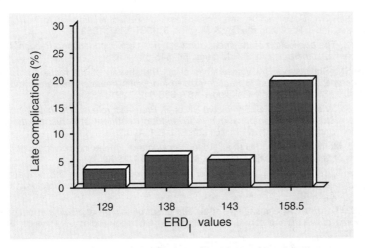

Figure 5. Late rectal complications correlated with extrapolated response dose (ERD$_l$) values, linear quadratic model: α/β and μ values were taken as 2.5 Gy and 0.46/h: statistical significance P > 0.08.

using a repair constant (μ) value of 0.46 h^{-1}, (Dale 1985). The total ERDs delivered to the rectum showed a correlation with the rectal complications for all stages. However, the correlation was not statistically significant (P>0.08), Figure 5.

Conclusions

The influence of intracavitary dose rate on the clinical outcome was definitely observed, although not statistically significant. However, it could be of greater significance in cases treated radically with intracavitary brachytherapy alone such as in early stage disease.

An increase in dose/fraction for hypofractionated treatments with external irradiation was found to have an adverse effect both on tumour control and on late normal tissue injury. While the classical models, NSD and TDF, failed to predict late normal tissue injury, the results shown with the linear quadratic model was found to be very promising. On the basis of our results, changes were made to our subsequent strategies and radiation therapy protocols.

References

Alcock CJ & Toplis PJ, *The influence of pelvic node disease on survival for stage I and II carcinoma of the cervix*, Clinical Radiology, **38**, 13-16, 1987.

Tata Memorial Hospital Cancer Registry, *Annual Report 1989*, Tata Memorial Hospital:Bombay, 1991.

Barendsen GW, *Dose fractionation, dose rates and isoeffect relationship for normal tissue responses*, Int. J. Radiation Biology & Physics, **8**, 1931-1997, 1982.

Dale RG, *The application of the linear quadratic dose effect equation to fractionation and protracted radiotherapy*, Brit. J. Radiology, **58**, 515-528, 1985.

Deore SM, Shrivastava SK, Viswanathan et al, *The severity of late rectal and recto-sigmoid complications related to fraction size in irradiation treatment of carcinoma cervix, stage III B.*, Strahlentherapie Onkologie, **167**, 638-642, 1991.

Deore SM, Viswanathan PS, Shrivastva SK et al, *Predictive role of TDF values in late rectal and recto-sigmoid complications in irradiation treatment of cervix cancer*, Int. J. Radiation Oncology Biology & Physics, **24**, 271-221, 1992.

Eifel PJ, Morris M, Oswald MJ et al, *Adenocarcinoma of the uterine cervix: prognosis and patterns of failure in 367 cases*, Cancer, **65**, 2507-2514, 1990.

Kamura T, Tsukamota N, Tsuruchi J et al, *Multivariate analysis of the histopathologic prognostic factors of cervical cancer in patients undergoing radical hysterectomy*, Cancer, **69**, 181-186, 1992.

Kovalic JJ, Perez CA, Grigsby PW et al, *The effect of volume of disease in patients with carcinoma of the uterine cervix*, Int. J. Radiation Oncology Biology & Physics, **21**, 905-910, 1991.

Lee Yi-Nan, Wang KL, Lin Ming-Huei et al, *Radical hysterectomy with pelvic lymph node dissection for treatment of cervical cancer: a clinical review of 954 cases*, Gynaecologic Oncology, **32**, 135-142, 1989.

Mendenhall WM, McCarty PJ, Morgan LS et al, *Stage IB or IIA-B carcinoma of the intact uterine cervix 6 cm in diameter: is adjuvant extrafascial hysterectomy beneficial ?*, Int. J. Radiation Oncology Biology & Physics, **21**, 899-904, 1991.

O'Brien DM & Carmichael JA, *Presurgical prognostic factors in carcinoma of the cervix, stages IB and IIB*, Amer. J. Obstetrics Gynecology, **158**, 250-254, 1988.

Orton CG, *Time dose factors (TDF) in brachytherapy*, Brit. J. Radiology, **47**, 603-607, 1974.

Orton CG & Ellis F, *A simplification in the use of the NSD concept in practical radiotherapy*, Brit. J. Radiology, **46**, 529-537, 1973.

Perez CA, Fox S, Lockett MA et al, *Impact of dose in outcome of irradiation alone in carcinoma of the uterine cervix: analysis of two different methods*, Int. J. Radiation Oncology Biology & Physics, **21**, 885-898, 1991.

Singh K, *Two regimens with the same TDF but differing morbidity used in the treatment of stage III carcinoma of the cervix*, Brit. J. Radiology, **51**, 357-362, 1978.

Turesson I & Notter G, *The influence of fraction size in radiotherapy on the late normal tissue reactions II. Comparison of the effects of daily and once week fractionation on human skin*, Int. J. Radiation Oncology Biology & Physics, **10**, 599-618, 1984.

10

Carcinoma of the Cervix Treated with Radiotherapy Alone: Results & Prevention of Complications

J.C. Horiot[1], D. Fric[1], I. Barillot[1],
J. Pigneux[2], S. Schraub[3], H. Pourquier[4],
N. Daly[5], M. Bolla[6], R. Rozan[7],
E. Barthelme[8] & R. Keiling[9]

[1] Centre Georges François Leclerc, Dijon, France.
[2] Fondation Bergonié, Bordeaux, France.
[3] Hopital Universitaire Jean Minjoz, Besancon, France.
[4] Centre Val d'Aurelle - Paul Lamarque, Montpellier, France.
[5] Centre Claudius Regaud, Bordeaux, France.
[6] Hopital Universitaire La Tronche, Grenoble, France.
[7] Centre Jean Perrin, Clermont Ferrand, France.
[8] Hopital Bon Secours, Metz, France.
[9] Hospices Civils, Strasbourg, France.

Introduction

1530 patients with cervix carcinoma were accrued from 1970 to 1983 in a multi-institutional cooperative study, Horiot et al (1988). They were treated with radiotherapy alone using external megavoltage radiotherapy followed by brachytherapy applications in 87% of the series, by external radiotherapy alone in 10% and by brachytherapy alone in 3%.

Treatment schedules were adapted from Gilbert Fletcher protocols of the (M.D. Anderson Hospital, Houston) MDAH guidelines based upon the volume of tumour rather than upon the stage of disease. Further refinements of treatment techniques and dose prescription were allowed by computer dosimetry and from 1975 by definition and use of reference points to reduce dose to normal tissues and organs such as bladder and rectum (Chassagne & Horiot 1977, Horiot et al 1977). This method was later adopted in 1985 in the ICRU Report No. 38.

Analysis of locoregional control and survival by stage was reported earlier by Horiot et al (1988,1989). This analysis is now updated with more patients and a longer follow-up: five years minimum and 21 years maximum follow-up. Moreover, since results of locoregional control and survival remain unchanged, we shall focus this presentation on correlating results with tumour volume in 1007 stages I and II patients. Lastly, sequelae and complications will be reported according to the French-Italian glossary (Chassagne et al 1993) and guidelines will be given to prevent complications.

Locoregional Control & Survival

Locoregional control and survival are described in Figures 1 and 2. These results are equal to those of the best series treated by a combination of brachytherapy and surgery for stages I and IIa. The advantage of radiotherapy over a radiosurgical approach becomes obvious in stages IIb and III with five-year local control rates of 76% in IIb, 50% in IIIa and 42% in IIIb resulting in survival rates of 70% in IIb, 48% in IIIa and 42% in IIIb.

However, the prognostic factors are not satisfactorily dealt with in the UICC-FIGO staging since the major prognostic factor, the volume of the cancer is still

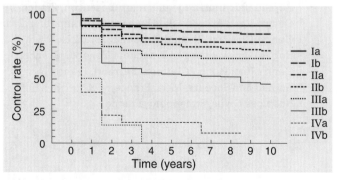

Figure 1. Locoregional control (UICC-FIGO stages).

ignored in this system. Stage Ib may be anything from a few mm^3 to more than 200 cm^3 in some bulky cervical tumours without vaginal or parametrial infiltration.

The comparison between UICC-FIGO staging and MDAH modified staging (Table 1) allows a much better separation of two groups with different prognosis in stage III disease.

Table 1
Comparison of the two staging systems UICC-FIGO and MDAH.

UICC-FIGO Staging		MDAH Staging	
Ia	Micro-invasive	IA	Micro-invasive
Ib	Clinical invasive confined to the cervix	IB	Invasive <1 cm or 2 positive quadrant biopsies
		IC	>1 cm confined to the cervix
IIa	Upper $^2/_3$ of the vagina	IIA	Upper vagina and/or medial parametrium
IIb	Parametrium not fixed to the pelvic wall	IIB	Lesion occupying more than half of the pelvis or barrel shaped endovervix (≥6 cm)
IIIa	Lower $^1/_3$ of the vagina	IIIA	Fixed to one pelvic wall or lower third of the vagina
IIIb	Fixed to pelvic wall and/or non functioning kidney caused by tumour	IIIB	Both pelvic walls or one pelvic wall and lower third of the vagina
IVa	Bladder or rectum mucosa and/or extending beyond the true pelvis	IVA	Biopsy proven bladder or rectum
IVb	Spread to distant organs	IVB	Distant metastases

However, it should be emphasised that in the MDAH staging system, stage IIIA accounts for the lower-third of the vagina only or for single parametrium involvement while IIIB describes bilateral parametrium involvement or combination of parametrium and lower-third of the vagina.

Comparing these two staging systems is not feasible in stages I and II since some patients with stage I UICC-FIGO are classified IIB in the MDAH substaging. We shall return later to this subset.

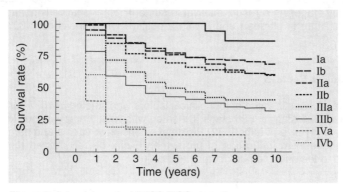

Figure 2. Actuarial survival (UICC-FIGO stages).

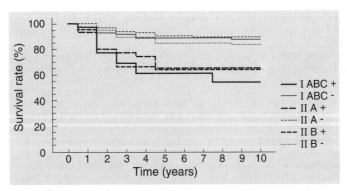

Figure 3. Actuarial survival rates by stage (MDAH stages I-II) correlated with lymphangiogram status.

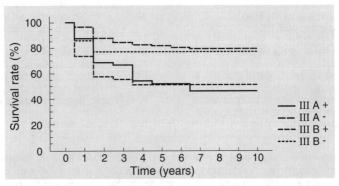

Figure 4. Actuarial survival rates by stage (MDAH stage III) correlated with lymphangiogram status.

The predictive value of a lymphangiogram is again demonstrated in stages I to III: Figures 3 and 4. When positive, a 25% reduction in survival is observed, stage by stage. As a result, survival in stage III with negative lymphangiogram is better than in stages I and II with a positive lymphangiogram: 80% versus 65%.

Prognostic Factors

The prognostic value of four clinical factors was studied in 1007 cervical carcinomas (321 stage I, 686 stage II) treated with radiotherapy alone. These factors were **[1]** Size of tumour. **[2]** Proximal extension to vagina and parametrium. **[3]** Endocervical infiltration of more than 6 cm: barrel shaped tumour. **[4]** Spread to the endometrium: corpus and collum.

Volume of Tumour

The volume of tumour by stage is shown in Table 2 using the MDAH staging. Tumour size was recorded in 77% of the 1090 cases. In stage IC (tumour larger than 1 cm), 72% of the patients had a tumour larger than 3 cm. The clinical determination between proximal and distal stage II is well documented by a three-fold incidence of tumours larger than 5 cm in stage II distal: 34.5% versus 10.5%.

Table 2
Distribution of tumour size with stage: quoted as percentages.

Stage Size	IA,B (52 patients)	IC (259 patients)	IIA (288 patients)	IIB (242 patients)
< 3 cm (248 patients)	100	28	30.5	15
3 - 5 cm (460 patients)	-	65	59	50.5
> 5 cm (133 patients)	-	7	10.5	34.5

Table 3
Correlation ($P < 0.001$) of positive lymphangiograms with tumour size.
Data was available on tumour size when a lymphangiogram was performed and could be interpreted for 582/714 (81.5%) patients.

Tumour size	Positive lymphangiograms	
	No. of patients	% of patients
< 3 cm	17/142	12
3 - 5 cm	80/341	23.5
> 5 cm	45/99	45.5

Table 4
Stage I and II carcinoma of the cervix. Correlation ($P < 0.001$) of all failures (locoregional and distant) with tumour size. Data is available on tumour size and follow-up for 824/1090 (76%) stage I and II patients.

Tumour size	No. of patients	% of patients
< 3 cm	39/248	16
3 - 5 cm	101/447	23
> 5 cm	44/125	33.5

The relationship between tumour volume and nodal risk is shown in Table 3 with a significant increase of positive lymphangiograms from 12% in stages I-II of less than 3 cm, to 45.5% in stages I-II of larger than 5 cm. Treatment failures (locoregional and distant) also correlate well with tumour volume, Table 4, with a regular increase in failure rates with increasing tumour size, from 16% to 35.5%: P<0.001.

Also of interest is the fact that the influence of tumour size is less marked in case of negative lymphangiograms with five-year survival rates of respectively 94%, 86% and 89% for tumour sizes of less than 3 cm, 3-5 cm and larger than 5 cm: P=0.05.

At equal volumes, the location of the cervix tumour (exocervix *versus* endo-cervix) influences the nodal risk, Table 5. A nearly three-fold higher nodal spread is observed in tumours of less than 3 cm when endocervical origin is compared to exocervical origin: 29.5% *versus* 11%.

Table 5
Positive lymphangiograms in stages I & II.
Does the location exocervix/endocervix influence the nodal spread?

Size	Excocervix		Endocervix	
	No. of patients	% of patients	No. of patients	% of patients
< 3 cm	12/108	11	5/17	29.5
3 - 5 cm	51/273	19	28/29	33
> 5 cm	13/40	32.5	32/69	46.5

Proximal versus Distal Extension in Stage II

Locoregional control, metastases and five-year survival rates were studied in 181 stage II proximal vagina, 225 stage II proximal parametrium and 264 stage II distal parametrium cases, Table 6. As expected, there is no difference between the two types of proximal spread. This again points out the absence of a rationale in the UICC-FIGO criteria used for subdividing stage II according to vaginal or parametrial extension.

Table 6
Prognostic value of proximal and distal spread in stage II.

Extension	No. of patients	Locoregional failure rate (%)	Metastatic rate (%)	5-year survival rate (%)
Proximal vagina	181	12	14	88
Proximal parametria	225	16.5	16	87
Distal parametria	264	21	21	83

Locoregional and metastatic failure rates are higher in cases with distal parametrium involvement although the five-year survival rate in our series remains high: 83%. These results compare favourably to stage II treated with surgery alone or with combination of brachytherapy and surgery, respectively 75% and 69%, collected from 1982 to 1986 in the FIGO (1991) Annual Report. This suggests the range of the potential gain resulting from the strategy of radiotherapy alone with external irradiation first followed by brachytherapy applications.

Endocervical Infiltration of >6 cm Diameter (Barrel Shaped Tumours) & Spread to the Endometrium (Corpus & Collum)

These two clinical entities, ignored by the UICC-FIGO, are classified as stage Ib unless the MDAH staging is used in which case these clinical presentations are stage IIB. In our series, barrel shaped tumours were clinically identified, usually after examination under general anaesthesia by several specialists. More recently, CT scans and ultrasonography are used to confirm clinical diagnosis and to provide an objective measurement of tumour regression.

Endometrial spread was rarely biopsy proven since usually the endocervical canal could not be probed. Hence it was in most cases diagnosed by clinical examination and diagnostic radiology procedures: hysterography, CT scans and ultrasonography. The corpus and collum presentation is defined as a tumour (of squamous or glandular origin) in which symmetrical spread to endometrium and endocervix cannot allow the distinction between cervical or endometrial origin.

Using these criteria, 128 stage I and II UICC-FIGO were identified: pure barrel shaped and pure corpus and collum are rare: respectively 20 and 16 patients. In 92 patients, barrel shaped and corpus and collum were diagnosed as a common entity, often in combination with parametrium involvement.

Table 7 analyses locoregional failures, metastases and five-year survival rates for the three presentations. Marked differences in locoregional failure rate are seen with excellent results for pure barrel shaped tumours: 5% versus 18.5% for corpus and collum and 31.5% for combined presentations.

Table 7
Cervical carcinoma stage IIB barrel and/or endometrial spread
with or without spread to the parametrium.

	No. of patients	Locoregional ± metastases rate (%)	Metastatic rate (%)	Total failure rate (%)	5-year survival rate (%)
Pure barrel	20	5	25	25	74
Corpus & collum	16	18.5	31	37.5	66
Combinations ± parametrium	92	31.5	26	38	68

The metastatic rate is about the same in the three groups, 25%-31%, because of the increased lymphatic risk linked to massive endocervical spread. Pure barrel shaped tumours have a better five-year survival, 74% *versus* 67%, due to better pelvic control of disease. It is therefore logical to reconsider stage II disease by grouping proximal spread (either vaginal or parametrial) as stage

IIA, to include only distal parametrial spread or spread to the middle-third of the vagina as IIB, and finally to create a stage IIC to acknowledge the poorer prognosis of most patients with barrel shaped tumours and/or endometrial spread.

Complications of Treatment

Charts of 1530 patients (including all stages) were reviewed to report complications using the French-Italian glossary (Chassagne et al 1993). This glossary allows an accurate identification of the grade of early and late normal tissue damage using five grades of increasing severity (G0 - G4) and describing each grade of complication per tissue or organ at risk. For example, rectal complications G1 include five definitions of signs and symptoms (G1a - G1e) corresponding to different types of morbidity of about the same inconvenience for the patient. The glossary was also designed to register and analyse signs and symptoms induced by different types of treatment: radiotherapy, surgery and chemotherapy.

We can then compare the incidence and severity of sequelae and complications, and moreover identify unambiguously each type of complication that otherwise would remain hidden behind the scoring of complications. This should, at last, lead to objective comparisons between series treated with different strategies, when authors comply with the rules and definitions of this glossary.

Distribution of Complications by Grade

No complication (G0) was reported in 922/1530 patients: 60%. This probably underestimates the occurrence of G1 symptoms, especially for acute reversible toxicity due to treatment that is often considered by radiotherapists as a 'normal symptomatology'. 1384 complications of all grades were reported in 608 patients: an average of 2.3 complications per patient with complication.

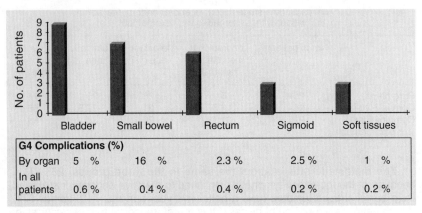

G4 Complications (%)				
By organ 5 %	16 %	2.3 %	2.5 %	1 %
In all patients 0.6 %	0.4 %	0.4 %	0.2 %	0.2 %

Figure 5. Lethal complications by organ or tissue of origin: 28 complications in 1530 patients (1.8%).

46% of these complications were G1, 39% were G2 and 13% were G3. 28 patients (1.8 % of the group of 1530 patients) had G4: death directly or indirectly induced by treatment complication. These lethal complications are detailed in Figure 5. The incidence of lethal complications for a given tissue or organ shows that, although death from small bowel complications only represents 0.4% of patients, lethal complications account for 16% of small bowel complications.

Distribution of Complications by Tissue or Organ

Gynaecological tract and pelvic soft tissues are the most frequent sites of sequelae and complications, in respectively 26% and 19% of patients. Then follows rectum (17%), bladder (20%), sigmoid (7%) and small bowel (3%).

Rectal complications by grade and type are described in Figure 6 which includes the score and type of complication in a summarised form. Most G1 complications were G1b: minor rectorragia. G3 rectal complications are mostly

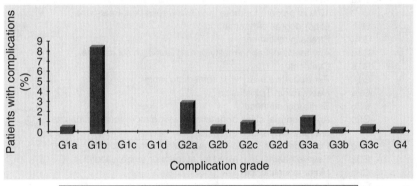

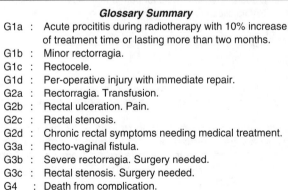

Glossary Summary

G1a : Acute procititis during radiotherapy with 10% increase of treatment time or lasting more than two months.
G1b : Minor rectorragia.
G1c : Rectocele.
G1d : Per-operative injury with immediate repair.
G2a : Rectorragia. Transfusion.
G2b : Rectal ulceration. Pain.
G2c : Rectal stenosis.
G2d : Chronic rectal symptoms needing medical treatment.
G3a : Recto-vaginal fistula.
G3b : Severe rectorragia. Surgery needed.
G3c : Rectal stenosis. Surgery needed.
G4 : Death from complication.

Figure 6. Rectal complications by grade and type.

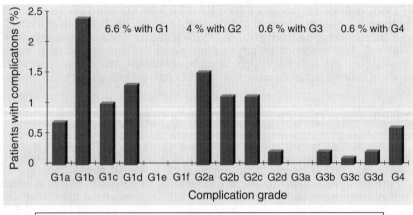

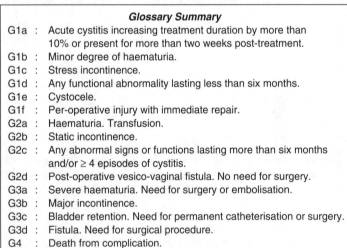

Glossary Summary

G1a : Acute cystitis increasing treatment duration by more than 10% or present for more than two weeks post-treatment.

G1b : Minor degree of haematuria.

G1c : Stress incontinence.

G1d : Any functional abnormality lasting less than six months.

G1e : Cystocele.

G1f : Per-operative injury with immediate repair.

G2a : Haematuria. Transfusion.

G2b : Static incontinence.

G2c : Any abnormal signs or functions lasting more than six months and/or $\geq$ 4 episodes of cystitis.

G2d : Post-operative vesico-vaginal fistula. No need for surgery.

G3a : Severe haematuria. Need for surgery or embolisation.

G3b : Major incontinence.

G3c : Bladder retention. Need for permanent catheterisation or surgery.

G3d : Fistula. Need for surgical procedure.

G4 : Death from complication.

Figure 7. Bladder complications by type.

represented by G3a (recto-vaginal fistulae: 1.6%) from a total of 2.5% G3 rectal complications. Death occurred because of rectal complication in 0.4% of patients.

A similar breakdown of complication data is available for each tissue and organ and will now be summarised. Most sigmoid complications were G2a, bowel symptoms of moderate intensity reported from sigmoid origin in 4.3% from a total of 5.2%. G3 was observed in 1.3% (bowel occlusion in most instances) and G4 in 0.2%.

Bladder complications are shown in Figure 7. Severe complications are rare: 0.6% of G3 and 0.6% of G4. Most G1 and G2 sequelae (2.4% and 1.5%) were due to minor or moderate degrees of haematuria.

Treatment induced signs or symptoms from the gynaecological tract and pelvic soft tissues were reported in 26% of patients. 3% are severe and occurred in patients cured from disease extending down to the lower-third of the vagina. Most G1 complications (13%) are represented by a decrease of about 50% of the original vaginal size while most of the 8.6% G2 correspond to vaginal stenosis and/or dyspareunia.

Prevention of Complications

Prevention of complications is based upon treatment individualisation. The general treatment guidelines are modified patient by patient depending upon the initial extent of disease, the quality of regression during external irradiation and last by modelling dose distribution of brachytherapy. Reference points for bladder, rectum (reference and mean) and reference volume for 60 Gy combined isodose curves of external and intracavitary radiation therapy have been described (Chassagne & Horiot 1977, Horiot et al 1977, Pourquier et al 1987) and used since 1975 (Combes et al 1985).

The ICRU Report No. 38 published in 1985 adopted nearly the same recommendations as those described in our earlier proposal. More recently (Barillot et al 1993), the definition of bladder reference points was further improved from individual measurements by ultrasonography to record the maximum and mean dose delivered to the bladder mucosa.

Prevention of complications was effectively achieved by plotting all grades of complications on scattergrams analysing the relationship between the 60 Gy reference volume and reference dose to critical organs (Crook et al 1987, Esche et al 1987, Esche et al 1987). Using this concept at the time of the last brachytherapy application enables one to foresee the incidence, type and score of complications to which the planned dose/volume exposes the individual patient. Then, the radiotherapist has to decide whether or not treatment planning should be modified to bring back the patient in a safer area by either reducing the duration of application or by changing the radioactive length and/or activity.

The experience collected throughout the past two decades is reflected in the decreasing incidence of grade 3 complications from 14.5% before 1979 to 6% since 1980, while the pelvic failure rate remained unchanged: 15% *versus* 13%. The complication rate is even lower when selecting stage I and II patients with favourable anatomy (eg. when brachytherapy could be performed with standard applicators), in whom the rate of grade 3 complications fell below 2%, (Esche et al 1987).

Conclusions

In summary, a combination of external megavoltage radiotherapy followed by intracavitary brachytherapy applications (an average of two) with respective contributions based upon the initial volume of disease, and individually adjusted according to tumour regression and dose distribution to critical organs, is now the standard approach for bulky stage I and for all stages II, III and IV. This treatment strategy should be the control arm when comparing other modalities of treatment in a controlled clinical trial.

The results of this series were obtained despite an unfavourable selection of patients due to two factors. [1] 44% of the patients had associated medical problems (such as diabetes, hypertension, obesity and cardiovascular disease) that would have resulted in an increased risk for surgical procedures. [2] As detailed earlier, at least 50% of stage I and II of this series had tumour sizes larger than 3 cm. Comparisons with other series of the literature should be made whenever possible using the same subgroups by stage and by volume of disease.

References

Barillot I, Horiot JC, Maingon P, Bone-Lepinoy MC, Vaillant D & Feutray S, *Maximum and mean bladder dose defined by ultrasonography. Comparison with the ICRU reference in gynaecological brachytherapy.* Radiotherapy & Oncology, In press, 1994.

Chassagne D & Horiot JC, *Propositions pour une définition commune des points de référence en curiethérapie gynécologique*, J. Radiologie Electrologie, **58**, 371-373, 1977.

Chassagne D, Sismondi P, Horiot JC, Sinistrero G, Bey P, Zola P, Pernot M, Gerbaulet A, Kunkler I & Michel G, *A glossary for reporting complications of treatment in gynaecological cancers*, Radiotherapy & Oncology, **26**, 195-202,1993.

Combes PF, Daly NJ, Horiot JC, Achille E, Keiling R, Pigneux J, Pourquier H, Rozan R, Schraub S & Vrousos C, *Results of radiotherapy alone in 581 patients with stage II carcinoma of the uterine cervix*, Int. J. Radiation Oncology Biology & Physics, **11**, 463-471, 1985.

Crook JM, Esche BA, Chaplain G, Isturiz J, Sentenac I & Horiot JC, *Dose-volume analysis and the prevention of radiation sequelae in cervical cancer*, Radiotherapy & Oncology, **8**, 321-332, 1987.

Esche BA, Crook JM & Horiot JC, *Dosimetric methods in the optimization of radiotherapy for carcinoma of the uterine cervix*, Int. J. Radiation Oncology Biology & Physics, **13**, 1183-1192, 1987.

Esche BA, Crook JM, Isturiz J & Horiot JC, *Reference volume, milligram-hours and external irradiation for the Fletcher applicator*, Radiotherapy & Oncology, **9**, 255-261, 1987.

FIGO (International Federation of Gynecology and Obstetrics), *Annual report on the results of treatment in gynaecological cancer. Twenty-first volume: Statements of results obtained in patients 1982 to 1986, inclusive 3 and 5-year survival up to 1990*, F. Pettersson (Ed), Int. J. of Gynecology & Obstetrics, **36**, 1991.

Horiot JC, Jampolis S, Pipard G, Schroeder P, Sentenac I, Ibrahim E & Aupecle P, *Evolution des critères dosimétriques de la curiethérapie des cancers du col utérin*, J. Radiologie Electrologie, **58**, 379-386, 1977.

Horiot JC, Pigneux J, Pourquier H, Schraub S, Achille E, Keiling R, Combes P, Rozan R, Vrousos C & Daly N, *Radiotherapy alone in carcinoma of the intact uterine cervix according to G.H. Fletcher guidelines: a French cooperative study of 1383 cases*, Int. J. Radiation Oncology Biology & Physics, **14**, 605-611, 1988.

Horiot JC, Pourquier H, Schraub S, Pigneux J, Brosens M & Loiseau D, *Current status of the management of cancer of the cervix in daily practice and in clinical research*, in:*Brachytherapy 2*, Mould RF (Ed), 199-214, Nucletron:Leersum, 1989.

ICRU (International Commission on Radiation Units and Measurements), *Dose and volume specification for reporting intracavitary therapy in gynaecology, ICRU Report No. 38*, ICRU:Bethesda, 1985.

Pourquier H, Delard R, Achille E, Daly NJ, Horiot JC, Keiling R, Pigneux J, Rozan R, Schraub S & Vrousos C, *A quantified approach to the analysis and prevention of urinary complication in radiotherapeutic treatment of cancer of the cervix*, Int. J. Radiation Oncology Biology & Physics, **13**, 1025-1033, 1987.

11

HDR Brachytherapy for Endometrial Cancer

K. Rotte

Universitäts-Frauenklinik,
Strahlenabteilung,
Josef Schneider Strasse 4,
7800 Würzburg,
Federal Republic of Germany.

Introduction

Endometrial carcinoma is the most common invasive genital malignancy. In contrast to cervical cancer, its incidence is increasing and it is much more difficult to establish the size of the target volume. In addition, a wide variety of individual shapes and widths of the cavum uteri causes severe problems to the radiotherapist's desire for a homogeneous dose distribution within the target volume. These difficulties are probably one of the reasons that in endometrial cancer contrary to carcinoma of the cervix uteri, the treatment results of primarily irradiated cases are worse than the results of surgical procedures.

Therefore, the usual treatment of endometrial carcinoma is hysterectomy and bilateral salpingo-oophorectomy. However, if a patient is not fit for surgery, radiotherapy as the primary treatment should be employed. Therefore primary radiotherapy plays an important role for patients with obesity, an age of more than 60 years, diabetes and/or high blood pressure: all of which magnify the risk of an operation.

At the Gynaecological Clinic of the University of Würzburg approximately 20% of the patients treated are found to be unfit for surgery, Figure 1. In these cases usually a combination of brachytherapy and teletherapy is performed.

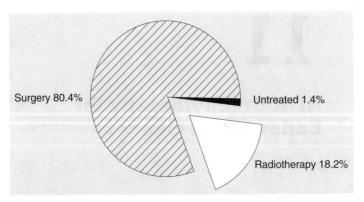

Figure 1. Method of treatment for 2017 cases of carcinoma of corpus uteri 1972-1991 at the Universitäts-Frauenklinik, Würzburg.

Requirements

For adequate brachytherapy there are three principal requirements, Table 1. The first requirement was achieved by the classical Heyman technique which allowed packing of the uterine cavity with radium sources in an almost optimal way. The second requirement however, concerning radiation protection, could not be fulfilled by this technique, as is well known. Also, being a low dose rate technique with a duration of treatment lasting 30 hours or more, clinical complications which were mainly venous thrombosis, occurred rather frequently and especially in combination with hypertension, obesity and diabetes mellitus which are typical findings in patients with endometrial carcinoma. In our department for example, thromboembolic complications were found in 7% of the cases when using the classical Heyman packing, (Rotte 1990).

Table 1
Brachytherapy requirements for endometrial carcinoma.

- A dose distribution adapted to the individual situation
  with dose concentration in the target volume and minimising
  the dose to the organs at risk.
- A practical technique with regard to radiation protection
  and to reproducibility of source positioning.
- A dose rate which minimises clinical complications
  without reducing therapeutic efficiency.

Techniques

These problems were solved by introducing different high dose rate (HDR) afterloading techniques. Initially we preferred a double-rod-shaped applicator. In none of our patients treated with this applicator was thromboembolism observed.

All these new techniques had a rather insufficient individual dose distribution due to the rigid applicators we used and this was a clear disadvantage in comparison to the classical Heyman packing (Joslin et al 1967, Kucera et al 1990, Rauthe et al 1988, Riippa et al 1985). In order to perform optimal brachytherapy it was consequently necessary to combine selectively the advantages of Heyman packing with remote afterloading techniques using HDR.

In order to overcome the disadvantages concerning radiation protection Simon & Silverstone (1976) developed a modified Heyman packing method.with hollow capsules that were manually afterloaded with caesium-137 sources. Using this system as a substitute for the original Heyman radium applicators the staff exposure is reduced considerably but not completely eliminated, whereas the treatment time remains unchanged in comparison to the radium method. The accuracy in the placement of the applicators is considerably enhanced, as the placing of the (at that time empty) applicators into the uterine cavity is without any risk of radiation hazard to the staff.

Only with the introduction of remote controlled and fractionated HDR afterloading it was it possible to combine total treatment protection and short treatment times avoiding clinical complications such as thromboembolic diseases and also provide for reproducible source positioning.

HDR afterloading has now been in use for nearly 30 years (Joslin 1989). During this time a variety of techniques for primary brachytherapy of endometrial carcinoma were introduced (Bauer et al 1981, Henschke et al 1966, Joslin et al 1967, Kucera et al 1990, Rauthe et al 1988, Riippa et al 1985, Rotte 1975).

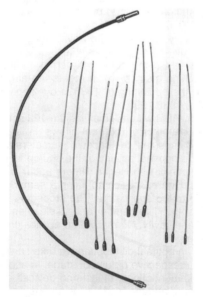

Figure 2. Small shaped applicator capsules (four sizes) for simulating the Heyman technique with remote controlled HDR afterloading.

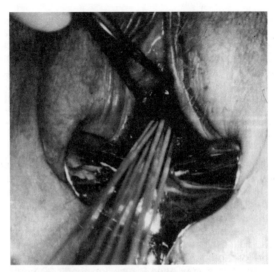

Figure 3. Capsules in situ after application.

Nearly all of these techniques used rigid applicators, resulting in a rather insufficient individual dose distribution irrespective of the type of applicator. This was a clear disadvantage in comparison to the techniques of Heyman (1941) and of Simon & Silverstone (1976).

The aim of selectively combining the advantages of Heyman packing with those of HDR remote afterloading was eventually realised by the development of afterloading equipment using sufficiently small radiation sources. Such a modified Heyman packing method which meets the above outlined provisions has been used since the beginning of 1988 in our department (Herbolsheimer et al 1988,1989, Rotte, 1988,1990).

The microSelectron-HDR with its small iridium-192 source (external diameter of 1.1 mm and active diameter of 0.6 mm) allows us to pack the uterine cavity with a maximum of 18 capsules, the capsule diameters available being 8, 6, 5, or 4 mm, Figure 2. The nominal activity of the source is 10 Ci (370 MBq). After dilation of the uterine cervix with Hegar dilators under general anaesthesia the capsules are inserted, Figure 3. Each contains a semi-rigid dummy to facilitate the correct placement of the applicators. The procedure is supported by percutaneous ultrasound control. The number of capsules needed of course depends on the size of the uterine cavity. Normally 6-10 applicators are necessary to sufficiently pack the uterus.

In order to obtain an optimal distribution we take care to place an additional capsule in the cervix, irrespective of tumour stage. In accordance with the ICRU report 38 (1985) recommendations, measuring devices are inserted in the rectum (using five detectors) and the bladder (using one detector in the centre of a Foley catheter balloon). Finally, vaginal gauze packing is applied to hold the applicators in place. The whole procedure lasts about 8-10 minutes and thus anaesthesia is restricted to a relatively short time.

Treatment Planning

After the application of the capsules is performed, isocentric orthogonal radiographs of the pelvis are made to visualise the relationship of the applicators to the organs at risk and to the bony structures of the pelvis, Figures 4a, 4b. By digitising these images and using a computer planning system, an individual dose distribution in three dimensions is produced. In some cases isocentric stereoscopic images can facilitate the digitising procedure. The doses measured directly by the rectal and bladder probes can be compared with those calculated using the planning system. Differences of more than ± 5% will not be tolerated without the physicist in charge rechecking the entire procedure.

In order to facilitate the planning procedure a standard planning program is stored in the computer. Optimisation according to the individual case can be performed by changing the time weights of the individual capsules. Each capsule can be distinguished by the different shapes of the dummies they contain. This plays an important role in cases where infiltration of the cervical canal or a deep infiltration of the myometrium is detected by clinical examination or imaging procedures, and also especially in those rare cases where the calculated doses within the organs at risk are too high.

We apply five fractions of 10 Gy, 10 days apart, to a reference isodose running through a so-called point MY (the abbreviation of myometrium) which is situated 2 cm below and lateral to the top of the dose distribution axis, ie. the axis of the uterine cavity. Thus our reference volume approximates the outline of the serosa of the uterus.

The doses calculated by the planning system within the rectum and the bladder are compared with those measured directly by rectal and bladder probes, as already mentioned. If there are no relevant differences, the calculated doses at the reference points in organs at risk, as recommended by ICRU (1985) are reliable and confirm a correct correlation between the radiation plan and the dose which is actually delivered, Figure 5a, 5b.

Nevertheless, the dose delivered to point MY is only an approximation, even if we perform an optimal packing of the uterus. Nuclear magnetic resonance images especially produce distinct pictures of the uterine cavity and of the outer

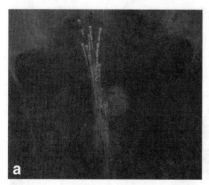

Figure 4. Orthogonal radiographs showing the applicator bundle, rectum and bladder probes, **(a)** anterior-posterior view, **(b)** lateral view.

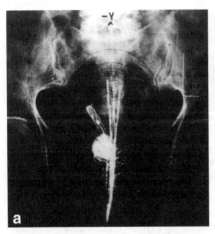
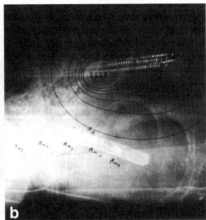

Figure 5. Projection of isodoses onto the radiographs shown in **Figures 4a,b,** (a) anterior-posterior view, (b) lateral view.

shape of the uterus. Since May 1992 we have access to MR equipment. Therefore since that time we always measure the thickness of the uterus by MR imaging and make our treatment planning accordingly, Figure 6a, 6b.

The doses at the rectum and the bladder should not exceed 7 Gy/fraction, namely 60 Gy within six weeks, including the teletherapy contribution. Because of the relatively great distance to the uterine applicators the average dose range is 3-5 Gy/fraction, so in contrast to primary irradiation of cervical cancer there are usually no problems to overcome.

The intracavitary applications are scheduled within a course of megavoltage treatment to the pelvic lymphatics, which are irradiated using 10 MV photons from a linear accelerator utilising bisegmental arc techniques with two isocentres. We apply 25 fractions of 2 Gy to the maximum dose point and the target volume must be enclosed at least by the 80% isodose.

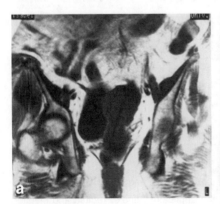
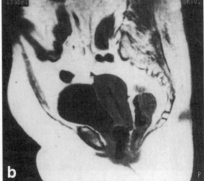

Figure 6. MR images of the uterus, (a) coronal view, (b) sagittal view.

Planning is supported by computer tomography in several slice positions. The target volumes are defined with regard to the individual anatomy and to the area that is irradiated by afterloading. The contribution of teletherapy to the brachytherapy reference volume should not exceed 10 Gy. Field sizes and distance between the isocentres conform to these requirements.

From 1972 onwards HDR afterloading increasingly replaced Heyman packing with radium in our department and from 1983 onwards HDR was used exclusively. The reason as already stated, was that with radium therapy, which is LDR, we encountered a total of eight cases (7.5%) of thromboembolism with two lethal outcomes. No such sequelae occurred with HDR afterloading. With radium the overall dose was applied in three equal fractions and with HDR afterloading in five equal fractions. The correction factor used to achieve isodose effects between the two forms of treatment was 0.8 during the whole period. The additional external beam therapy as outlined before was carried out in such a way as to keep the overall dose distribution in both treatment arms similar. We apply a total dose of 50 Gy with a weekly dose of 10 Gy.

Results

During 1972-1977 we used rigid double-rod shaped applicators for the intracavitary HDR brachytherapy, (Rotte 1988). From the beginning of 1988 we changed entirely to the previously outlined remote controlled HDR packing technique. Up to the end of 1991 a total of 53 patients were treated in this manner. Since that time the total number of applications in these cases is 265. Patients who received a previous treatment with different fractionation, total dose, overall time or teletherapy were not taken into consideration in this analysis irrespective the reasons causing the previous schedules. The mean age of the patients was 77 years.

As shown in Table 2 we have to date one local recurrence which occurred in a stage III tumour within 12 months after treatment. It was associated with rapidly progressing metastases of the lung and pleural effusion. The patient died a few weeks later. Acute side effects are restricted to a mild cystitis or diarrhoea. These are seen in about 70% of our patients, the diarrhoea being primarily related to external beam irradiation. Severe early complications have not occurred to date, Table 2.

Our overall treatment results and icidence of side effects in bladder and rectum from 1972-1991 in patients with endometrial cancer who were treated with radiotherapy alone are shown in Tables 3 and 4. Concerning late side effects, only those patients who have a follow-up time of more than 24 months (N=327) were taken into account. In these cases no severe side effects such as fistulae or ulcers have to date been observed.

Discussion & Conclusions

Summarising our experience in the last 15 years we conclude that utilising the possibilities of computer planning systems for changing the time weights of one or more capsules results in an additional improvement of the dose distribution with regard to the tumour as well as to the organs at risk.

Table 2
Preliminary results of primary radiotherapy with HDR afterloading
using a modified Heyman packing technique: 1988-1991.
Minimum follow-up period of seven months.

FIGO stage	Number of cases	Number free of local disease	Number of local recurrences	Number of distant metastases	Number of late side effects
I	21	21	0	0	0
II	23	23	0	0	0
III	9	8	1	0	0

Table 3
Recurrence free survival following primary radiotherapy:
367 cases treated 1972-1991.

Stage	Radium, LDR,1972-1982	Double-rod shaped applicator, HDR, 1972-1987	Heyman capsules, HDR, 1988-1991
I	76.9% (30/39)	72.7% (72/99)	100% (21/21)
II	73.9% (34/46)	72.4% (76/105)	100% (23/23)
III	28.5% (6/21)	35.3% (6/17)	89% (8/9)
Minimum follow-up period	9 years	5 years	7 months

Table 4
Incidence of late side effects to bladder and rectum following primary radiotherapy:
367 cases treated 1972-1991.
(No vesico-vaginal or recto-vaginal fistulae were observed).

	Radium, LDR, 1972-1982	Double-rod shaped applicator, HDR,1972-1987	Heyman capsules, HDR, 1988-1991
Bladder	1.8% (2/106)	1.7% (4/221)	0/53
Rectum	5.6% (6/106)	5.2% (11/221)	0/53
Total no of lesions	7.5% (8/106)	7.0% (15/221)	0/53
Minimum follow-up period	9 years	5 years	7 months

Irradiation under the conditions of HDR afterloading requires the patient to be immobilised only for a short time. This minimises the risk of thromboembolism and guarantees a reliable source position during treatment. It does not result in a higher rate of recurrences or in a greater incidence of side effects when compared with protracted radiation if radiobiological aspects are taken into account (Baier 1979, Dale 1990, Fowler 1989, Warmelink et al 1989).

In spite of the well known mobility of the uterus we do not consider brachytherapy as a boost that is given to homogeneous external beam radiation of the pelvis. Instead, we distinguish two separate target volumes in order to avoid reduced brachytherapy doses within the uterus. We are convinced that the high central doses surrounded by steep dose gradients are the reason for the very good clinical results in gynaecological radiotherapy (Baier 1979).

In using a biaxial arc technique in teletherapy we avoid the sharply defined dose profiles that occur with opposing fixed fields with central shielding. We believe that the relatively smooth transition between the two dose profiles (brachytherapy and external beam therapy) is a good technique for parametrial tumour infiltration. The treatment planning is supported by computer tomography in several planes and the target volumes are individually defined at each plane. This is necessary to define the isocentres with respect to individual uterine positions and to reduce the treatment volumes.

I want to stress that an individual procedure as outlined is absolutely practical under daily routine conditions. Although of course a specialised staff and suitable equipment is required. Thus, although surgical treatment of endometrial cancer will be the first choice of therapy at least in the foreseeable future, for the group of patients with high surgical risk, which in our hospital consists of about 20% of the overall figure, primary irradiation is an alternative to be considered seriously.

References

Baier K, *HDR afterloading und biologische Therapieplanung*, in:*Medizinphysik, Annual Proceedings*, Leetz HK (Ed), 75-79, 1979.

Bauer M, von Fournier D, Fehrentz F, Kuttig H, zum Winkel K & Neldner F, *Afterloading-Methode zur Simulation der intrauterinen Packmethode beim Korpuskarzinom*, Strahlentherapie, **157**, 793-800, 1981.

Dale R, *The use of small fraction numbers in high dose rate gynaecological afterloading: some radiobiological considerations*, Brit. J. Radiology, **63**, 290-294, 1990.

Fowler JF, *The linear quadratic formula and progress in fractionated radiotherapy, a review*, Brit. J. Radiology, **62**, 679-694, 1989.

Henschke UK, Hilaris BS & Mahan GD, *Intracavitary radiation therapy of the uterine cervix by remote afterloading with cycling sources*, Amer. J. Roentgenology, **96**, 45-51, 1966.

Herbolsheimer M, Baier K, Gall P, Löffler E & Rotte K, *Ferngesteuerte intrauterine Nachlade-Packmethode beim Endometriumkarzinom*, Röntgen-Berichte, **17**, 226-234, 1988.

Herbolsheimer M, *Intrauterine packing by remote HDR afterloading in endometrial carcinoma*, in:*Changes in brachytherapy*, Rotte K & Kiffer J (Eds), 130-138, Wachholz:Nürnberg, 1989.

Heyman J, Reuterwall O & Brenner S, *The Radiumhemmet experience with radiotherapy in cancer of the corpus of the uterus. Classification, method of treatment and results*, Acta Radiologica, **22**, 11-98, 1941.

ICRU, *Dose and volume specification for reporting intracavitary therapy in gynaecology*, ICRU Report No.38, ICRU:Bethesda, 1985.

Joslin CA, O'Connell D & Howard NW, *The treatment of uterine carcinoma using the Cathetron III. Clinical considerations and preliminary reports on treatment results*, Brit. J. Radiology, **40**, 899-904, 1967.

Joslin CA, Henschke memorial lecture, E*ndocurietherapy Hyperthermia Oncology*, **5**, 69-81, 1989.

Kucera H, Vavra N & Weghaupt K, *Zum Wert der alleinigen Bestrahlung des allgemein inoperablen Endometriumkarzinoms mittels High Dose Rate Iridium-192*, Geburtsh. u. Frauenheilk, **50**, 610-613, 1990.

Rauthe G, Vahrson H & Giers G, *Five year results and complications in endometrium cancer HDR afterloading vs. conventional radium therapy*, in:*High dose rate afterloading in the treatment fo cancer of the uterus, breast and rectum*, Vahrson H & Rauthe G (Eds), 240-245, Urban & Schwarzenberg:Munich, 1988.

Riipa P, Kivinen S & Kauppila A, *Comparison of Heyman packing and Cathetron afterloading methods in the treatment of endometrial cancer*, Brit. J. Radiology, **58**, 437-441, 1985.

Rotte K, *Technik, Strahlenbiologie und Ergebnisse der Afterloading-Behandlung gynäkologischer Karzinome, Röntgen-Berichte*, **4**, 251-266, 1975.

Rotte K, *Long time results of HDR afterloading in comparison with radium therapy and in endometrium cancer*, in:*High dose rate afterloading in the treatment of cancer of the uterus, breast and rectum*, Vahrson H & Rauthe G (Eds), 218-221, Urban & Schwarzenberg: München, Wien, Baltimore, 1988.

Rotte K, *Technique and results of HDR afterloading in cancer of the endometrium*, in:*Brachytherapy HDR and LDR*, Martinez AA, Orton CG & Mould RF (Eds), 68-79, Nucletron:Columbia, 1990.

Simon N & Silverstone SM, *Afterloading with miniaturised 137-caesium sources in the treatment of cancer of the uterus*, Int. J. Radiation Oncology Biology & Physics, **1**, 1017-1021, 1976.

Warmelink C, Ezzell G & Orton CG, *Use of time dose fractionation model to design high dose rate fractionation schemes*, in:*Brachytherapy 2*, Mould RF (Ed), 41-48, Nucletron:Leersum, 1989.

12

Role of Brachytherapy in Treatment of Head & Neck Cancers: Institut Gustave-Roussy Experience with 1140 Patients

A. Gerbaulet, C. Haie-Meder, H. Marsiglia, U. Kumar, A. Lusinchi, J-L. Habrand, G. Mamelle, F. Flamant & D. Chassagne

Institut Gustave-Roussy,
Rue Camille Desmoulins,
94805 Villejuif Cedex,
France.

Introduction

Brachytherapy utilises the delivery of ionising radiation using sealed radionuclides from very close distances to malignant tumours, in contrast to external beam irradiation where radiation is delivered from greater distances. Today, brachytherapy has a very significant and clearly defined role in the management of neoplasms and plays an important role in the cure of many of them. The brachytherapy of head and neck cancers predominantly utilises the various techniques of interstitial brachytherapy and it is this subject which will be discussed in some detail.

Historical Notes

The origins of brachytherapy began almost immediately after the discovery of X-rays by Röntgen in November 1895 when in March 1896 Henri Becquerel discovered the natural radiation emissions from uranium crystals. Then in December 1898 Marie and Pierre Curie announced that they had isolated radium from pitchblende, having previously (July 1898) discovered radioactive polonium.

In 1903 the first radium implants for the treatment of cancer were independently reported by Robert Abbe in New York and by Strebel in Munich. Subsequently, there was a host of developments in this sphere but with primitive equipment and dosimetry and with manually preloaded sources. In the early 1930s the Manchester system was devised and the Paterson-Parker rules of implantation and of dosimetry then entered routine clinical practice.

From 1950 onwards, rapid technical evolution of external radiotherapy made the practice of brachytherapy relatively uncommon. The high energy teletherapy machines with sophisticated treatment planning, dosimetric methods, good depth dose delivery and radiation safety made indications for interstitial radium brachytherapy decrease significantly.

Fortunately, brachytherapy staged a revival with the discovery of artificial radioactivity by Irene Curie and Frédéric Joliot, in 1933, because with the later developments of the nuclear reactor and of particle accelerators, the production of radionuclides for medical use has now become routine. Some of the improvements responsible for the present day status of interstitial brachytherapy were: afterloading system development (reducing radiation hazards to personnel), radioactive iridium-192 wires as an alternative to radium needles and the evolution of the Paris system as a guide for clinical brachytherapy, amongst others. The main advantages of iridium-192 are:

- Very thin, flexible source wires with a maximum diameter of 0.5 mm
- Conveniently short half-life of 74 days
- Low gamma energy of 0.35 MV facilitating relatively easy shielding and protection of operating personnel
- Afterloading application systems: either remote or manual. Ensures better implantation geometry and avoids unnecessary radiation exposure to staff.

Advantages of Brachytherapy

A radioactive substance delivers a high dose of radiation within the tumour volume and beyond. At the same time, there is a rapid fall-off of the dose intensities as one moves away from the sources. This allows, in a given implant system, a very high dose of radiation to be delivered to the target area with a considerable sparing of the surrounding normal tissue around this area.

This therefore allows the brachytherapist to deliver a tumouricidal dose of radiation to a relatively small volume with precision as the very high doses are delivered immediately around each source when the radioactive material is placed within the tumour. This form of localised radiotherapy is not possible with external beam radiotherapy.

Also, from the radiobiological view point, brachytherapy delivers continuous radiation during an overall short duration of about six days. This is in contrast to external radiotherapy.

The Radioactive Source: Iridium -192

The radioactive material used for implantation at the Institut Gustave-Roussy is routinely iridium-192 wires. It has many advantages in the treatment of head and neck cancer. It is supplied as wire of iridium-platinum alloy (25:75).

It can have a diameter of either 0.3 mm or 0.5 mm depending on the technique of application. The lengths of the wires are cut according to clinical necessity.

At our centre, we store in a large 'iridium safe' different wire lengths of various dose intensities. In any given clinical situation, therefore, the sources for implantation can be readily chosen from this safe, with the desired length and intensity.

The Paris System

The early 1960s saw the birth of the Paris system of dosimetry and by 1970 its foundation was laid, based on the clinical experience of the French school of brachytherapy. After 25 years of use the system has proved to be simple, reliable and clinically efficacious. The Paris system advocates the following four main guidelines:

[1] Linear activity of the sources must be uniform along the lines and identical in all the lines used

[2] Sources must be straight, parallel and equidistant from each other

[3] The central plane is defined as the plane including the midpoint of all the sources and at right angles to the axes of the sources.

[4] The distances between sources may vary from implant to implant, but in a given implant must be identical between the lines.

In the central plane the following two dose rates are calculated:

[1] **Basal dose rate** which is the average lowest dose rate between a set of lines

[2] **Reference dose rate** which is the dose rate equal to 85% of the basal dose rate of the given implantation system.

Depending on the number of active wires and their planar configuration, in volume implants (which are the most common type in head and neck cancers) the implantation can be subdivided geometrically into triangles. The minimal dose received in each such triangle is called basal dose. Basal dose is thus calculated for each triangle and the average of the basal doses for the triangles in the implant plan gives us the mean basal dose. 85% of this dose is taken as the reference dose. Based on clinical experience, which is found to fit very closely to the desired target volume, the prescribed tumour dose is delivered at the level of this reference isodose.

Afterloading Interstitial Brachytherapy

After a full diagnostic work-up the patient is taken into the operation theatre and prepared for interstitial brachytherapy with the usual surgical asepsis. Depending upon the type of procedure performed, the anaesthesia is either local or general. With good visualisation and assisted by fluoroscopy with an image intensifier, the hollow guide needles are introduced in and around the patient's lesion according to the guidelines of the Paris system. This is achieved as accurately as possible. After a satisfactory implantation of the target volume a radiographic verification film is taken before the patient leaves the operating theatre. Subsequently, predictive dosimetry is made. The patient is either manually or remotely afterloaded with iridium-192 sources. This is followed by both computerised and manual dosimetry and based on this, the tumour dose is prescribed and the time duration is decided. During the given time of irradiation, which routinely takes 4-7 days for a radical implant, the patient is kept in a protected room with full radiation safety precautions. On completion of irradiation, the radioactive wires first and the source carriers (tubes, needles) next, are removed with the usual precautions and asepsis.

The technique of interstitial brachytherapy utilises many types of procedures depending on anatomical and tumoural factors. The four commonly used procedures at the Institut Gustave-Roussy are as follows:

[1] Plastic tube technique
[2] Guide gutter technique
[3] Hypodermic needle technique
[4] Silk suture technique

Plastic Tube Technique

In the plastic tube technique the target volume with overlying skin and mucosa is fixed so it cannot move, by the implantation of plastic tubes (which will later contain the radioactive iridium-192 wire), which remain in the tissue for the duration of the implant. The plastic tube has an outer diameter of 1.6 mm and an inner diameter of 1.2 mm.

Initially, the target area is implanted by needles, to be substituted subsequently by plastic tubes using stainless steel or nylon obturators. The arrangement of the lines can be verified radiologically after the needles are placed within the tissue, and if found satisfactory, can be substituted by the plastic tubes.

For certain tumours, for instance carcinoma of the tongue and of the floor of the mouth, it is necessary to encompass the lesion by making a series of loops with the tubes over the surface of the lesion to deliver adequate doses to the surface of the lesion. On completion of substitution, the plastic tubes are trimmed and plastic tube spacers are placed between them to initially secure the system at each end and it is then finally secured by metal buttons to ensure immobilisation.

Guide Gutter Technique

This system is rapid and convenient and utilises the principles of manual afterloading. The gutters are available (from 3-5 cm) either double or single guides, of various lengths and shapes. Accordingly the radioactive iridium-192 wires are used as hairpins or as single pins, of corresponding lengths but with a diameter of 0.5 mm and unsheathed. The parallel guides of the double gutter are usually 12 mm apart and are linked on the top by a metal band which is inverted, facilitating a good grip of the gutter during the implantation.

A typical implantation begins with introduction of the guide gutters to a desired pattern, verified fluoroscopically for corrections of malposition, if necessary. Typically, this procedure is performed under local anaesthesia to benefit from an almost normal muscle tone with good cooperation of the patient. After a satisfactory guide implantation, sutures are placed under the horizontal metal bridge (at the top) of the gutters for subsequent fixation of radioactive lines into place.

Next, corresponding iridium-192 hairpins are removed from their lead containers and quickly slid into the guide gutters and the latter removed over the iridium hairpins, all in one smooth motion. The brachytherapist performs this standing behind a lead screen. The procedure is repeated for the remaining gutters. On complete substitution, the previously placed sutures are secured by long handle forceps to firmly keep the iridium-192 pins in place during the whole period of irradiation. The patients tolerate this system very well and removal after the duration of irradiation is very simple and uneventful.

Hypodermic Needle Technique

This technique employs hypodermic needles with an external diameter of 0.8 mm bevelled at both ends. The needles are kept in place during the whole period of treatment with the iridium-192 source within it.

When the target volume is adequately implanted by the needles, tailor-made spacing templates or plastique or plastic tubing are slipped over both ends of the needles to retain optimal spacing. The iridium-192 sources are then advanced into these hollow needles with adequate protection (manual afterloading). Lead caps are crimped over the needle tips to retain the system in situ. This system is used for external lesions such as carcinoma of the lip or nose where the elasticity of the soft tissue structures would bunch together any other system of brachytherapy.

Silk Suture Technique

For small surface lesions of the face which need to be treated by brachytherapy which conforms to the anatomical curvatures and at the same time treats the lesion, the silk suture technique is ideal. This procedure makes use of a braided silk thread (4,-0), which has a small potentially cylindrical cavity within it. Into this space is introduced a given length of steel wire of 0.3 mm diameter and this portion of the thread is hardened by dipping it into an organic chemical compound. After drying, the steel wire is removed and this leaves the suture material with a cannula into which the iridium-192 source is passed and kept in place by a knot upon the silk suture. Subsequently, the suture is placed in the lesion by threading it through the tissues using a needle, as in any surgical procedure, Figure 5. Once the source moves into place, the extra suture material is cut and the ends of the sutures are tied together and taped to the skin to ensure them being in place through out the duration of irradiation. This technique is commonly used for lesions of the lower eyelid, nasal bridge and alae nasi where anatomical curvatures are to be respected.

Results

To illustrate the role of brachytherapy in the treatment of head and neck carcinoma, 1140 patients treated at Institut Gustave-Roussy are reported, Table 1.

Table 1
Patient workload.

Site		No.of cases
Nasal vestibule		36
Lip		231
Floor of mouth		206
Mobile tongue		269
Oropharynx		312
Base of tongue	: 106	
Tonsil	: 86	
Ant. oropharynx	: 75	
Soft palate	: 45	
Nasopharynx		47
Children with head & neck cancer		39
All sites		1140

All these patients were treated with low dose rate brachytherapy according to the rules of the Paris system using iridium wires, Figure 1, manually afterloaded with the techniques indicated in Table 2, which are cross-referenced to the appropriate Figures 2-6.

These different systems are presented to illustrate the technical aspects of brachytherapy we have used according to the treatment sites. For each tumour site the following data is given: patient population, TNM distribution, treatment protocol, technical aspects of brachytherapy and results: disease-free survival, local control, complications rates.

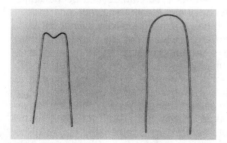

Figure 1. Iridium-192 wires which are loaded into a guide gutter (left) or into a plastic tube (right)

Table 2
LDR brachytherapy manual afterloading techniques.

Technique	
Plastic tubes	:see Figure 2
Guide gutters	:see Figure 3
Hypodermic needles	:see Figure 4
Silk threads	:see Figure 5
Moulded applicators	:see Figure 6

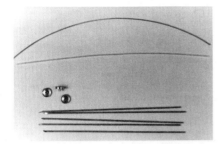

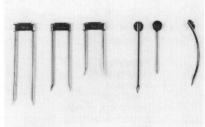

Figure 2. Materials used for a plastic tube implantation.

Figure 3. Different types of guide gutter: double, simple, straight, curved.

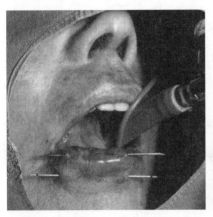

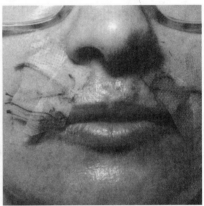

Figure 4. Hypodermic needles used for treatment of a lip carcinoma.

Figure 5. The silk thread technique.

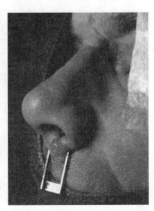

Figure 6. Moulded applicator for a naso-pharynx cancer.

Figure 7. Nasal pyramid implanted with three planes of plastic tubes.

Figure 8. Double guide gutter technique for a nasal vestibule cancer.

Table 3
Nasal Vestibule.

Parameter		Parameter value	
Population			
No.of patients		36	
Mean age		66 yrs	
Age range		44-82 yrs	
Percentage of males		83%	
TNM stage	T1:	45%	
	T2:	45%	
	T3:	10%	
	N0:	93%	
	N1N2:	7%	
Treatment protocols			
	Brachytherapy:	93%	
	External+Brachy:	7%	
Brachytherapy afterloading technique			
	Plastic tubes:	20%	[see Figure 7]
	Hypodermic needles:	54%	
	Guide gutters:	40%	[see Figure 8]
	Silk threads:	6%	
Mean dose		72 Gy	
Results			
5-yr disease free survival		68%	
Local control rate		86%	
Complications			
	Grades I & II:	33%	
	Grade III:	8%	

 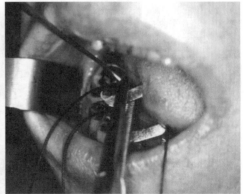

Figure 9. Lip cancer: triangular implantation with hypodermic needles.

Figure 10. Guide gutter implantation under local anaesthesia for a floor of mouth cancer.

Table 4
Lip.

Parameter		Parameter value
Population		
No.of patients		231
Mean age		65 yrs
Age range		28-90 yrs
Percentage of males		85%
TNM stage	T1:	82%
	T2:	13%
	T3:	3%
	T4:	2%
	N0:	80%
	N1:	12%
	N2:	5%
	N3:	3%
Treatment protocols		
	Brachytherapy ± CND:	97%
	External+Brachy:	3%
(CND=Cervical node dissection)		
Brachytherapy afterloading technique		
	Plastic tubes:	40%
	Hypodermic needles:	56% [see Figure 9]
	Silk threads:	14%
Mean dose		76 Gy
Results		
5-yr disease free survival		66%
Local control rate		95%
Complications		
	Mucosal necrosis:	13%
Cosmetic results		
	Grade I:	70%
	Grade II:	16%
	Grade III:	14%

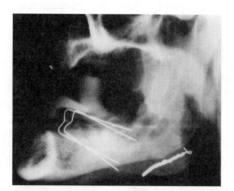

Figure 11. Floor of mouth cancer: radiographic control with two double iridium-192 hairpins.

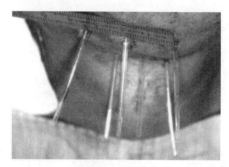

Figure 12. Plastic tube technique: check of the distance between the different lines during the brachytherapy implantation for a mobile tongue cancer.

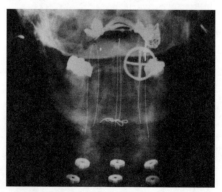

Figure 13. Radiographic control for the brachytherapy application.

Table 5
Floor of Mouth.

Parameter		Parameter value
Population		
No.of patients		206
Mean age		53 yrs
Age range		31-85 yrs
Percentage of males		4%
TNM stage	T1:	42%
	T2:	50%
	T3:	6%
	T4:	2%
	N0:	70%
	N1:	18%
	N2:	13%
	N3:	0
Treatment protocols		
Brachytherapy ± CND:		87%
External+Brachy:		13%
Brachytherapy afterloading technique		
Brachytherapy alone		
	Plastic tubes:	21%
	Guide gutters:	79% [see Figures 10 and 11]
Mean dose		65 Gy
External + Brachytherapy		
	Plastic tubes:	19%
	Guide gutters:	81%
Brachy mean dose		27 Gy
Results		
Brachytherapy alone		
5-yr disease free survival		74%
Local control rate		89%
External+Brachytherapy		
5-yr disease free survival		30%
Local control rate		59%
Second malignancies		30%
Complications		
	Mucosal necrosis:	11%
	Bone necrosis:	21%

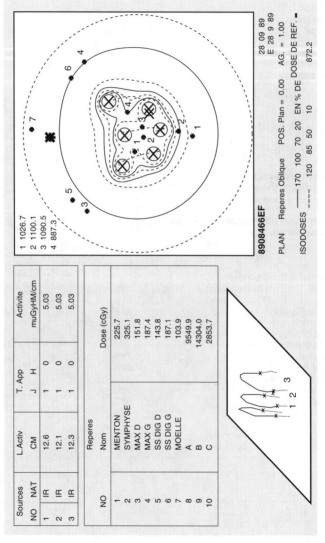

Figure 14. Dose distribution calculated by computer in the reference plane: same patient as in Figure 13.

Table 6
Tongue.

Parameter		Parameter value	
Population			
No.of patients		269	
Mean age		55 yrs	
Age range		25-87 yrs	
Percentage of males		77%	
TNM stage	T1:	31%	
	T2:	55%	
	T3:	14%	
	N0:	81%	
	N1:	16%	
	N2:	3%	
	N3:	0	
Treatment protocols			
Brachytherapy ± CND:		72%	
External+Brachy:		28%	
Brachytherapy afterloading technique			
Brachytherapy alone			
	Plastic tubes:	21%	[see Figures 12,13 and 14]
	Guide gutters:	79%	
Mean dose		71 Gy	
External + Brachytherapy			
	Plastic tubes:	51%	
	Guide gutters:	49%	
Brachy mean dose		27 Gy	
Results			
Brachytherapy alone			
5-yr disease free survival		62%	
Local control rate		87%	
External + Brachytherapy			
5-yr disease free survival		30%	
Local control rate		49%	
Second malignancies		12%	
Complications			
Mucosal necrosis:		11%	
Bone necrosis:		8%	

Table 7
Oropharynx.

Parameter		Parameter value
Population		
No.of patients		312
Mean age		58 yrs
Age range		38-86 yrs
Percentage of males		85%
Tumour site		
	Base of tongue:	34%
	Tonsil:	28%
	Ant. oropharynx:	24%
	Soft palate:	14%
TNM stage	T1:	25%
	T2:	40%
	T3:	35%
	N0:	50%
	N1:	26%
	N2:	7%
	N3:	17%
Treatment protocols		
	Brachytherapy:	11%
	External+Brachy:	89%
Brachytherapy afterloading technique		
	Plastic tubes:	26% [see Figures 15 and 16]
	Guide gutters:	74%
Mean dose		75 Gy
Note: In this retrospective study guide gutters were used more often than plastic tubes. Nowadays we essentially use plastic tubes.		
Results		
5-yr disease free survival		
	Base of tongue:	26%
	Tonsil:	37%
	Ant. oropharynx:	40%
	Soft palate:	37%
Local control rate		
	Base of tongue:	68%
	Tonsil:	79%
	Ant. oropharynx:	69%
	Soft palate:	93%
Complications		
	Grades I & II:	27%
	Grade III:	7%

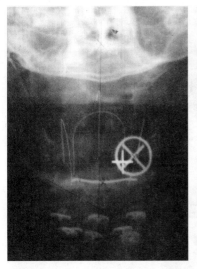 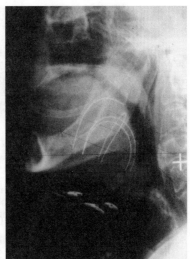

Figure 15. AP view radiograph.   **Figure 16**. Lateral view radiograph.

Table 8
Nasopharynx.

Parameter	Parameter value
Population	
No.of patients	47
Mean age	42 yrs
Age range	26-57 yrs
Percentage of males	70%
TNM stage	
Cases treated with a first line brachy as a boost after external	33
Cases treated for a recurrence in a previously treated area	14

Brachytherapy afterloading technique
A moulded nasopharyngeal applicator was made for each patient.
This applicator [see Figures 17 and 18] was afterloaded with iridium-192 wires.
Mean dose for first line brachy after external dose of 45 Gy was 30 Gy. Mean dose for salvage brachytherapy was 60 Gy.

Results
5-yr disease free survival

	First line brachy:	42%
	Salvage brachy:	17%
Local control rate		
	First line brachy:	74%
	Salvage brachy:	50%

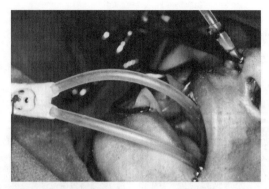

Figure 17. Nasopharynx carcinoma endocavitary brachytherapy with a moulded applicator. These are constructed on an individual basis for each patient.

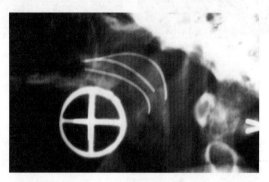

Figure 18. Lateral control radiograph with the three iridium-192 sources adapted to the topography of the tumour.

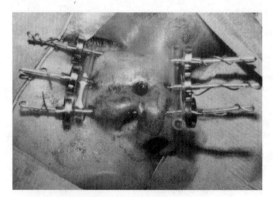

Figure 19. Rhabdomyosarcoma of the nasolabial sulcus in a boy two years old: plastic tube technique.

Table 9
Paediatric head & neck malignancies.

Parameter		Parameter value
Population		
No.of patients		39
Mean age		5 yrs
Age range		3 mths - 15 yrs
Main tumour sites		
Nasolabial sulcus:		31%
Oral cavity:		21%
Neck:		15%
Ear:		10%
Percentage of cases with		
rhabdomyosarcoma	:	70%
TNM stage	T1:	61%
	T2:	36%
	TX:	3%
	N0:	56%
	N1:	41%
	NX:	3%

Treatment protocols
For children the approach was quite different to that with adults and included chemotherapy in most cases. External radiotherapy was given in 31% of cases.

Indications for brachytherapy
Brachytherapy was indicated in two different situations.
First line brachytherapy: 64%
Salvage brachytherapy: 36%

Brachytherapy afterloading technique
Plastic tubes [see Figure 19] alone or combined with hypodermic
needles and/or guide gutters : 95%
Guide gutters ± hypodermic needles : 5%
Brachy performed perioperatively : 31%
Mean dose
First line brachytherapy : 68 Gy
Salvage brachytherapy : 56 Gy

Results
First line brachytherapy
5-yr disease free survival : 76%
Local control rate : 84%
Severe complications : 24%
Salvage brachytherapy
5-yr disease free survival : 50%
Local control rate : 64%
Severe complications : 21% [see Figure 20]

Conclusions

This retrospective study of some 1140 patients treated in the Institut Gustave-Roussy with brachytherapy for head and neck carcinoma shows that 60% of the patients received brachytherapy alone as treatment for their primary tumour and 40% received brachytherapy combined with external radiotherapy.

In the first group (exclusively brachytherapy) the five-year disease free survival was 71% and local control 90%. In the second group (combined external radiotherapy & brachytherapy) the figures are 35% and 63% respectively. The complication rate was smaller than 10% with brachytherapy as the only treatment and higher than 20% with brachytherapy as a boost after external radiotherapy.

In head and neck cancers, brachytherapy provides excellent local control and improves survival in selected tumours. The main selection criteria are: accessibility, moderate size and well defined margins.

Brachytherapy advantages have been clearly demonstrated in this analysis: good patient tolerance, short treatment time and an important role in conservative approach.

Successful brachytherapy depends, however, upon a close collaborative effort, careful assessment of the patient, precise planning and technique respecting the rules of a system.

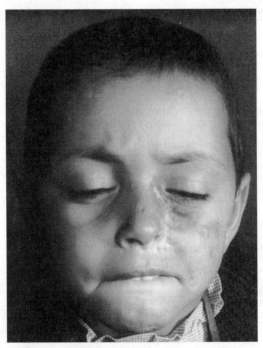

Figure 20. Cosmetic sequelae after brachytherapy for a nasolabial sulcus rhabdomyosarcoma.

References

Chassagne D, Janvier L, Pierquin B & Flaisler A, *La plésio-curiethérapie des cancers du cavum avec support moulé et iridium-192*, Ann. Radiology, **6**, 719-726, 1963.

Chassagne D, Monchmov M, Sahatchiev A & Pierquin B, *Techniques d'endo-curiethérapie par fils de soie radioactifs dans les épithéliomas cutanés*, Journal Radiology, **54**, 849-851, 1973.

Chassagne D, Cronier C & Gerbaulet A, *Place de la curiethérapie dans les sarcomes embryonnaires de la tête et du cou de l'enfant*, Cah. ORL Chir. Cervico-fac, **10**, 527-530, 1975.

Chassagne D & Gerbaulet A, *Brachytherapy applications in cancer of the oral cavity*, in: *The scope of brachytherapy in head and neck tumors*, 23-48, Brachytherapy update: New-York, 1988.

Chirat E, Gerbaulet A, Lusinchi A, Haie-Meder C, Vandenbrouck C, Eschwege F & Chassagne D, *La curiethérapie dans le cancer de la lèvre. A propos de 231 cas traités à Institut Gustave-Roussy*, Bulletin Cancer, **75**, 632, 1988.

Dutreix A, Marinello G & Wambersie A, *Dosimétrie en curiethérapie,* Masson: Paris, 1982.

Dutreix J, *Expression of the dose rate effect in clinical curietherapy* , Radiotherapy & Oncology, **15**, 25-37, 1989.

Esche B, Haie-Meder C, Gerbaulet A, Eschwege F, Richard JM & Chassagne D, *Interstitial and external radiotherapy in carcinoma of the soft palate and uvula*, Int. J. Radiation Oncology Biology & Physics, **1**, 619-625, 1988.

Eschwege F, Haie C, Gerbaulet A, Richard JM, Mamelle G, Wibault P & Chassagne D, *Brachytherapy of carcinoma of the tongue and floor of mouth, in:Head and neck cancer,* **1**, Proc. International Conference Baltimore, July 1984, Society of head & Neck Surgeons and American Society for Head & Neck Surgery, Chretien PB, Johns ME, Shedd DP, Strong EW & Ward PH, (Eds), 352-355, Mosby:St. Louis, 1985.

Flamant F, Caillaud JM, Gerbaulet A, Revillon Y & Pellerin D, *Tumeurs mésenchymateuses malignes*, in: *Encyclopédie des cancers: cancers de l'enfant*, Lemerle J, **25**, 428-456, Flammarion: Paris, 1991.

Gerbaulet A, Chassagne D, Hayem M, Vandenbrouck C & Schlienger M, *L'épithélioma de la lèvre. Une série de 335 cas*, Journal Radiology, **59**, 603-610, 1978.

Gerbaulet A & Chassagne D, *Progres techniques en curietherapie ORL*, in:*i tumori della testa e del collo*, Veronesi U, Bocca E, Molinari R & Emanuelli H, (Eds), 49-52, Ambrosiana:Milan, 1979.

Gerbaulet A, Panis X, Flamant F & Chassagne D, *Iridium afterloading curietherapy in the treatment of pediatric malignancies.* The Institut Gustave-Roussy experience, Cancer, **56**, 1274-1279, 1985.

Gerbaulet A & Pernot M, *Le carcinome épidermoïde de la face interne de la joue. A propos de 748 malades*, J. Eurology Radiotherapy, **6**, 1-4, 1985.

Gerbaulet A, Panis X, Flamant F & Chassagne D, *Iridium afterloading curietherapy in the treatment of pediatric malignancies*, Cancer year book, 352-354, 1987.

Gerbaulet A, Marsiglia H, Haie C, Mamelle G. Eschwege F & Chassagne D, *Brachytherapy in floor of mouth carcinoma. Experience of the Institut Gustave-Roussy concerning 206 patients*, Journal Cancer Research Clinical Oncology, **116**, 798, 1990.

Gerbaulet A, Habrand JL, Haie-Meder C. L'Helgouach G, Panis X, Esche B, Flamant F & Chassagne D, *The role of brachytherapy in the conservative treatment of paediatric malignancies: experience of the activity*, **5**, 85-90, 1991.

Gerbaulet A & Briot E, *La curiethérapie in: Techniques d'irradiation des cancers*, Mazeron JJ, Locoche T & Maugis A (Eds), 101-119, Vigot: Paris, 1992.

Gerbaulet A & Bridier A, *Tumeurs pédiatriques*, in: *Manual pratique de curiethérapie*, Pierquin B & Marinello G (Ed), 250-264, Hermann: Paris, 1992.

Haie C, Gerbaulet A, Wibault P, Chassagne D & Marandas P, *Résultats de la curiethérapie et de l'association radiothérapie transcutanée - curiethérapie dans 155 cas de cancers de la langue mobile*, in: *Actualités de carcinologie cervico-faciale: cancers de la langue*, 53-57, Masson: Paris, 1983.

Lambin P, Haie-Meder C, Stas N, N'Guyen J, Delapierre M, Petit C, Briot E, Chassagne D & Gerbaulet A, *Curietherapie des tumeurs de la cavité buccale: dosimetrie in vivo avec appareil de protection*, Bulletin Cancer/Radiothrapy, **78**, 489, 1991.

Lambin P, Haie-Meder C, Gerbaulet A & Chassagne D, *Curietherapy versus external irradiation combined with curietherapy in carcinoma of the mobile tongue*, Radiotherapy & Oncology, **23**, 55-56, 1992.

Lusinchi A, Eskandari J, Son Y, Gerbaulet A, Haie C, Mamelle G, Eschwege F & Chassagne D, *External irradiation plus curietherapy boost in 108 base of tongue carcinomas*, Int. J. Radiation Oncology Biology & Physics, **17**, 1191-1197, 1989.

Marandas P, Gerbaulet A & Luboinski B, *Tumeurs malignes du plancher de la bouche*, in. Encycl. Med. Chir. Editions techniques Oto-Rhino-Laryngologie, **16**, Paris 20627 D10, 1991,

Marsiglia H, Haie-Meder C, Mamelle G, Eschwege F & Chassagne D, *Résultats de la curiethérapie à propos de 206 cancers du plancher bucccal*. Expérience de l'Institut Gustave Roussy, Bulletin Cancer/Radiothrapy, **79**, 391, 1992.

Pierquin B, Chassagne D & Gasiorowski M, *Présentation technique et dosimétrique de curiethérapie par fils d'or 198*, Journal Radiology Electrology, **40**, 690-693, 1959.

Pierquin B & Chassagne D, *Techniques d'endo et de plésio-curiethérapie par radio-éléments artifiels*, Annals. Oto-Laryngol, **79**, 413-420, 1962.

13

HDR Brachytherapy with Special Reference to Nasopharyngeal Cancer

P.C. Levendag[1], A.G. Visser[2], I.K. Kolkman-Deurloo[2], W.M.H. Eijkenboom[1] & C.A. Meeuwis[3]

[1]Departments of Radiation Oncology, [2] Radiation Physics & [3]Head and Neck Surgery.
Dr. Daniel den Hoed Cancer Center,
Groene Hilledijk 301,
3075 EA Rotterdam,
The Netherlands.

Introduction

Brachytherapy has been used in the Dr. Daniel den Hoed Cancer Center/Academic Hospital Rotterdam-Dijkzigt (DDHCC/AZR-Dijkzigt) routinely over the past years for a number of tumour sites in the head and neck. Since 1985 there has been an evolution in treatment techniques and we have changed from rigid iridium-192 single pins and hairpins to flexible afterloading catheters for iridium-192 wire sources. In 1987 we introduced the microSelectron-LDR, in 1991 the microSelectron-HDR and in 1992 the microSelectron-PDR has been implemented in our brachytherapy programme.

The purpose of our two chapters is to report on preliminary experience with high dose rate (HDR) and pulsed dose rate (PDR) endocavitary and interstitial brachytherapy for tumours of the nasopharynx and the base of tongue. A total of 81 patients (eight sites) were treated from January 1991 to June 1992, Table 1. However, since follow-up is very short, the data reported can evidently only have limited meaning. The main emphasis will therefore be on treatment protocols, treatment techniques and preliminary results with regard to control at the implanted site. Also presented will be side-effects for patients with primary or recurrent cancers of the nasopharynx and oropharynx: the two largest site subgroups.

Table 1
Summary of HDR/PDR brachytherapy results: January 1991 - June 1992.

Site	No.of primary cases	Crude control rate	No. of recurrent cases	Crude control rate
Nasopharynx	24	23/24	5	2/5
Nasal vestibule	6	6/6	0	
Base of tongue	7	7/7	2	2/2
Neck	0		12	6/12
Pharyngeal wall	1	1/1	1	0/1
Tonsil &/or soft palate	13	13/13	3	2/3
Mobile tongue	5	5/5	0	
Skin	0		2	2/2
All sites	56	55/56	25	14/25

Epidemiology

Nasopharyngeal carcinoma (NPC) is a clinical entity quite different in a number of ways from other epidermoid carcinomas of the head & neck. Firstly, its peculiar geographical distribution, with a special predilection for the south eastern provinces of China and in Europe for the Mediterranean basin. In China the incidence has been reported to be the highest, 30-80 per 100,000 population per year. NPC is an epidermoid cell lineage of the head & neck with a variety of morphological degrees of differentiation with the undifferentiated type being by far the most frequent. NPC is known for its special serological and biological relationship to the Epstein-Barr virus and clinical and experimental data suggest that this virus is an aetiological factor.

However, environmental factors such as ingestion of salted foods among the Chinese and Eskimos and an augmented family risk in the endemic areas are of particular importance in NPC. Patients with NPC frequently present with unilateral hearing loss, large lymh nodes in the neck and/or signs of cranial nerve deficiencies such as abducens paralysis.

External Beam Radiotherapy

The nasopharynx is a cuboid space in direct continuity with the nasal cavity, oropharynx, eustachian tubes and middle ears as well as with the base of skull. Due to these anatomical conditions the nasopharynx is, in contrast to other head & neck sites, generally unsuitable for either primary or salvage surgery. Moreover even though NPC is associated with a high incidence of systemic metastatic disease, locoregional control remains an extremely important therapeutic goal in early as well as in advanced cases. Because of this feature, external beam radiation therapy (EXRT) remains the mainstay for the treatment of NPC. Classical treatment guidelines for $T_{1-4}N_0$,+ NPC are to treat the neck in conjunction with the primary tumour by EXRT to a dose of 50 Gy. Subsequently the primary tumour and neck nodal metastases are boosted to a cumulative dose of about 70 Gy. However, many small deviations of this standard treatment approach can be encountered when considering the protocols for NPC in different institutions.

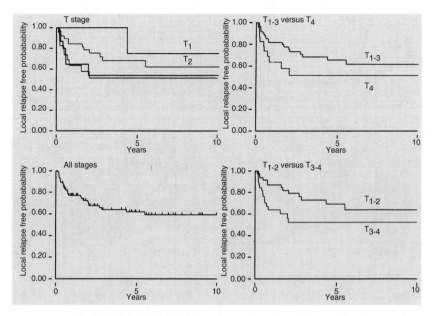

Figure 1a. External beam radiotherapy for NPC, 1965-1985: local relapse free survival results.

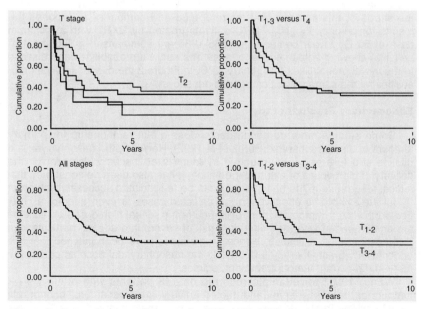

Figure 1b. External beam radiotherapy for NPC, 1965-1985: disease free survival results.

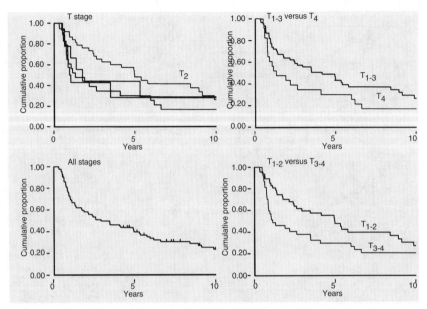

Figure 2. External beam radiotherapy for NPC, 1965-1985: overall survival results.

Regarding the efficacy of EXRT for NPC, extensive data has been reported in the literature on local control and survival. To review this literature is beyond the scope of this chapter. But for reference and comparison purposes the results for primary $T_{1-4}N_0,+$ NPC patients treated by EXRT with a minimum dose of 50 Gy in our center from 1965-1985 are summarised in Figures 1(a) and 1(b) showing actuarial local relapse free survival probabilities and disease free survival probabilities for primary NPC. In Figure 2 the overall survival probabilities for the same patient categories are shown.

Endocavitary Brachytherapy

Some studies have demonstrated a dose-effect relationship for primary tumours of the nasopharynx (Perez et al 1992). However, the nasopharynx is a midline structure and is surrounded by many vital tissues which prohibit the delivery of high doses of external irradiation. It has also been demonstrated that a local recurrence in the nasopharynx can be re-irradiated successfully in order to palliate symptoms effectively or, in selected cases to even attempt a cure. For worthwhile symptomatic control in recurrent disease, high doses of radiation are again needed with their attendant risk of severe late effects, particularly in previously irradiated tissues. Hence programmes have been initiated that use endocavitary brachytherapy for boosting the nasopharyneal dose as part of primary and recurrent tumour treatment regimes.

Wang (1991) for example reported on 146 patients with primary T_{1-3} tumours of the nasopharynx and quoted a five-year actuarial local control rate of 91% (where the boost was given by means of By) compared to 60% (where the boost was given by means of EXRT). This result is statistically significant, P=0.0002.

Pryzant et al (1992) published data on 53 patients with recurrent NPC, showing a five-year disease free survival of 44% (By boost) compared to 14% (EXRT boost), P=0.19, and a five-year overall survival of 60% (By boost) compared to 16% (EXRT boost), P=0.029.

The results of patients with NPC treated between 1965-1985 in our Center by EXRT alone, see Figures 1 and 2, were found in retrospect to be less than optimal: in particular when one compares the data to some of the results published in the current literature (Wang 1991). We considered therefore that a better local control and survival could possibly be obtained by using higher doses of radiation for the primary tumour, preferably using brachytherapy.

Treatment Protocol & Techniques

After the introduction of our microSelectron-HDR in the DDHCC we changed our protocol for patients with NPC from EXRT only to EXRT combined with endocavitary brachytherapy. The treatment protocol of the Rotterdam Head & Neck Cooperative Group for patients with $T_{1-4}N_0+$ NPC is currently that of Table 2.

Table 2
NPC protocol of the Dr. Daniel den Hoed Cancer Center/Academic Hospital Rotterdam.
(EXRT= external beam radiotherapy, BY= brachytherapy)

Tumour	Technique	Cumulative dose (Gy)
Primary NPC and neck	EXRT	46
Primary NPC and postive neck nodes	EXRT	60
Postive neck nodes & parpharyngeal mass	EXRT	70
Primary NPC	BY*	78-82

* microSelectron-HDR BY is prescribed as follows: 2 fractions each of 3 Gy/day, six hour interval, total of 4x3 Gy or 6x3 Gy. If the primary tumour has been treated by EXRT to 70 Gy (parapharyngeal extension and/or T_4 tumour), 4x3 Gy is given for a total dose of 82 Gy. In other cases when the primary tumour has been treated by EXRT to 60 Gy, 6x3 Gy is given for a total dose of 78 Gy.

To perform the brachytherapy on an outpatient basis in a busy clinic using the microSelectron-HDR and optimisation with the NPS computer planning system, a simple silicone mould called the Rotterdam nasopharynx applicator was designed, Figure 3. This device can be easily introduced under topical anaesthesia, Figure 4.

AP and lateral radiographs, Figure 5, are subsequently taken and the dose is calculated in different tumour tissue and normal tissue points: column [A] in Table 3. Usually the dose in the nasopharynx is prescribed at 0.75 cm from the source axis at the NA tumour point, Figure 5. In cases with an unsatisfactory dose distribution in a number of dose-points (* in column [A] in Table 3) a recalculation (termed optimisation) is performed using the NPS planning system for the microSelectron-HDR by changing the dwell times for the iridium-192 point source, see column [B] in Table 3.

Table 3
The dose to the nasopharynx is prescribed at 0.75 cm from the source axis.
This table shows normal tissue dose points and dose points in the nasopharynx and at
Rouviere's node. This dose point distribution is computed for every patient with
nasopharyngeal carcinoma treated by brachytherapy. The dose points are indicated
on lateral and AP radiographs. If the dose point distribution for normal tissue is
considered to be less than satisfactory, the relative dose distribution can be altered
to a certain extent by using the NPS planning system optimisation program:
compare columns [A] and [B].
(* indicates that the dose is considered to be excessive in the non-optimised distribution.)

Dose point location	Percentage dose	
	[A] Non-optimised	[B] Optimised
Retina,right	29	21
Retina,left	56*	24
Opticchiasm	38	25
Pituitary glan	28	22
Nose,left	334*	94
Nose,right	69*	92
Foramen ovale,right	37	47
Foramen ovale,left	59	61
F.O./F.L.,right	49	60
F.O./F.L.,left	76	75
Foramen lacerum,right	56	68
Foramen lacerum,left	89	87
Nasopharynx,right	100	104
Nasopharynx,left	100	90
Palate,right	204*	110
Palate,left	121	96
Spinal cord	46	87
Rouviere's node	158*	116

R: Retina, O: Optic chasm, H: Pituitary gland, NO: Nose, FO:
Foramen ovale, FL: Foramen lacerum, NA: Nasopharynx,
P: Palate, M: Spinal cord, C: Rouviere's node.

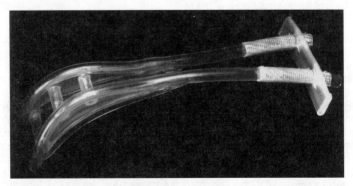

Figure 3. The silicone Rotterdam nasopharynx applicator: outer diameter
5.5 mm and inner diameter 3.5 mm.

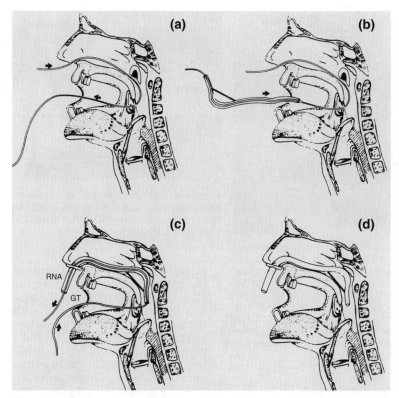

Figure 4. After decongestion (R/Xylometazoline HCl 1%) and topical anaesthesia (R/Cocaine hydrochloride 7%) of the nasal mucosa and nasopharynx, guide tubes (outer diameter 2 mm) are introduced through the nose and exit through the mouth. The Rotterdam nasopharynx applicator (RNA) is guided intraorally over the guide tubes (GT) by pulling on the nasal part of the guide tubes. The applicator is finally placed in situ into the nasopharynx and nose. To facilitate positioning of the applicator into the nasopharynx, gently pushing the oral parts of the guide tubes intraorally by some standard type of forceps can sometimes be of additional help, as in (c). By using a silicone flange the Rotterdam nasopharynx applicator is secured in the correct position for the duration of the treatment, for example 3-4 days.

Dosimetry

When the Rotterdam nasopharynx applicator is used with the microSelectron-HDR, planning of the dose distribution is performed using optimisation and dose prescription on 'patients points'. The location of these points is defined by the anatomy of the patient and geometry of tumour. For reconstruction purposes a pair of orthogonal radiographs is made with the patient points indicated on the lateral radiograph, Figure 5. The patient points are transferred to the AP radiograph using the appropriate magnification and placed at prescribed distances laterally from the sagittal midplane of the patient.

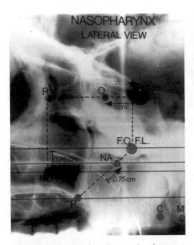

Figure 6. Patient with silicone Rotterdam nasopharynx applicator in situ and connected to the microSelectron-HDR for outpatient brachytherapy treatment.

Figure 5. Lateral radiograph of target volume in the case of an endocavitary brachytherapy boost dose to the nasopharynx. On the lateral and AP radiographs a number of tumour tissue points (NA, F.O, F.L, C) as well as normal tissue points (H, O, R, No, P, M) are shown. The notation for these dose points are explained in Table 3.

At the base of the applicator the separation between the centres of the tubes is 22.5 mm. Towards the nose the separation between the centres of the tubes decreases to 14 mm due to anatomical constraints. This means that the two tubes of the applicator are positioned in two slightly converging planes which are generally situated symmetrically at the left and right side of the sagittal midplane of the patient. On the lateral radiograph the tubes are projected on a sagittal plane.

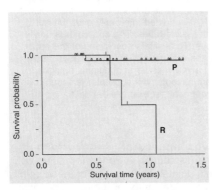

Figure 7. Actuarial local relapse free survival probability for (P) primary and for (R) recurrent (R) NPC: treatment given January 1991-June 1992 external beam radiation and fractionated HDR brachytherapy.

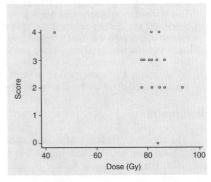

Figure 8. Scoring distribution for early side effects, grades 0-4, for mucosa in related to dose for primary NPC.

In this sagittal plane one first locates the projections of the palate points (P) and the foramina points (F.O, F.O/F.L, F.L). A line is drawn which connects these projections. On this line the projection of the reference points is drawn at a distance of 0.75 cm from the projection of the central axis of the tube. These reference points are called the NA (nasopharynx) points. Next, these points are transferred to the AP radiograph. For the foramina points this means that both F.O points are located at 2 cm from the midplane with the F.O/F.L points at 1.5 cm and the F.L points at 1 cm. The palate points (P) are situated at 1 cm later-ally from the midplane. The reference points, ie. the NA left and right points, are located at 1.5 cm right and left from the midplane. On the same lateral radio-graph the projections of the retina (R), of the pituitary gland (H), of the node of Rouviere (C) and the myelum/spinal cord (M) are indicated. As can be seen in Figure 5, a line drawn connecting the projections of the pituary gland (H) and the retina (R), the projection of the optic chiasm (O) are defined on this line at 1 cm ventrally from the pituitary gland. The projection of the nose points (NO) is drawn on the line departing from the projection of the retina perpendicular to the tubes at 0.75 cm caudally from the tubes. Analogous to the procedure described for the foramina, the palate and the nasopharynx, the projections of the R and NO points are transferred onto the AP radiograph. The lateral sepa-ration from the R and NO projections from the midplane of the patient onto the AP radiograph are 2 cm and 1 cm. The pituitary gland, opticum chiasm, node of Rouviere and the myelum/spinal cord are projected on the AP radiograph on the midline of the patient.

The NA points are used for dose specification. For optimisation purposes, usually the NA, NO and C points are used, ie. the dose distribution is optimised to deliver 100% of the reference dose to these 5 points (NA-right, NA-left, NO-right, NO-left, C). The node of Rouviere is also included in this procedure as this limits the dose in the spinal cord. The dose distribution is evaluated using a table of the resulting doses in all specified patients points, see Table 3. Depending on the resulting dose distribution one is able to vary the relative weight of each patient point in the optimisation procedure, in order to arrive at the desired doses as shown in the example of Table 3. Column [A] represents the non-optimised dose distribution and column [B] represents the resulting doses in the optimised case.

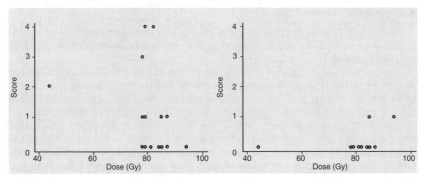

Figure 9. Scoring distribution for late side effects, grades 0-4, for mucosa **(Left)** and for skin **(Right)** related to dose for primary NPC.

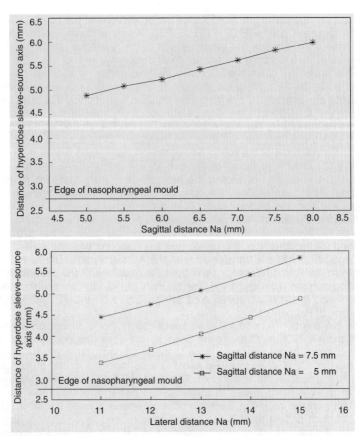

Figure 10. Diameter of the hyperdose sleeve (200 %) as a function of dose prescription distance. **(Top)** Lateral distance from NA=15 mm. **(Bottom)** Sagittal distances from NA=7.5 mm and 5 mm. The applicator edge is indicated.

In the non-optimised case the dose distribution was considered to be unsatisfactory as both nose points, the left retina, the right palate and the node of Rouviere receive too high a dose.

As can seen from column [B] the overdosage in these points is considerably reduced through the optimisation procedure. From this example it is clearly seen that for this type of application the main merit of the optimisation procedure is the reduction of the dose in overdosed regions: tumour tissue, but particularly in the normal tissues. That is, the dose to the dose prescription points can be brought close to the desired value and the dose to neighboring normal tissues can be reduced. It is mandatory of course that during the simulation procedure the radiographs are taken at very well defined angles relative to the patient and that patient movements are absolutely minimised, eg. immobilisation by head strap.

Preliminary Results

After the computer planning procedure the HDR irradiation can be started by simply inserting standard afterloading catheters into the Rotterdam nasopharynx applicator and connecting the catheters to the microSelectron-HDR, Figure 6. For twice daily ease of insertion of the afterloading catheters in the silicone mould a lubricant spray (R/Silisonde) is preferred.

A total of 29 patients were treated, 24 with a primary cancer and five were re-irradiated for a local recurrence. For the primary cancer patients the mean age was 56 years with a range 5-92 years: 19 males and five females. The mean follow-up was 261 days with a range 114-481 days. Only one patient failed locally.

For the five patients whose tumour had recurred after previous irradiation the mean age was 54 years and the range 39-67 years: three males and two females. The mean follow-up was 278 days with a range of 217-386 days. 3/5 patients experienced a local failure after the fractionated HDR. Figure 7 shows the actuarial local relapse free probability and overall survival probability for these two groups of patients: primary (N=24) and recurrent (N=5) cancer.

For all brachytherapy patients with a minimum follow-up of three months, acute and late side- effects were scored according to a modified RTOG scoring system: grades 0-4. For the acute side-effects maximum grading was scored during the first three months after completion of treatment for skin (S), mucosa (M), dysphagia (D), wound healing (W), xerostomia (X) and pain (P). Only the mucosa (M) scores relate to total dose to the primary cancer are shown in Figure 8.

For the period after three months following treatment, all side effects were considered late effects. A maximum score was assigned to late side effects of the skin (S), subcutaneous tissues (T), mucosa (M), xerostomia (G), cord (C), eye (E) and pain (P). Figure 9 shows late effects related to total dose to the primary tumour. It is also noted that some patients experienced synechy of the mucosal linings in the nose due to the 'hyperdose sleeve (200% of $D_{reference}$)' around the source axis Figures 9 and 10. To prevent this type of side effect one could either change the dose prescription point (ie. distance from the source axis of the NA point) and/or insert fatty gauzes (R/optule) in the nose temporarily for 1-2 weeks after having removed the Rotterdam nasopharynx applicator.

Conclusions

The silicone Rotterdam nasopharynx applicator which is used in conjunction with EXRT for NPC is designed to be relatively easily applied under topical anaesthesia for outpatient brachytherapy and the material is tissue (nasal mucosa) friendly. Into the silicone mould two standard afterloading catheters can be inserted at the time of irradiation and in this way the applicator is suitable for different types of radioactive sources for manual or (preferably) remote controlled afterloading. It can be used with the microSelectron-LDR/MDR or with the microSelectron-HDR in conjunction with the NPS optimisation program. It can be sterilised by steam (134 °C/273 °F) and is re-usable. Although follow-up is still short our preliminary results with fractionated HDR show excellent local control rates for NPC and if dosimetry is performed properly, few side-effects are encountered.

Reference

Wang CC, *Improved local control of nasopharyngeal carcinoma after intracavitary brachytherapy boost*, Amer. J. Clinical Oncology, **14 (1)**, 5-8, 1991.

Chapter

14

HDR & PDR Brachytherapy with Special Reference to Base of Tongue Cancer

P.C. Levendag[1], A.G. Visser[2], I.K. Kolkman-Deurloo[2], W.M.H. Eijkenboom[1] & C.A. Meeuwis[3]

[1]Departments of Radiation Oncology, [2]Radiation Physics & [3]Head and Neck Surgery, Dr. Daniel den Hoed Cancer Center, Groene Hilledijk 301, 3075 EA Rotterdam, The Netherlands.

Introduction

Interstitial brachytherapy with or without EXRT has been used for some 80 years as part of standard treatment regimes. Most of the data on interstitial brachytherapy for head & neck cancer refers to its use for early tumour stages. To date the vast majority of cases have been treated by LDR brachytherapy. In recent years a renaissance was seen in brachy-therapy applications. This was mainly due to sophisticated technology in computer planning and remotely controlled HDR afterloading machines. Also, radiobiological research stimulated new routes to explore and this has finally led to the concept of pulsed dose rate (PDR) brachytherapy, (Brenner & Hall 1991).

The recent renovations in our department of brachytherapy paralleled the historical developments elsewhere in brachytherapy. In 1985 we changed our policy of using the guide gutter technique. Now, all our implants in the head & neck region are performed with standard flexible afterloading catheters. This allows us to use interstitial brachytherapy in larger tumours and/or to perform implants in more complex anatomical structures. In fact, for a number of sites interstitial brachytherapy with or without surgery and EXRT has now become a standard treatment option in our center for patients with advanced/recurrent tumours. This is particularly true if patients are found to be inoperable and/or if surgery would seem too morbid a procedure.

LDR for Recurrent & Advanced Tumour

As a point of reference, we will briefly summarise the results obtained in our center with LDR brachytherapy for advanced tumours: T_3/T_4 base of tongue, and with re-irradiation of recurrent cancers.

The advanced T_3/T_4 base of tongue tumours carry a grave prognosis. Previously these cancers were treated by means of EXRT. However, since 1986 LDR interstitial brachytherapy (BY) has been incorporated into the treatment protocols. According to the current protocol EXRT to the primary tumour and neck of 46 Gy is followed, in the case of neck nodes, by a unilateral or bilateral neck dissection and a BY boost dose of 30 Gy to the primary cancer. Table 1 summarises our results with a series of 63 T_3/T_4 primary squamous cell cancer of the base of tongue treated 1975-1991.

Table 1
Results for 63 cases of T3/T4 base of tongue tumours treated 1975-1991.

Period & Treatment protocol	Crude local control rate	Local relapse free survival rate	Overall survival rate
1974-85 EXRT	11/33	25% at 5 yrs	20% at 5 yrs
1986-87 EXRT:optional	2/6	-	-
1986-87 EXRT+BY:optional	6/8	-	-
1988-91 EXRT+BY	11/15	73% at 3 yrs	55 % at 3 yrs

Re-irradiation is only offered to patients with advanced recurrent tumours or in-field second primaries unsuitable for surgery and/or chemotherapy as a first line of salvage. To establish the role of re-irradiation in head & neck cancer we analysed a 13-year experience with patients re-irradiated in the DDHCC, Levendag et al (1992).

The re-irradiation was performed 1970-1980 using EXRT (N=55) and 1985-1988 using BY with or without EXRT (N=18). The large majority of our patients were in a poor medical condition and/or had advanced stage III/IV lesions: 48/73 had stage III/IV disease and 16/18 of the BY±EXRT cases and 32/55 of the EXRT cases had $rT_{3,4}N_0,+$ tumours at the time of recurrence. The results are summarised in Table 2.

Even in advanced base of tongue and for cases of re-irradiation, improvements in local control and (for base of tongue) survival has been observed when using BY. However, being immobilised and connected for extended periods of time to a microSelectron-LDR can be extremely tiresome and awkward for a patient. Moreover, dosimetry of large volume implants is complicated and the dose distributions obtained are far from optimal.

In our view this was to some extent reflected in the morbidity some of our patients experienced, such as severe mucositis, pain and ulceration. It was anticipated at the time that by modern brachytherapy technology such as HDR/PDR afterloading machines and optimisation, a gain in terms of patient wellfare can be obtained. That is, more flexibility in doctors/nursing/family care and more freedom of movement for patients as they can be disconnected from the afterloading machines between fractions. Also, a decrease in side effects can be expected because of optimisation and hence improvement in the dose distribution and the elimination of 'hot spots'.

Table 2
Results for head & neck re-irradiation cases: 1970-80 versus 1985-88.
(The side effect data is given for controlled lesions)

Period & Treatment protocol	Crude local control rate	Overall survival rate	Incidence of side effects
1970-80 EXRT	16/55 (29%)	20% at 5 yrs	4/16
1985-88 BY ± EXRT	9/18 (50%)	20% at 5 yrs	3/9

Fractionated HDR Policy

Previously, brachytherapy in the DDHCC/AZR-Dijkzigt has been given mostly by means of a microSelectron-LDR. Because of technological advantages, (eg. no source preparation, more flexibility in patient care for cases treated using HDR afterloading machines, optimisation capabilities of the NPS computer planning system) as from January 1991 we embarked on a pilot study giving the brachytherapy part in all cancers of the head & neck by means of fractionated HDR or PDR. With fractionated HDR the brachytherapy is given in two fractions of 3 Gy/day using the microSelectron-HDR, with an interval of six hours between fractions. At the beginning, for a small number of early (T_1/T_2) tumours, a somewhat high fraction dose was given of 5 Gy. Soon afterwards we changed that particular treatment policy and started to use a fixed fraction size of 3 Gy with a fixed interval (6 hours). Every working day two fractions are given until the local dose prescribed by the Head & Neck Protocol of the Rotterdam Head & Neck Cancer Cooperative Group has been applied. At present, due to a shortage of technicians we are not able to use the microSelectron-HDR during the weekends. The total number of fractions depends on the site and on the T-stage as well as on whether a full course or a boost dose (BY combined with EXRT) is to be given by brachytherapy.

As a reference guide the total number of HDR fractions for 3 Gy/fraction/twice per day, is determined by our calculations to be equivalent to a given dose of EXRT, see Table 3.

PDR Policy

In 1992 a microSelectron-PDR with a 1 Ci source was installed in the DDHCC. We considered that, in contrast to the pilot study with the microSelectron-HDR, more fractions of smaller fraction size were advantageous. However, our basic concept in contrast to suggestions made by Brenner & Hall (1991) was not to divert from the three hour interval. This way, at least during the day time, patients could be disconnected from the microSelectron-PDR and walk about freely. We decided on a fraction size of 1 Gy (8 fractions/day) for the boost dose and a fraction size of 1.5 Gy (8 fractions/day) for a full course of brachytherapy treatment.

As we were not acquainted sufficiently enough with the reliability of the machine, firstly a pilot study was launched: for the first 10-15 patients the microSelectron-PDR will only be used during the day time with a fraction size of 2 Gy: 2 Gy/fraction & 4 fractions/day with a three hour interval in between fractions (daytime regime).

After completion of this initial phase, we will continue with an eight fractions of 1 Gy (Boost) or 1.5 Gy (full course) study (8 hours/day). Due to its automatic set-up capabilities the microSelectron-PDR will give us an extra advantage over the microSelectron-HDR by being able to continue the irradiation protocol during weekends.

As a reference guide: the total number of PDR fractions (for 1 Gy or 1.5 Gy/fraction/eight times per day) is considered by our calculations to be equivalent to a given dose of EXRT, see Table 3.

Table 3
Fractionation schemes for fractionated HDR and for PDR brachytherapies. HDR is given in two fractions of 3 Gy twice daily with a minimum interval of six hours between fractions. PDR is given in eight pulses (fractions) per day with an interval of three hours. ETD is the extrapolated tolerance dose in Gy. Parameters used for the calculation are $T_{1/2}$, repair (acute damage [tumour] & late normal tissue damage) = 3 hours and α/β = 10 Gy (tumour), 3 Gy (late effects)*.

EXRT reference dose	ETD (Gy)	Equivalent LDR (50 cGy/hour)	Fractionated HDR (2 fr/day, 6h intervals) N x d = d	ETD	PDR (8fr/day 3 h intervals) N x d	ETD
5x2 = 10 Gy	12	18.0 h = 9.0 Gy	3x3.0 = 9.0 Gy	12.4	9x1.0 Gy	11.3
8x2 = 16 Gy	19.2	28.1 h = 14.1 Gy	5x3.0 = 15.0 Gy	20.7	15x1.0 Gy	19.1
10x2 = 20 Gy	24	34.8 h = 17.4 Gy	6x3.0 = 18.0 Gy	24.8	19x1.0 Gy	24.3
11x2 = 22 Gy	26.4	38.2 h = 19.1 Gy	7x3.0 = 21.0 Gy	29.0	21x1.0 Gy	26.9
12x2 = 24 Gy	28.8	41.5 h = 20.8 Gy	7x3.0 = 21.0 Gy	29.0	22x1.0 Gy	28.2
13x2 = 26 Gy	31.2	44.9 h = 22.5 Gy	8x3.0 = 24.0 Gy	33.1	24x1.0 Gy	30.8
15x2 = 30 Gy	36	51.6 h = 25.8 Gy	9x3.0 = 27.0 Gy	37.3	28x1.0 Gy	36.0
16x2 = 32 Gy	38.4	54.9 h = 27.5 Gy	9x3.0 = 27.0 Gy	37.3	30x1.0 Gy	38.6
17x2 = 34 Gy	40.8	58.3 h = 29.2 Gy	10x3.0 = 30.0 Gy	41.4	32x1.0 Gy	41.2
18x2 = 36 Gy	43.2	61.6 h = 30.8 Gy	10x3.0 = 30.0 Gy	41.4	34x1.0 Gy	43.8
25x2 = 50 Gy	60	85.1 h = 42.6 Gy	14x3.0 = 42.0 Gy	58.1	28x1.5 Gy	60,0
27x2 = 54 Gy	64.8	91.8 h = 45.9 Gy	16x3.0 = 48.0 Gy	66.4	30x1.5 Gy	64.3
28x2 = 56 Gy	67.2	95.1 h = 47.6 Gy	16x3.0 = 48.0 Gy	66.4	31x1.5 Gy	66.5
30x2 = 60 Gy	72	101.8 h = 50.9 Gy	17x3.0 = 51.0 Gy	70.6	34x1.5 Gy	73.0
31x2 = 62 Gy	74.4	105.2 h = 54.3 Gy	18x3.0 = 54.0 Gy	74.4	35x1.5 Gy	75.2
32x2 = 64 Gy	76.8	108.5 h = 54.3 Gy	19x3.0 = 57.0 Gy	78.7	36x1.5 Gy	77.4
33x2 = 66 Gy	79.2	118.8 h = 55.9 Gy	19x3.0 = 57.0 Gy	78.7	37x1.5 Gy	79.5
34x2 = 68 Gy	81.6	115.2 h = 57.6 Gy	20x3.0 = 60.0 Gy	82.9	38x1.5 Gy	81.7
35x2 = 70 Gy	84	118.5 h = 59.3 Gy	20x3.0 = 60.0 Gy	82.9	39x1.5 Gy	83.9
36x2 = 72 Gy	86.4	121.9 h = 61.0 Gy	21x3.0 = 63.0 Gy	87.0	40x1.5 Gy	86.0
37x2 = 74 Gy	88.8	125.2 h = 62.6 Gy	21x3.0 = 63.0 Gy	87.0	41x1.5 Gy	88.2

*As of May, 1993, $T_{1/2}$ repair acute (tumour) = 1 hour, late effects 3 hours

Treatment Techniques

Previously all our implants were performed using continuous LDR with iridium-192 wire sources of activity approximately 1mCi/cm. Techniques were fairly standardised and have been described previously by Levendag & Putten (1990). In one plane (subjectively the most representative plane with regard to tumour volume: referred to as the 'central plane') the dose is computed and prescribed to 85% of the mean dose in the centres of gravity, see Figures 1 and 2.

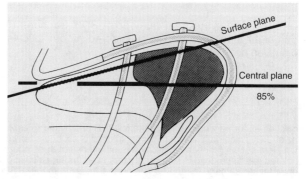

Figure 1. Base of tongue implant: only one sagittal plane of the volume implant is shown. Parts of the implanted catheters are actually loaded with iridium-192 wire sources. This is shown as grey areas in catheters. Note that one catheter is running over the dorsum of the tongue. The part forming the intersection between the two catheters with buttons in each sagittal plane is loaded with a continuous iridium-192 wire source. This type of volume implant was used for LDR interstitial brachytherapy for base of tongue cancers to mid-1991.

In a number of other planes the dose was also computed in order to obtain some three-dimensional view of the dose distribution over the entire target volume. The homogeneous dose distributions in these types of complex volume implants were often difficult to obtain, and laborious (in terms of computer planning as well as in terms of doctors/technicians time) but best approximation technique to eliminate too large a hot spot, for example, was to differentially unload. Moreover, for patients with head & neck implants to remain connected to the microSelectron-LDR for 3-7 days (depending on the total dose) appears to cause significant discomfort.

At present, commercially available brachytherapy afterloading catheters (outer diameter 2 mm) in conjunction with the microSelectron-HDR or microSelectron-PDR are used for all our head & neck implants. Because of its optimisation capabilities and because of the direct interface with the treatment unit (by means of the program card) we now perform all dose calculations using the NPS computer planning system and from May 1993 the PLATO system. It should be noted that careful planning is mandatory and that multiple sagittal planes are required for calculation purposes. Examples of changes in dose distribution by geometric optimisation are discussed later.

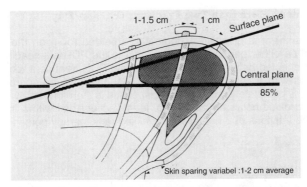

Figure 2. Base of tongue implant showing one sagittal plane of the volume implant. Parts of the implanted catheters are shown with the iridium-192 stepping source dwell positions of the microSelectron-HDR. These are shown as grey areas. Note that one catheter is running over the dorsum of the tongue: part of it is 'inactive': compare with **Figure 1**. The lower dose on the dorsum/surface of the tongue, because of this 'inactive part', is compensated for by using longer dwell times in the top positions of the two catheters with buttons (in each sagittal plane). As a clinical consequence, the side effects such as mucositis and ulcers due to the dose distribution in the surface plane are less severe, or even absent, as opposed to the frequently encountered side effects (due to the high surface dose) with the LDR implant technique, **Figure 1**. This volume implant technique and loading pattern was used for fractionated HDR & PDR interstitial brachytherapy for base of tongue cancer from mid-1991.

Using the optimisation programme we readily found some clinical advantages. For example, in the past (viz. LDR loading pattern for Figure 1) long lasting severe mucositis and pain in the mucosal surface of the base of tongue were frequently observed. This was undoubtedly due to the large hot spots because of the loading patterns (ie. long trajectories of the catheters running over the mucosal surface). By standard unloading of some parts of the catheters this side effect has practically disappeared. Underdosage to the surface of the tongue site of the tumour is prevented by using longer dwell times in the top positions of other catheters, see Figure 2.

Calculation of Equivalent Fractionation Schemes for HDR & PDR

Fractionated HDR Schemes: One or a Maximum of Two Fractions/Day.

In the latter case a minimum interval of six hours between the fractions should be maintained. This type of treatment in given in our brachytherapy department, ie. either on an outpatient basis or by transporting the patients from rooms on the ward to the treatment room in the brachytherapy department.

PDR Schemes : More than Two Fractions (Pulses)/Day

This treatment is given in a dedicated shielded room on the ward. The patient can be either permanently connected to the PDR afterloading machine or be disconnected between fractions. Because PDR treatment requires multiple fractions with a constant interval it is essential that the source transport mechanism is completely reliable. Our test phase is therefore only with fractions given during office hours of 0800-1800, ie. 4 fractions/day with a fixed interval between the fractions of 3 hours, with qualified radiotherapy personnel present.

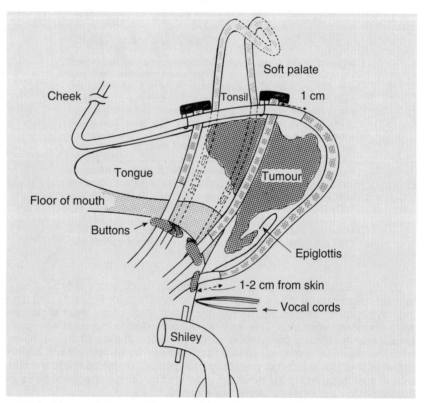

Figure 3. Base of tongue and tonsillar fossa implant showing the parts of the implanted catheters actually loaded (stippled grey zones) and with variable dwell times using the iridium-192 stepping source of the microSelectron-HDR or microSelectron-PDR. Note the catheters running over the dorsum of the tongue; parts of this catheter are not loaded: compare with **Figure 1**. The dose on the surface of the tongue, because of these inactive parts, is compensated for by using longer dwell times in the top positions of the other two catheters: this is the case in each sagittal plane. As a consequence, the long-lasting mucositis (and possibly a radiation ulcer) is less severe or even absent in the situation described in **Figure 2** as opposed to **Figure 1**. This type of volume implant and loading pattern has been used for fractionated HDR interstitial brachytherapy or for PDR base of tongue implants as from 1991.

Only after extensive testing of the equipment and the procedure, continuous treatment (constant interval over the whole treatment period, ie. 8 fractions/day with an interval of three hours between fractions) will be applied. Both situations have been considered in the calculations of possible fractionation schemes. A summary of fraction size and interval for the different fractionation regimes that are in use at the present time in the DDHCC/AZR-Dijkzigt for patients with tumours in the head & neck is given in Table 4.

Table 4
Fractionation regimes: 1991-1992.

Treatment type	Fractionation policy	BY boost EXRT: dose/fraction (Gy)	BY as full course/single treatment: dose/fraction (Gy)
Fractionated HDR	2 fractions/day, minimum 6h interval	3.0	3.0
PDR test phase	4 fractions/day, 3h interval, treatment only during day-time (8-18h)	2.0	2.0
PDR continuous treatment	8 fractions/day 3h interval, treatment 24 hours/day	1.0	1.5

Calculation of Equivalent Fractionated Schemes

For these calculations the linear quadratic (LQ) model is used taking into account incomplete repair of sublethal damage in the limited time between fractions and also taking into account the finite duration of each radiation fraction. The formulation described by Brenner & Hall (1991) has been used. However, in one aspect the method of Brenner & Hall (1991) has not been followed, ie. the total PDR dose has not been chosen to equal the total LDR dose. We used the following procedure.

Firstly the total LDR (50 cGy/hour) dose was calculated which should be equivalent to a chosen dose fractionation scheme as used for conventional EXRT, ie. EXRT with one fraction of 2.0 Gy/day given 5 days/week. For this step the incomplete repair model was used. Next, after having made an arbitrary choice for the PDR fraction size of 1 Gy or of 1.5 Gy, and the interval between PDR fractions: 3 hours. The number of fractions was calculated which would result in the same ETD as with the EXRT, ie. the same level of survival. This means that the total PDR dose and the overall time of the PDR treatment are usually somewhat different from the total LDR dose for our PDR fractionation regimes. This contrasts with the PDR concept proposed by Brenner & Hall (1991) as in our fractionation regimes there is no strict condition that the PDR dose must be equal to the LDR dose. There is less need for extreme fractionation, ie. there is less need for very short intervals between fractions and small fraction doses. However, to keep the probability of late effects in normal tissues as low as possible it remains essential to choose the overall treatment time of the PDR comparable to or longer than the application time of the corresponding LDR scheme. Trying to shorten the overall treatment time should not be attempted. With regard to the calculations, the following parameters were used, Table 5.

Table 5
Parameters used for calculations PDR (and HDR) schemes of equivalent fractionation.

- Tumour effect α/β = 10 Gy, α = 0.3 Gy-1
- Late effects (normal tissues): α/β = 3 Gy, α = 0.3 Gy-1
- Half-time for repair of sublethal damage: T   = 3.0 h for both early effects (tumour effect) and late effects (damage to normal tissues)
  [from May 1993 we have used $T_{1/2}$ = 1h for each effects and 3h for late effects]
- Pulse duration: 5 min. This choice is not very relevant as long as the chosen repair half-time is long compared to the pulse duration. For small PDR pulses this will mostly be the case.

A summary table of the computed equivalent schemes currently in use is presented in Table 3 which gives PDR treatment schemes as a function of a reference EXRT (2 Gy/day) regime with which they should be equivalent. This table also gives the ETD of the reference EXRT scheme and the equivalent LDR scheme, ie. the application time and the resulting total dose. This is given for continuous irradiation with a dose rate of 50 cGy/hour. The final two columns in Table 3 present the equivalent fractionated HDR & PDR regimes and their corresponding ETDs. To obtain an impression of the consequences of a particular scheme regarding the probability of the occurrence of late effects in normal tissues, the ratio of the ETD values for the HDR (PDR) scheme and the corresponding LDR scheme (as given in Table 3) can be computed easily. A ratio <1 would then indicate that the PDR scheme is expected to produce fewer late effects and a ratio >1 indicates that more late effects might be expected with respect to LDR. A ratio of <1 is in principle possible because the overall time for the PDR schemes has not been chosen to be identical with the LDR value: and usually it is somewhat longer.

Dosimetry for Base of Tongue Implants

For a comparison of the dose distributions of base of tongue implants obtained in LDR treatment using iridium-192 wires with those obtained in fractionated HDR treatment using a single iridium-192 stepping source, the results of optimised and non-optimised dose distributions have been evaluated. For this evaluation a specific implant of a patient which can be considered to be representative has been used. The configuration of this implant is shown in Figures 1-3. Basically it consists of three sagittal planes. Each sagittal plane consists of one catheter entering either posteriorly through the base of tongue proper (vallecula) or through the larynx (if covering of the epiglottis was necessary), depending on tumour extension. It subsequently runs over the dorsum of the tongue with two blind-ended catheters with buttons sutured to it.

The main direction of the implant is defined as the main direction of the blind-ended catheters which run approximately parallel. We usually define a central plane (Figure 4) perpendicular to this main direction and passing through the centre of the implant. The orientation of the central plane is illustrated in Figures 1-2 together with a 'surface plane' (Figure 5) which is chosen to investigate the dose distribution over the surface of the tongue. The intersection of the catheters and the central plane form triangles, the geometric centres of which are taken as reference points. This method can be seen as a generalisation of the Paris system for dose specification for this type of implant. The reference points for defining the 'basal dose' are chosen in the geometrical centres of the triangles in the central plane. This is because generally these will be the locations of the local minima in the dose distribution in the central plane. The average of the doses in these reference points is defined as the basal dose and the reference dose is taken to be 85% of this basal dose. In Figures 4-5 the resulting dose distributions in the central plane and in the surface plane are shown.

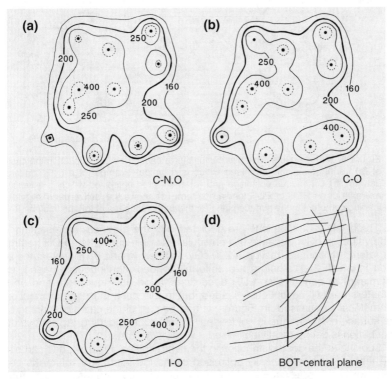

Figure 4. Central plane dose distributions for a base of tongue implant in the case of **(a)** continuous, non-optimised which is a typical example of a LDR loading pattern, **(b)** continuous optimised and **(c)** interrupted optimised which is a typical example of an HDR or PDR loading pattern. **(d)** shows the 'active parts' of afterloading catheters in the central plane for this particular base of tongue implant.

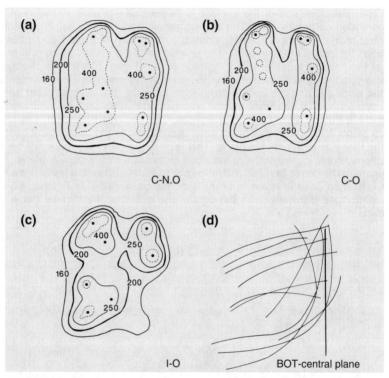

Figure 5. Surface plane dose distributions for a base of tongue implant in the case of **(a)** continuous, non-optimised which is a typical example of a LDR loading pattern, **(b)** continuous optimised and **(c)** interrupted optimised which is a typical example of an HDR or PDR loading pattern. **(d)** shows the 'active parts' of after-loading catheters in the surface plane for this particular base of tongue implant.

Three different situations are depicted with the numbers representing iso-dose values in cGy. Because this particular example concerns a PDR treatment the reference isodose/fraction is 200 cGy. Figures 4a and 5a represent the situation in which the catheters are uniformly loaded (continuously loaded, non-optimised) to simulate an LDR dose distribution. In Figures 4b and 5b the catheters are still continuously loaded, but in this case the dose distribution is geometrically optimised. In Figures 4c and 5c part of the catheter running over the surface of the tongue is not loaded: an interrupted loading. Again, this dose distribution is geometrically optimised.

Looking at the dose distribution in the central plane, Figure 4, one can easily see that in the geometrically optimised cases the implanted volume is better covered by the reference isodose. As expected, continuously or interrupted loading has little or no effect on the dose distribution in the central plane, Figure 4 and Table 6.

This aspect should of course also be investigated for the dose distribution in the surface plane, Figure 5. In this plane the difference between the three situations is more pronounced. In Figure 5a it can clearly be seen that the overdosed region, eg. the region covered by the 400 cGy isodose, is quite large. This over-dosed region can be considerably reduced through an optimisation procedure, see Figure 5b.

Table 6
Dose distribution in the central plane: LDR (CNO) versus fractionated HDR or PDR (IO).

Dose points in centres of gravity	Dose (CNO)		Dose (CO)		Dose (IO)	
	Gy	%	Gy	%	Gy	%
1	270	135	223	112	245	122
2	227	113	237	118	236	118
3	240	120	266	133	247	124
4	281	140	281	140	255	128
5	228	114	233	116	229	115
6	202	101	208	104	224	112
7	211	105	192	96	204	102
8	196	98	216	108	235	118

CNO: continuous, non optimized: typical example of a LDR treatment
CO: continuous, optimized
IO: interrupted, optimized: typical example of a HDR or a PDR treatment

In certain cases interrupted loading could be advantageous in giving a larger reduction of the overdosed region. In this special case this is not so pronounced as part of the volume is not covered any more by the reference isodose, see Figure 5c. The resulting dwell times in a number of positions of catheters 1, 2 and 3 are presented in Table 7. This shows the non-optimised dose distribution with equal times in each dwell position, followed by the two geometrically opti-mised cases.

The most interesting feature is to compare the dwell times of catheters 2 and 3 (the two blind-ended catheters with buttons sutured to catheter 1) and especially the dwell positions 1 and 2 for the two geometrically optimised con-figurations. In the configuration with the continuously loaded catheter, ie. the catheter running over the dorsum of the tongue, these positions show relatively short times to compensate for the contribution of the 'dorsum running' catheter. In the case of interrupted loading these positions show relatively much longer dwell times. This is a typical situation for a base of tongue implant consisting of several blind-ended parallel catheters, Table 7. In general for this type of vol-ume implant, we now choose interrupted loading because of the reduction of overdosed volume especially at the dorsum of the tongue. This reduction is expected to result in reduced side effects in terms of the probability of occur-rence of long lasting mucositis and/or ulcers.

During the planning stage the dose distributions are very carefully analysed, both in the central and the surface plane and more importantly also in sagittal planes in between the sagittal planes containing the catheters. If for whatever reason the resulting dose distribution seems to be unsatisfactory, eg. if substan-tial cold spots occur, ie. areas of dose below the reference dose, one can sub-sequently decide to load one or more parts of the 'inactive sections' of the dor-sum running catheters and to re-optimise the dose distribution.

Table 7
Sagital plane surface dose distribution: LDR (CNO) versus fractionated HDR or PDR (IO).

Source position	Catheter 1 Weight	Catheter 1 Sec.	Catheter 2 Weight	Catheter 2 Sec.	Catheter 3 Weight	Catheter 3 Sec.	Treatment
1	1.00	5.9	1.00	5.9	1.00	5.9	
2	1.00	5.9	1.00	5.9	1.00	5.9	CNO
3	1.00	5.9	1.00	5.9	1.00	5.9	
4	1.00	5.9	1.00	5.9	1.00	5.9	
etc.			etc.		etc		
1	0.14	2.5	0.23	4.1	0.21	3.8	
2	0.16	2.9	0.22	4.0	0.30	5.5	CO
3	0.17	3.0	0.29	5.3	0.35	6.4	
4	0.20	3.6	0.32	5.9	0.38	6.8	
etc.			etc.		etc		
1	0.27	4.6	0.57	9.9	0.59	10.2	
2	0.25	4.4	0.49	8.6	0.51	8.9	IO
3	0.28	4.9	0.45	7,8	0.47	8.2	
4	0.39	6.7	0.42	7.3	0.47	8.1	
etc.			etc.		etc		

CNO: continuous, non optimized: typical example of a LDR treatment
CO: continuous, optimized
IO: interrupted, optimized: typical example of a HDR or a PDR treatment
Catheter 1: afterloading catheter running over dorsum of the tongue
Catheter 2 & 3: blind ended afterloading catheters sutured with button to catheter 1

Preliminary Results

A total of 46 patients with a variety of tumours in the head & neck were treated by interstitial HDR or PDR brachytherapy, with or without external beam radiation therapy and surgery: 26 had a primary cancer and 20 a recurrent

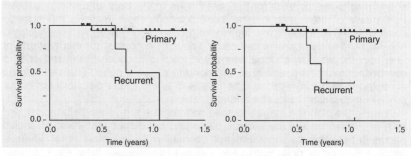

Figure 6. Actuarial local relapse free survival probability **(Left)** for (P) primary and for (R) recurrent tumours of the head & neck treated between January 1991 and June 1992 by external beam radiation and/or HDR or PDR interstitial brachytherapy. **(Right)** shows the actuarial overall survival probability for the same patient groups.

tumour after previous irradiation. For the primary cancers subgroup the mean age was 59 years with a range of 35-88 years: 23 males and three females. The mean follow-up period was 132 days with a range of 101-152 days. None of the patients failed at the implanted site.

For the subgroup of 20 patients who recurred after fractionated HDR or PDR irradiation the mean age was 66 years with a range of 39-67 years: 13 males and seven females. The mean follow-up period was 187 days with a range of 0-483 days. 8/20 experienced a local failure.

Figure 6 shows the actuarial local relapse free survival and overall survival results for the two patient subroups: primary and recurrent cancers.

For all brachytherapy patients with a minimum follow-up of three months, acute and late side effects were scored according to a modified RTOG scoring system: grades 0-4. For the acute side effects maximum grading was scored during the first three months after completion of treatment for skin (S), mucosa (M), dysphagia (D), wound healing (W), xerostomia (X) and pain (P). In this review the M and S scores are given in relation to the total dose in Figures 7 and 8. This is seen for the primary cancers subgroup in Figure 7 (Left) and Figure 8 (left). For the recurrent tumour subgroup the data is given in Figure 7 (right) and Figure 8 (Right).

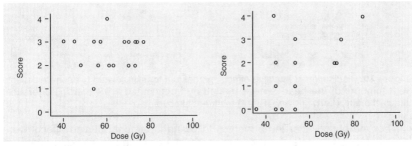

Figure 7. Distribution of early side effects, grades 0-4 for mucosa related to dose for patients with tumours of the head & neck treated by fractionated HDR or by PDR interstitial brachytherapy: **(Left)** primary cancers, **(Right)** recurrent tumours.

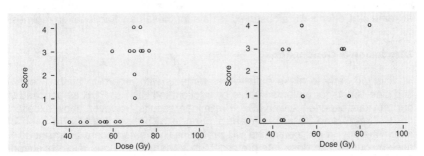

Figure 8. Distribution of early side effects, grades 0-4 for skin related to dose for patients with tumours of the head & neck treated by fractionated HDR or PDR interstitial brachytherapy. **(Left)** primary cancers, **(Right)** recurrent tumours.

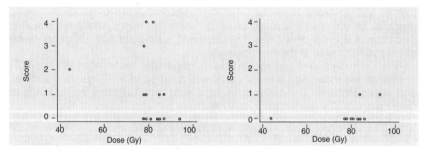

Figure 9. Distribution of late side effects, grades 0-4 for mucosa related to dose for patients with tumours of the head & neck treated by fractionated HDR or PDR interstitial brachytherapy. **(Left)** primary cancers, **(Right)** recurrent tumours.

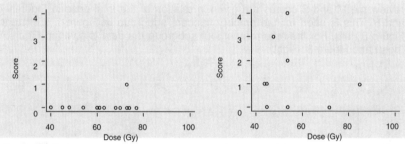

Figure 10. Distribution of late side effects, grades 0-4 for skin related to dose for patients with tumours of the head & neck treated by fractionated HDR or PDR interstitial brachytherapy. **(Left)** primary, **(Right)** recurrent tumours.

For the period after three months following treatment, all side effects were considered late effects. A maximum score was assigned to late side effects of the skin (S), subcutaneous tissues (T), mucosa (M), xerostomia (G), cord (C), eyes (E) and pain (P). As an example, Figures 9 and 10 show late effects for M and S in relation to the total dose for both patient subgroups. Although the follow-up period is much too short for scoring late side effects, again no obvious extreme side effects were observed to date for these new fractionation regimes.

Discussion & Conclusions

It is too early to make definitive statements with regard to tumour control and side effects for patients treated by fractionated HDR or PDR as opposed to our previous experience with LDR. Preliminary results, however, show excellent control rates and do not warrant a change of policy. That is, in case of brachytherapy in our centre we will preferentially treat cancers of the head & neck by our 'pulsed dose rate protocol'. Since there is only one microSelectron-PDR in the DDHCC, in case of unavailability of this microSelectron-PDR due to logistical reasons we will treat our patients according to the fractionated HDR protocol.

It should be emphasised that both treatment protocols are experimental and should be evaluated cautiously relative to the worldwide experience with LDR brachytherapy, with regard to tumour control as well as with respect to the late side effects.

The experimental fractioned HDR and PDR approach which the DDHCC has taken is somewhat different to the approach on PDR as proposed by Brenner & Hall (1991). Problems such as establishing the correct values for half-times of repair for acute (tumour) and late (normal tissue) damage remain to be solved. At the time of writing this chapter we had arbitrarily chosen a $T_{1/2}$ of 3 hours for early and late effects to study the influence of half-times of repair values, the ratio of the total doses of PDR and LDR has been calculated as a function of the linear-quadratic parameter /b and the time constant $T_{1/2}$ for the repair of sublethal damage. An example is given in Figure 10, where for a specific LDR scheme of 51.5 hours at 50 cGY/hour for D=20.8 Gy, the equivalent PDR schemes have been calculated, using an interval of three hours and a pulsed dose of 1.0 Gy.

From Figure 11 we can conclude that for early effects (α/β approximately 10 Gy) and for repair times ranging from one to three hours, the PDR/LDR dose ratio varies from 105% to 110%. That is, PDR has to be chosen somewhat higher than the LDR dose. For this scheme the PDR/LDR dose ratio for late effects (α/β approximately 3 Gy) is found to be higher: 110%/120%. This means that an overdosing of late effects in normal tissues is not to be expected with this scheme. From May 1993 we have used for all our fractionation regimes a $T_{1/2}$ of 1 hour (acute effects/tumour) and T1/2 of 3 hours (late effects).

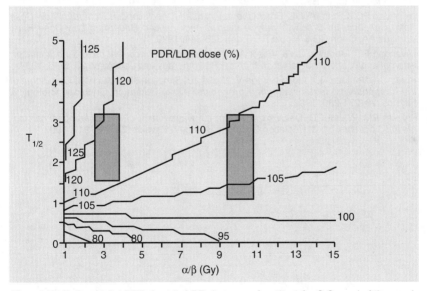

Figure 11. Ratio of total PDR dose to LDR dose as a function of α/β Gy and of the repair time constant for repair of sublethal damage. The shaded regions indicate parameter ranges for early effects (α/β =10Gy) and late effects (α/β = 3Gy), LDR: 50 cGy/hour, T = 41.5 hour, D = 20.8 Gy. PDR: 3 hour interval, 1.0 Gy pulses.

Advantages of using fractionated HDR and PDR when compared to LDR include no source preparation, outpatient basis treatment (useful for small implants treated by fractionated HDR), higher throughput of patients (for HDR although not for PDR), optimisation feasibility, more patient-friendly : disconnecting patients from machine with HDR and for PDR in the case of long intervals in between fractions, such as six or three hours. However, it has also been our experience that the sophistication in treatment techniques evidently accompanies the need for more and better trained technicians!

Acknowledgements

The authors acknowledge the great help of Mr. D. Sipkema, brachytherapy technician in the DDHCC, for running some of the computer planning examples used in this chapter. Also, we acknowledge the expertise in patient care of the members of the Rotterdam Head & Neck Oncology Group: Drs M. de Boer, P.P.M. Knegt, M. Scholtemeyer, L.L. Visch & S.J.M. Wijthoff; as well as from the referring physicians of the different head & neck groups in The Netherlands. In particular the close cooperation with head & neck oncologists of the Academic Hospital Groningen and Leiden has been much appreciated.

References

Brenner D & Hall E, *Conditions for the equivalence of continuous to pulsed low dose rate brachytherapy*, Int. J. Radiation Oncology Biology & Physics, **20**, 181-190, 1991.

Levendag PC & Putten WJL, *Brachytherapy in head & neck cancer: Rotterdam Low Dose Rate experience,*in: *Brachytherapy in head & neck cancer: Rotterdam Low Dose Rate*, Martinez AA, Orton CG & Mould RF (Eds), 325-344, 1990.

Levendag PC, Meeuwis CA & Visser AG, *Re-irradiation in recurrent head & neck cancer: external and/or interstitial radiation therapy*, Radiotherapy and Oncology, **23**, 6-15, 1992.

Perez CA, Venkata RD, Marcial-Vega V, Marks JE, Simpson JR & Kucik N, *Carcinoma of the nasopharynx: factors affecting prognosis*, Int. J. Radiation Oncology Biology & Physics, **23**, 271-280, 1992.

Pryzant RM, Wendt CD, Delclos L & Peters LJ, *Retreatment of nasopharyngeal carcinoma in 53 patients*, Int. J. Radiation Oncology Biology & Physics, **22**, 941-947, 1992.

15

Long Duration Moderate Interstitial Hyperthermia & HDR Brachytherapy for Newly Diagnosed Malignant Gliomas

D.M. Garcia[1], J.A. Marchosky[2], G.H. Nussbaum[3], M.A. Mackey[3] & R.E. Drzymala[3]

[1]Radiation Oncology Department,
[2]Neurosurgery Department,
 Missouri Baptist Medical Center,
 3015 N. Ballas Road,
 St. Louis,
 MO 63131,
 USA.

[3]Mallinckrodt Institute of Radiology,
 Washington University School of Medicine,
 St Louis,
 MO 63108,
 USA.

Introduction

Glioblastoma multiforme is among the most aggressive of all brain tumours and is almost invariably fatal within two years of initial diagnosis. Conventional treatment with varying degrees of surgery and post-operative external irradiation has resulted in a median survival of nine months with less than 5% of patients surviving to two years, Walker et al (1978). Anaplastic astrocytomas have a more favourable prognosis but the median survival is only two years with surgery alone and five years with surgery and post-operative irradiation, Garcia et al (1985).

In an attempt to improve local tumour control and thus prolong survival, we have opted for an approach employing long duration, moderate temperature interstitial hyperthermia in combination with HDR interstitial brachytherapy. Technical details of the planning of treatment with this approach have been reported by Garcia et al (1992) and Marchosky et al (1990, 1991). In this chapter, emphasis will be placed on the stereotactic technique for implantation of catheters under CT guidance, the treatment protocol and the preliminary clinical results obtained to date.

Materials & Methods

Stereotactic Implantation Technique

Stabilisation Frame. A head stabilisation frame developed for CT-guided needle biopsies of the brain (Marchosky & Moran 1983, Moran et al 1984) was used for the volumetric implantation of multiple catheters into malignant brain tumours (Moran et al 1984, Simpson et al 1987, Marchosky et al 1990). The device consists of a support base attached to the CT table, a ring shaped frame, a head support attached to the frame and adjustable nylon pads to stabilise the head and eliminate the need for perforation of the scalp to secure the head position.

Figure 1. CT-mounted stereotactic frame for interstitial catheter implantation. Adjustable pads support the patient's head and eliminate the need for perforation of the skull.

Template. A custom designed acrylic template which is attached to the head stabilisation frame was used to guide the twist drill used to make the perforations, to guide the catheters. That is, to maintain the desired spacing of the various catheters selected in the planning phase. The template contains parallel rows of apertures with adjacent rows separated by 7.5 mm. Each row contains apertures for hyperthermia catheters and brachytherapy catheters.

In a given application, up to four of the brachytherapy catheter holes may be used for thermometry catheters. Across each row the pattern repetition of holes is as follows: 'hyperthermia' - 8.67 mm gap - 'brachytherapy' - 8.67 mm gap - 'brachytherapy' - 8.67 mm gap - 'hyperthermia'. Successive rows are staggered right and left relative to one another by 13 mm. Thus the linear map of holes in every other row (eg. rows 1, 3 & 5 or 2, 4 & 6) is exactly the same.

In a particular clinical application a repetition pattern is created in which hyperthermia catheters are implanted at the corners of equilateral triangles of side 15 mm and brachytherapy catheters are placed at the centres of these triangles. This positions them 8.67 mm from each of the three nearest hyperthermia catheters. Dedicated thermometry catheters are placed in judiciously chosen unoccupied brachytherapy catheter holes.

Figure 2. A sterilised plastic template attached to the stereotactic frame is used to guide the drill and catheters and to maintain the desired inter-catheter spacing.

Catheters. The hyperthermia catheters employed in this protocol are 2.2 mm in diameter with an overall length of 22 cm. Active heating lengths (lengths of internal, coaxial heating coils) of 2, 3, 4, 5, 6, 7 or 8 cm could be selected. As discussed in earlier reports by Babbs et al (1990) and DeFord et al (1990,1991a,b), heat is generated by the passage of direct current under computer control through the electrically resistive heating coils. Tissue temperature is then elevated through the transfer of heat directly to the tissue from the heated catheters.

The brachytherapy catheters are 1.8 mm in diameter and are 20 cm in length and marked at 1.0 cm intervals. The dedicated thermometry catheters are 1.2 mm in diameter and contain four thermistor sensors spaced 1 cm apart.

Up to four thermometry catheters, which equate to 16 temperature sensors, are used in a given application.

Implantation. The catheters were implanted percutaneously in the CT suite using interactive CT scanning and surgery. After induction of general anaesthesia the patient's head was secured in the stereotactic frame and the scalp was shaved, prepared with antibacterial solution and draped. A sterile 1/16" silicone sheet was stapled to the scalp over the area of the tumour and the template was secured to the stabilisation frame. Contrast enhanced CT scans were made in planes 7.5 mm apart corresponding to the successive rows of apertures in the template. This permitted planning of catheter placement. The target volume for implantation was the contrast enhancement plus a 1.0 cm margin.

Using the CT scanning software a line intersecting a portion of the tumour was projected through each appropriately positioned template aperture. The implantation depth was determined by the scanning software from the distance along the line from the surface of the template to the deepest tumour (plus an appropriate margin) point. The software was also used to determine the treatment length (active length of hyperthermia and brachytherapy implants) by measuring the distance traversed by the line across the tumour. Implantation depth and treatment length for a given aperture were both recorded on a template diagram.

Once the three-dimensional placement of all of the hyperthermia and brachytherapy catheters was determined and the implantation depths and treatment distances for these catheters were recorded, locations for the dedicated thermometry catheters were selected and their implantation depths were calculated. Using the information recorded on the template diagram and guidance provided by the rigid acrylic template, the silicone sheet, scalp, skull, and dura were perforated with a sterile battery operated twist drill. The semi-rigid catheters were implanted to the indicated depths and the accuracy of their placement was verified by CT scans. Repeat CT scanning allowed necessary adjustments to be made immediately.

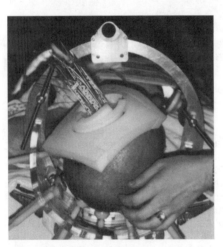

Figure 3. Layered foam dressing with central well of silicone elastomer used to secure the brachytherapy and hyperthermia catheters.

Once the catheters were satisfactorily positioned, the template was carefully withdrawn. Cyanoacrylate ester cement was used to initially anchor the catheters to the silicone sheet. The catheters were further secured by building a foam well and filling the centre with silicone elastomer. The patient was then removed from the head stabilisation frame and taken to the post-anaesthesia recovery unit.

Brachytherapy Treatment Technique

Once stabilised, the patient was brought to the Radiation Oncology Department for simulation films using dummy sources within each catheter. These films are required for computerised brachytherapy treatment planning. While the plan for the HDR treatment was prepared the patient was moved to the Neurosurgical Intensive Care Unit where preparations were made for hyperthermia delivery. Typically, the patient returned to Radiation Oncology for the first of three HDR treatments after an initial three hour session of hyperthermia.

HDR treatments were administered using the spatially programmed microSelectron-HDR remote afterloading iridium-192 stepping source. In the protocol used in this study a total dose of 1500 cGy administered in three equal fractions was prescribed. As mentioned earlier, the three fractions were spaced approximately equally over the total period of heating with each fraction given during one of the one hour breaks between three hour heating intervals.

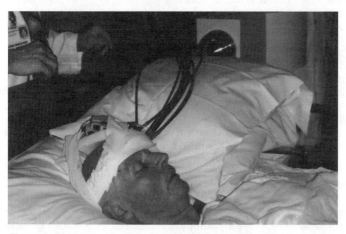

Figure 4. Patient prepared to receive high dose rate remote afterloading brachytherapy treatment with a microSelectron-HDR unit.

Hyperthermia Treatment Technique

The hyperthermia treatment was delivered in the neurosurgical Neurosurgical Intensive Care Unit with a commercially available, computer controlled system: the Cook VH-8500 hyperthermia treatment system. The treatment specification protocol was 48 hours of moderate hyperthermia to be delivered over a 64 hour period. To accomplish this the minimum tissue temperature was elevated to 41.5°C for three of every four hours. The one hour break between the three hour heating intervals allowed patient mobility and nursing care. During treatment, patients were continuously monitored for neurological function, vital signs, electrolytes and core body temperature. Appropriate medications, including steroids, antibiotics, and anticonvulsants were administered as needed.

Catheter Removal, Discharge & Follow-Up

Once treatment with hyperthermia and radiation was completed, catheters were removed in the CT suite and CT scans were obtained to assess haemostasis, mass effect and tumour status. When clinically indicated, the patients were discharged from the hospital. Follow-up was performed every two months and included neurologic function tests and CT scans. When the CT scans indicated a decrease in mass effect and edema, steroids were tapered but patients were maintained on anticonvulsants.

Patient Characteristics

Between April 1990 and February 1992 a total of 11 patients with newly diagnosed malignant glioma were treated with external irradiation to 4600 cGy in 23 fractions. This was followed after a two week break by long duration interstitial hyperthermia and interstitial HDR brachytherapy. 5/11 patients had undergone subtotal surgical resection of the tumour prior to receiving external irradiation.

The patient age range was 23-64 years with a mean of 40 years. The sex distribution was 5/11 females and 6/11 males. The range of pre-treatment Karnofsky scores was 85-100 with a mean of 93. The histological distribution was 7/11 with glioblastoma multiforme, 3/11 with astrocytoma with anaplastic features and 1/11 with an anaplastic oligodendroglioma. Tumour volumes determined from pre-treatment CT scans ranged from 2 cm^3 to 115 cm^3 with a mean of 27 cm^3. Tumour sites were respectively 5, 2, 1, 2 and 1 for frontal, temporal, fronto-temporal, parietal and corpus callosum lesions.

Summary of Treatment Characteristics

Patients received an average of 4600 cGy of external irradiation and 1500 cGy of interstitial HDR brachytherapy and required a mean of 11 brachytherapy and 10 hyperthermia catheters to treat the tumour volume. The average duration of the treatment delivery was 34 hours. Three patients required early termination of treatment at three, 21 and 27 hours due to increased intracranial edema and resultant deterioration in their neurological condition.

The average targeted minimum tissue temperature was 41.8°C. The average measured minimum tissue temperature was 41.4°C and the average maximum tissue temperature was 44.8°C. Since the hyperthermia delivered to this group of patients departs from classic hyperthermia in both a lower desired temperature (target) and a longer therapy delivery time, we considered it appropriate to describe thermal doses using the Dewey-Sapareto model (Sapareto & Dewey 1984).

This model provides a method of therapy quantification combining both time and temperature to calculate a thermal dose in equivalent minutes at 43°C. Using this model the patients received a mean of 231 equivalent minutes of therapy at 43°C.

Results

Response. 8/11 patients remain alive and 3/11 have died of tumour progression. A median survival for this patient group has not yet been reached. The length of follow-up is now in the range 30-99 weeks with a mean of 62 weeks. The 7/11 patients with glioblastoma multiforme have a mean follow-up time of 58 weeks with 4/7 remaining alive. The 4/11 with anaplastic astrocytoma or anaplastic oligodendroglioma have a mean follow-up of 71 weeks with all patients still alive. Post-treatment Karnofsky scores are in the range 40-100 with a mean of 78.

In an effort to quantify tumour response, tumour volumes were calculated from follow-up contrast enhanced CT scans. In this analysis 4/11 patients showed marked improvement with a greater than 75% decrease in tumour volume when compared to a pretreatment baseline CT scan. 3/11 showed partial improvement with a greater than 25% but less than 75% decrease in tumour volume. 1/11 had a stable response with a less than 25% decrease in the tumour volume. 1/11 had continued tumour progression with a greater than 25% increase in tumour volume. 2/11 patients could not be evaluated using follow-up CT scans as they required an immediate post-treatment debulking craniotomy to relieve mass effect.

Complications. Complications arose in 6/11 patients. 2/6 developed mass effect requiring craniotomy for decompression, 2/6 developed pulmonary emboli which cleared with medical management. 2/6 developed scalp infections which resolved with antibiotics.

Discussion

Technique. The technique employed in the present clinical study evolved over several years with experience interstitial brachytherapy in the brain without hyperthermia, (Abrath et al 1986, Simpson et al 1987) and subsequently with interstitial hyperthermia in the brain without radiation, (Marchosky et al 1991, Marchosky et al 1990). This initial experience demonstrated the ability of patients to tolerate volume implants without undue sequela.

In the present approach, conventional burr holes are replaced with small twist drill holes since this decreases surgical time and eliminates the need for suturing of the implant sites after removal of the catheters. The performance of the entire implant procedure in the CT suite is time saving, as it allows a CT guided needle biopsy to be performed, the treatment to be planned, catheters to be implanted and their placement to be verified without having to transfer the patient to the operating room. This CT based approach takes approximately two hours and obviates the need for double staffing and extra operating room time, thus increasing the cost-effectiveness of the procedure.

In opting for a combination of interstitial HDR brachytherapy and interstitial hyperthermia, our decision to use HDR brachytherapy rather than LDR (low dose rate) brachytherapy was dictated primarily by the needs of patients and the Neurological Intensive Care Unit clinical staff. As mentioned earlier, the long duration hyperthermia is administered to the patient in the Neurological

Intensive Care Unit because of the need to continuously monitor the condition of the patient and to provide nursing care to the patient over the entire heating period.

LDR Brachytherapy. The use of LDR interstitial brachytherapy, which would require radioactive sources to be present in the patient over the extended period of the implant, would expose to unacceptable levels of radiation the nursing staff, other patients in the Neurological Intensive Care Unit and visitors.

Prostate Cancer Clinical Trial. It is noted that in an ongoing clinical study at St. Luke's Hospital, St. Louis, Missouri, which employs interstitial hyperthermia and interstitial brachytherapy in treatment of recurrent tumours of the prostate, LDR irradiation is used and is given simultaneously with the hyperthermia over the entire heating period, (Garcia et al 1992). However, for this patient population, constant nursing care is not necessary and the combined simultaneous administration of heat and radiation takes place in a single occupancy patient room. For the patient population in the present study, the HDR brachytherapy is logistically appropriate, as it allows the radiation treatment to be delivered in just a few minutes in the shielded environment of the Radiation Oncology Department.

Survival. There is an urgent need to improve survival in patients with malignant gliomas, especially glioblastoma multiforme. The fact that these tumours can afflict children and young adults is particularly frustrating. Although therapeutic approaches employed to treat such tumours have used chemotherapy, hyperthermia, interstitial brachytherapy, radiation sensitisers and hyperfractionation, the *gold standard of treatment* remains some degree of surgery followed by post-operative external beam irradiation. Unfortunately, this standard approach yields a median survival of only nine months for patients with glioblastoma multiforme, (Walker et al 1978).

Presently, the patients in this protocol with glioblastoma multiforme are averaging a survival of over 12 months and the median survival in this group is expected to increase with 4/7 patients still living.

Local Tumour Failure. It is important to recognise that unlike the case for other malignancies treated primarily with radiation, local tumour failure is the principal reason for premature death from gliomas. In addition, attempts to sterilise the tumour in such treatment have been particularly challenging because of the limited tolerance of surrounding normal brain and critical structures.

Follow-up Assessment. The clinical protocol employed on the present study is a phase I/II protocol. Although in general, the level of complications has been acceptable for the patient population treated, the tumour response has been difficult to evaluate unequivocally. Neurological deterioration that can occur immediately post-implant may require months of rehabilitation before significant improvement is observed, and thus may be difficult to distinguish from tumour progression over that period.

Post-implant CT and MR scans can be difficult to interpret due to mass effect and necrotic changes that occur post-treatment and then only slowly resolve. While the treatment regimen has produced a few long-term survivors with excellent neurological function, death due to progression of tumour has occurred in about one-third (3/11) of the patients.

Prediction of Outcomes. We are currently exploring ways to predict the effectiveness of treatment in individual patients through measurement of levels of heat shock proteins (hsp 28 and hsp 70) and also of S-phase fraction before, during and after the treatment given on the present protocol. It is hoped that this study will ultimately provide a set of determinants (or predictors) of the likely effectiveness of the proposed treatment, allowing clinically useful decisions regarding changes in treatment and/or in patient selection to be made.

Tumour Control. Recent studies of the mechanism of cell killing during simulated long duration, moderate 41.5°C hyperthermia using HeLa cells in vitro have yielded insight into some of the processes which may contribute to tumour control in the clinic. The general observation is that perturbations in cell cycle progression during the heat treatments lead to the precocious entry of cells into mitosis before the completion of DNA replication, (Mackey et al 1992a). It is interesting to note that thermal radiosensitisation under these conditions appears to maximise before any significant cell kill commences from the heat treatment, (Mackey et al 1992b).

Furthermore, the characteristic reduction in the killing efficiency of ionising irradiation at low dose rates is obviated when such irradiation is delivered over a long duration, moderate hyperthermia exposure (Armour et al 1991). However, further study of the long duration, moderate hyperthermia response of a variety of other human cell lines is needed to generalise these in vitro results.

Patient Biopsy Studies. Since it is problematical to extrapolate from cell culture data to the clinical situation, basic biological investigations of the clinical effects of such treatment are also required. Such studies would be ideally performed using patient biopsy samples obtained before and during a standard course of long duration hyperthermia, with or without adjuvant radiotherapy.

The Future. Verification of the aforementioned effects of the long duration heat treatment upon cell cycle progression in clinical tumour samples, ultimately expressed as premature mitoses and cell death, could lead to routine use of predictive assays designed to tailor specific treatment regimens on a patient-by-patient basis.

Acknowledgments

The authors would like to thank Dr. Chris Moran for analysing the CT scan response and Mary Jane Schmitt for preparation of this manuscript.

References

Abrath FG, Henderson SD, Simpson JR, Moran CJ & Marchosky JA, *CT guided volumetric interstitial brachytherapy of brain tumors*, Int. J. Radiation Oncology Biology & Physics, **12**, 359-363, 1986.

Armour E, Wang Z, Corry P & Martinez A, *Equivalence of continuous and pulse simulated low dose rate irradiation in 9L gliosarcoma cells at 37C and 41C*, Int. J. Radiation Oncology Biology & Physics, **22**, 109-114, 1991.

Babbs CF, Fearnot NE, Marchosky JA, Moran CJ, Jones JT & Plantenga TD, *Theoretical basis for controlling minimal tumour temperature during interstitial conductive heat therapy*, IEEE Transactions in Biomedical Engineering, **37**, 662-672, 1990.

DeFord JA, Babbs CF, Patel UH, Bleyer MW, Marchosky JA & Moran CJ, *Effective estimation and computer control of minimum tumour temperature during conductive interstitial hyperthermia*, Int. J. Hyperthermia, **7**, 441-453, 1991a.

DeFord JA, Babbs CF, Patel UH, Fearnot NE, Marchosky JA & Moran CJ, *Accuracy and precision of computer simulated tissue temperatures in individual human intracranial tumours treated with interstitial hyperthermia*, Int. J. Hyperthermia, **6**, 755-770, 1990.

DeFord JA, Babbs CF, Patel UH, Fearnot NE, Marchosky JA & Moran CJ, *Design and evaluation of closed-loop feed back control of minimum temperatures in human intracranial tumors treated with interstitial hyperthermia*, Medical Biology Engineering Computing, **29**, 197-206, 1991b.

Garcia DM, Fulling KH & Marks JE, *The value of radiation therapy in addition to surgery for astrocytomas of the adult cerebrum*, Cancer, **55**, 919-927, 1985.

Garcia DM, Marchosky JA, Nussbaum G & Drzymala R, *Interstitial HDR brachytherapy and long duration interstitial hyperthermia in the treatment of newly diagnosed malignant gliomas*, Activity Selectron Brachytherapy Journal, **6**, 70-74, 1992.

Garcia DM, Nussbaum GH, Fathman AE, Drzymala RE, Bleyer MW, DeFord JA & Welsh DM, *Concurrent iridium-192 brachytherapy and long duration conductive interstitial hyperthermia for the treatment of recurrent carcinoma of the prostate: A feasibility study*, Endocurietherapy/Hyperthermia Oncology, **8**, 151-158, 1992.

Mackey MA, Anolik SL & Roti Roti JL, *Cellular mechanisms associated with the lack of chronic thermotolerance expression in HeLa S3 cells*, Cancer Research, **52**, 1101-1106, 1992a.

Mackey MA, Anolik SL & Roti Roti JL, *Changes in heat radiation sensitivity during long duration, moderate hyperthermia in HeLa S3 cells*, Cancer Research, **52**, 1101-1106, 1992b.

Marchosky JA, Babbs CF, Moran CJ, Fearnot NE, DeFord JA & Welsh DM, *Conductive hyperthermia: A new modality for treatment of intracranial tumors*, in:*Consensus on hyperthermia for the 1990s*, Bicher H, McLaren JR & Pigliucci GM (Eds), 124-144, Plenum Press:New York, 1991.

Marchosky JA & Moran CJA, *A simple stereotaxic CT controlled brain biopsy system for general neurosurgical use*, Contemporary Neurosurgery, **5**, 1-8, 1983.

Marchosky JA, Moran CJ, Fearnot NE & Babbs CF, *Hyperthermia catheter implantation and therapy in the brain*, Neurosurgery, **72**, 975-979, 1990.

Moran CJ, Naidich TP, Marchosky JA & Barbier JY, *A simple stabilisation device for intracranial aspiration procedures guided by computed tomography*, Radiology, **144**, 183-184, 1984.

Moran CJ, Naidich TP & Marchosky JA, *CT-guided needle placement in the central nervous system: Results in 146 consecutive patients*, Amer. J. Roentgenology, **143**, 861-868, 1984.

Sapareto SA & Dewey WC, *Thermal dose determination in cancer therapy*, Int. J. Radiation Oncology Biology & Physics, **10**, 787-800, 1984.

Simpson JR, Marchosky JA, Moran CJ, Devineni VR, Abrath FG & Henderson S, *Volumetric interstitial implantation of glioblastoma multiforme*, Endocurietherapy/Hyperthermia Oncology, **3**, 161-170, 1987.

Walker MD, Alexander E Jr., Hunt WE, MacCarty CS, Mahaley MS Jr., Mealey J Jr., Norell HA, Owens G, Ransohoff J, Wilson CB, Gehan EA & Strike TA, *Evaluation of BCNU and/or radiotherapy in the treatment of anaplastic gliomas*, Neurosurgery, **49**, 333-343, 1978.

16

Stereotactic Radiosurgery Treatment Planning

B. Bauer-Kirpes

Nucletron International B.V.,
Waardgelder 1,
3905 TH Veenendaal,
The Netherlands.

Introduction

Radiosurgery is a technique of external beam irradiation which operates on a similar principle to the beam configuration of the Gamma Knife and consists of the following.

- Multiple isocentric arcs at 4-11 couch rotation angles.
- Narrow circular fields.
- Stereotactic localisation of the target point.

The requirements for radiosurgery treatment planning systems differ in some aspects from conventional treatment planning systems, mainly due to the three-dimensional nature of the treatment setup. Radiosurgery planning is strongly image oriented because it is based on 3D patient anatomy information, usually provided by a stack of CT scans which typically range between 20 and 50 slices.

In many cases target volume information is based on two imaging modalities, such as CT and angiography for AVMs. Since all images are obtained with the stereotactic frame, image coordinates from different modalities can be related to the same stereotactic coordinate system. This process is called stereotactic localisation.

From the stack of CT scans, arbitrarily oriented sections must be reformatted, usually to generate sagittal and coronal sections. Additionally, sections in

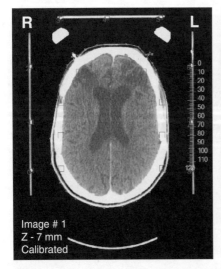 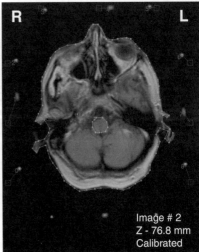

Figure 1. CT with stereotactic fiducials and ruler. **Figure 2.** MR with stereotactic fiducials.

the plane defined by the gantry arc are required. In these sections, graphical input and output is required, such as:

- Digitise target point in axial slice or reformatted section.
- Digitise beam arc in parasagittal section.
- Draw the target volume, isodoses, etc. in arbitrary sections.

Stereotactic Localisation

Stereotactic localisation is defined as a method to register each image in the stereotactic coordinate system, which is frame oriented. To visualise the stereotactic frame in the images, localisers are attached to the frame. These produce landmarks in the images from which the transformation matrix from image coordinate space to stereotactic space can be calculated. Once this is created, all anatomical information derived from the images can be expressed in stereotactic coordinate space.

The position of the stereotactic coordinate system in relation to the CT image coordinate system must be determined. Then, every CT pixel can be expressed in stereotactic coordinates. Since the images may not be perfectly parallel to the frame or shifted or tilted relative to each other, the software calculates a separate transformation matrix for each slice.

The markers have to be digitised in all slices and the transformation matrix is calculated and stored for each individual slice. This process can be automated while still leaving the possibility for manual manipulation.

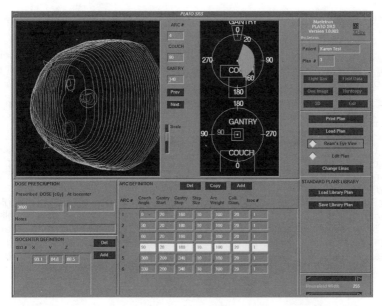

Figure 3. Field setup screen with linac diagram and beam's eye view.

Compatibility with CT Localisers

Most CT localiser frames use the same principal layout and consist of radio-opaque rods which are arranged in a fixed pattern. The software does not use internally stored frame geometry and therefore the frame geometry is stored in an external file. This allows to enter geometry data for virtually all frames.

Ring Alignment

The stereotactic frame does not need to be perfectly aligned with the CT scanner. All tilt, rotation or shift of the frame *versus* the CT coordinate system or scan plane will be detected by the CT localisation. This also means that the images do not need to be parallel to each other. In particular, variation in slice spacing throughout the scan series is possible and even encouraged. The head area which contains the lesion can be scanned with finer slice spacing, such as 1.5 mm-3 mm. This is in order to increase the accuracy of the CT localisation in the Z direction. The rest of the head up to the vertex is only needed for finding the beam entry points. Since this is not critical for the accuracy of the dose calculation a coarse slice spacing, such as 5 mm-8 mm, is sufficient.

The software will correct for misalignments of the stereotactic frame since all coordinates are now represented in stereotactic coordinates. In particular, all contour points for the 3D display, as well as all image pixels for the multi-planar reconstruction, are transformed into stereotactic space.

Field Setup

A treatment technique in radiosurgery consists of a combination of non-coplanar arcs. These arcs may all have different isocentres, weights, collimators and gantry angles. However, in most cases a standard technique will be employed as defined by the user.

Storing Plans

During a planning session many plans will be made and evaluated, among which the best will be used for the treatment. Each plan receives a new plan number and is stored in a file. All plans for a patient can be uniquely identified and retrieved.

Plans can also be stored in a patient independent form such that a plan library can be built up. These plans from the library can be used as a template for other patients. If, for example, a hospital uses a standard protocol of six arcs with table angle increments of 30°, this setup can be stored in the library. During the planning session, this technique can be retrieved and then the user does not have to enter these six arcs individually each time this plan is required.

Input Parameters

The target point is specified in X,Y,Z stereotactic coordinates. It can either be digitised in a CT scan or in a multiplanar reformatted section. Alternatively the stereotactic coordinates, for example obtained from radiographs, can be entered from the keyboard. Target points are maintained in a separate list which is independent from the arcs. Therefore, arcs can be assigned to an existing isocentre. With this technique, arcs can be grouped to one isocentre, which can be edited in the CT images or in the 3D view.

The collimators are uniquely defined by a collimator number. Additionally each collimator has a so-called isodose diameter, which is used in the beam's eye view, (see Figure 3), and in the 3D display to assess the diameter of the isodose. The isodose diameter can be defined freely by the user. Each arc can use a different collimator. The arc weight is a value relative to the weight of others arc. It is defined at the isocentre of the arc.

The couch angle is entered as a number with the definition of angles conforming to IEC specifications. The gantry rotation is specified by the first and last angle and by the angle increment between the fixed beams, which are used to simulate a continuous motion. The single beams are displayed in the oblique section as lines with a mark for the beam entry point. The single beams are also used in the beam's eye view as discrete positions for the gantry rotation.

Gantry and couch angles are visualised in the schematic linac diagram (see Figure 3) as soon as they are entered.

Beam Visualisation

Since for standard treatments, such as a four-arc technique, the high level isodoses are almost perfectly spherical, the dose distribution around an isocentre can be approximated as a sphere of a given diameter. This information can be used during field setup and isocentre definition to optimise the set up even before the dose has been calculated. Whenever a CT plane, either transversal or reformatted, is displayed, the isocentre can be represented by a circle. This allows the user to assess immediately whether the desired isodose will encompass the target volume. The 3D displays, beam's eye view and room's eye view particularly make use of this feature. The user can interactively move the isocenters and observe the correlation of the sphere with the target volume or other isocentres.

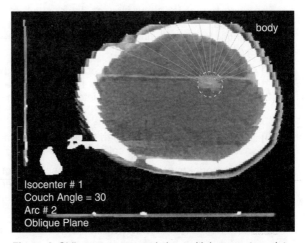

Isocenter # 1
Couch Angle = 30
Arc # 2
Oblique Plane

Figure 4. Oblique reconstructed plane with beam entry points.

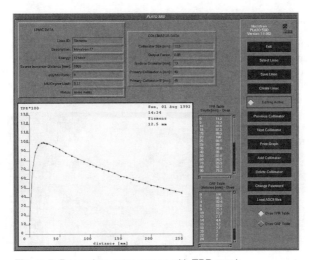

Figure 5. Beam data entry screen with TPR graph.

Dose Calculation

The dose model for small circular fields which are used for stereotactic radiosurgery can be as simple as possible. This speeds up the dose calculation in a 3D matrix for a large number of fixed beams. Three important simplifications can be made as follows:

[1] Corrections for sloped or curved surfaces can be neglected, because the field sizes are small, typically 1-3 cm in diameter.
[2] Inhomogeneities are not taken into account, because brain tissue has a water equivalent density and the influence of the skull on the dose distribution and absolute dose is below 3%.
[3] The fixed beams are assumed to be rotation symmetrical. This is a valid assumption when circular collimators are used.

The dose model uses measured depth dose data, off-axis profiles and output factor for each collimator in use. Arcs are calculated as a summation of a user definable number of fixed beams. This is a fast and proven dose model (Hartmann et al 1985, Kooy et al 1985), which is widely used for radiosurgery dose calculations.

Dose Visualisation

Evaluation of the dose distribution is an important and time-consuming task, because all brain tissue surrounding the target volume is considered as critical organ. The distribution must be checked for the following features.

- Complete coverage of the target volume in all slices.
- Dose outside the target volume.
- Appearance of hot spots.
- Dose to critical organs.

Point Dose

For a fast dose evaluation at critical points the dose at the cursor position can be calculated in real time. The cursor is not limited to the current dose matrix. With the display of the contributions of each arc, critical arcs can be determined and modified if necessary. For example, the beams eye view can be utilised to locate the gantry angles at which the arc hits the critical point.

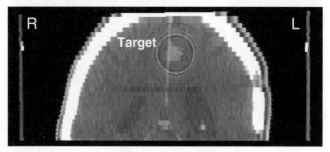

Figure 6. Coronal plane with isodoses.

2D Isodoses

Two-dimensional isodoses can be displayed in CT scans, coronal and sagittal reformatted sections, and in the arc planes. Since it is important to reduce the calculation time to a minimum, the area of dose calculation and the dose matrix resolution can be specified by the user. Limiting the dose matrix to the target area can reduce the calculation time dramatically. To view dose at critical organs, either the point dose feature is used, or the dose matrix is redefined so that it covers the critical organ.

3D Isodoses

Although 2D isodoses in multiple slices can provide the spatial information on whether the dose covers the target volume, the 3D isodose display illustrates the relationship between target surface and isodose surface, on a single viewing screen. Isodoses or organ surfaces can be made transparent for better visualisation of structures which might be hidden by others. The 3D model can be rotated, zoomed and moved interactively in real time, thus providing optimum visualisation from all sides. The 3D isodoses are calculated from a 3D dose matrix, for which the resolution can be chosen directly in mm. This makes the matrix independent of the CT pixel size and slice distance.

Dose-Volume Histograms

With dose-volume histograms, the user can evaluate the following.
- Minimum or maximum dose at the target and other organs
- Irradiated volume of organs
- Dose distribution within organs

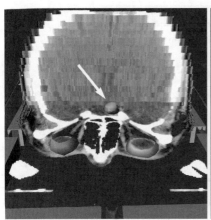 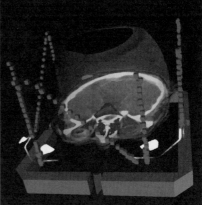

Figure 7. 3D display with CT cut-outs combined with isodose surface (arrow) **(left)** and frame fiducials **(right)**.

The histograms can be calculated for each defined organ using a random sampling technique. The number of points can be chosen by the user according to the preferences of calculation speed and accuracy.

Protocol

The protocol output must enable the user to set up the patient on the linear accelerator and to verify relevant data on safety, such as monitor units. Therefore it contains all relevant data for the following.

- Patient identification
- Beam data identification
- Plan identification
- Setup data for stereotactic frame and linear accelerator
- Calculation details for verification of monitor units

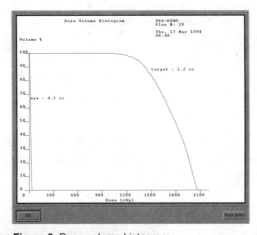

Figure 8. Dose-volume histogram.

Acknowledgement

Marco Luzzara, Enrico Ongania and Davide Casolino have worked extensively on the described software. Their ideas, skills and helpful criticisms have contributed significantly to this work. I am also grateful to Reginald Schreuders for his help in preparing this chapter.

References

Chierego G, Marchetti C, Avanzo RC, Pozza F & Colombo F, *Dosimetric considerations on multiple arc stereotaxic radiotherapy*, Radiotherapy & Oncology,**12**, 141-152.

Engenhart R et al, *Stereotactic single high dose radiation therapy of benign intracranial meningiomas*, Int. J. Radiation Oncology Biology & Physics, **19**, 1021-1026, 1990.

Gehring MA, Mackie R, Kubsad SS, Paliwal BR & Mehta MP, *A three-dimensional volume visualization package applied to stereotactic radiosurgery treatment planning*, Int. J. Radiation Oncology Biology & Physics, **21**, 491-500, 1991.

Gibbs F et al, *Measurement of mechanical accuracy of isocenter: in conventional linear-accelerator-based on radiosurgery*, Int. J. Radiation Oncology Biology & Physics, **25**, 117-122, 1993.

Hartmann GH et al, *Cerebral radiation surgery using moving beam irradiation at a linear accelerator*, Int. J. Radiation Oncology Biology & Physics, **11**, 1185-1192, 1985.

Hartmann GH et al, *Cerebral radiation surgery using moving beam irradiation at alinear accelerator*, Int. J. Radiation Oncology Biology & Physics, **21**, 683-693, 1991.

Hartmann GH et al, *Precision and accuracy of stereotactic convergent beam irradiations from a linear accelerator*, Int. J. Radiation Oncology Biology & Physics, **28**, 481-492, 1994.

Kooy H et al, *Treatment planning for stereotactic radiosurgery of intra-cranial lesions*, Int. J. Radiation Oncology Biology & Physics, **11**, 1185-1192, 1985.

Lutz W, Winston K & Maleki N, *A System for stereotactic radiosurgery with a linear accelerator*,.Int. J. Radiation Oncology Biology & Physics, **14**, 373-381, 1988.

Loeffler JS et al, *Stereotactic radiosurgery for arteriovenous malformations of the brain using a standard linear accelerator*, Int. J. Radiation Oncology Biology & Physics, **17**, 671-677, 1989.

Niemierko A & Goitein M, *Random sampling for evaluating treatment plans*, Medical Physics, **17**, 753-762, 1990.

Rice RK et al, *Measurements of dose distributions in small beams of 6 MV x-rays*, Physics in Medicin &.Biollogy, **32**, 1087-1099, 1987.

Saunders W et al, *Radiosurgery for arteriovenous malformations of the brain using a standard linear accelerator: Rationale and Technique*, Int. J. Radiation Oncology Biology & Physics, **15**, 441-447, 1988.

Schlegel W et al, *Computer systems and mechanical tools for stereotactically guided conformation therapy with linear accelerators*, Int. J. Radiation Oncology Biology & Physics, **24**, 781-787, 1992.

Serago C et al, *Stereotactic target point verification of an X-Ray and CT localiser*, Int. J. Radiation Oncology Biology & Physics, **20**, 517-523, 1991.

Siddon RL, *Solution to treatment planning problems using coordinate transformations*, Medical Physics, **8**, 766-774, 1981.

Siddon RL & Barth NH, *Stereotaxic localisation of intracranial targets*, Int. J. Radiation Oncology Biology & Physics, **13**, 1241-1246, 1987.

Tsai JS et al, *Quality assurance in stereotactic radiosurgery using a standard linear accelerator,* Int. J. Radiation Oncology Biology & Physics, **21**, 737-748, 1991.

17

Advances in Brain Tumour Treatment

W.R. Shapiro

Barrow Neurological Institute,
St. Joseph's Hospital & Medical Center,
350 West Thomas Road,
Phoenix,
AZ 85013,
USA.

Introduction

The Brain Tumor Cooperative Group (BTCG), previously named the Brain Tumor Study Group, has established that in the treatment of supratentorial malignant astrocytomas the concept of cytoreduction through multimodality therapy, including surgery, radiation therapy and chemotherapy, (Shapiro 1986).

Surgery

The role of surgical resection in the treatment of such tumours remains controversial even after 75 years of experience with primary malignant gliomas. No one disagrees that only surgery permits a pathological diagnosis to be established during life. However, many physicians consider that current methods of radiological diagnosis, including CT scanning and MR imaging, permit a diagnosis of malignant brain tumour without the necessity for operation, thus avoiding the risks of surgery. Such a view denies a role for surgery as "cancer" therapy.

There is evidence that surgical reduction of tumour to very small residual amounts can prolong survival and permit the patient to return to an active life for a year or longer. In one BTCG study, CT scans from brain tumour patients were studied at several times in their treatment courses and compared to ultimate outcome (Wood et al 1988). This study found no significant relationship between preoperative tumour size and prognosis. This indicated that the effect of the treatment received after the initial scan outweighed any effect that preoperative tumour size may have.

On the other hand there was a very strong relationship between post-operative size and survival. This was especially noticeable for patients with minimal or no residual enhancement. There was a statistically significant ordering of tumour size, such that those patients with very little residual enhancement (< 1 cm^2 in length x width dimensions) had the longest survival, followed by those with tumours 1-4 cm^2, and then by patients with tumours > 4 cm^2, (P=0.0001).

When the difference between preoperative and postoperative tumour size was evaluated, there was no significant relationship between percentage of tumour removed and survival. Although a trend toward longer survival was seen in patients whose tumours were reduced by 75% or more. Thus, the most beneficial effect of surgery is less the result of debulking than of leaving the least residual tumour possible. Nevertheless, these results strongly support the surgical removal of largest possible volume of tumour that safe operation allows.

There is little justification in performing only biopsy or limited resection of accessible tumours. If the surgeon confines his resection to the tumour itself, he rarely induces a major new neurological defect. On the contrary, patients are frequently able to return to a full, active life without the need for large doses of corticosteroid hormones to ameliorate incapacitating symptoms.

Radiation Therapy

The proper portals and doses of radiation therapy in the treatment of brain tumours have changed with the advent of better imaging techniques. The Brain Tumor Study Group (BTSG) reported in controlled studies that whole-brain radiation therapy increases the survival of patients over that which follows surgery alone (Walker et al 1978,1980). Other data from the BTSG showed that patients receiving 5500-6000 cGy live significantly longer than those receiving 5000 cGy or less (Walker et al 1979).

In the above cited BTCG study using CT scans, patients with no tumour enhancement after radiation therapy had a better survival than those with residual tumour (Wood et al 1988). Patients with larger tumours that shrank by more than 50% survived longer than those whose tumours shrank less than 50%. Those patients whose tumours enlarged during radiation therapy had a substantially worse outcome. Also, neither increased fractionation (twice daily) of radiotherapy nor addition of the radiosensitiser Misonidazole have thus far conferred any survival advantage over the conventional post-operative use of whole brain radiotherapy and BCNU (Deutsch et al 1989).

Radiation damages normal brain tissue: there is good evidence in experimental animals that doses of 6000 cGy produce damage to the normal brain (Nakagaki et al 1976). What is still not certain is the extent of such damage on patients and how it maybe made worse by associated chemotherapy.

A recently reported BTCG study compared whole-brain radiation therapy for malignant glioma with whole-brain and a coned down radiation boost (Shapiro et al 1989). Patients accrued in 1980 and 1981 were to receive 6020 cGy of whole-brain radiotherapy, while those accrued in 1982 and 1983 were randomly assigned to receive either whole-brain radiotherapy to 6020 cGy or 4300 cGy of whole-brain radiotherapy plus 1720 cGy coned down to the tumour volume. There was no statistical difference in survival between any of the groups, indicating that reduction of part of the radiotherapy to the tumour volume is as effective as full whole-brain irradiation.

Pathological observation suggests that damage can occur with radiation and chemotherapy (Burger et al 1979), and patients undergoing such treatment may show deficits in cognitive function (Hochberg & Slotnick 1980). The incidence of such complications, that is, the ratio of the number of patients who eventually develop the complication to those at risk, remains to be determined since most patients with this disease die in the first two or three years.

Among the newer techniques in radiotherapy is that of interstitial implantation of radioactive seeds. Substantially prolonged survival has been reported in patients with recurrent malignant gliomas treated with temporarily implanted iodine-125 sources (Gutin et al 1987). Another technique uses radiosensitisers: chemicals that sensitise the tumour cells to radiotherapy. These appear to be especially valuable in hypoxic tumour regions because radiation therapy is not as effective in the absence of oxygen. One of these, Misonidazole, was tested in a number of studies in the treatment of malignant gliomas, but in a BTCG study it was found not to add to the radiation effect (Deutsch et al 1989). In the same study, hyperfractionation (ie. more than one dose per day) was no more effective than a once daily fraction, although a number of hyperfractionation regimes are under active investigation. Studies of the efficacy of interstitial brachytherapy are underway and are described later in this chapter.

Chemotherapy

Chemotherapy completes the technique of multimodality treatment of malignant gliomas. The BTSG in 1983 reported that surgery plus radiation therapy and chemotherapy with BCNU (Carmustine) significantly added to the survival of patients with malignant glioma in comparison to surgery plus radiation therapy without chemotherapy (Green et al 1983). Patients with all three modalities had a median survival of 12 months whereas those with surgery plus radiation had a medial survival of 10 months. The 18-month survival rate was 2.5 times as high among the patients receiving Carmustine than among those without chemotherapy.

High dose Methyl-prednisolone does not lead to longer survival (Green et al 1983). Procarbazine and Streptozotocin have each showed similar effectiveness to BCNU (Deutsch et al 1989, Green et al 1983). Combination chemotherapy in Trial 8001 demonstrated again that BCNU was as effective as BCNU sequencing with Procarbazine, or BCNU plus Hydroxyurea sequencing with Procarbazine plus VM-26, (Shapiro et al 1989). Despite these results, IV BCNU was clearly not curative, and methods were sought to improve its efficacy using intra-arterial (IA) BCNU, as described below.

Prognostic Variables

A major consideration in the therapy of malignant glioma is the presence of prognostic variables that influence survival. The BTCG have determined that a number of such factors correlated with outcome (Green et al 1983). For example, patients younger than 45 years of age lived significantly longer than · patients over 65 years of age, irrespective of therapy. A defined death rate for comparison purposes (defined as: number of deaths/10 patient months) gave for patients under 45 years of age a value of 0.42, while for patients older than 65 years of age this death rate was 1.41 and is a highly significant difference. This effect of age on survival has been suggested in other studies and has been generally recognised by neurologists and neurosurgeons for many years.

Other important prognostic indicators included personality change (which when present yielded a higher death rate than when absent), duration of symptoms (ie, those patients whose symptoms exceeded six months before operation lived twice as long as patients whose duration of symptoms was under four months), and performance status postoperatively.

The performance status, based on a modification of a scale originally proposed by Karnofsky, semiquantifies the ability of the patient to handle normal living circumstances. The Karnofsky scale is measured in units of 10 from zero to 100. Generally, patients able to work have Karnofsky ratings of 80, 90 or 100, those whose symptoms prevent them from working but who otherwise can take care of themselves have Karnofsky ratings between 50 and 70; and patients who are clinically ill with their disease have Karnofsky ratings of 40 and below. In the above mentioned studies, patients whose Karnofsky scales were between 70 and 100 had a death rate (as defined earlier) of 0.7-0.55, as compared to a death rate of 1.52 for Karnofsky ratings between 10 and 40.

An important prognostic variable was the histopathological category; patients with glioblastoma multiforme had twice the death rate of patients with other malignant (mostly grade III) gliomas. Subsequent studies have confirmed the important prognostic variables of age, Karnofsky performance status and pathology, (Deutsch et al 1989, Shapiro et al 1989). To these must be added the extent of residual tumour postoperatively (Wood et al 1988).

Trial 8301: Intraarterial BCNU, 5-Fluorouracil

The rationale for "regional" chemotherapy via IA drug administration has been well presented by Collins (1984) who noted that drugs with high first-pass extraction (usually highly lipid soluble) and high total body clearance (eg. rapid metabolism) were especially good candidates for IA administration. Both higher local drug concentration and reduced systemic toxicity would result from the administration of lower doses of such drugs into the arterial supply of the tumour.

Malignant glioma is an excellent example of a tumour system which IA chemotherapy would be likely to be effective. Such tumours can be well localised by CT and by MR imaging and their arterial supply, identified by arteriography, consists usually of one or two feeding arteries. Both laboratory (Levin et al 1978) and clinical (Greenberg et al 1981, 1984, Hochberg et al 1985,

Madajewicz et al 1981) studies have suggested that higher concentrations of BCNU maybe achieved in tumour by "regional" chemotherapy consisting of IA drug infusion.

The relatively short in vivo half-life of BCNU (5-10 minutes) provides a rationale for the first-pass benefit of an IA infusion (Collins 1984). Levin et al (1978b) had demonstrated that BCNU concentrations in monkey brain could be increased by a factor of four by administering the drug through the carotid artery rather than via IV infusion. Fenstermacher & Cowles (1977) and Fenstermacher & Gazendam (1981) using a mathematical model, predicted that carotid administration of BCNU would produce as high as a 10-fold greater drug concentration in brain tissue than would IV administration, while bone marrow levels of BCNU were predicted to be equivalent to those following IV administration.

Several trials in small numbers of patients have reported clinical efficacy of IA BCNU. While eye toxicity and encephalophathy were reported, their incidence was considered low enough to be acceptable for human trials, especially if the dose was kept below $400mg/m^2$, (Feun et al 1984, Greenberg et al 1981, Madajewicz et al 1981, Safdari et al 1985).

To test the assumption that IA BCNU was both safe and effective, in December 1983 the BTCG began accrual of patients to Trial 8301, a randomised phase III trial comparing IA BCNU versus IV BCNU, each regime without or with IV 5-Fluorouracil (5-FU). The combination of BCNU plus 5-FU had been found to be the most effective of four regimes tested earlier by the BTSG (unpublished data) and was also reported to be effective in studies by Levin et al (1978a). The sequential 5-FU added a cell-cycle specific agent and was designed to improve the efficacy of BCNU alone. As noted below, IA BCNU was found to be too toxic to the brain and accrual to BCNU IA was stopped in October 1986. Accrual to the remaining arms ended in March 1987. Because of the finding of brain toxicity a preliminary report was published, warning of the danger of the regime (Shapiro & Green 1987). Final results have recently been published (Shapiro et al 1992).

Patients were to be entered in the study within three weeks of definitive surgical treatment for the primary tumour. Eligible patients had histologically proven supratentorial malignant glioma, were at least 15 years of age, and had a Karnofsky performance status of 40 or greater at the time of randomisation.

Radiotherapy consisted of combined whole brain irradiation to 4300 cGy followed by a coned-down boost of an additional 1720 cGy to the tumour plus a 2 cm margin for a total tumour dose of 6020 cGy. Patients were randomly assigned to receive either IV or IA BCNU ($200 mg/m^2$) once every eight weeks. Patients in each of these two groups were also randomly assigned to receive BCNU alone or BCNU followed 14 days later by the addition of IV 5-FU ($1 gm/m^2/day$) for three days, every eight weeks. Those randomised with equal probability to one of the four groups in this 2x2 factorial design were considered part of the "full randomisation".

Some patients were found not to be eligible to receive the IA BCNU, usually because of evidence of severe arteriosclerosis in the artery to be infused. These patients were to receive IV BCNU and in addition were randomised to receive or not to receive the 5-FU. They were considered part of the "limited randomisation". Chemotherapy was begun concomitant with the start of radiation therapy. IV BCNU was administered in a single dose dose of $200 mg/m^2$

over 30-60 minutes. IA or IV BCNU was repeated at eight week intervals with doses adjusted for haematological depression.

IA BCNU was administered through a catheter placed into the femoral artery. For internal carotid infusion the catheter tip was located above the carotid artery bifurcation. No attempt was made to pass the tip to a point above the ophthalmic artery take-off. For vertebral infusion the tip was located in the appropriate vertebral artery. BCNU was made up in the standard fashion, dissolving 100 mg of the drug in 3 ml absolute ethanol to which sterile water for injection was added to make the total 30 ml. The BCNU was infused at 4 ml/minute or slower if during internal carotid infusions the eye on the ipsilateral side became painful. Patients were also given narcotic analgesics and ice was applied to the eye as needed.

During the course of the study a serious toxicity occurred in the IA group. By May 1985, 13 patients had developed encephalopathy. All 13 patients had received at least two courses of IA BCNU and the encephalopathy was documented in the 3rd-7th months of therapy. Because of the occurrence of encephalopathy the BTCG acted in May 1985 to decrease the dose of IA BCNU to 100 mg/m^2 beginning in Course 3, with the remaining 100 mg/m^2 given by the IV route. In July 1985 it was decided to change Course 2 in a similar manner.

The results are as follows. The total randomised population (RP) numbered 505, with an age range of 18-79 years (median age of 56). There were 448 patients in the Valid Study Group (VSG). Of the 57 patients excluded from the VSG, 40 did not have malignant glioma on review of slides by the neuropathology review, 15 did not have adequate material available for neuropathology review and two patients were randomised in error. In general, the patients in the several groups were quite comparable. Overall, 75% of the patients in the VSG had glioblastoma multiforme and 78% of the patients had a Karnofsky performance status of 70 or greater.

Survival data were analysed for both the RP and the VSG. For patients eligible for the full randomisation (all four arms), there was statistically significant heterogeneity across the four curves (P=0.03), and the longest surviving group was that receiving IV BCNU. (For the VSG the heterogeneity was slightly less, P=0.06) When the survival data were grouped by randomised assignment of IA versus IV BCNU, the group randomised to BCNU IA had a statistically lower survival (P=0.002 for the RP and P=0.03 for the VSG). In the VSG, the median survival times were 11.2 months for the group randomised to IA BCNU and 14.0 months for the IV BCNU group, with 0.13 and 0.25 respective 2-year survival probabilities calculated using a life-table method. 5-FU had no influence on survival and the survival curves for the assigned 5-FU groups were practically superimposable (P=0.84 for the RP and P=0.96 for the VSG).

Analyses of other variables in these data showed that histopathological category, age at randomisation and Karnofsky performance status at randomisation were all markedly significant prognostic variables (P<0.00001 for each variable when considered separately). This is consistent with results in previous studies.

Applying a Cox proportional hazards model to study survival in the VSG we found that although age was quite important prognostically in both histopathological subgroups, the effect of age was more pronounced in the non-glioblastomas. The three prognostic variables were all significantly predictive when included together in the model, but the treatment variables were not statistically significant. The model did indicate a significant interaction between BCNU assignment and histopathology (P=0.003). While there was similar survival for the two BCNU groups (IA slightly worse) among the glioblastomas, the IA group had considerably worse survival among the non-glioblastomas.

No unexpected adverse events occurred with respect to haematological or systemic toxicity. However, the most serious adverse reaction associated with IA BCNU was encephalopathy which occurred in 16 patients. The symptoms developed only after two or more courses of IA BCNU and were associated with or preceded by severe ocular toxicity progressing to visual loss in a majority of patients. A total of 11 patients had both encephalopathy and visual loss, five had encephalopathy alone and 15 others had visual loss.

The encephalopathy was manifested by the subacute development of repeated seizures, hemipareses contralateral to the perfused hemisphere and progressively deteriorating mental status. The clinical picture resembled tumour progression but differed in the higher frequency of seizures and the failure of corticosteroid therapy to delay the progression of the encephalopathy in most of the patients. CT scanning revealed hypodensity of the white matter of the perfused hemisphere with mass effect including shift and ventricular compression. MR imaging revealed widespread increased T2 signal in the white matter along with mass effect. The neuropathological findings were initially described by Mahaley et al (1986) and in detail in six such patients by Rosenblum et al (1989).

In the latter study four brains had no evidence of tumour and a fifth had only a microscopic focus of tumour. Only one patient's brain demonstrated progressive tumour growth. The principal pathological finding was disseminated miliary foci of necrosis with mineralising axonopathy restricted to the internal carotid artery distribution and involving primarily the white matter, which was edematous. In three cases the process had progressed to a histologically dissimilar, massive necrotising leukoencephalopathy indistinguishable from pure radionecrosis.

The most important finding in this study was that IA BCNU administered in the doses described did not increase survival of newly diagnosed patients with malignant glioma over that afforded by IV BCNU. The addition of 5-FU was also not efficacious. In addition, the study demonstrated substantial toxicity produced by the IA BCNU including blindness and fatal encephalopathy. Indeed, one especially tragic result was that patients likely to live longer, those with anaplastic astrocytoma, actually had shorter survival if randomised to IA BCNU.

The mechanism of the encephalopathy remains to be elucidated. The neuropathological findings from several of our cases have been published (Rosenblum et al 1989). The appearance is quite similar to that of the lesions produced by irradiation, and indeed most of the patients in these series had received radiation therapy in addition to the IA BCNU. However, the encephalopathy can occur in the absence of radiation therapy (Bashir et al 1988), although it appears to be more common when both therapies are combined.

It has been proposed that streaming in the arterial tree produces uneven distribution of a poorly mixed drug resulting in focally damaging high concentrations in the brain. Lutz et al (1986) and Blacklock et al (1986) have suggested that the current catheters and slow infusions could account for non-uniform high drug concentrations that would produce focal areas of necrosis. However, this would not explain the large, generally contiguous white matter lesions observed in the pathological specimens.

Positron emission tomographic (PET) studies by Junck et al (1989) using IA $^{15}O-H_2O$ in humans demonstrated diffuse distribution of the isotope, not focal hot spots. Saris et al (1991) also using $^{15}O-H_2O$ in PET studies demonstrated intravascular streaming in patients given the isotope into the supraophthalmic segment of the internal carotid artery but not in patients given isotope into the infraophthalmic segment. The authors thought the larger diameter of the internal carotid artery in the neck reduced the likelihood of streaming. Hence, streaming alone does not appear to explain the pathogenesis of the encephalopathy.

Whatever the pathogenesis of the encephalopathy, IA BCNU is neither effective nor safe at least by the techniques used in this trial.

Trial 8420: IV PCNU versus IA Cisplatinum

While it is clear from the results of Trial 8301 that IA BCNU at doses likely to be advantageous in regional therapy is too toxic for use in brain tumours, other drugs maybe less toxic. Among the agents administered IA in brain tumour chemotherapy, Cisplatinum has had the most use (Stewart et al 1982, Mahaley et al 1989). Newton et al (1989) reported CNS toxicity following Cisplatinum treatment of patients who had failed previous IA BCNU and the IA combination of the two drugs maybe quite toxic.

In BTCG Trial 8420, IA Cisplatinum was tested in a Phase II randomised study comparing it to IV PCNU and preliminary results have been presented (Green et al 1989). IA Cisplatinum, 60 mg/m^2 was given every four weeks, versus IV PCNU, 100 mg/m2 every eight weeks. Overall, 311 patients were randomised, 156 to receive intravenous PCNU, 155 to receive intraarterial Cisplatinum.

The median age was 45 years, 56% had glioblastoma multiforme, most of the remainder had anaplastic astrocytoma and a few had recurrent low-grade glioma. 63% of the patients were men and 79% had a Karnofsky performance status of 70 or better. In general, both regimens were well tolerated although patients receiving IA Cisplatinum had fewer treatments. The overall incidence of encephalopathy associated with IA Cisplatinum was 3.9% and the incidence of severe encephalopathy was 1.5% as compared to 9.5% seen for IA BCNU. For the randomised population, the difference in survival was of borderline statistical significance (P=0.06) with the group randomised to PCNU having the better survival; for the VSG, P=0.07.

The median survival times were 10.0 months for the group randomised to Cisplatinum and 13.0 months for the PCNU group with respectively 0.25 and 0.28 2-year survival probabilities calculated using a life-table method. The observation that the overall survival was similar and the IA Cisplatinum was better tolerated than IA BCNU has led BTCG to combine IA Cisplatinum with IV BCNU in a new protocol: Trial 8901 (see next section).

Finally, several other drugs have been administered IA in brain tumour patients with variable results, including ACNU (Roosen et al 1989, Yamashita et al 1983), PCNU (Stewart et al 1987), HECNU (Fauchon et al 1990, Poisson et al 1990) and combination BCNU, Cisplatinum, VM-26 (Stewart et al, 1984).

Current BTCG Studies in Malignant Glioma

Trial 8701

Trial 8701 randomises newly diagnosed patients to receive (A) postoperative temporary iodine-125 seed implantation in the residual tumour bed followed by standard external beam radiotherapy plus IV BCNU or (B) external radiotherapy plus BCNU without the iodine-125 seed implantation. The primary purpose of this trial is to test in a well controlled trial the value in newly diagnosed patients of adding an additional 60 Gy in the form of brachytherapy to the 60 Gy delivered by external irradiation. Prolonged survival has been reported in patients with recurrent malignant gliomas treated with temporarily implanted iodine-125 (Gutin et al 1987). However, it is apparent that selection plays an important role in such results (Florell et al 1992) and only prospective controlled trials can assess the value of brachytherapy. As of April 1992 a total of 210 patients have been accrued to Trial 8701.

Trial 8901

Trial 8901 randomises newly diagnosed patients and those previously diagnosed but not treated with chemotherapy to receive (A) standard IV BCNU, (B) combination IV BCNU plus IA Cisplatinum or (C) the new agent 10-Ethyl-10-deaza-aminopterin (EDAM). This trial is designed for newly diagnosed patients not eligible for Trial 8701 and for patients who have received radiation therapy but no chemotherapy. It tests standard IV BCNU against a combination of IV BCNU and IA Cisplatinum and in addition introduces a new concept in clinical chemotherapy trials for gliomas: the use of new agents in Phase III trials using relatively small numbers of patients for the new drug. Arms (A) and (B) have the standard number of patients of about 150 per arm, while arm (C) is changed to a new drug when about 60 patients are accrued. It is thus designed as a "screening protocol" in newly diagnosed patients or those previously diagnosed but not treated with chemotherapy. The first drug in this series, EDAM, previously showed efficacy in breast cancer and non-small cell lung cancer patients. By the end of 1991 a total of 237 patients had been accrued to this protocol and arm (C) was changed to the new Adriamycin-like drug Piroxantrone.

Trial 9210 and Trial 9220

The newest program under development is to randomise eligible patients with recurrent gliomas who have not had brachytherapy to receive iodine-125 seeds without or with the radiosensitiser SR 2508. These patients will then be randomised together with others not eligible for iodine-125 seeds, to receive one of three drug protocols: Tamoxifen, combination Etoposide plus IA Cisplantin or the new drug Topotecan.

References

Aronin PA, Mahaley MS Jr, & Rudnick SA et al, *Prediction of BCNU pulmonary toxicity in patients with malignant glioma. An assessment of risk factors.* New England J. Medicine, **303**, 183-188, 1980.

Bashir R, Hochberg FG, Linggood RM & Hottleman K, *Pre-irradiation internal carotid artery BCNU in treatment of glioblastoma multiforme,* J. Neurosurgery, **68**, 917-919, 1988.

Blacklock JB, Wright DC & Dedrick RL et al, *Drug streaming during intra-arterial chemotherapy,* J. Neurosurgery, **64**, 284-291, 1986.

Burger PC, Mahaley MS & Dudka L et al, *The morphological effects of radiation administered therapeutically for intracranial gliomas: a postmortem study of 25 cases,* Cancer, **44**, 1256-1272, 1979.

Collins JM, *Pharmacologic rationale for regional drug delivery,* J. Clinical Oncology, **2**, 498-504, 1984.

Cox DR, *Regression models and life tables,* J. Royal Statistical Society (B), **34**, 187-202, 1960.

Cutler SJ & Ederer F, *Maximum utilization of the life table method in analyzing survival,* J. Chronic Disease, **8**, 699-712, 1975.

Dedrick RL, *Arterial drug infusion: pharmacokinetic problems and pitfalls,* J. National Cancer Institute, **80**, 84-89, 1988.

Deutsch M, Green SB & Strike TA et al, *Results of a randomized trial comparing BCNU plus radiotherapy, streptozotocin plus radiotherapy, BCNU plus hyperfractionated radiotherapy, and BCNU following misonidazole plus radiotherapy in the postoperative treatment of malignant glioma,* Int. J. Radiation Oncology Biology & Physics, **16**, 1389-1396, 1989.

Fauchon F, Davila L & Ghatellier G et al, *Treatment of malignant gliomas with surgery, intra-arterial infusions of 1-(2-hydroxyethyl) chloroethylnitrosourea and radiation therapy; a phase II study,* J. Neurosurgery, **27**, 231-234, 1990.

Fenstermacher JD & Cowles AL, *Theoretic limitations of intracarotid infusions in brain tumour chemotherapy,* Cancer Treatment Reports, **61**, 519-526, 1977

Fenstermacher JD & Gazendam J, *Intra-arterial infusions of drugs and hyperosmotic solutions as ways of enhancing CNS chemotherapy,* Cancer Treatment Reports, **65** (Suppl 2), 27-37, 1981.

Feun LG, Wallace W & Yung W-KA et al, *Phase-I trial of intracarotid BCNU and cisplatin in patients with malignant intracerebral tumours,* Cancer Drug Delivery, **1**, 239-245, 1984.

Florell RC, Macdonald DR & Irish WD, Bernstein M, Leibel SA, Gutin PH & Cairncross JG, *Selection bias, survival, and brachytherapy for glioma,* J. Neurosurgery, **76**, 179-183, 1992.

Green SB, Byar DP & Walker MD et al, *Comparisons of carmustine, procarbazine, and high-dose methylprednisolone as additions to surgery and radiotherapy for the treatment of malignant glioma,* Cancer Treatment Reports, **67**, 121-132, 1983.

Greenberg HS, Ensminger WD & Chandler WR et al, *Intra-arterial BCNU chemotherapy for treatment of malignant gliomas of the central nervous system,* J. Neurosurgery, **61**, 423-429, 1984.

Greenberg HS, Ensminger WD, & Seeger JF et al, *Intra-arterial BCNU chemotherapy for the treatment of malignant gliomas of the central nervous system: a preliminary report,* Cancer Treatment Reports, **65**, 803-810, 1981.

Gutin PH, Leibel SA & Wara WM et al, *Recurrent malignant gliomas: survival following interstitial brachytherapy with high-activity iodine-125 sources,* J. Neurosurgery, **67**, 864-873, 1987.

Hochberg FH, Pruitt AA & Beck DO et al, *The rationale and methodology for intra-arterial chemotherapy with BCNU as treatment for glioblastoma*, J. Neurosurgery, **63**, 876-880, 1985.

Hochberg FH & Slotnick B, *Neuropsychological impairment in astrocytoma survivors*, Neurology (Minnep), **30**, 172-177, 1980.

Junck L, Koeppe RA & Greenberg HS, *Mixing in the human carotid artery during carotid drug infusion studies with PET*, J. Cerebral Blood Flow Metabolism, **9**, 681-689, 1989.

Levin VA, Kabra PM & Freeman-Dove MA, *Pharmacokinectics of intracarotidartery 14C-BCNU in the squirrel monkey*, J. Neurosurgery, **48**, 587-593, 1978.

Lutz RJ, Dedrick RL & Boretos JW et al, *Mixing studies during intracarotid artery infusion in an in vitro model*, J. Neurosurgery, **64**, 277-283, 1986.

Madajewicz S, West CR & Park HC et al, *Phase II study: intra-arterial BCNU therapy for metastatic brain tumours*, Cancer, **47**, 653-657, 1981.

Mahaley MS Jr, Hipp SW & Dropcho EJ et al, *Intracarotid cisplatin chemotherapy for recurrent gliomas*, J. Neurosurgery, **70**, 371-378, 1989.

Mahaley MS Jr, Whaley RA, Blue M & Bertsch L et al, *Central neurotoxicity following intracarotid BCNU chemotherapy for malignant gliomas*, J. Neuro-Oncology, **3**, 287-314, 1986.

Mantel N, *Evaluation of survival data and two new rank order statistics arising in its consideration*, Cancer Chemotherapy Reports, **50**, 163-170, 1966.

Nakagaki H, Brunhart G & Kemper TL et al, *Monkey brain damage from radiation in the therapeutic range*, J. Neurosurgery, **44**, 3-11, 1976.

Newton HB, Page MA, Junck L & Greenberg HS, *Intra-arterial cisplatin for the treatment of malignant gliomas*, J. Neuro-Oncology, **7**, 39-45. 1989.

Poisson M, Chiras J, & Fauchon et al, *Treatment of malignant recurrent glioma by intra-arterial, infra-ophthalmic infusion of HECNU 1-(2-choloroethyl)-1-nitroso-3-(2-hydroxy-ethyl) urea*, J. Neuro-Oncology, **8**, 255-262, 1990.

Roosen N, Kiwit JCW, Lins E et al, *Adjuvant intraarterial chemotherapy with nimustine in the management of World Health Organisation grade IV gliomas of the brain*. Cancer, **64**, 1984-1994, 1989.

Rosenblum MD, Delattre J-Y, Walker RW & Shapiro WR, *Fatal necrotizing encephalopathy complicating of malignant gliomas with intra-arterial BCNU and irradiation: A pathological study*, J. Neuro-Oncology, **7**, 269-281, 1989.

Safdari Gh H, Mompeon B & Dubois JB et al, *Intraarterial 1,3-bis(2-chloroethyl)-1-nitrosourea chemotherapy for the treatment of malignant gliomas of the brain; a preliminary report*, Surgery Neurology, **24**, 490-497, 1985.

Saris SC, Blasberg RG & Carson RE et al, *Intravascular streaming during carotid artery infusions. Demonstration in humans and reduction using diastole-phased pulsatile administration*, J. Neurosurgery, **74**, 763-772, 1991.

Shapiro WR, *Therapy of adult malignant brain tumours: what have the clinical trials taught us?*, Seminars Oncology, **13**, 38-45, 1986.

Shapiro WR & Green SB, *Neurosurgical Forum. Letter to the editor: reevaluating the efficacy of intraarterial BCNU*, J. Neurosurgery, **66**, 313-315, 1987.

Shapiro WR, Green SB & Burger PC et al, *Randomized trial of three chemotherapy regimens and two radiotherapy regimens in postoperative treatment of malignant glioma: Brain Tumour Cooperative Group Trial 8001*, J. Neurosurgery, **71**, 1-9, 1989.

Shapiro WR, Green SB & Burger PC et al, *A randomized comparison of the intraarterial (IA) versus intravenous (IV) BCNU, without or with IV 5-fluorouracil (5-FU) for newly diagnosed patients with malignant glioma*. J. Neurosurgery, **76**, 772-781, 1992.

Stewart DJ, Grahovac Z & Benoit B et al, *Intracarotid chemotherapy with a combination of 1,3-bis(2-chloroethyl)-1-nitrosourea (BCNU), cisdiammine-dichloroplatinum (cisplatin) and 4'-O-demethyl-1-O-(4,6-O-2-thenylidene-β-D-glucopyranosyl) epipodophyllotoxin (VM-26) in the treatment of primary and metastic brain tumours.* Neurosurgery, **15**, 828-833, 1984.

Stewart DJ, Grahovac Z & Russel NA et al, *Phase I study of intracarotid PCNU.* J. Neuro-Oncology, **5**, 245-250, 1987.

Stewart DJ, Wallace S & Feun L et al, *A Phase I study of intracarotid artery infusion of cis-diamminedichloroplatinum (II) in patients with recurrent malignant intracerebral tumors,* Cancer Research, **42**, 2059-2062, 1982.

Walker MD, Alexander E Jr & Hunt WE et al, *Evaluation of BCNU and/or radiotherapy in the treatment of anaplastic gliomas. A cooperative clinical trial,* J. Neurosurgery, **49**, 333-343, 1978.

Walker MD, Green SB & Byar DP et al, *Randomized comparisons of radiotherapy and nitrosoureas for the treatment of malignant glioma after surgery,* New England J. Medicine, **303**, 1323-1329, 1980.

Walker MD, Strike TA & Sheline GE, *An analysis of dose-effect relationship in the radiotherapy of malignant gliomas,* Int. J. Radiation Oncology Biology & Physics, **5**, 1725-1731, 1979.

Wood JR, Green SB & Shapiro WR, *The prognostic importance of tumour size in malignant gliomas: a computed tomographic scan study by the Brain Tumor Cooperative Group,* J. Clinical Oncology, **6**, 338-343, 1988.

Yamashita J, Handa H & Tokuriki Y et al, *Intra-arterial ACNU therapy for malignant brain tumors,* J. Neurosurgery, **59**, 424-430, 1983.

18

Remote Afterloading Brachytherapy for the Local Control of Endobronchial Carcinoma

B.L. Speiser[1] & L. Spratling[2]

[1] St. Joseph's Hospital & Medical Center, Department of Radiation Oncology, 350 West Thomas Road, Phoenix, Arizona 85013, USA.

[2] 500 West Tenth Place, Suite 6, Mesa, Arizona, USA.

Introduction

An earlier paper entitled *Intermediate dose rate remote afterloading brachytherapy for intralumenal control of bronchogenic carcinoma* by Speiser & Spratling (1990) reported on 45 patients treated with a dose rate between those classified as LDR and HDR. This initial series used a standard LDR afterloading unit modified to allow one or two source trains long enough to be placed in catheters of sufficient length to be used in the tracheal bronchial tree. This also allowed higher activities per cm, that is, 20 mCi/cm, to achieve the higher than customary dose rate. This unit was used until the new microSelectron-HDR was available and placed into active clinical use.

In another publication entitled *Comparison of intermediate versus high dose rate remote afterloading brachytherapy in the control of endobronchial carcinoma* by Speiser & Spratling (1988), a comparison was made of the first 45 patients treated with intermediate dose rate (IDR) with the first 45 patients using HDR. Results of that analyses showed no significant difference in the initial clearing of obstructive disease.

The purpose of this chapter is to update the report on all patients treated with IDR (47 cases) and to report on patients treated with HDR brachytherapy (295 cases).

Methods & Material /Patient Workload

Starting on 24 October 1986 and ending on 29 July 1987, all patients fulfilling the following eligibility requirements were treated using a modified IDR afterloading unit. In the earliest reports two patients who had received two courses of treatment, the first with IDR and the second with HDR, were excluded from the analysis. These two patients are included in the present analysis. Following the clinical acceptance of the microSelectron-HDR all subsequent patients were treated with HDR brachytherapy. These 295 patients received treatment between August 1987 and August 1991.

Patient Selection Criteria

Patient selection criteria remained the same through all the phases of this study and consisted of the following. [a] Involvement of proximal airways which were defined as the trachea, mainstem and lobar bronchi. Disease only involving segmental bronchi did not fulfil the selection criteria. [b] All patients must have intralumenal disease visualised and biopsy proven by bronchoscopy. [c] All patients must have endolumenal disease leading to obstruction with clinically significant symptomatology which included dyspnea, haemoptysis, cough, and/or the signs and symptoms of obstructive pneumonia. Neodymium-yttrium-aluminum-garnet laser photoresection was optional for all highly obstructing lesions immediately prior (usually within 24 hours) to brachytherapy. Patients were placed in one of the following treatment arms.

Protocol Group [1.0] Curative Intent

This group included patients who fulfilled the following criteria [1.1-1.5] which are now defined [1.1] Those with inoperable non-oat cell lung cancer. [1.2] Those who had received no prior radiation. [1.3] Those who were T1, 2, 3, N0, 1, 2, 3, and N0 categories. [1.4] Those whose performance category using the Host or ECOG scale (Stanley 1980) was N0, 1, 2. [1.5] Those with weight loss less than 10% of body weight for the six months preceding diagnosis (Feinstein & Wells 1990).

The first group of patients treated using IDR were initially placed into the curative category based on the physician's indication of whether he thought the patient curable. The above criteria were retroactively used for analysis in this group of patients to conform to the HDR studies. Treatment consisted of external radiation of 6000 cGy in 30 fractions given during weeks 1-6, with appropriate shielding and/or field changes, so that the spinal cord dose was equal to or less than 4500 cGy. Brachytherapy was performed during weeks 1, 3 and 5.

Protocol Group [2.1] Palliative Intent

This group included the following. [2.11] Those with primary lung carcinoma: non-oat cell histology. [2.12] Those who were T4 and/or M1 disease categories. [2.13] Patients with a lesser stage of disease but with a Host performance status of H3 or H4, or who had weight loss greater than 10% of body weight in the six months preceding diagnosis and who were ineligible for the curative intent protocol.

Protocol Group [2.2] Palliative Intent

This group included the following patients. **[2.21]** Those with oat cell carcinoma with significant respiratory distress. **[2.22]** Patients with non-lung primaries metastatic to the endobronchial mucosa. **[2.23]** Those with lung primaries with intrapulmonary spread. Treatment consisted of brachytherapy during weeks 1, 2 and 3.

Optional radiation therapy could be delivered for group [2.1] patients of 250 cGy/day for a total of 3750 cGy in 15 fractions. For non-lung primaries or for oat cell carcinoma, concurrent chemotherapy using the same regimen in effect prior to the brachytherapy, could be continued at the option of the medical oncologist during brachytherapy.

Protocol Group [3] Recurrent Tumours

Patient criteria for those to be treated for a recurrence included the folllowing. **[3.1]** All histologies for **[3.2]** patients who had received a prior course of curative intent radiation therapy. These patients received brachytherapy only, at weeks 1, 2 and 3.

Levels of Brachytherapy

Brachytherapy was delivered as three fractions and there were three levels of brachytherapy dose used. Group **[1]** patients consisted of all patients treated with an IDR (200-1000 cGy/hour) and who received 1000 cGy calculated at a 5 mm depth per fraction for three planned fractions. Group **[2]** patients, of whom there were a total of 144, received HDR brachytherapy: 1000 cGy calculated at a 10 mm depth for each of three fractions. Group **[3]** patients, of whom there were a total of 151, received HDR of 750 cGy delivered at a 10 mm depth, for each of three fractions.

Catheter Placement

The original technique for catheter placement has been described in a previous publication by Speiser & Spratling (1990). The technique was later modified so that the catheters could be placed further distally than the margin needed for tumour treatment, in order to allow better anchoring of the distal end but not to the pleural surface. In addition, 1-4 catheters were used.

Stepping Source & Optimisation

The initial modified-LDR treatment machine contained fixed length iridium-192 sources but the microSelectron-HDR afterloader uses a stepping source and dwell position/time technique which is coupled with computerised dosimetry and optimisation software.

Evaluation Techniques

Evaluation techniques consisted of the obstruction score which has been described by Speiser & Spratling (1990): the Host or ECOG performance scale, a symptom index that rated severity of symptoms including haemoptysis, pneumonia/elevated temperature, dyspnea, cough, see Table 1, and oxygen saturation levels. All were obtained immediately prior to each brachytherapy procedure and prior to the first follow-up bronchoscopy procedure (Speiser 1990).

Table 1
Symptom index scoring system.

Dyspnea

Score	Definition
0	None
1	Dyspnea on moderate exertion
2	Dyspnea with normal activity, walking on level ground
3	Dyspnea at rest
4	Requires supplement oxygen

Cough

Score	Definition
0	None
1	Intermittent, no medication necessary
2	Intermittent, non-narcotic medication
3	Constant or requiring narcotic medication
4	Constant, requiring narcotic medication but without relief

Haemoptysis

Score	Definition
0	None
1	Less than 2x/week
2	Less than daily but greater than 2x/week
3	Daily, bright red blood or clots
4	Decrease of Hb/Hct.>10%, greater than 150 cc, requiring hospitalisation, leading to respiratory distress, or requiring > 2 units transfusion

Pneumonia/Elevated Temperature

Score	Definition
0	Normal temperature, no infiltrates, WBC less than 10,000
1	Temperature greater than 38.5 and infiltrate, WBC less than 10,000
2	Temperature greater than 38.5 and infiltrate and/or WBC greater than 10,000
3	Lobar consolidation on radiograph
4	Pneumonia or elevated temperature requiring hospitalisation

Results

Patient Characteristics

The combined group of 342 patients consisted of 217 males (63%) and 125 females (37%). Their age range was 31-90 years with mean of 66.6 years. Neodymium-yttrium-aluminium-garnet laser photoresection was used in 24% of the patients. Histologies consisted of squamous cell (49%), large cell undifferentiated (16%), adenocarcinoma (14%), small cell undifferentiated (11%) and other histologies (10%).

The division of patient numbers into curative, palliative and recurrent protocol groups was 20%, 48% and 32%, respectively. Although T1, T2, and N0 categories were included in the protocol there was only one patient who fell within these early stage categories. 3% of the patients had T1-T2,N1 disease, 21% had T3,N0 disease or T1-3,N2 disease, 11% had either N3 disease or T4 disease and 25% had metastatic (M1) disease at presentation. Patients with local recurrences of their primary but without evidence of metastatic disease comprised 23% of the study with an additional 10% with synchronous local recurrence and metastatic disease. Non-lung primaries metastatic to the endobronchial lining made up 6% and the last 2% had intrapulmonary spread of a lung primary to the contralateral lung.

Analysis Group Definitions

Analysis Group I patients (N=47) consisted of those individuals treated with IDR brachytherapy: 1000 cGy at 5 mm depth. **Analysis Group II** patients (N=144) were treated with HDR: 1000 cGy at a 10 mm depth. **Analysis Group III** patients (N=151) were treated with HDR: 750 cGy at a 10 mm depth.

External Irradiation

External radiation was used concurrently for all patients treated in the curative intent group, as well for 43% of the patients in the palliative group. In total there was a 41% rate of concurrent external radiation in the entire series of 342 patients. Also, 5% of the patients in this study received additional radiation for metastatic disease at some point after entry into the study.

Symptoms

All patients had symptoms secondary to obstruction. Cough was the most common: occurring in 99% of the patients and was based on patient history. The only patient in the series who indicated that he did not have cough, in reality did have cough but because of prior brain damage leading to a severe short term memory deficit, could not remember his cough episodes. Dyspnea was the second most common symptom and occurred in 95% of the complete series. Haemoptysis occured in 66% and obstructive pneumonia occurred in 48%.

Because of the varying degrees of symptomatology observed in the initial study of Group [1] patients, a symptom index, Table 1, was devised and used for subsequent portions of the study for Groups [2] and [3]. Patients received a score prior to each brachytherapy and at the time of their follow-up bronchoscopy.

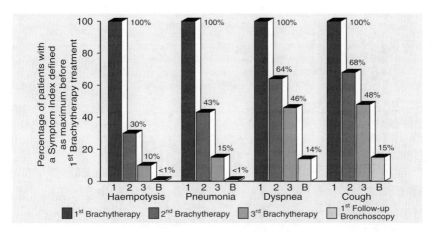

Figure 1. Symptom Index response expressed as percentage of a weighted index at each brachytherapy and at first follow-up bronchoscopy. The scores are weighted and normalised to 100% for the first score.

Figure 1 is a composite diagram summarising the symptom index responses. The initial symptom index scores prior to the first brachytherapy were weighted and normalised to 100% and the subsequent weighted scores were then stated as a percentage of the initial score. This Figure 1 shows the percentage reduction in the overall scores at each brachytherapy (1st, 2nd, 3rd) and at the first follow-up bronchoscopy, (B).

The first symptom shown is haemoptysis for which was observed the most dramatic decrease in scores of 70, 90 and >99%. The second most impressive result was for the pneumonia index with decreases of 57%, 85 and >99%. Observations for the dyspnea scores showed decreases of 36, 54 and 86% and the observed response for cough exhibited decreases of 32, 52 and 85%. Both the dyspnea and the cough scores showed less impressive responses in part due to pre-existing pulmonary disease and radiation bronchitis.

Obstruction Scores

The obstruction scoring system was used as a semiquantitative measure with the mean obstruction scores normalised to 100% and subsequent mean scores then stated as a percentage of the initial mean score. Figure 2 is a composite diagram for the subgroups: pre-treatment and post-treatment for curative, palliative and recurrent groups patients. This is regardless of whether laser was used or not, or whether concurrent external radiation was used or not. The data showed no significant difference with the addition of laser and/or external radiation to brachytherapy when the assessment is only judged by the reduction of the obstruction score. Although, there is a significant decrease of clearing of disease in the recurrent protocol versus patients in the curative and palliative groups. There was no differentiation made for radiation bronchitis membrane which was included with residual neoplasm as obstruction.

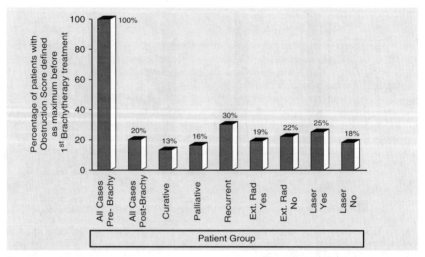

Figure 2. Decrease of obstruction score expressed as mean scores: pre-brachytherapy scores normalised to 100%. Post-brachytherapy scores quoted as a percentage residual for all patients, and for the curative, palliative and recurrent groups of protocol patients and also for concurrent external radiation (Yes/No) and pre-brachytherapy laser treatment (Yes/No).

HOST Performance Status

The Host performance status was used for stratification within the protocol and also for evaluation. The patients were scored prior to each of their three brachytherapy HDR treatment fractions and also prior to their first follow-up bronchoscopy. The results were weighted and normalised to 100%. After the first brachytherapy procedure there was a decrease in severity of the performance score of 24% to performance levels of lesser severity. The decrease was 52% at the third brachytherapy fraction and was 93% by the time of the first follow-up bronchoscopy.

Brachytherapy Fractions/Patient

Table 2 gives the number of brachytherapy treatment fractions performed per patient: although the protocol actually called for three brachytherapy fractions per patient. 11% of the group had two procedures with the third procedure eliminated either with sufficient improvement in the endobronchial appearance of the carcinoma or with significant clinical deterioration of the patient. This was not considered to be a protocol violation.

The 6% of the total group with more than three fractions, Table 2, consisted of patients with premortem local failure, defined as recurrence in or contiguous to an area of disease which was previously treated by brachytherapy. Treatments for these patients constituted of partial or full retreatment by brachytherapy for a recurrence.

Table 2
Number of brachytherapy procedures per patient.

No. of procedures	No. of patients	% of patients	
2	38	11	
3	281	82.5	
4	12	3.5	} 6.5% local failure
5	4	1.0	requiring 1-3 additional
6	6	2.0	brachytherapy procedures
Totals	341	100.0	

Table 3
Survival results.

Patient status	Group I		Group II		Group III		All groups	
	No. of patients	% of patients	No. of patients	% of patients	No. of patients	% of patients	No. of patients	% of patients
Alive	1	2	2	1	32	21	35	10
Dead	46	98	136	94	118	78	300	88
Lost to follow-Up	0	0	6	5	1	1	7	2
Totals	47	100	144	100	151	100	342	100

Table 4
Causes of death.

Cause of death	Group I		Group II		Group III		All groups	
	No. of patients	% of patients	No. of patients	% of patients	No. of patients	% of patients	No. of patients	% of patients
Loco-regional carcinoma	9	20	65	47	49	42	123	41
Metastatic carcinoma	27	59	46	34	39	33	112	37
Intercurrent disease	7	15	14	10	4	3	25	8
Unknown	3	7	11	8	26	22	40	13
Totals	46	101	136	99	118	100	300	99

Survival

Table 3 gives the survival of each of the three analysis groups defined earlier. Table 4 gives a breakdown of the causes of death of the 88% of the series who in Table 3 have been reported to have died at the time of analysis. Loco-regional is defined as death from any death from intrathoracic carcinoma.

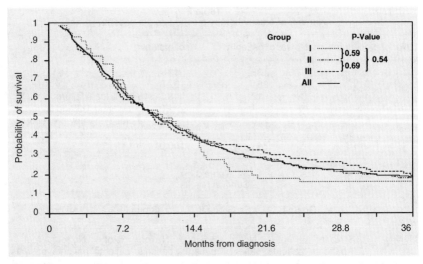

Figure 3a. Probability of survival and Mantel-Haenszel test results for equality of curves for groups I, II, III and for all groups combined: survival calculated from date of diagnosis.

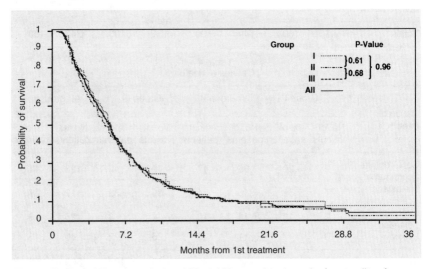

Figure 3b. Probability of survival and Mantel-Haenszel test results for equality of curves for groups I,II, III and for all groups combined: survival calculated from date of first brachytherapy treatment.

Survival was measured from date of diagnosis and from date of first brachytherapy treatment. Groups I, II and III had statistically identical survivals both from date of diagnosis, Figure 3a, and from the date of their first treatment, Figure 3b.

For the treatment categories of curative, palliative, and recurrent, only the recurrent category showed a statistically improved survival when analysed from date of diagnosis, Figure 4a. Within this group, patients only with a local recurrence and with no metastatic disease fared better than those patients with both local disease and distant recurrence.

However, when analysed from the date of first brachytherapy treatment, only the curative group showed a statistically improved survival, Figure 4b.

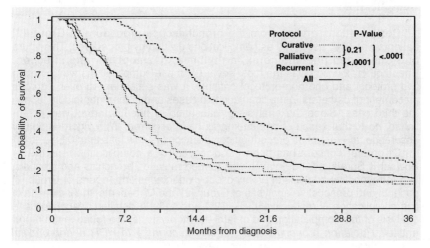

Figure 4a. Probability of survival and Mantel-Haenszel test results for equality of curves for curative, palliative and recurrent patient groups: survival calculated from date of diagnosis.

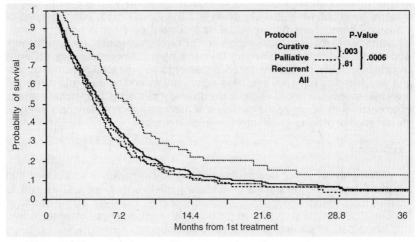

Figure 4b. Probability of survival and Mantel-Haenszel test results for equality of curves for curative, palliative and recurrent patient groups: survival calculated from date of first brachytherapy treatment.

Within the recurrent group there was no difference in survival between local and local-distant recurrence groups. In this group of advanced, but potentially curable patients, the mean survival time from date of diagnosis was 10.8 months and from the first brachytherapy was 9.5 months. For palliative patients the survival was respectively 14.0 months and 5.6 months and for recurrent patients respectively 25.6 months and 6.2 months.

Complications

Complications arising from the bronchoscopy procedure in Group [1] patients was 3% : assessed as complications divided by procedures. This figure of 3% included pneumothorax, arrhythmia, haemoptysis and infection. Pneumothorax which was the most severe of these complications was noted in two protocol and one non-protocol patients. It was secondary to over vigorous placement of catheters in the lingula in two cases and in the right middle lobe in the third case. Since the analysis of causation of pneumothorax was established, no further cases of pneumothorax have occurred. With vigorous quality assurance, the rate of all procedural complications is now less than 0.5%.

Of greater concern has been the discovery of a complication reported by Speiser & Spratling (1989) which was termed radiation bronchitis and stenosis. In a retrospective analysis of bronchoscopy videotapes and reports of Group [1] patients and prospective analyses of Group [2] and [3] patients, the incidence of this complication is respectively 9%, 12% and 11%. A detailed description and analysis of this complication and of fatal haemoptysis can be found in the report entitled *Radiation bronchitis and stenosis secondary to HDR endobronchial brachytherapy* by Speiser & Spratling (1992).

The other major sequelae to the disease and/or treatment which has been noted has been that of massive and lethal haemoptysis. In all cases patients who developed massive haemoptysis died immediately. The overall rate of massive haemoptysis leading to death is 7.3%. In all cases, patients dying of massive haemoptysis had residual or recurrent carcinoma seen on bronchoscopy, post-mortem examination and/or radiographic studies. One patient who developed massive bleeding from the right pulmonary artery during a bronchial dilatation procedure underwent emergency right total pneumonectomy and was found to have full thickness carcinoma extending from just below the bronchial mucosa fibrinoid necrotic membrane into the right pulmonary artery. In no case could we prove the existence of necrosis into the pulmonary artery in the absence of residual or recurrent neoplastic disease.

Discussion

With the initial use of remote afterloading brachytherapy it was hoped that this modality would be both an excellent palliative tool, as well as one to improve local control and thus the probability of cure. However, by the design of the protocol, restricting its use to patients with central airway disease, a bias was introduced for patients with higher stage disease.

The use of significant symptomology likewise biased the study by introducing severity factors which, in addition to the stage of disease have been shown by Feinstein & Wells (1990) to decrease the probability of ultimate five-year survival. This leads to the question of what should be the primary role of radiation for patients with relatively advanced local disease but with severity factors indicating a low probability of cure. It is for that reason that inclusion of those patients who are symptomatic into the protocol remains justified. This subgroup of patients still receive excellent palliation from the brachytherapy portion of their treatment.

The use of the symptom index scoring system has shown to be a reproducible way of grading severity of symptoms and their subsequent response. The system was set up on a five-tier basis to coincide with the HOST or ECOG system which ranks severity in the range 0-4. The obstruction score after initial revision continues as a reliable semi-quantative measure of immediate neoplastic cell destruction. By its use it can be shown that concurrent external radiation or prior YAG photoresection does not have a significant effect over and above that obtained with brachytherapy at the present dose and fraction levels used for endobronchial disease. It also shows that the use of laser does not necessarily improve the local clearing of disease and therefore we have now relegated YAG photoresection to those instances where it is the pulmonologist's decision that a brachytherapy catheter could not be safely passed or tolerated without the use of YAG laser. The palliative results obtained by the technique we have described have been excellent. There are multiple factors why this may be the case for this study. Selection criteria included significant obstruction signs and symptoms: which is a pivotal portion of the study.

There are patients treated by protocol, but not eligible for the protocol at the same treatment facilities, who had non-significant obstructive signs and symptoms and who had a lesser degree of response. They had a minor degree of endobronchial involvement with the majority of the disease extrabronchial. These patients early on in our study were considered to be poor candidates for endobroncial brachytherapy with its very limited range of dose penetration. These patients with extrinsic compression tend to have continued symptomatology which is not improved upon by brachytherapy.

Other areas of potential influence in the study are the higher doses we have used compared to those at some other centres, or the use of multiple fractions: three versus one. We have found that placement of the catheter or catheters may be less than optimal during the first procedure but improves during the second and third. In addition, it is common for patients to have two or three catheters placed for the most optimal dosimetry, especially if disease crosses into two airways, requiring at least two catheters for optimal treatment of all sites visualised.

The results of palliation cannot be shown to be significantly different with different applied doses. The dose-fractionation search currently underway is an attempt to find the lowest dose of endobronchial radiation or optimal number of fraction sizes that will provide the desired level of endobronchial clearing with lowest incidence of short-term and of long-term complications.

It is hoped in our fourth protocol that this dose-fractionation search can be completed and the most optimal level can be identified. At this point, the most optimal level is our third protocol which prescribes 750 cGy at a 10 mm depth for three fractions. This has the ability to clear endobronchial disease at the same rate as the higher dose but with a decreased rate of the more severe forms of radiation bronchitis and stenosis.

Survival has been reported for all three Analysis Groups [I-III]. However, in spite of the use of severity factors to reallocate certain patients with advanced but local disease into palliative categories, it still has not been possible to properly identify a subpopulation of patients with lung cancer with a reasonable probability of survival.

The long survival of patients with recurrent disease is definitely a selection process. An analysis was performed both from date of diagnosis and from the date of first brachytherapy treatment. When analysed from the date of treatment, recurrent patients have survival compatible with the palliative group patients. A patient who lives long enough after a prior course of radiation to have recurrent disease without succumbing to regional and metastatic disease, is definitely in a select group of patients who ultimately will have a median survival greater than newly diagnosed patients referred for radiation therapy.

Patients treated in the curative intent group with the addition of brachytherapy, have no longer survival than patients treated by standard external radiation. Patients treated according to protocol, who by definition are cases with central airway disease, are more advanced and should be compared to similar series with external radiation. At this time, the addition of brachytherapy to external radiation cannot be shown to improve long-term survival, but as mentioned earlier, is justified as an excellent means of palliating a group of patients whose overall five-year survival is low with any means of treatment presently available. However, because of these concerns, the current protocol recognised the limitations of the endobronchial brachytherapy contribution for curative intent patients and we now decrease its overall role by reducing the dose to 500 cGy/fraction calculated at 10 mm depth for a total of 1500 cGy in three fractions: while simultaneously increasing the dose of external radiation from 60 Gy to 64 Gy.

The complication of radiation bronchitis and stenosis has led to a dose-fractionation search to find a brachytherapy schedule which will provide similar benefits of excellent immediate relief, low recurrence rates with reduced incidence and/or severity of this complication.

Table 5
Publications which quote the
incidence of massive fatal haemoptysis
within the range 0-50%.

Reference
Schray et al (1985a,b,1988)
Seagren et al (1985)
Macha et al (1987)
Mehta et al (1989,1990)
Burt et al (1990)
Roach et al (1990)
Bedwinek et al (1991)
Khanavkar et al (1991)
Aygun et al (1992)
Lo et al (1992)
Garcia et al (1993)
Gauwitz et al (1993)

Table 6
Treatment scheme.

Curative Intent-Protocol 1.0

Weeks	1	2	3	4	5	6	7	8	9	10	11	12	Dose
External 200 cGy/Fx	‖	‖‖	‖	‖‖	‖	‖‖	‖‖						6400 cGy/32 Fx
	Brachy #1		Brachy #2		Brachy #3							F/U Bronch	
Internal 500 cGy/Fx													1500 cGy/3 Fx

Palliative Intent Protocol 2.1

Weeks	1	2	3	4	5	6	7	8	9	10	11	12	Dose
External (Optional) Dose 250 cGy/Fx	‖	‖‖	‖	‖									3750 cGy in 15 Fx
	Brachy #1	Brachy #2	Brachy #3						F/U Bronch				
Internal 500 cGy/Fx													2000 cGy/4 Fx

Palliative Intent-Protocol 2.2

Weeks	1	2	3	4	5	6	7	8	9	10	11	12	Dose
Internal 500 cGy/Fx x 4 or 750 cGy/Fx x3	Brachy #1	Brachy #2	Brachy #3	Brachy #4									2000 cGy/4 Fx or 2250 cGy/3 Fx
				Chemotherapy Optional					F/U Bronch			

Recurrent-Protocol 3.0

Weeks	1	2	3	4	5	6	7	8	9	10	11	12	Dose
Internal 500 cGy/Fx	Brachy #1	Brachy #2	Brachy #3	Brachy #4						F/U Bronch			2000 cGy/4 Fx

I = Day of Treatment by External

Massive fatal haemoptysis has become a controversial complication of the disease and/or treatment with its incidence reported between 0% and 50%: from a review of papers listed in Table 5.

By selection of patients with significant endobroncial disease it could be assumed that these patients if left untreated would have very high incidence of infiltration into pulmonary vasculature and fatal haemoptysis. It then becomes a question of whether haemoptysis in these cases is the result of too much treatment or the opposite: insufficient treatment allowing disease to progress.

One of the most instructive cases was briefly discussed in the **Results** section and was a patient with recurrent squamous cell carcinoma of the right lung who had received two courses of external radiation and laser photoresection before he presented for brachytherapy. The patient had received one full course of intermediate dose rate brachytherapy and upon recurrence, a second partial course of high dose rate brachytherapy. The patient developed radiation bronchitis and stenosis requiring balloon dilatation. He was receiving the second of such dilatation procedures when the balloon ruptured into the pulmonary artery. The emergency right pneumonectomy averted immediate death but it was with the grim realisation that pathologically the fibrotic-fibrinoid necrotic membrane was a surface effect, with the rest of the tissues showing extensive replacement by carcinoma extending full thickness into the pulmonary artery. This patient died approximalety one month later from a continued growth of carcinoma and exsanguination and should be considered a failure of treatment.

Conclusions

The use of HDR remote afterloading brachytherapy provides excellent palliation in a group of patients where cure is either not attainable or has low probability and palliation should be the principle goal of therapy of patients with such intralumenal neoplastic disease. It would seem reasonable that delivering the highest dose directly to the neoplasia would be the most advantageous form of therapy as shown in this study. The initial dose of radiation was initially considered to be quite safe with a low rate of complications, thus justifying the escalation of dose.

There was no significant gain in Group [II] patients in terms of an initial clearing of disease although the recurrence rate was lower for this group. Group [III] patients had a reduction of dose but maintained the same number of fractions. To date this group has shown a decrease in severity in radiation bronchitis but not in its incidence.

Future Study

In our study, Group [IV], which started August 1991, see Table 6, the major changes are as follows. [a] The brachytherapy dose has been reduced to 500 cGy at 10 mm depth. [b] There is an increase to four fractions.

It is hoped that this decrease of total dose (2250 cGy to 2000 cGy), fraction size (750 cGy to 500 cGy), and increase of fraction number (3 to 4) will be evidenced by continued excellent palliation with a decreased rate and severity of radiation bronchitis and stenosis.

References

Aygun C, Weiner S, Scariato A, Spearman D & Stark L, *Treatment of non-small cell lung cancer with external beam : radiotherapy and high dose rate brachytherapy*, Int. J. Radiation Oncology Biology & Physics, **23**, 127-132, 1992.

Bedwinek J, Bruton C, Petty A, Sofield J & Lee L, *High dose rate endobronchial brachytherapy and fatal pulmonary haemorrhage*, Int. J. Radiation Oncology Biology & Physics, **22**, 23-30, 1991.

Burt PA, O'Driscoll BR, Notley HM, Barber PV & Stout R, *Intralumenal irradiation for the palliation of lung cancer with the high dose rate micro-Selectron*, Thorax, **45**, 765-768, 1990.

Feinstein AR & Wells CK, *A clinical severity staging system for patients with lung cancer*, Med., **69**, 1-33, 1990.

Garcia DM, Drzymala R & Potts D, *High dose rate brachytherapy in the management of enbronchial carcinoma*, Endocurietherapy/Hyperthermia Oncology, In press, 1993.

Gauwitz M, Ellerbroek N, Komaki R, Putman JB, Ryan MB, Decaro L, Davis M & Cundiff J, *High dose rate endobronchial irradiation in recurrent bronchogenic carcinoma*, Int. J. Radiation Oncology Biology & Physics, In press, 1993.

Knanavkar B, Stern P, Alberti W, Nakhosteen JA, *Complications associated with brachytherapy alone or with laser in lung cancer*, Chest., **99**, 1062-1065, 1991.

Lo T, Beamis J, Weinstein R, Costey G, Andrews C, Webb-Johson D, Girshovich L & Leibenhaut M, *Intralumenal low dose rate brachytherapy for malignant endobronchial obstruction*, Radiotherapy & Oncology, **23**, 16-20, 1992.

Macha HN, Koch K, Stadler M, Schumacher W & Kurmhaar D, *New technique for treating occlusive and stenosing tumours of the trachea and main bronchi: endobronchial irradiation by high dose iridium-192 combined with laser canalization*, Thorax, **42**, 511-515, 1987.

Mehta MP, Shababi S, Jarjour NN & Kinsella TJ, *Endobronchial irradiation for malignant airway obstruction*, Int. J. Radiation Oncology & Physics, **17**, 847-851, 1989.

Mehta MP, Shababi S, Jarjour NN, Steinmetz M, & Kubsad S, *Effect of endobronchial radiation therapy on malignant bronchial obstruction*, Chest, **97**, 662-665, 1990.

Roach M, Leidholt EM, Tatera BS & Joseph J, *Endobronchial radiation therapy (EBRT) in the management of lung cancer*, Int. J. Radiation Oncology Biology & Physics, **18**, 1449-1454, 1990.

Schray MF, McDougal JC, Martinez A, Edmundson GK & Cortese DA, *Management of malignant airway obstruction: clinical and dosimetric considerations using an iridium-192 afterloading technique in conjunction with the neodymium-yag laser*, Int. J. Radiation Oncology Biology & Physics, **11**, 403-409, 1985.

Schray MF, Martinez A, McDougall JC, Edmundson GK, Cortese DA & Brutinel WM, *Malignant airway obstruction: management with temporary intralumenal brachytherapy and laser treatment*, Endocurietherapy/Hyperthermia Oncology, 1, 237-245, 1985.

Schray MF, McDougall JC, Martinez A, Cortese DA & Brutinel WM, *Management of malignant airway compromise with laser and low dose rate brachytherapy*, Chest, **93**, 264-269, 1988.

Seagren SL, Harrell JH & Horn RA, *High dose rate intralumenal irradiation in recurrent endobronchial carcinoma*, Chest, **88**, 810-814, 1985.

Speiser B & Spratling L, *Comparison of intermediate versus high dose rate remote afterloading brachytherapy in the control of endobronchial carcinoma*, in:Brachytherapy 2, Mould RF (Ed), 469-480, Nucletron:Leersum, 1988.

Speiser B & Spratling L, *High dose rate remote afterloading endobronchial carcinoma*, in:Brachytherapy HDR and LDR, Martinez AA, Orton CG & Mould RF (Eds), 10-26, Nucletron:Columbia, 1989.

Speiser B & Spratling L, *Intermediate dose rate remote afterloading brachytherapy for intralumenal control of bronchogenic carcinoma*, Int. J. Radiation Oncology Biology & Physics, **18**, 1443-1448, 1990.

Speiser B, *Protocol for local control of endobronchial carcinoma using remote afterloading HDR brachytherapy*, Activity Selectron Brachytherapy Journal, Supplement 1, 16-19, 1990.

Speiser B & Spratling L, *Radiation bronchitis and stenosis secondary to high dose rate endobronchial carcinoma*, Int. J. Radiation Oncology Biology & Physics, 1992.

Stanley KE, *Prognostic factors for survival in patients with inoperable lung cancer*, J. National Cancer Institute, **65**, 25-32, 1980.

19

Single Dose Brachytherapy for Endobronchial Cancer

R. Stout
on behalf of P. Barber, P. Burt &
The Department of Radiotherapy

Christie Hospital Trust,
Wilmslow Road,
Manchester M20 9BX,
United Kingdom.

Introduction

The development of a miniature high activity iridium-192 source for use in the microSelectron-HDR remote afterloading system, has overcome many of the problems previously associated with endobronchial brachytherapy, so that intralumenal radiotherapy in the proximal and distal airways is now feasible, practical, well tolerated and widely applicable.

Endobronchial brachytherapy has always been attractive because any adverse effects on normal tissues are confined to those within the immediate vicinity of the bronchus. Where the aim of treatment in advanced cancer is palliation, intralumenal radiotherapy alone may achieve the same relief of haemoptysis, cough and breathlessness as conventional X-ray therapy but with less morbidity.

If more radical treatment is considered appropriate, brachytherapy may be combined with X-ray therapy to boost the dose to the primary tumour since the trachea and bronchi are relatively resistant to radiation injury, being composed largely of fully developed cartilage, a post-mitotic cellular system. For the same reason, brachytherapy may be given to patients who have relapsed after previous external beam irradiation given to tolerance for the lung, oesophagus or spinal cord.

Practical Application

Insertion of the treatment catheter(s) is performed under local anaesthesia using flexible bronchoscopy. Almost all patients are discharged from hospital the same day.

Current Practice

Our first objective after the installation of the microSelectron-HDR was to determine the effectiveness and morbidity of a single intralumenal treatment for palliation in advanced disease. Between April 1988 and March 1989, 77 patients presented with inoperable unilateral tumours who had received no previous treatment. Their symptoms were limited to haemoptysis, breathlessness and cough. Each was treated with one catheter prescribing a single dose of 1500-2000 cGy at 10 mm from the source.

Symptom relief was assessed at six weeks. Haemoptysis was relieved in 86% of cases, breathlessness in 61% and cough in 51%. Re-expansion of pulmonary collapse was achieved in 46%, Figure 1.

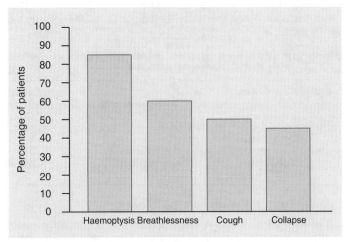

Figure 1. Histogram showing the percentage of patients out of a total of 77, with unilateral inoperable tumours, who at six weeks follow-up had their symptoms assessed as 'Better' on a scale of 'Better, Same, Worse'.

Early morbidity was minimal and there has been no observable late morbidity with a minimum follow-up of 28 months. Duration of response is best illustrated in patients who presented with haemoptysis. Only 7/39 responders (18%) have required further treatment for recurrent haemoptysis between three and 16 months after brachytherapy. Three more patients had a massive terminal haemorrhage at three, four and 12 months.

25 patients have required external beam therapy for persistent, recurrent or new thoracic symptoms, with the remainder, 52/77 (68%) who obtained good palliation using brachytherapy alone. The survival rate was 50% at six months and 5% at two years.

A single HDR intralumenal treatment can achieve good palliation with minimal morbidity and durable response. Its ease of administration commends it both to patient and clinician.

It may also prove curative for small endobronchial tumours. Six patients were encountered during the same year who were considered unsuitable for surgery even though they had bronchoscopically operable tumours. All six are alive 30-36 months after a single dose treatment with 3/6 without evidence of local or distant relapse.

Future Directions

The practice of endobronchial brachytherapy worldwide is already diverse. The evaluation of different protocols in clinical trials is essential if the optimum treatment for different patient groups is to be defined. Two prospective randomised trials are well underway in Manchester and should be completed by the end of 1992, Table 1. In each trial the intralumenal dose is 1500 cGy at 10 mm from the source and the X-ray therapy dose is 3000 cGy in eight fractions over 10 days.

Table 1
Randomised trials of single dose intralumenal brachytherapy in advanced bronchial carcinoma.

Trial 1	X-ray therapy or Brachytherapy	**for patients with**	Haemoptysis Breathlessness Cough
Trial 2	X-ray therapy or X-ray therapy + Brachytherapy	**for patients with additional**	Chest pain or Dysphagia

The aims of Trial 1 are to compare the following:

(1) The alleviation of cough, haemoptysis and dyspnoea in patients with endobronchial carcinoma of the lung using either a single intralumenal treatment or external irradiation.

(2) The quality of life in both groups of patients in terms of psychological, functional and physical status, (that is, symptoms of disease and treatmentside effects).

(3) The acute and late effects of treatment.

(4) Survival.

In Trial 2 the aim is to compare the alleviation of all thoracic symptoms in patients with advanced carcinoma of the lung using external irradiation plus intralumenal therapy or external irradiation alone. The quality of life and end points of treatment are assessed as for Trial 1.

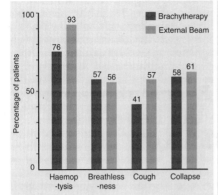 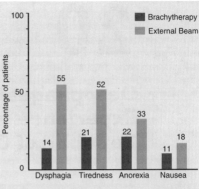

Figure 2. Histogram from Trial 1 showing the percentage of patients out of a total of 76, with unilateral inoperable tumours, who at two months follow-up had their symptoms assessed as 'Better' on a scale of 'Better, Same, Worse'.

Figure 3. Histogram from Trial 1 showing the percentage of patients out of a total of 76, with unilateral inoperable tumours, who at one month follow-up had their symptoms assessed as 'Worse' on a scale of 'Better, Same, Worse'.

76 patients have now been entered into Trial 1 and 49 patients into Trial 2. A preliminary analysis of symptom relief and acute morbidity reveals equivalent response rates in the two treatment arms in each trial and less morbidity in patients receiving brachytherapy. This is illustrated in Figures 2 and 3 from Trial 1. The improvement in haemoptysis, breathlessness, cough and pulmonary collapse with brachytherapy alone also confirms the findings of our non-randomised study, Figure 1.

A detailed study of the quality of life assessments, late effects of treatment and survival awaits completion of the trials. As yet we have not observed any obvious increase in late morbidity in the combined treatment arm in Trial 2.

20

Oesophageal Brachytherapy: Experience in the People's Republic of China

Liu Tai Fu

Department of Radiation Oncology,
Cancer Hospital of Shanghai Medical University,
270 Dong An Road,
Shanghai 200032,
People's Republic of China.

Epidemiology

Cancer of the oesophagus is relatively frequent in all parts of the People's Republic of China, with a predominance in the northern provinces and the highest incidence rising to 258 per 100,000 population in Lin County, Henan. Many factors have been incriminated but nutrition seems to play an important role with anaemia as a dominant factor. In our hospital, oesophageal cancer is one of the main tumours treated in the Department of Radiation Oncology with an average annual patient workload of more than 700 cases, Figure 1.

The incidence of oesophageal carcinoma in Shanghai itself is not very high and therefore most of our patients are from neighbouring provinces. In spite of all efforts, the results of external radiation therapy alone have remained poor with the majority of cases presenting for radiation treatment in the late stages of disease.

A review of the five-year survival rates from some of the larger radiotherapy centres in the People's Republic of China has shown that they rarely exceed 10% with the variation in the data probably due to differences in the proportions in each series of the stage distribution of patients accepted for radiotherapy, rather than in the techniques used.

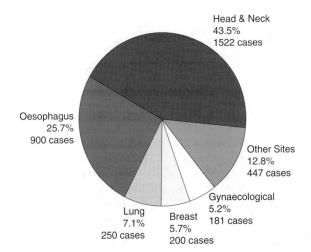

Figure 1. Distribution by site of 3500 cases treated by radiotherapy in 1991 in the Cancer Hospital of the Shanghai Medical University.

Clinical Staging

The first problem we experienced was the method of clinical staging. The new UICC classification of 1987 is appropriate for patients treated surgically where the actual extent of disease can be determined at operation, including wall penetration and lymph node spread (Hishikawa et al 1991). However, such a method cannot be applied to cases treated by radiotherapy when the extension of disease can be determined only by endoscopy, radiography or CT. The criteria originally proposed by the UICC in 1980 for pre-treatment clinical classification and staging are more relevant to radiotherapy where the length, obstructive status, involvement of circumference and oesophageal spread are the main considerations. This method of staging has been used throughout the People's Republic of China in reporting results of radiotherapy.

External Beam Radiotherapy

The techniques of external beam radiotherapy have been more or less similar in all our radiotherapy departments: with an anterior direct field and two posterior angled fields to avoid overdosage to the spinal cord. The doses to the axis of the oesophagus ranged from 50 Gy to 70 Gy. The length of the fields was determined by the length of the lesion as seen on radiographs, with an adequate margin for subclinical disease. Recent studies by our oesophageal cancer group comparing radiographs and CT scans of the same patients, have shown that in many cases the routinely used anterior field width of 5 cm is not adequate when extra-oesophageal extension occurs (Yao et al 1992). Wider anterior direct fields of 7-8 cm are required.

Tumour Length & Site

From our past experience we have found that the most important factor in treatment was the length of the oesophageal lesion at first treatment and that tumours smaller than 5 cm in length had a better prognosis. We also observed that the higher the site in the oesophagus, the better was the prognosis. This led us to consider the question as to what role intralumenal brachytherapy can play in the radiation treatment of oesophageal carcinoma.

Local Tumour Dose

Local dosage to the oesophageal lesion has been the focus of investigation by all authors in our country but in several large series of cases the conclusions have been controversial. Most authors believe 60 Gy to be optimal and that an increase of dose to over 70 Gy has not improved five-year survivals: even though there seemed to be better local control (Sun 1989). Other authors have shown that doses of 50 Gy have achieved similar results to those in 70 Gy groups (Wan et al 1990, Sha et al 1990), Table 1.

Table 1
Survival results as a function of dose.

Reference	5-year survival results for a given dose	
	50 Gy	70 Gy
Wan et al (1990)	18/108 (16.7%)	7/99 (17.2%)
Sha et al (1990)	9/100 (9%)	8/100 (8%)

Of the failures, 50-60% have been due to local recurrence at the primary site. Efforts have been made to boost the local primary dose by small field external irradiation but with no improvement in results. Zhang (1990) used a technique of 50-55 Gy by large field external irradiation followed by coned down fields which were adapted to the decrease in length of the lesion as indicated on follow-up radiographs. The total local dose reached 80 Gy. No improvement in local control or survival rate was found, Table 2.

Table 2
Follow-up results for two patient subgroups: those who received only routine treatment and those who in addition received a local boost.

Follow-up	Patient subgroup	
	Routine	Boost
Local recurrence rate	142/774 (18.3%)	33/145 (22.8%)
1-year survival rate	393/774 (50.8%)	53/145 (36.5%)

Intralumenal Brachytherapy as Sole Method of Treatment

Intralumenal brachytherapy for oesophageal carcinoma was first used for large numbers of patients by Guisez (1925) but due to radiation hazards with radium sources the method was not widely accepted in the 1920s and 1930s. In the People's Republic of China the earliest reported series of relatively large numbers of patients treated by intralumenal brachytherapy was reported by Yin (1985) who during the period 1970-1974 treated 203 cases using cobalt-60 pellet sources of activities equivalent to a range of 83-112 milligrams radium. His reference point was 0.5 cm below the surface of the oesophageal mucosa and details of the technique have been reported by Yin (1989). However, the five-year survival rate was only 8.4%.

Complications were not frequent and were mostly varying degrees of oesophagitis, although a few cases of radiation ulcer were observed, especially when the dose per treatment fraction was 10-15 Gy. Local bleeding was also observed but its frequency was not higher than that experienced in cases treated by external irradiation alone. The incidence of oesophageal perforation was also similar for both intralumenal brachytherapy alone and for external irradiation alone.

Intralumenal Brachytherapy Combined with External Irradiation

It is evident that intralumenal brachytherapy alone is not adequate as a method of radiotherapy for oesophageal carcinoma. The combination of external irradiation and intralumenal brachytherapy (using caesium-137) is much more encouraging as shown by the four-year survival results of Wang & Zhao (1987). However, in a subsequent report from the same group with an accrual of 200 randomised cases, Zhao et al (1990), although the three-year survival rates were much better with the combined modality treatment, 31% *versus* 19%, at five years the comparative survival rates had fallen to 17% *versus* 10%, Table 3.

Table 3
Survival results for a randomised trial, with 100 patients in each subgroup, of external irradiation combined with intralumenal brachytherapy *versus* external irradiation alone: after Zhao et al (1990).

T-year	T-year survival results for a treatment subgroup	
	External + brachytherapy	Brachytherapy alone
1	78/100 (78%)	56/100 (56%)
2	31/100 (31%)	19/100 (19%)
3	15/88 (17%)	9/89 (10%)

HDR Brachytherapy

The advent of high dose rate (HDR) remote afterloading brachytherapy equipment has brought about a radical change in our concepts on intralumenal brachytherapy. Although oesophageal carcinoma has been treated by radiotherapy throughout the People's Republic of China by external irradiation for more than 40 years, the widespread use of intralumenal brachytherapy was not feasible generally, due to lack of equipment with adequate therapeutic capabilities as well as sufficient radiation protection. The introduction of the microSelectron-HDR into the People's Republic of China has fulfilled the above basic requirements and thus brought about a renaissance in oesophageal brachytherapy.

Due to the small size of the iridium-192 source used in the microSelectron-HDR we have not experienced any difficulties in placing the source at the required oesophageal positions. Although the follow-up time is currently too short to present any long-term results, we have already gained significant experience in the application of intralumenal HDR brachytherapy in the treatment of oesophageal cancer and we present below a survey of the current experience in the People's Republic of China.

P.R. China Current Experience with HDR Brachytherapy

With regard to physical aspects, the most important is the reference point used in calculating dosage. The majority of centres have used as reference a point 1.0 cm from the source. However, a few centres prefer to use a point 0.5 cm below the surface of the oesophageal mucosa.

Recently, Bai et al (1992) have used an intralumenal balloon to decrease the relative dose to the normal oesophageal mucosa, based on the concept that normal areas will be distended away from the radiation source, whilst areas infiltrated by tumour tend to remain rigid. In this instance, the reference point is 0.5 cm below the surface, regardless of the distance to the axis of the radiation source. It is thus evident that to define accurately the dosages being used in oesophageal brachytherapy and especially to exchange experiences, we will have to decide on a uniform definition of a reference point or points. This is all the more important in HDR brachytherapy where differences of a few millimetres in source point distance may describe very different values of physical dose.

HDR brachytherapy for oesophageal cancer is well accepted by the patient due to the short irradiation times involved. However, this also brings with it the radiobiological problem of defining the optimum time-dose-fractionation protocol. Most of our thinking on brachytherapy has been based on radium low dose rate (LDR) techniques and therefore our current HDR techniques are essentially empirical.

HDR brachytherapy is given in combination with external irradiation and the doses used are in the range 7-10 Gy for each treatment fraction which is prescribed once per week for a total of 2-3 fractions. The sequence of external irradiation and intralumenal brachytherapy varies: giving brachytherapy before, during or after external irradiation. However, in most cases the brachytherapy was given as boost after external irradiation. Zhu et al (1992) of Tianjin have also tried the use of increasing the number of fractions, ie. 250-350 cGy/fraction twice a day with 4-6 fractions per week: a type of hyperfractionated brachytherapy.

The immediate and short term results have been quite encouraging with over 90% of the patients treated having varying degrees of improvement in deglutition after brachytherapy. Objectively, as seen on post-treatment radiographs, 80% showed improved passage of barium whilst in 40% the lesion was no longer visible.

Recurrent Oesophageal Cancer after External Irradiation

An important application of our microSelectron-HDR has been in the treatment of recurrent oesophageal cancer after external radiotherapy. In the past, such cases were rarely considered for re-treatment by radiation due to the hazards involved. In Shanghai we have so far treated 27 cases, all proven by biopsy. The exact location of the recurrent lesion was determined on a simulator and two films were taken at 90° degrees to each other and the optimum dose distribution was obtained using the NPS planning system. The reference point was placed at 1.0 cm from the source axis and a dose of 8 Gy given per fraction to a total of 16-24 Gy at weekly intervals.

Of the 27 patients a total of 25 had amelioration in deglutition with an accompanying improvement in their general condition. There was some prolongation of median survival time although at one year 23/27 were already dead, but it should be noted that only 10/23 had recurrent oesophageal obstruction as the cause of death, whilst the remaining 13/23 died of other complications, mostly due to the poor condition when accepted for treatment.

The Cancer Hospital of the Chinese Academy of Medical Sciences has had a similar experience with a series of 24 cases of which 20/24 were residual or recurrent following radiation therapy. Their immediate results were about the same as our results in Shanghai. On X-ray examination there was complete disappearance of visible lesion in 8% and partial control in 67%. They found the optimum doses to be 14-21 Gy delivered in 2-3 fractions. When the dose was raised to 20-30 Gy per fraction, 2/10 cases had ulceration. Pain was not a serious complication in this series as most could be relieved by suitable medical measures.

Recently we have just started a randomised study on the combination of external irradiation and HDR brachytherapy using the microSelectron-HDR for the routine intralumenal brachytherapy treatment. To date a total of 46 cases have completed the protocol. The external irradiation was delivered using a telecobalt machine and a three-field technique. The control group received 70 Gy/35 fractions/49 days whilst the two HDR brachytherapy groups A and B, received 60 Gy external irradiation.

The HDR brachytherapy was given after a rest period of one week and patients were divided into two groups. Group A received a single dose of 8 Gy calculated at 1.0 cm from the source axis and group B received 10 Gy at 5 Gy per fraction separated by an interval of one week.

The follow-up time is still too short to make any statisticaly significant inferences but preliminary analysis shows that for the 28 cases receiving intralumenal treatment the immediate results appear to be similar. Because of this observation one might in the future either consider increasing the external irradiation dose or the intralumenal HDR brachytherapy dose to boost the local effects of radiation. The alternative is to wait and see if the lower external irradiation will decrease the late effects and thus indirectly contribute to improving the results of treatment.

Conclusions

HDR brachytherapy for oesophageal carcinoma is receiving an increasing amount of attention in the People's Republic of China. Due to the fact that an enormous number of cases of oesophageal carcinoma are being treated annually by radiotherapy throughout our country, there is great potential to plan well designed studies to determine the role of HDR brachytherapy in the radiation treatment of this cancer. A more rational combination of external radiation and brachytherapy to enhance results would be a logical outcome of such studies and would add much to our knowledge of how to treat this difficult type of cancer, not only to increase survival but also to improve the quality of life of the patients.

References

Bai FQ, Liu EC & Zhu XD, *Application of a new oesophageal balloon applicator*, in:*Brachytherapy in the People's Republic of China*, Mould RF (Ed), (in Chinese & English), E-123, Nucletron:Veenendaal,1992.

Guisez J, *Malignant tumours of the oesophagus*, J. Laryngology Otology, **40**, 213-222, 1925.

Hishikawa Y, Kurisu K & Taniguchi M, *High dose rate intralumenal brachytherapy for oesophageal cancer: 10 year experience in Hyogo College of Medicine*, Radiotherapy & Oncology, **21**, 107-114, 1991.

Sha YH, Li YH & Wang CH, *Dosage study radiotherapy for oesophageal carcinoma*, China J. Radiation Oncology, **4**, 3-5, 1990.

Sun DR, *Ten-year follow-up of oesophageal cancer treated by radical radiation therapy: analysis of 869 patients*, Int. J. Radiation Oncology Biology & Physics, **16**, 329-334, 1989.

Wan J, Kao SZ & Guo BZ, *Dose study and remote results in radiotherapy for oesophageal carcinoma*, Chinese J. Radiation Oncology, **4**, 2-3, 1990.

Wang RZ & Zhao RF, *Combined intracavitary and external radiotherapy for oesophageal carcinoma - a prospective randomised clinical trial on 128 patients*, Chinese J. Radiation Oncology, **1**, 41-43, 1987.

Yao WX, Shi XH & Liu TF, *Study on improving results in the treatment of oesophageal cancer patients, Doctorate thesis*, Cancer Hospital of Shanghai Medical University, 63-75, 1992.

Yin WB, *Brachytherapy of carcinoma of the oesophagus in China*, in:*Brachytherapy 2*, Mould RF (Ed), 439-441, 1989.

Zhao RF, Zhang PG & Zhang GG, *Combination of external irradiation and intracavitary caesium-137 radiotherapy for oesophageal carcinoma - analysis of 200 cases*, Chinese J. Radition Onocology, **4**, 85-87, 1990.

Zhang XC, *Evaluation of boost irradiation in cancer of the oesophagus, Cancer Research Preventative Treatment*, (in Chinese), **4**, 43-48, 1990.

Zhu XD, Bai FQ & Rong JM, *Combination of HDR intracavitary brachytherapy with external irradiation in the treatment of oesophageal carcinoma*, in:*Brachytherapy in the People's Republic of China*, Mould RF (Ed), (*in Chinese & English*), E-119, Nucletron:Veenendaal, 1992.

21

Cancer of the Oesophagus

A.D. Flores

British Columbia Cancer Agency,
600 West 10th Avenue,
Vancouver,
British Columbia,
Canada V5Z 4E6.

Introduction

The prognosis of patients with carcinomas of the oesophagus and cardia is extremely poor. An extensive review of the world literature by Earlam & Cunnha-Melo (1980) showed that only 4-6% of patients survived to five years. Treatment results were equally poor regardless of the type of treatment used. Improvements in operative techniques, operative mortality or technological advances to deliver external beam radiotherapy did not translate into better survival and most investigators now believe that improvement of quality of life rather than survival should be the main goal of therapy.

Researchers have for a long time recognised the need for better treatment protocols and during the last decade, conscious efforts have been made to improve results by using a combination of treatment modalities.

Although overall statistics are still poor (Matthews & Waterhouse 1987, Desai et al 1989), encouraging preliminary results have been reported using chemotherapy as an adjuvant treatment to radiotherapy and/or surgery (Keane et al 1985, Seydel et al 1987, Herskovic et al 1991, Forrastiere et al 1990, Kelsen et al 1990, Coia et al 1991).

The last decade has also seen the renaissance of brachytherapy as a treatment with real potential to improve the therapeutic ratio of external irradiation and the recognition of a need for optimisation in the treatment programmes for oesophageal malignancies.

Patterns of Failure & Prognostic Factors

The study of the natural history of the disease reveals that when the diagnosis is made, most of the patients are old, frail, malnourished, in very poor general condition and that when the disease is already advanced they are probably incurable.

An analysis of the patterns of failures at several institutions including our own (Mantravadi et al 1982, Isono et al 1982, Mandard et al 1981, Ruol et al 1988, Flores et al 1989) shows that most patients die with local recurrence and obstruction caused by the persistent cancer.

In British Columbia during the decade 1970-1980 a total of 401/483 (83%) patients seen had T2 or larger than 5 cm primary tumours when first seen and in 288/483 (60%) of these patients the disease had extended beyond the oesophageal wall. Most patients fail to be cured due to the simple fact that they are diagnosed with extensive tumours and also with metastases.

New Therapeutic Trends

The theory behind systemic chemotherapy as an adjuvant treatment to radiation was the hope that it could improve local control by radiosensitisation and also could affect microscopic systemic metastatic disease. In recent reports (Herskovic et al 1991, Coia et al 1991), an improvement in local control and even survival has been suggested using adjuvant chemotherapy to radiotherapy. These conclusions have not been shared by others (Kavanagh et al 1992, Araugo et al 1991).

There is, however, a consensus among authors that present chemotherapy regimens have not affected metastases or the development of metastases in oesophageal malignancies (Seydel et al 1987, Herskovic et al 1991, Forrastiere et al 1990, Kelsen et al 1990, Kavanagh al 1992). Better systemic therapy is clearly needed to enhance tumour response and hopefully survival.

Pre-operative external irradiation has also been used in the past and the treatment results have also been mixed. Two European phase III studies (Launois et al 1981, Gignoux et al 1987) comparing oesophagectomy alone *versus* pre-operative external irradiation suggested no advantage with the treatment combination. In these trials, however, the radiotherapy schedule was short, unusual and complications, even perioperative mortality, were high. Three more recent phase III studies, comparing oesophagectomy alone with a more standard preoperative external irradiation, reported significant benefit in the group receiving pre-operative irradiation (Huang et al 1988, Wang et al 1988, Yin 1989).

Brachytherapy alone or in combination with external irradiation has been employed only sporadically in the past using low dose rate radioactive materials. Patients had to be admitted to hospital in view of the long treatment time and there was the inevitable problem of radiation exposure to the staff.

In the last few years, the development of safer and higher specific activity radioactive sources has permitted the fabrication of improved miniaturised sources which in turn has translated into a shorter treatment time and in an improved treatment delivery by remote afterloading systems, Table 1. This technology has made intracavitary irradiation a feasible, easy and attractive complement to external irradiation in oesophageal malignancies.

Table 1
Linear activities of radionuclide sources.

Source	Linear activity	
	mCi/cm	MBq/cm
Caesium-137 tubes	21	770
Caesiums-137 Selectron-LDR		
pellets, 4 pellets/cm	126	4660
Iridium-192 (10 Ci/4 mm)	20	74000

The rationale of adding brachytherapy to radiotherapy is based on the fact that the amount of irradiation that can be safely given by external irradiation is limited by the tolerance of the peri-oesophageal tissues. Brachytherapy on the other hand, due to its rapid dose fall-off can increase the amount of irradiation to the intralumenal disease without affecting significantly the adjacent normal tissues. Therefore the effectiveness or therapeutic ratio of external irradiation is enhanced.

Vancouver Experience

Prior to 1984 intracavitary irradiation for oesophagus was employed only sporadically and only for recurrent disease. It consisted of LDR radium-226 or caesium-137 tubes placed in tandem in the oesophagus and a dose of 3000

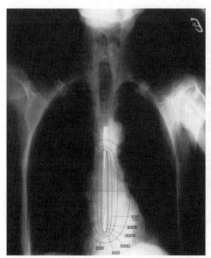 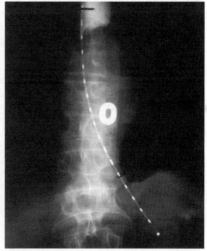

Figure 1. Oesophageal tube with dummy sources to simulate caesium-137 pellets: HDR of 1000 cGy/hr.

Figure 2. Similar oesophageal tube with dummy sources to simulate iridium-192 source positions: HDR of greater than 20,000 cGy/hr.

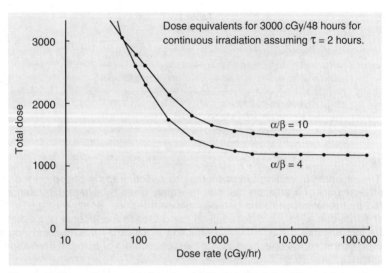

Figure 3. Theoretical model of acute and late isoeffects for different dose rates.

cGy at 1 cm from the axis delivered in 48 hours. This treatment was well tolerated but had only a brief palliative effect since most patients had advanced and/or recurrent disease. An oesophageal applicator (Rowland & Pagliero 1985) became available to us in February 1985. This device could be connected to a remote afterloading system containing caesium-137 pellets of 4 mm diameter. Each pellet had an activity of 40 milligram-radium-equivalent and when placed in tandem (40 pellets required for a 10 cm linear source) could deliver a dose rate of 1000 cGy/hr at 1cm from the axis of the source. A similar device could be used with an HDR iridium-192 remote afterloader, Figures 1 and 2.

As higher biological effects are expected with higher dose rates it was felt necessary to estimate equivalent doses for higher dose rates against safer and well tried LDR regimens for the design of new treatment protocols. This was accomplished using a linear quadratic model (Dale 1985).

Figure 3 shows that 3000 cGy given with LDR radioactive materials is equivalent to 1500 cGy given with HDR if one assume an α/β ratio of 4 for late effects and 10 for acute effects. It also can be seen that while the biological effect changes significantly when changing from a dose rate of 100 cGy/hr to 1000 cGy/hr, the isoeffect curve flattens and there is practically no change in effect beyond 1000 cGy/hr.

In 1975 a phase I study was started in Vancouver to evaluate external beam radiotherapy of 4000 cGy given in three weeks plus brachytherapy of 1500 cGy at 1 cm axis, Figure 4, for oesophageal and cardia carcinomas. The main goals of this initial programme were to evaluate the toxicity and effectiveness of this treatment and to assess quality of life of the patients treated. Only patients with or impending bronchial or tracheal fistula were excluded from the study. It became rapidly evident that brachytherapy for oesophagus was a tolerable, fea-

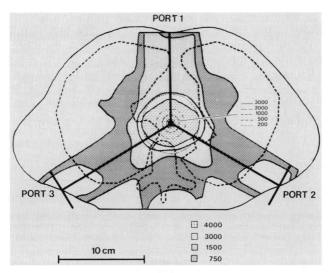

Figure 4. External irradiation plus brachytherapy boost isodoses.

sible and effective treatment. An analysis of the first 171 patients treated (Gignoux et al 1987), showed that intracavitary irradiation was a feasible out-patient treatment with acceptable morbidity and no mortality. The quality of life of patients treated by brachytherapy, as measured by their performance status, swallowing ability and pain was significantly better after treatment.

As dysphagia was the major symptom of these patients there is a practical advantage to starting treatment with intracavitary irradiation in patients with severe obstruction. The oesophageal applicator is also a mild dilator and dysphagia can immediately improve after brachytherapy. Brachytherapy on the other hand may be more effective after an initial course of external irradiation as shrinkage of the tumour bulk allows better a dose at the base of the tumour.

In order to determine the best timing of brachytherapy, a phase III study was started in 1987 to compare two groups of patients: one group of patients receiving brachytherapy before external radiotherapy with another group receiving brachytherapy after external radiotherapy. The brachytherapy dose was 1500 cGy at 1 cm from the axis and the external irradiation component was of 4000 cGy given in 15 treatment days in three weeks overall time. The endpoints of this study were to compare local control, survival and quality of life of the patients. This trial has now accrued 200 patients and has been closed. An interim analysis, though, is not yet possible.

During the period 1985-1992 more than 600 patients with carcinomas in the oesophagus and/or cardia have been treated at the Cancer Agency in Vancouver with intracavitary irradiation. Of these patients, the first 150 patients were treated with caesium-137 pellets providing a dose rate of 1000 cGy/hr. All subsequent patients (450) received treatment with an HDR iridium-192 source providing a dose rate in the range 20,000-50,000 cGy/hr. The dose given at 1 cm from the source was, however, the same as estimated by the linear quadratic model or 1500 cGy.

Since we have not seen any significant difference in acute or late effects among patients treated with either LDR (radium, caesium-137), MDR (caesium-137 pellets) or HDR (iridium-192), we have to assume that the linear quadratic formula has reasonably predicted the isoeffect values for different dose rates.

During the period 1985-1989 a total of 297 patients with carcinomas of the oesophagus and cardia were treated at our institute with radiotherapy and brachytherapy and were eligible for an analysis with a minimum follow-up of at least three years from treatment. The site distribution, clinical status at presentation, type of treatment and outcome of all these cases is shown in Table 2. 93/297 of the patients had their tumour located above the tracheal bifurcation and were treated only by radiotherapy as this is the policy in our centre. 40 had only palliative treatment and 53 had radical treatment by radiotherapy and

Table 2
Summary chart for oesophageal and cardia carcinomas, their treatment and outcome.
(BY = Brachytherapy, L.ADV = Locally advanced, INOP = Inoperable,
DM = Distant metastases, 4000 = 4000 cGy External radiotherapy).

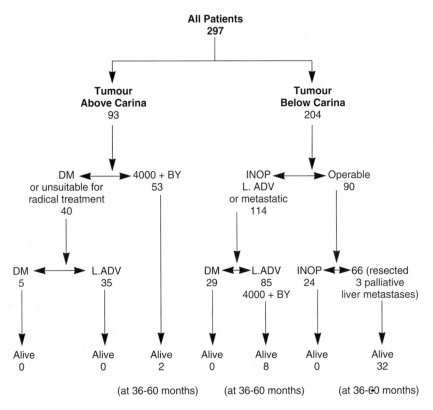

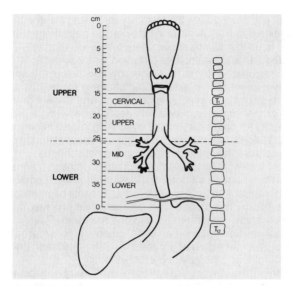

Figure 5. Schematic diagram for clinical trial protocols. If the centre of the tumour is above the carina radiotherapy based protocols are proposed. If it is below the carina then surgical based protocols will predominate.

brachytherapy. Only two of these patients survived the disease to five years. Most patients, 204/297, had their tumour located below the tracheal bifurcation.

The majority of them had an inoperable tumour, locally advanced disease or metastatic disease and received only radiotherapy (external + brachytherapy). 8/85 were alive with no evidence of disease at the time of our analysis. Only 90/297 of patients had a potentially resectable lesion and 66/90 of them had their tumour actually resected following radiotherapy and brachytherapy. Only one patient died due to complications related to this treatment. Three of the patients had liver metastasis at the time of the operation and none of them survived more than four months. Of the 63 patients who had a resection with curative intent, 32 are still alive with no evidence of disease for more than three years, with a median survival time of 43 months.

Discussion

As most patients with cancer of the oesophagus and cardia have advanced disease and a very poor prognosis, the main goal of treatment should be an improvement of their quality of life. While some degree of morbidity is acceptable, it is entirely unjustified to accept a palliative treatment which has the potential risk of perioperative mortality. The simplicity of intracavitary irradiation, the convenience of the short treatment time, plus the radiation safety provided by the remote afterloading system, makes this treatment ideal for palliative situations such as cancer of the oesophagus.

Our clinical experience over the last six years using the combination of intra-cavitary and external irradiation for cancer of the oesophagus and cardia, has demonstrated to us that this treatment is safe, has low morbidity and appears to provide an adequate and reasonable palliation for these patients' symptoms.

The combination of external radiotherapy and brachytherapy has obvious advantages over conventional external radiotherapy alone. It is also superior to surgery in metastatic or unresectable conditions and since it does not increase the morbidity or mortality associated with oesophagectomy, it provides a better selection of cases for oesophagectomy by limiting its use in only potentially cur-able cases. It is known that the morbidity and mortality related to oesophagecto-my increases as the level of the tumour is in the oesophagus.

In Canada it was agreed to use the tracheal bifurcation (carina) to divide the oesophagus in two specific sites for the design and development of clinical tri-als, Figure 5. Patients with tumours above the tracheal bifurcation could be allo-cated to radiotherapy based protocols and adjuvant programmes which could include chemotherapy, hyperthermia and/or sensitisers. Patients with tumours below the tracheal bifurcation, however, could be considered for surgically based protocols with an adjuvant programme using irradiation pre-operatively in the form of external radiotherapy and brachytherapy.

Although there are many surgical options of oesophagectomy, our prefer-ence is to use transhiatal total oesophagectomy with extrathoracic anastomosis in the neck for patients receiving pre-operative irradiation. This has the advan-tage of minimising morbidity associated with leaks and pulmonary complications and adequately removing proximal oesophageal mucosa to reduce the possibili-ty of local recurrence at the level of the anastomosis.

Since there is no difference in the survival rates or local control obtained by the so-called radical en bloc oesophagectomy with mediastinal dissection ver-sus transhiatal oesophagectomy, we feel that this latter procedure should be preferred after irradiation given preoperatively.

Conclusions

[1] Brachytherapy is an effective palliative treatment for patients with carcinomas of the oesophagus and cardia.
[2] The addition of brachytherapy to external irradiation permits enhancement of local control without increasing operative morbidity nor mortality.
[3] The value of systemic chemotherapy as an adjuvant treatment to radiotherapy and brachytherapy needs to be explored.

References

Araugo CM, Souhami L, Gil RA, Carvalho R et al, *A randomised trial comparing radiation therapy versus concomitant radiation therapy and chemotherapy in carcinoma of the thoracic oesophagus,* Cancer, **67**, 2258-2261, 1991.

Coia LR, Engstrom PF, Paul AR, Stafford PM & Hanks GE, *Long term results of infusional 5-FU, mitomycin-C and radiation as primary management of the oesophageal carcinoma,* Int. J. Radiation Oncology Biology & Physics, **20**, 29-36, 1991.

Dale RG, *The application of the linear quadratic dose-effect equation to fractionated and protracted radiotherapy,* Brit. J. Radiology, **58**, 515-528, 1985.

Desai PB & Vyas JJ et al, *Current status of surgical treatment of cancer of oesophagus*, Seminars of Surgical Oncology, **5**, 359-364, 1989.

Earlam R & Cunnha-Melo JR, *Oesophageal squamous carcinoma: a critical review of surgery*, Brit. J. Surgery, **67**, 381-390, 1980.

Earlam R & Cunnha-Melo JR, *Oesophageal squamous carcinoma: a critical review of radiotherapy*, Brit. J. Surgery, **67**, 457-461, 1980.

Flores A, Nelems B, Evans K, Hay J, Stoller J & Jackson S, *The impact of new radiotherapy modalities on the surgical management of cancer of the oesophagus and cardia*, Int. J. Radiation Oncology Biology & Physics, **17**, 937-944, 1989.

Forrastiere A, Orringer MB, Perez-Tamayo C, Urba S, et al, *Concurrent chemotherapy and radiation therapy followed by transhiatal oesophagectomy for local-regional cancer of the oesophagus*, J. Clinical Oncology, **8**, 119-127, 1990.

Gignoux M, Roussel A, Paillot B et al, *The value of preoperative radiotherapy in oesophageal cancer. Results of the EORTC*, World J. Surgery, **11**, 426-432, 1987.

Herskovic A, Martz K, Al-Sarraf M, Leichman L, et al, *Intergroup Oesophageal study: comparison of radiotherapy to radio-chemotherapy combination*: a phase III trial, Abstract, Proceedings ASCO, **135**, 1991.

Huang GJ, Gu X, Wang L et al, *Combined preoperative irradiation and surgery for oesophageal carcinoma*, in:*International trends in general thoracic surgery, oesophageal carcinoma*, 315-318 Wilkins EW & Wong J (Eds), Saunders:Philadelphia, 1988.

Isono K, Onoda S, Ishikawa T, Sato H & Nakayama K, *Studies on the causes of death from oesophageal carcinoma*, Cancer, **39**, 2173-2179, 1982.

Kavanagh B, Anscher M, Leopold K, Deutch M, et al, *Patterns of failure following combined modality therapy for oesophageal cancer*, 1984-1990, Int. J. Radiation Oncology Biology & Physics, **24**, 633-642, 1992.

Keane TJ, Harwood AR et al, *Radiation therapy with 5-FU infusion and mitomycin-C for oesophageal squamous carcinoma*, Radiotherapy & Oncology, **4**, 205-210, 1985.

Kelsen DP, Bains M & Burt M, *Neoadjuvant treatment for cancer of the oesophagus*, Seminars in Surgical Oncology, **6**, 268-273, 1990.

Launois B, Delarue D, Campion J & Kerbaol M, *Preoperative radiotherapy for carcinoma of the oesophagus*, Surgery Gynecological Obstet, **2**, 690-692, 1981.

Mandard AM, Chasle J, Marnay J, Villedieu B et al, *Autopsy findings in 111 cases of oesophageal cancer*, Cancer, **48**, 329-335, 1981.

Mantravadi RVP, Lad T, Briele H & Liebuer EJ, *Carcinoma of the oesophagus, sites of failure*, Int. J. Radiation Oncology Biology & Physics, **8**, 1897-1901, 1982.

Matthews HR & Waterhouse JA, *Cancer of the oesophagus*, Clinical Monograph, **1**, MacMillan:London, 1987.

Rowland CG & Pagliero M, *Intracavitary irradiation in palliation of carcinoma of the oesophagus and cardia*, Lancet, **2**, 981-983, 1985.

Ruol F, Segalin A, Castoro C, et al, *Patterns of neoplastic recurrence after radical and palliative resection of the oesophagus*, in:*Diseases of oesophagus*, Sievert (Ed), 714-716, Springer:Berlin, 1988.

Seydel H, Leichman K, et al, *The Radiation Therapy Oncology Group, Preoperative radiation and chemotherapy for localised squamous cell carcinoma of the oesophagus: a RTOG study*, Int. J. Radiation Oncology Biology & Physics, **14**, 33-35, 1987.

Wang Mei, Gu Xian-zhi, et al, *Randomised clinical trial on the combination of preoperative irradiation and surgery in the treatment of the oesophageal carcinoma. Report on 206 patients*, Int. J. Radiation Oncology Biology & Physics, **16**, 325-327, 1988.

Yin Wei-bo, *Brachytherapy of carcinoma of the oesophagus in China*, in:*Brachytherapy 2*, Mould RF (Ed), 139-141, Nucletron:Leersum, 1989.

Chapter

22

Preoperative Radiotherapy for Rectal Cancer Using Intralumenal HDR Brachytherapy

N. Kamikonya[1], Y. Hishikawa[1], M. Izumi[1], K. Kurisu[1], M. Taniguchi[1], H. Yanagi[2], M. Kusunoki[2] & J. Utsunomiya[2]

Hyogo College of Medicine,
[1] Department of Radiology,
[2] Second Department of Surgery,
1-1 Mukogawa-cho,
Nishinomiya,
Hyogo 663,
Japan.

Introduction

High dose rate intracavitary brachytherapy using a remote afterloader was developed originally for the treatment of cervical cancer but recently this technique has been utilised intralumenally in the treatment of cancers of the oesophagus (Hishikawa et al 1987) and of the biliary tract (Yoshimura et al 1989): as well as routinely in many centres worldwide for endobronchial cancer.

In the Department of Radiology, Hyogo College of Medicine, we initiated in October 1986 with the Second Department of Surgery, a clinical study of the use of HDR brachytherapy as pre-operative therapy for rectal cancer, (Kamikonya 1991).

Patient Series

From 1986-1990 a total of 52 patients with rectal cancer were pre-operatively treated with HDR intralumenal brachytherapy. The median follow-up was 3.33 years with a range of 1.5-5.6 years. The sex ratio was male:female 35:17 and the mean age was 60.9 years with a range of 37-87 years. Staging according to Dukes' classification was A:11 cases, B:16 cases and C:25 cases with a mean tumour length of 4.4 cm and a range of 2.0-7-0 cm. The tumour site distribution above and below the peritoneal reflection was respectively 14 and 36: 2/52 were sited at the anus. The histological differentiation of these 52 adenocarcinoma cases was as follows: well 36/52, moderate 14/52, poor 1/52 with 1/52 being a mucinous adenocarcinoma.

HDR Brachytherapy
Technique

The HDR remote afterloading machine was a Toshiba RAL4OA using the radionuclide cobalt-60. The source could be remotely moved over a distance of 15 cm and for the rectal cancer treatments it was moved at 1 cm intervals. Insertion tubes consisted of

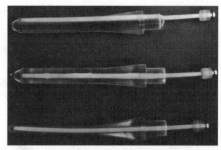

Figure 1. Three types of outer tube for intralumenal HDR brachytherapy for rectal cancer. Type C-1 is 2 cm in diameter and fixes the inner tube in an off-centre position. Type C-2 is also 2 cm in diameter but fixes the inner tube in the centre. Type C-3 is 1 cm in diameter and fixes the inner tube in the centre.

inner and outer tubes and the inner was connected directly to the machine and used as the path for the radiation source. The outer tube containing the inner tube is inserted into the rectum. The inner tube is made of polyethylene 5 mm in diameter and the outer tube is made of silicone: three designs have been made, namely types C-1, C-2 and C-3, Figure 1.

The source was moved beyond the superior and inferior margins of the tumour by 1 cm and its position was determined by endoscopy on a simulation table and the position of the endoscope observed by fluoroscopy, was marked on the skin surface. The purpose of the hip shell, Figure 2, is to ensure the fixation of tubes and also keeps the treatment position of the patient. The shell is constructed of thermal plastic resin and is made at the time when the source position is determined. Dosage is evaluated at a point 5 mm from the surface of the outer tube.

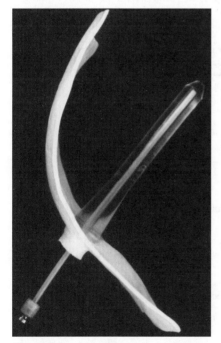

Figure 2. The hip shell and the outer tube. A shell is prepared for each individual patient.

The outer tube is inserted into the rectum with the patient in the left recumbent position as at endoscopy. The inner tube is then inserted into the outer tube and this is followed by the insertion of dummy sources. Thin wires are placed on the marks which are made on the body. When it is confirmed that the positioning is correct the intralumenal HDR brachytherapy can be delivered.

Results

The patients were divided into three groups according to treatment dose. The high dose (50-80 Gy) group contained 15 patients, the medium dose (30-40 Gy) group contained 35 patients and the low dose (16-20 Gy) group contained two patients. Histopathological response was evaluated from resected specimen and these responses were divided into three groups defined by the viability of the irradiated cancer cells. The poor response group showed minimal cellular changes present but a majority of the cells appeared viable. The moderate response group showed cellular changes and partial destruction of the tumour. The good response group showed only non-viable tumour cells present or viable cells nests present only in small areas. In the medium and high dose groups most patients showed good response, Table 1. The pattern of treatment success and failure is given in Table 2 from which it is seen that at the time of writing 33/35 cases who received a medium dose are alive without disease.

Table 1
Histopathological response by dose group.

Response	No.of cases with a given response for the low, medium & high dose groups		
	Low	Medium	High
Poor	-	-	-
Moderate	2/2	13/35	4/15
Good	-	22/35	11/15

Table 2
Treatment outcomes.

Outcome	No.of cases with a given outcome for the low, medium & high dose groups		
	Low	Medium	High
Alive & well	1/2	33/35	12/15
Local disease	1/2	-	1/15
Distant disease	-	1/35	2/15
Local+distant	-	1/35	-

No complications were observed between the start of HDR brachytherapy and the end of surgery. However, postoperative complications were observed: both major and minor. Anal skin trouble and poor wound healing were classed as minor complications and all patients with minor complications subsequently healed. Major complications consisted of fistula, pelvic abscess and anastomotic leakage. All patients with major complications were surgically treated. A higher incidence of major complication was recognised in the high dose group, $P < 0.01$, 5/15 versus 1/35 for the medium dose group and 0/2 for the low dose group. The incidence of minor complications were 1/2 for low dose, 15/35 for medium dose and 5/15 for high dose.

Conclusions

Dose level was found to be an important factor with this patient series with a significantly higher incidence of complications occuring in the high dose group who received 50-80 Gy. We consider that the optimum results were obtained with 30/40 Gy given by intralumenal HDR brachytherapy but that for a future study there should be a randomised trial of pre-operative radiotherapy: intralumenal HDR brachytherapy *versus* external beam radiotherapy.

References

Hishikawa Y, Kamikonya N, Tanaka S et al, *Radiotherapy of oesophageal carcinoma: Role of high dose rate intracavitary irradiation*, Radiotherapy & Oncology, **9**, 13-20, 1987.

Kamikonya N, *Fundamental and clinical studies of preoperative radiotherapy with high dose rate intraluminal brachytherapy*, Nippon Acta Radiology, **51**, 950-961, 1991.

Yoshimura H, Sakaguchi H, Yoshioka T et al, *Afterloading intracavitary irradiation and expanding stent for malignant biliary obstruction*, Radiation Medicine, **7**, 36-41, 1989.

23

Combined External Beam Radiation & Conformal HDR Real Time Iridium-192 Brachytherapy Dosimetry for Locally Advanced Adenocarcinoma of the Prostate

A.A. Martinez[1], G.K. Edmundson[1], J. Gonzalez[2],
J. Hollander[2], D. Brabbins[1], J. Stromberg[1], W. Spencer[2] &
F. Vicini[1].

[1]Department of Radiation Oncology,
[2]Department of Urology,
William Beaumont Hospital,
601 W. 13 Mile Road,
Royal Oak,
Michigan 48073,
USA.

Introduction

In 1991 there were estimated to be 122,000 new cases of carcinoma of the prostate with 32,000 expected to die from the disease and that approximately 59% of patients with prostatic carcinoma had at presentation, disease localised to the prostatic region, (Boring et al 1991).

The treatment options for patients with localised prostatic carcinoma include observation, (George 1988) radical prostatectomy (Culp 1968, Jewett 1975, Zinke 1981, Paulson 1990), radiation therapy, (Bagshaw 1980, Larramore 1985, Perez 1986, Pilepich 1987, Hanks 1987), hormonal therapy, (Blackard 1975, Smith 1987) and combinations of these modalities.

With observation only, progression will occur in 84% (George 1988). Hormonal therapy is usually reserved for known metastatic or presumed metastatic disease (Blackard 1975 & Smith 1987). Radical prostatectomy and radiotherapy are arguably equivalent treatments in the management of carcinoma confined to the prostate (T1, T2) with very similar times to disease progression (Paulsen 1982, Pilepich 1987).

Radiation therapy has historically been the preferred treatment for locally advanced disease (T3) but the results are less than ideal (Perez 1987) with a range of five-year and 10-year survival rates of 40-75% and 35-55% respectively (Bagshaw 1980, Perez 1986, Pilepich 1987, Hanks 1987). The recurrence rate in the pelvis is at least 30% at five years in patients with locally advanced disease (Bagshaw 1980, Perez 1986, Pilepich 1987, Hanks 1987).

Controversy exists as to the significance of positive prostate biopsies following radiation therapy. Biopsy positivity ranges from as low as 21% to as high as 71% post-external beam irradiation (Leach 1982, Scardino 1986, Schellhammer 1987, Kahalin 1989). Investigators have shown increased local failure, increased distant metastases and decreased survival among patients with positive biopsies (Scardino 1986, Cox 1983). Consequently, improving local control becomes of most important.

Another reported explanation for local failure has been the underestimation of the treated volume. Technical advances in imaging, in particular with ultrasonography, have allowed a more accurate assessment of disease involvement and delineation of normal anatomy.

The significant problem with local failure as determined by biopsy or progression clinically, and the premise that local failure may lead to decreased survival and the possible increased incidence of metastases, has led to the development of alternative treatments with the goal of improved local control.

In order to improve local control, hormonal therapy has been added to radiation therapy without benefit being shown. (Cox 1983, Byar 1972, van der Werf-Messing 1976, Beilor 1981, Neolia 1977). Different brachytherapy procedures have been utilised and will be discussed later in this chapter.

Alternative types of radiation to photons, such as neutrons, have also been used (Larramore 1985). The RTOG neutron trial has reported improved local control and survival, though follow-up is short. Confirmatory trials are necessary to prove the beneficial effect of neutron therapy. In addition, the high cost of neutron therapy makes this option unrealistic at present.

The *gold standard* for radiation therapy remains conventional external photon beam radiation to the prostate and pelvis but the use of regional nodal irradiation is controversial (Bagshaw 1977, McGowan 1981, Asbell 1988). Also, retrospective reviews have suggested a beneficial effect from irradiating larger volumes (Bagshaw 1977, McGowan 1981) although a randomised study has not confirmed this benefit (Asbell 1988).

Dose response data suggests that for locally advanced prostatic adenocarcinoma an external beam dose equal to or greater than 7000 cGy is necessary to achieve a reasonable rate of local control (Perez 1986, Hanks 1988). Unfortunately, with increasing external beam doses over 7000 cGy one sees an increasing frequency of gastrointestinal and genitourinary complications (Perez 1986, Hanks 1988, Pilepich 1986, Andur 1990): the main organs effected being the bowel and bladder.

Attempts to increase the dose to the prostate, maintaining a similar complication rate using brachytherapy techniques, have been made with mixed results. Permanent iodine-125 seed implantation has been tried in the early stages of the disease, with results very similar to the results achieved with external beam irradiation (Kandzar 1986, Schellhammer 1987). The rate of positive biopsy post-implantation was in the range 33%-64% for stage B2 and C lesions respectively. This apparent lack of improvement in the MSKCC iodine-125 trial is considered to be a function of the biological and physical characteristics of the radionuclide iodine-125. In a recent update the lack of local control was correlated with an increase in distant metastases and lower survival (Fuks 1991).

Low dose rate (LDR) iridium-192 implantation has had the most favourable positive biopsy rate: in the low range 15%-22% at 18 months (Puthawala 1985, Martinez 1985,1990). This technique was pioneered at Mayo Clinic and William Beaumont Hospital and has rendered the best pathologically confirmed local control and best survival rates for patients with stages C and D1. The incidence of severe complications using this technique are in the range 10%-20% and were felt to be related to the required surgery and to implant technical factors. After technical modifications the incidence of severe rectal complication rate fell below 8% (Martinez 1990).

In order to decrease rectal complications from transperineal template implants, new equipment has been developed to place transperineally and under ultrasound guidance, needles in the prostatic gland. The ultrasound guided transperineal implant allows us a degree of control on needle placement never available before by permitting us direct and continuous visualisation of the relationship between rectal wall and the prostatic tumour.

Ultrasonically guided HDR brachytherapy using iridium-192 has also been utilised (Bertermann 1990) and we believe that the advantages of HDR iridium-192 applications are those given in Table 1.

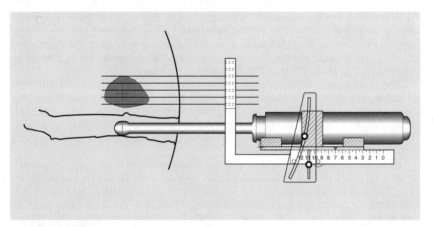

Figure 1. Schematic diagram of the ultrasound probe inside the rectum and the needles passing through the template and patient's perineum into the prostate.

Table 1
Advantages of HDR iridium-192 brachytherapy in the treatment of cancer of the prostate.

- Outpatient treatment requiring no hospitalisation.
- This very short treatment is given under spinal anaesthesia without the risks which can accompany general anaesthesia and abdominal surgery.
- The needles are precisely positioned under ultrasound guidance.
- The dose is optimised with our on-line dosimetry programme to maximise tumour coverage and to minimise normal tissue treatment.
- The HDR afterloading unit offers complete radiation protection for medical and paramedical staff.

Conversion of External Beam Boost to HDR Brachytherapy Boost

In order to find a biological comparison between an external beam boost (10 fractions of 200 cGy) and an interstitial implant boost, a mathematical formula is utilised: the linear quadratic model. This makes the assumptions that the repair half-time for both normal tissues and prostatic carcinoma cells is equal and $\alpha/\beta = 4$ Gy for late rectal wall damage and $\alpha/\beta = 10$ Gy for tumour damage (prostate carcinoma cells); then an HDR fraction of 550 cGy x 3 once weekly will increase damage to rectal mucosa by 2.6% and underdose the tumour by 5%. A dose of 570 cGy x 3 will increase the rectal mucosa damage by 4.8% and underdose the tumour by 3.3%. A dose of 614 cGy will achieve equal tumour control to that obtained using external beam but might increase normal tissue injury by 10%. This biological model provides us with a guideline and not with an equivalent regimen.

Unfortunately, it appears to overstate rectal injury because it makes the assumption that treated volumes and dose distributions are equivalent. In fact, the implanted volume is much smaller than the external beam boost volume and the dose gradient is much sharper in the implant case. However, this model is probably our best approximation for biological comparison of the two regimens.

Trial Design

The implications local failure have on the potential well-being of the patient, metastatic rate and survival, makes it mandatory that attempts continue to be made to control the tumour locally and to maintain minimal morbidity. It appears that brachytherapy offers this potential with a fractionated HDR iridium-192 technique under ultrasound guidance and using online dosimetry. For this reason, we began a prospective non-randomised trial looking at local control and morbidity in 40-75 treated patients with stages B2, C carcinoma of the prostate using ultrasound guided real-time dosimetry HDR applications in conjunction with external beam irradiation to the pelvis. Our protocol stated that patients must meet the eligibility criteria in Table 2.

Table 2
Eligibility criteria for patient entry into the trial.

[1] Histological confirmation of prostatic adenocarcinoma, AJC stages T2b-T4, with or without pelvic nodal disease but without evidence of para-aortic nodal or other distant metastases.
[2] Both lobes of the prostate gland should be biopsied and consequently the final stage is a pathological stage.
[3] All patients must be a candidate for spinal anaesthesia.
[4] Treatment should be initiated within 15 weeks following diagnosis.
[5] All patients must have an abdominal pelvic CT scan to rule out obvious para-aortic nodal metastases and/or intra-abdominal spread. Bipedal lymphangiogram is recommended but is not mandatory. Patients must not have bone scan evidence of disseminated disease.
[6] All patients must have pretreatment transrectal ultrasound and prostate specific antigen.
[7] All patients must have had no prior malignancy within the previous five years: except for basal cell or squamous cell carcinoma of the skin.
[8] All patients must be informed of the investigational nature of this programme and informed consent by our Internal Review Board should be signed.

Treatment Plan

This is summarised below in Table 3.

Table 3
Treatment plan.

Week 1 External beam radiation daily x 4 + 1st brachytherapy on Day 5
Week 2 External beam radiation daily x 4 + 2nd brachytherapy on Day 10
Week 3 External beam radiation daily x 4 + 3rd brachytherapy on Day 15
Week 4 External beam radiation daily x 5
Week 5 External beam radiation daily x 7

Fractionation	Pelvis	Prostate
200 cGy x 4 + 550 HDR	800 cGy	550/1350 cGy
200 cGy x 4 + 550 HDR	800/1600 cGy	550/2700 cGy
200 cGy x 4 + 550 HDR	800/2400 cGy	550/4050 cGy
180 cGy x 12	2160/4560 cGy	2160/6210 cGy

Brachytherapy

The first 22 patients will be treated with the microSelectron-HDR and receive 550 cGy weekly x 3 to the prostate and medial half of seminal vesicles as determined by prostate ultrasound. For complete information on technical description and dosimetric considerations see Edmundson et al (1993).

Standard homogeneity criteria for dose prescription of transperineal template implants will be utilised. If rectal, urethral and/or bladder severe toxicity occurred but did not exceed 20%, then the dose is increased to 600 cGy weekly x 3 to the target volume for the remaining 25 patients.

Brachytherapy procedures will be performed in the Radiation Oncology Brachytherapy Suite under spinal anaesthesia following the standard William Beaumont Hospital protocol for spinal anaesthesia. At least one, but preferably three flexible cystoscopies should be performed after the needle placement prior to the actual HDR treatment.

Study Calendar

Table 4 describes the study calendar for our combined external beam and brachytherapyu protocol for T2B,3,4;N0,N1,M0 adenocarcinoma of the prostate.

Monitored Toxicities

The toxicity scoring system that has been used for this study is given in Table 5. It is based on a grades 0-4 and is equivalent to none, mild, moderate, severe & life-threatening.

Table 4
Study calendar.

Required studies	Pre	Treatment					Off Treatment								Δ
	Study	Wk 1	Wk 2	Wk 3	Wk 4	Wk 5	Mo 3	Mo 6	Mo 9	Mo 12	Mo 15	Mo 18	Mo 24	Mo 30	Mo 36
Physical															
History & physical exam	X						X	X	X	X	X	X	X	X	X
Weight & performance status	X	X		X		X	X	X	X	X	X	X	X	X	X
Tumor measurement	X						X	X		X	X	X	X	X	X
Toxicity notation		X	X	X	X	X	X	X	X	X	X	X	X	X	X
Laboratory															
CBC/differential/platelets	X		X	X	X	X	X	X	X	X	X	X	X	X	X
Alkaline phosphatase	X							X		X			X		X
Prostatic specific antigen	X						X	X	X	X	X	X	X	X	X
Needle biopsy prostate √		X											X		
X-rays & Scans															
Chest X-ray	X											X			X
CT pelvis	X														
Bone scan	X											X			X
Transrectal ultrasound	X							X		X		X		X	X
Treatment															
Radiation therapy Ω		X	X	X	X	X									
HDR brachytherapy			X	X	X										

Δ Patients will be followed yearly thereafter. Follow-up is performed with these tests.
√ Under transrectal ultrasound (TRUS) guidance is possible.
Ω Radiation therapy should be delayed for six weeks following TURP must begin
  ≤ 15 weeks from diagnosis.

Brachytherapy

The first 22 patients will be treated with the microSelectron-HDR and receive 550 cGy weekly x 3 to the prostate and medial half of seminal vesicles as determined by prostate ultrasound. For complete information on technical description and dosimetric considerations see Edmundson et al (1993).

Standard homogeneity criteria for dose prescription of transperineal template implants will be utilised. If rectal, urethral and/or bladder severe toxicity occurred but did not exceed 20%, then the dose is increased to 600 cGy weekly x 3 to the target volume for the remaining 25 patients.

Brachytherapy procedures will be performed in the Radiation Oncology Brachytherapy Suite under spinal anaesthesia following the standard William Beaumont Hospital protocol for spinal anaesthesia. At least one, but preferably three flexible cystoscopies should be performed after the needle placement prior to the actual HDR treatment.

Study Calendar

Table 4 describes the study calendar for our combined external beam and brachytherapyu protocol for T2B,3,4;N0,N1,M0 adenocarcinoma of the prostate.

Monitored Toxicities

The toxicity scoring system that has been used for this study is given in Table 5. It is based on a grades 0-4 and is equivalent to none, mild, moderate, severe & life-threatening.

Table 5
Monitoring of toxicities.

Haematological.	White cell count, haemoglobin and platelet count.
Gastrointestinal.	Nausea, vomiting, diarrhea, tenesmus, rectal pain, small bowel obstruction, rectal ulcer and fistula.
Bladder.	Dysuria, urinary retention, incontinence, urgency, frequency, haemorrhagic, cystitis, urethral stricture and fistula.

Preliminary Results

Since November 1991 a total of 80 implants have been performed on 20 protocol and five non-protocol patients with newly diagnosed bx/C prostatic adenocarcinoma. We began the treatment programme initially utilising an HDR dose of 550 cGy. Patients were treated with [a] 4560 whole pelvis four-field irradiation and [b] three HDR fractions of 550 cGy each to the target volume.

The mean age of this patient group was 67 years and the mean Gleason score was 6.7. Those with prior TURPs were not excluded. Under spinal anaesthesia, transperineal needle implants utilising real-time ultrasound guidance with online isodose distributions were performed weekly on an outpatient basis during weeks 1, 2 and 3 of external irradiation.

The brachytherapy target volume included the entire prostate gland and the medial aspects of the seminal vesicles. An average of 14 needles were required to adequately cover this volume. Rectal dose calculations and TLD measurements were performed. Acute toxicity was recorded weekly during treatment and at 1.5, three and six months following treatment using modified RTOG/EORTC grading criteria. Prospective prostatic rebiopsis at 18 months are planned in all patients who have not failed distantly.

The mean follow-up from treatment completion is six months. No significant intraoperative or perioperative complications occurred. Grade 3 toxicity was encountered in three patients: two with dysuria and one with diarrhea. All toxicities were otherwise grade 1 or 2 and were as expected from pelvic external irradiation: haaemorrhagic cystitis (18%), bladder spasms (5%), implant related toxicities included urinary retention (41%), haematospermia (18%), perineal pain (27%).

SWOG performance status changed from 0 to 1 in two patients (7%). The mean calculated rectal dose per fraction was 58% of the HDR dose with an acceptable agreement demonstrated by TLD measurements within the limitations of iridium-192 TLD dosimetry. PSA levels obtained at three months showed a greater than 50% reduction in 83% of patients.

The acute toxicity encountered to date with this clinical trial has been minimal. Consequently, dose escalation will proceed. The preliminary results from this unique approach utilising conformal HDR iridium-192 brachytherapy boost for locally advanced prostatic carcinoma are encouraging and further follow-up will permit comparison to results obtained with conventional irradiation, conformal external beam and other brachytherapy techniques.

References

Andur RJ, *Adenocarcinoma of the prostate treated with external beam radiation therapy: 5-year minimum follow-up*, Radiotherapy & Oncology, **18**, 235, 1990.

Asbell SO, *Elective pelvic irradiation in stage A2 B carcinoma of the prostate: Analysis of RTOG 77-06*, Int. J. Radiation Oncology Biology & Physics, **15**, 1307, 1988.

Bagshaw MA, *Evaluation of extended field radiotherapy for prostatic neoplasms. 1976 progress report.*, Cancer Treatment Reports, **61**, 27, 1977.

Bagshaw MA, *External radiation therapy of carcinoma of the prostate*, Cancer Supplement, 1912, 1980.

Beilor D, *Radical external radiotherapy for prostatic carcinoma*, Int. J. Radiation Oncology Biology & Physics, **7**, 855, 1981.

Bertermann H, *Ultrasonically guided interstitial high dose rate brachytherapy with iridium-192: Technique and preliminary results in locally confined prostate cancer*, in:*Brachytherapy HDR and LDR*, Martinez AA, Orton CG & Mould RF (Eds), 281-303, Nucletron:Columbia, 1990.

Blackard CE, *The veteran's administration cooperative urological research group studies of carcinoma of the prostate: A review*, Cancer Chemotherapy Reports, **59**, 225, 1975.

Boring CB, Squire TS & Tong T, *Cancer Statistics*, CA-A Journal for Clinicians, **41**, 19-28, 1991.

Byar DP, *The VACURG studies of cancer of the prostate*, Cancer, **30**, 513, 1972.

Cox J, *Do prostatic biopsies twelve months or more after external irradiation for adenocarcinoma, stage III predict long term survival*, Int. J. Radiation Oncology Biology & Physics, **9**, 299, 1983.

Culp OS, *Radical perineal prostatectomy: Its, past, present and future*, J. Urology, **98**, 618, 1968.

Edmundson GK, Rizzo NR, Teahan M, Brabbins D, Vicini FA & Martinez A, *Concurrent treatment planning for outpatient high dose rate prostate template implants*, Int. J. Radiation Oncology Biology & Physics, In press, 1993.

Fuks Z et al, *The effect of local control on metastatic dissemination in carcinoma of the prostate: Long-term results in patients treated with iodine-125 implantation*, Int. J. Radiation Oncology Biology & Physics, **21**, 537-547, 1991.

George NIR, *Natural history of localised prostate cancer managed by conservative therapy alone*, The Lancet, 494-497, 1988.

Hanks GE, *A ten year follow-up of 682 patients treated for prostate cancer with radiation therapy in the United States*, Int. J. Radiation Oncology Biology & Physics, **13**, 499, 1987.

Hanks GE, *The effect of dose on local control of prostate cancer*, Int. J. Radiation Oncology Biology & Physics, **15**, 1299, 1988.

Jewett HJ, *The present status of radical prostatectomy for stages a & b prostatic cancer*, Urological Clinics of North America, **2**, 105, 1975.

Kahalin JN, *Identification of residual cancer in the prostate following radiation therapy: Role of transrectal ultrasound guided biopsy and prostate specific antigen*, J. Urology, **142**, 326, 1989.

Kandzar SJ, *Post-irradiation, biopsy and histological effects in early stage prostatic cancer treated with iodine-125 implants*, Prostate, **9**, 319, 1986.

Larramore GE, *Fast neutron radiotherapy for locally advanced prostate cancer: results of an RTOG randomised study*, Int. J. Radiation Oncology Biology & Physics, **11**, 1621, 1985.

Leach GE, *Radiotherapy for Prostatic Carcinoma: Post-irradiation prostatic biopsy and recurrence patterns with long term follow-up*, J. Urology, **128**, 505, 1982.

Martinez A, *Combination of external beam irradiation and multiple site perineal applicator (MUPIT) for the treatment of locally advanced or recurrent prostatic, perineal and gynaecologic malignancies*, Int. J. Radiation Oncology Biology & Physics, **11**, 391, 1985.

Martinez A, *Use of a remote afterloading LDR apparatus for patients undergoing interstitial implantation of the prostate with iridium-192 combined with external beam irradiation*, in: *Brachytherapy HDR and LDR*, Martinez AA, Orton CG & Mould RF (Eds), 304-316, Nucletron:Columbia, 1990.

McGowan DE, *The value of extended field radiation therapy in carcinoma of the prostate*, Int. J. Radiation Oncology Biology & Physics, **7**, 1333, 1981.

Neolia W, *Megavoltage radiation therapy for carcinoma of the prostate*, Int. J. Radiation Oncology Biology & Physics, **2**, 873, 1977.

Paulsen DF, *Radical surgery versus radiotherapy in adenocarcinoma of the prostate*, J. Urology, **128**, 502, 1982.

Paulsen DF, *Radical prostatectomy for clinical stage T1-2, N-0, M-0 prostatic adenocarcinoma: Long term results*, Journal Urology, **144**, 1180, 1990.

Perez CA, *Tumour control in definitive irradiation of localised carcinoma of the prostate*, Int. J. Radiation Oncology Biology & Physics, **12**, 523, 1986.

Perez CA, *Carcinoma of the prostate, in:Principles and practice of radiation oncology*, Perez CA & Brady LW (Eds), Lippincott:Philadelphia, 1987.

Pilepich MV, *Definitive radiotherapy in resectable (Stage A2 + B) carcinoma of the prostate - results of a nationwide overview*, Int. J. Radiation Oncology Biology & Physics, **13**, 659, 1987.

Pilepich MV, *Radical prostatectomy or radiotherapy in carcinoma of the prostate*, Urology, **30**, 18, 1987.

Pilepich MV, *Correlation of radiotherapeutic parameters and treatment related morbidity in carcinoma of the prostate: Analysis of RTOG study 75-06*, Int. J. Radiation Oncology Biology & Physics, **13**, 351, 1987.

Puthawala AA, *Temporary iridium-192 implant in the management of carcinoma of the prostate*, Endocurietherapy/Hyperthermia Oncology, **1**, 25, 1985.

Scardino PT, *The prognostic significance of post-irradiation biopsy results in patients with prostatic cancer*, J. Urology, **135**, 510, 1986.

Schellhammer PF, *Prostate biopsy after definitive treatment by interstitial iodine-125 implant or external beam radiation therapy*, J. Urology, **137**, 897, 1987.

Schellhammer PF, *Prostate biopsy after definitive treatment by interstitial iodine-125 implant or external beam radiation oncology*, J. Urology, **137**, 897, 1987.

Smith JA, *Hew methods of endocrine management of prostatic cancer*, J. Urology, 137, **1**, 1987.

van der Werf-Messing B, *Localised advanced carcinoma of the prostate: radiation therapy versus hormonal therapy*, Int. J. Radiation Oncology Biology & Physics, **1**, 1043, 1976.

Zincke H, *Radical retropubic prostatectomy and pelvic Lymphadenectomy for high stage cancer of the prostate*, Cancer, **47**, 1901, 1981.

24

Bladder Implantation:
Fact or Fiction?

J.J. Battermann

Department of Radiotherapy,
University Hospital Utrecht,
P.O. Box 85500,
3508 GA Utrecht,
The Netherlands.

Introduction

The original description of bladder implantation was by Cade (1929) in his book *Radium treatment of cancer*, where he quoted Barringer reporting 75% cures after bladder implantation of which the majority survived more than five years when the histology was papillary carcinoma. A figure of 35% cures was quoted for infiltrating carcinoma. Barringer considered radium as the method of election in the treatment of bladder carcinoma, Figure 1.

Wallace et al (1952) of the Royal Marsden Hospital, London described a technique using tantalum-182 hairpin wires which were removable through the urethra. In The Netherlands, Breur (1956) realised the advantages of applying a high local dose in primary malignancies of the bladder using radium needles. His technique was followed by van der Werf-Messing (1981) and by Battermann (1986) although for radiation safety reasons caesium-137 needles eventually replaced radium. One of the disadvantages of this implantation technique was the radiation exposure to staff and patients' visitors, even when using caesium-137. Furthermore, there was often a delayed wound healing with infection.

A different technique was applied in France by Mazeron et al (1985) using iridium-192 wires after local excision of the tumour. This technique of implantation with separate plastic tubes gives the opportunity for afterloading and was adopted by us to overcome some of the disadvantages of the needle implantation method. This chapter describes the technique of implantation using remote afterloading and the preliminary results in 39 patients.

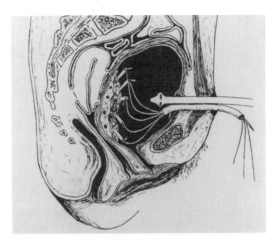

Figure 1. Open suprapubic method of irradiation for carcinoma of the bladder. The needles are introduced into and around the growth. In the drawing the needles are shown half-introduced, but should be entirely buried in the growth. Threads are brought out through a separate rubber tube at the side of the De Pezzer catheter. 10-12 needles are necessary. The total quantity of radium applied varies between 6 mg and 10 mg. The needles are left in position 10 days for a total average dose average dose of 2,500 milligram-hours, Cade(1929).

Material & Methods

In the period August 1988 to March 1992 a total of 39 patients have been implanted. The male to female ratio was 3:1 with an age range of 34-78 years and a mean age of 62 years. Candidates for bladder implantation should fulfil the eligibility criteria given in Table 1.

Table 1
Eligibility criteria for bladder implantation.

- Solitary lesion.
- Diameter less than 5 cm.
- Tumour stage T1, T2, T3A.
- No previous bladder malignancy.
- Fit for surgical procedure.

Table 2 gives a breakdown according to T-stage and G-stage. Only patients with a poorly differentiated T1 tumour or local recurrence after transurethral resection were included.

Table 2
T and G staging of 39 patients
treated by bladder implantation.

| T-stage | G-stage | | Total |
	G2	G3	cases
T1	2	2	4
T2	16	12	28
T3A	2	3	5
T3B	0	1	1
T4	0	1	1
T1-T4	20	19	39

The majority of patients had a T2 tumour, but it should be noted that the differentiation between T2 and T3A remains difficult and often can only be determined on palpation during the operation, with one finger in the bladder lumen and one finger outside the bladder wall, Figure 2. Inspite of the eligibility criteria, one patient was included who had a previous implant almost 10 years earlier for a T2 lesion. Since he refused a total cystectomy a second implant was performed. One other patient had a T4 lesion: growth into the vaginal wall. She received a higher external irradiation dose and a local implantation through the vaginal wall without opening the abdomen.

38/39 patients received preoperative external irradiation with a dose equivalent of 30 Gy (mostly 12 x 235 cGy) using megavoltage X-rays to irradiate the true pelvis. Implantation followed within one week of completion of the external therapy. Under general (or sometimes spinal) anaesthesia, the abdomen was opened through a lower laparotomy incision. After inspection and palpation of the regional nodes (which were not suspect in any of our cases) the bladder

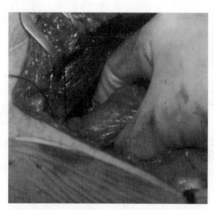

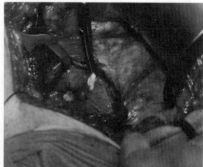

Figure 3. The bladder is opened in the midline and the tumour area visualised. The diameter is estimated, including the necrotic TUR effect. In this patient there is still oedema around the tumour area visible.

Figure 2. Palpation of the tumour infiltration in the bladder wall by one finger in the bladder lumen and one finger on the outside.

was opened as far as possible from the tumour site. In general the bladder could be opened in the midline.

The tumour was located in the side walls in 28/39 patients, in the posterior wall or base of the bladder in 7/39 and in the dome of the bladder in 4/39. In 3/4 cases with tumour in the dome, a partial resection was performed followed by implantation in the scar. In all other patients the whole procedure was a retroperitoneal one. The tumour area was always visualised and the diameter confirmed, Figure 3. In 23/39 patients the diameter was less than 3 cm, in 14/39 was 3-5 cm and in 2/39 was greater than 5 cm.

According to the exact localisation of the tumour and its size, combined with the shape of the bladder, the curvature and length of the thoracic needle is chosen to implant the flexible plastic tubes for afterloading. The number of tubes implanted was in the range two to five, with 19/39 receiving three tubes and 14/39 receiving four tubes. If possible, the tubes are placed in the bladder wall and do not enter the lumen. With this 'tunnelling technique' urinary leakage is minimised together with the chances of infection. In some cases however, it is not possible to tunnel the tubes straight on. In these cases the tubes enter the bladder lumen at a distance from the tumour site and are subsequently tunnelled through the tumour area.

After positioning all tubes the lengths of the active sources are estimated by the introduction of dummy sources. The length of the active sources varied from 4 cm to more than 5 cm, with 12/39 having a length of 4.5 cm and 19/39 a length of 5 cm. After the introduction of the dummy sources the bladder is closed and then the leading ends of the tubes are passed through the abdominal wall ,Figure 4. A drain is placed in Retzius' space and the abdominal wall is

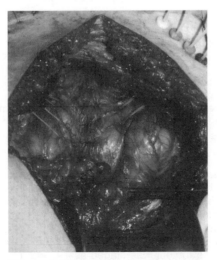

Figure 4. The flexible plastic tubes are brought separately through the abdominal wall. The tubes are fixed by buttons. Using separate loops, urine leakage and infection are minimised.

closed after a final check of the positioning of the tubes with the dummy sources in place. The tubes are fixed on both sides with buttons. Finally, a Foley catheter is introduced to drain the urine from the bladder.

After recovery, the patient is brought to the simulator room for localisation films. We use a stereo-shift method to visualise the positioning of the dummy sources and the afterloading technique allows some rearrangement of sources if the geometry is not ideal and the localisation films are used for the planning of the dose distribution lines.

The Nucletron planning system allows the display of the isodose lines in the X, Y and Z directions independent of the position of the implant in the body of the patient and perpendicular to the Y direction a number of cross sections are taken to calculate the final distribution. From these dose distribution displays the total treatment time is calculated. Depending on the external beam dose, the brachytherapy dose varied from 40Gy to 60 Gy: 40 Gy was delivered to 29/39 patients. In general the dose rate was between 40 cGy/hour and 50 cGy/hour and thus the total time varied from 80 hours to 120 hours. The actual treatment is given in a lead shielded room, where the remote afterloading offers full radiation protection to the nursing staff. In general the patient requires some spasmolytics and pain medication.

After completion of the treatment time the patient is disconnected from the microSelectron-LDR/MDR machine. Removal of the flexible tubes is easy and without any problems. From the shielded room the patient is taken to the urogical ward. The drain in Retzius' space is removed one to two days later and the Foley catheter is removed 10-12 days after the date of operation.

Results

All patients are regularly seen by the urologist and radiation oncologist for cystoscopy. In general, four cystoscopies are undertaken in the first year, three in the second year, two in the third year and one every other year. Routine blood examination is performed every year as is a chest X-ray. Urography and/or echography is undertaken when there is a suspicion of ureter obstruction according to the original tumour site.

The follow-up ranged between a few months and 48 months but patients with a follow-up of less than 12 months are not included in this analysis: 6/39 cases. 1/39 is still alive 14 months after implantation but refuses to come for follow-up cystoscopy.

23 patients are alive, 21 patients have no evidence of disease with a follow-up of 13-48 months: mean of 26 months. 2/23 are alive with a local recurrence: one of these already had multiple lesions during the operation (this was the patient who had a previous bladder implant) but he was implanted because he first refused cystectomy. Since there was progression of the lesions after the new implantation he finally underwent a total cystectomy. He is alive and well now 24 months after cystectomy. Another patient had a recurrence six months after implantation: the tumour was staged as TA and treated by transurethral resection. He is alive and well with a follow-up of 20 months.

Nine patients died: 4/9 with a local recurrence with an interval of six months (two patients), seven months and 21 months. All patients had a T3 lesion. One patient had a salvage cystectomy, but she died of intercurrent disease seven months after operation. At autopsy there was no tumour found. Two other patients refused a cystectomy or their condition did not allow a cystectomy. They died after 12 and 14 months. The last patient had distant spread of the tumour when the local recurrence was diagnosed. He died six months after the diagnosis of recurrent tumour. Four patients died of distant spread only with an interval of 3, 9, 11 and 17 months. In two patients there were bone metastases, in one patient brain metastases and in one patient nodal metastases in the para-aortic region. It is also recorded that one patient died of complications after the operation. He was re-admitted to the hospital with a pelvic infection due to a lymphocèle and died of terminal kidney function.

The hospitalisation varied from 10 to more than 31 days with a mean of 13 days. 30/39 patients were discharged 10-14 days from the day of implantation, for 2/39 this was 15-20 days, for 2/39 this was more than 20 days and 5/39 were referred elsewhere. 3/39 had a psychosis during their actual treatment but one of these patients was known to have a psychiatric history. Another of these three patients had a psychosis due to a CVA. The third in this subgroup already had symptoms of Alzheimer's disease and he was referred to a psychiatric institution after his psychosis presented, but recovered in about six months.

In 2/39 an ileus was encountered during the treatment and in these patients there was some delay in the total treatment time although both could be treated conservatively. 1/39 had heart discomfort and a local infection of the wound, 1/39 had stomach bleeding that could also be treated conservatively and 3/39 had to be re-admitted due to an infection. In 2/3 of these cases this was an abscess in the abdominal wall and they were also treated conservatively. Also, as mentioned previously, 1/39 died due to complications.

During follow-up cystoscopies it is common to encounter a radiation ulcer at the site of implantation and in general this appears after six months and disappears in another 6-9 months. The majority of our patients had no radiation ulcers. Although all patients have urinary discomfort during the first months after treatment, the bladder capacity returned to normal in all our patients. In 3/39 a persistent ulcer was observed for more than 12 months, albeit without the patient considering that this was a serious complaint. 2/39 had a ureter obstruction and in one of these cases a neo-implantation had to be performed. There were no signs of recurrent tumour in these two patients.

Discussion

One of the treatment modalities in the management of localised bladder cancer is implantation of radioactive material. Although excellent results have been reported (van der Werf-Messing et al 1981, 1983, Mazeron et al 1985, Wijnmaalen & van der Werf-Messing 1986, Battermann & Tierie 1986, Battermann & Boon 1988, 1991) this treatment technique is ignored by many urologists.

It is often stated that bladder cancer is a multicentric disease and thus local implantation will not prevent the onset of new primaries in the bladder mucosa. After transurethral resection alone the recurrence rate is 50%-70%. Also, of more importance, 5%-10% of TA tumours and 20%-50% of T1 tumours progress in stage and/or grade, (Jakse et al 1987, Jenkins et al 1989).

Intravesical chemotherapy and immunotherapy gained wide acceptance in the postoperative treatment, since it was shown that this additive treatment reduces the recurrence rate and prolongs the interval free period, (Green et al 1984, Herz et al 1987, Heney 1988, Martinez-Pineiro et al 1990).

In particular, the series from van der Werf-Messing et al (1981) and from Battermann & Tierie (1986) indicate a low incidence of second primaries in the bladder mucosa. Since no random biopsies were taken in these series the radiation technique must have an influence on the reduction of second tumours. We have to keep in mind, though, that the series described are selected in respect of tumour site (in general, locations in the bladder neck and prostatic urethra were excluded), size (tumour diameter of less than 5 cm), multifocal appearance (only solitary lesions or pluriform lesions situated within a range of 4 cm), and no previous bladder tumours elsewhere in the bladder (only local recurrences after TUR are included).

On the other hand, the majority of our 39 patients had a moderately or poorly differentiated tumour, or a recurrence after previous TUR. Thus it should be concluded that the treatment technique itself plays a role in the reduced recurrence rate. It could therefore be advocated that patients should also be included who had recurrences at other sites previously treated by transurethral resection.

Not only for T1 lesions, but especially for T2/T3A lesions the results of implantation are excellent with regard to local control and survival (van der Werf-Messing et al 1983, Wijnmaalen & van der Werf-Messing 1986, Battermann & Boon 1988). Although as mentioned previously we have to keep in mind that this group of patients is highly selected, nevertheless, the results are at least comparable with the best results obtained after radical cystectomy with conservation of the anatomical and functional integrity of the lower urinary tract. Also, yet again, the majority of patients had a moderately or poorly differentiated tumour.

It is clear that for these tumours a local treatment of transurethral resection alone or one which is combined with intravesical therapy is insufficient, (Klimberg & Wajsman 1986). Therefore T2 tumours are particularly suitable for implantation. Also, even in larger T3 tumours (van der Werf-Messing 1980) this implantation technique could be an alternative to total cystectomy. However, in these patients a higher external beam treatment is advised, followed by an local implantation with a reduced brachytherapy dose.

Although the original needle implantation technique seemed very simple, the complication rate was high and the hospitalisation was generally long: Battermann & Boon (1991) mention a mean hospitalisation of over 30 days. Also, the removal of the active needles is quite often hampered and in about 10% of the cases in the Battermann & Boon (1991) series, reopening had to be performed to extract a needle.

With the technique we have described, afterloading flexible tubes are separately tunnelled under the mucosa and this enables the bladder to be closed completely after the positioning of the tubes. This avoids urinary leakage and thus reduces the infection rate. Also, removal of the active sources and the plastic tubes does not present any problems. In our current series of patients the mean hospitalisation is reduced to 13 days including 4-6 days of actual irradiation. Furthermore the remote afterloading technique offers full radiation protection to medical and nursing staff and to patients' visitors.

Experience with definitive external beam therapy shows a lower local control rate and reduced survival when compared with total cystectomy and when compared with interstitial brachytherapy techniques, (Shipley & Rose 1985, Duncan & Quilty 1986, Quilty & Duncan 1986). Of course the advantage of external beam radiotherapy is that treatment can be given on an outpatient basis. On the other hand the total treatment period varies within the range 5-7 weeks and the initial and late complication rates seem considerably higher than after interstitial brachytherapy. The experience, especially in the United Kingdom with definitive radiation therapy combined with further surgery, (Hope-Stone et al 1984, Quilty et al 1986), is also applicable to the interstitial brachytherapy experience.

Apart from the afterloading technique we have described with low dose rate brachytherapy and the previous interstitial needle technique, one could also consider direct implantation through the cystoscope. Ralston Paterson in his book *The treatment of malignant disease by radiotherapy*, had by the time of this writing in 1963, already abandoned the technique of gold-198 grain or radon-222 seed implant because "it is technically impossible to secure a properly spaced and planned implant with any reliability". In Paterson's view "the only means of achieving an accurate implant is at open operation and even then it is difficult enough".

A new concept is the use of high dose rate (HDR) brachytherapy in place of low dose rate (LDR) brachytherapy. Until now, though, there is no experience with HDR in the treatment of bladder cancer. The advantages of HDR in a fractionated scheme (or ultimately in a pulsed dose rate scheme) are clear and are described by Mazeron et al (1992). Using one high activity remote afterloading iridium-192 stepping source for all tubes can probably further optimise the treatment plan. The most important advantage however, could be the psychological impact for the patient who with this technique is not isolated for the entire treatment period. However, clinical experience is still required to determine whether HDR brachytherapy offers the same results as LDR brachytherapy in different tumour sites, including the bladder.

Conclusion

The remote afterloading technique we have described for the treatment of localised bladder cancer offers a similar local control probability when compared with our earlier method of needle implantation. It does though, offer reduced hospitalisation and full radiation protection.

References

Battermann JJ & Tierie AH, *Results of implantation for T1 and T2 bladder tumours*, Radiotherapy & Oncology, **5**, 85-90, 1986.

Battermann JJ & Boon TA, *Interstitial therapy in the management of T2 bladder tumours*, Endocurietherapy/Hyperthermia Oncology, **4**, 1-6, 1988.

Battermann JJ & Boon TA, *Remote controlled afterloading technique for the treatment of bladder cancer*, Endocurietherapy/Hyperthermia Oncology, **7**, 151-154, 1991.

Breur K, *De radio-chirurgische behandeling van blaascarcinoom*, Nederlands Tijdschrift van Geneeskunde, **100**, 1052-1061, 1956.

Cade S, *Radium treatment of cancer*, Churchill:London, 1929.

Duncan W & Quilty PM, *The results of a series of 963 patients with transitional cell carcinoma of the urinary bladder primarily treated by radical megavoltage X-ray therapy*, Radiotherapy & Oncology, **7**, 299-310, 1986.

Green DF, Robinson MRG, Glashan R, Newling D, Dalesio O & Smith PH, *Does intravesical chemotherapy prevent invasive bladder cancer?* J. Urology, **131**, 33-35, 1984.

Heney NM, *Intravesical chemotherapy: How effective is it?* Urology, **31**, 17-19, 1988.

Herr HW, Laudone VP & Whitmore WF, *An overview of intravesical therapy for superficial bladder tumors*, J. Urology, **138**, 1363-1368, 1987.

Hope-Stone HF, Oliver RTD, England HR & Blandy DM, *T3 bladder cancer: salvage rather than elective cystectomy after radiotherapy*, Urology, **4**, 315-320, 1984.

Jakse G, Loidl W, Seeber G & Hofstadter F, *Stage T1 grade 3 transitional cell carcinoma of the bladder, an unfavourable tumour?*, J. Urology, **137**, 39-43, 1987.

Jenkins BJ, Nauth-Missir RR, Martin JE, Fowler CG, Hope-Stone HF & Blandy JP, *The fate of G3pT1 bladder cancer*, Brit. J. Urology, **64**, 608-610, 1989.

Klimberg IW & Wajsman Z, *Treatment for muscle invasive carcinoma of the bladder*, J. Urology, **136**, 1169-1175, 1986.

Martinez-Pineiro JA, Leon JJ, Martinez-Pineiro L Jr., Fiter L, Mosteiro JA, Navarro J, Matires MJG & Carcamo P, *Bacillus Calmette-Guerin versus doxorubicin versus thiotepa: a randomised prospective study in 202 patients with superficial bladder cancer*, J. Urology, **143**, 502-506, 1990.

Mazeron JJ, Boisserie G & Baillet F, *Pulsed LDR brachytherapy: current clinical status*, in:*International Brachytherapy*, Mould RF (Ed), 42-45, Nucletron:Veenendaal, 1992.

Mazeron JJ, Marinello G, Leung S, Le Bourgeois JP, Abbou CC, Auvert J & Pierquin B, *Treatment of bladder tumours by iridium-192 implantation. The Creteil technique*, Radiotherapy & Oncology, **4**, 111-119, 1985.

Paterson R, *The treatment of malignant disease by radiotherapy*, Arnold:London, 1963.

Quilty PM & Duncan W, *Primary radical radiotherapy for T3 transitional cell cancer of the bladder: an analysis of survival and control*, Int. J. Radiation Oncology Biology & Physics, **12**, 853-860, 1986.

Quilty PM, Duncan W, Chisholm GD, Fowler JW, Hargreave TB, Newsam JE & Tolley DA, *Results of surgery following radical radiotherapy for invasive bladder cancer*, Brit. J. Urology, **58**, 396-405, 1986.

Shipley WU & Rose MA, *Bladder cancer: The selection of patients for treatment by full-dose irradiation*, Cancer, **55**, 2278-2284, 1985.

Wallace DM, Stapleton JE & Turner RC, *Radioactive tantalum wire implantation as a method of treatment for early carcinoma of the bladder*, Brit. J. Radiology, **25**, 421-424, 1952.

van der Werf-Messing BHP, Star WM & Menon RS, *T3NxM0 carcinoma of the urinary bladder treated by the combination of radium implant and external irradiation*, Int. J. Radiation Oncology Biology & Physics, **6**, 1723-1725, 1980.

van der Werf-Messing BHP, *Carcinoma of the urinary bladder (category T1NxM0) treated either by radium implant or by transurethral resection only*, Int. J. Radiation Oncology Biology & Physics, **7**, 299-303, 1981.

van de Werf-Messing BHP, Menon RS & Hop WCJ, *Carcinoma of the urinary bladder category T2T3 (NxM0) treated by interstitial radium implant: 2nd report*, Int. J. Radiation Oncology Biology & Physics, **9**, 481-485, 1983.

Wijnmaalen AJ & van der Werf-Messing BHP, *Factors influencing the prognosis in bladder cancer*, Int. J. Radiation Oncology Biology & Physics, **12**, 559-565, 1986.

25

Skin Dose Due to Breast Implantation for Early Breast Cancer

V.J. de Ru, P. Hofman, H. Struikmans, M.A Moerland, M.J.H. Nuyten-van Deursen & J.J. Battermann.

Department of Radiotherapy,
University Hospital Utrecht,
P.O. Box 85500,
3508 GA Utrecht,
The Netherlands.

Introduction

An important goal of breast conserving therapy (BCT) is to preserve a good cosmesis and it is therefore of interest to determine the radiation dose delivered to the skin. Treatment after breast conserving surgery consists usually of a dose of 50 Gy delivered to the whole breast followed by a boost dose to the former tumour volume. The method of delivery and the level of this boost dose are considered to be significant factors in determining the cosmetic outcome of the radiation treatment.

In our institution the radiotherapy part of BCT consists, when less than three lymph nodes of the axillary node dissection are tumour positive, of external beam irradiation of the entire breast by two tangential opposing wedge fields (25 x 200 cGy fractions, five fractions per week, prescription to the isodose line around the target volume: mostly 90% to 95%), followed by a boost dose to the former tumour volume.

This boost can be given by external irradiation using wedged photon beams, electron beams, or it can be given interstitially using a LDR afterloading technique with caesium-137 pellet sources. We use two levels of boost dose: 14 Gy or 20 Gy. The indications for the 20 Gy boost dose are: **[1]** Incomplete surgical resection and **[2]** Extensive intraductal component (EIC). Also, we prefer to deliver the 20 Gy boost dose using LDR interstitial brachytherapy. This is because the interstitial technique delivers a high localised dose to the former tumour volume and enables a relative sparing of the surrounding normal tissues. These factors provide for the probability of a better cosmetic outcome when compared to what can be expected using external beam techniques. The contraindications for a breast implant are given in Table 1.

Table 1
Contraindications for a breast implantation boost.

- The breast is too small and therefore not suitable for an implant.
- Surgical clips (left in situ during surgery to outline the former tumour volume) are found to be close to the chest wall.
- The former tumour volume (plus tumour free margin) cannot be encompassed in a two-plane or three-plane volume implant.

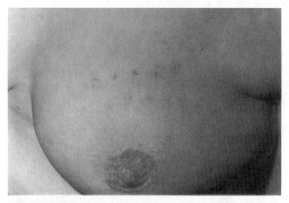

Figure 1. Marked skin reaction around the needle points as late sequelae of a breast implant.

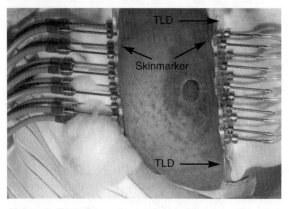

Figure 2. Typical two-plane implant using templates and stainless steel needles. The skin marker buttons and TLD placement can be seen.

As one of the aims of BCT is to preserve a good cosmesis, the skin dose delivered by the boost treatment should be kept reasonably low. This means with an interstitial technique that the skin dose should be kept below 20 Gy: otherwise scars occur on the skin surface round the needle entry and exit points, Figure 1.

To determine more precisely the skin dose in breast implants we placed specially developed skin markers at the entrance and exit skin openings over the implant needles. The markers were reconstructed from the isocentric stereo radiographs of the implant and the skin dose was calculated. In addition the calculated skin dose was verified by TLD measurements.

Material & Methods

The skin dose was calculated for 23 patients who were implanted in the breast either under local or general anaesthesia. Local anaesthesia of the skin was applied by means of a field block with lidocaine/epinephrine. A two-plane implant was performed using two templates and 7-9 stainless steel needles, Figure 2.

Special skin marker buttons were developed so that we could calculate the dose to a marker from the isocentric stereo radiographs. These marker buttons are placed over the needles at the surface of the skin and are under the templates, Figure 2. The templates and needles are fixed to each other by very small screws. The distance between the needle entrance and exit openings in the skin can then be measured using calipers.

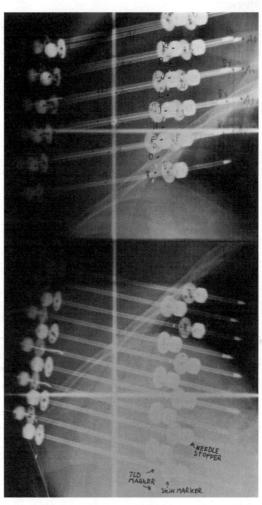

As the implant is performed after the breast conservation surgery and tumour marker clips are not always placed by the surgeon, it is often difficult to define the exact target volume. We therefore find it necessary to start the active length of the sources at 7.5 mm from the skin entrance/exit openings and we have available a set of caesium-137 pellets with defined active lengths between 55 mm and 105 mm so that all eventualities can be accomodated. Although the use of the 55 mm sources is restricted to a maximum of four.

After isocentric stereo radiographs are taken, Figure 3, the reference dose rate is calculated according to the Paris

Figure 3. Isocentric stereo radiograph of an implant. The skin markers and TLD are indicated.

system and from the same radiographs the dose per skin button is calculated. When the skin dose exceeds 20 Gy the needle is re-positioned to correct this dose. Finally, the patient is connected to the microSelectron-LDR/MDR and the treatment is started.

As the uncertainty of the skin dose calculations will be critical especially at the cranial border of the breast (the larger gap between the template and the breast tissue allows more movement of the button) the calculations were verified by TLD measurements.

Results

The active length of the applied sources used were in the range 55-105 mm, Table 2, and a total of 422 points was used to calculate a mean skin dose per patient of 9.5 Gy: range 5.5-17.0 Gy. The mean skin dose per active source length was 9.8 Gy: range 9.0-10.5 Gy. (Originally, the calculated skin doses were on average 15% low at the medial side and 15% high at the lateral side when compared to the results of the TLD measurements. We determined the source of this error and the skin dose calculations were corrected accordingly).

Table 2
Distribution of active source lengths.

Length (mm)	Frequency of use
55	55
65	75
75	57
85	34
95	38
105	8

For needles giving rise to skin doses higher than 15 Gy (42 points) the entrance dose is plotted versus the exit dose, Figure 4, and those needles can be determined for which it was possible to correct the skin dose by pushing or pulling the needle: points in Figure 4 which lie close to the ordinate or abscissa axes.

Furthermore a region can be determined (this is to the right of the line Q in Figure 4) for needles giving rise to a high skin dose at both the entrance and exit points. This latter region consists of a total of 21 points dominated by the small active source lengths: 6/21 points have an active length of 55 mm and 10/21 points an active length of 65 mm.

Repositioning of these needles will not help to reduce the skin dose and therefore the only solution is the use of shorter active source lengths. Although the numbers of these patients are small, it is possible that the use of more 55 mm and even of 45 mm active length sources will result in lower skin doses, thus improving the cosmetic outcome of this BCT brachytherapy boost technique.

Discussion

Our mean measured skin dose per patient of 9.5 Gy (range 5-17 Gy) is in accordance with the data of Habibollahi et al (1988) who found a mean skin

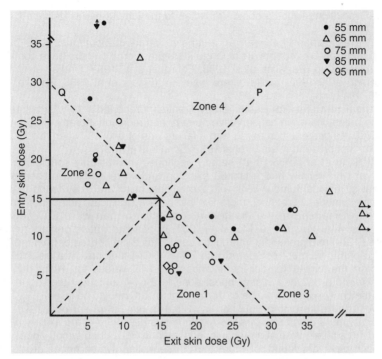

Figure 4. Entrance skin dose versus exit skin dose. Points to the left of the line Q can be lowered by repositioning. Points to the right of line Q can be lowered by using a shorter active length for the source.

dose due to a 20 Gy iridium-192 boost implant of 8.7 ± 2.2 Gy in the upper half of the breast and 9.9 ± 2.6 Gy in the lower half of the breast. They found unfavourable cosmetic results predominantly in the lower half of the breast (the mean dose of the unfavourable group was 10 ± 3 Gy), although no relationship was demonstrated between skin dose and the final cosmetic result after 3-5 years follow-up.

The follow-up for our series of patients is still too short to be able to evaluate the cosmetic outcome. As only 21/442 points received a dose higher than 15 Gy without the possibility of repositioning the needle we do not expect any serious skin problems. However, we have adjusted our caesium-137 source assembly stock which now contains active lengths in the range 35-95 mm: with six sources of each length.

The question can be posed: *"What about our indications for a higher (20 Gy) boost dose?"* No doubt exists in the literature about the need for a higher boost dose if a microscopically positive margin of invasive tumour is present, Kurtz et al (1990). Previously, re-resection was always advised and certainly for macroscopic residual disease this is still obligatory (Recht et al 1986) but for microscopic positive margins it is no longer strongly advised: provided that postoperative irradiation including boost irradiation to the tumour bed is delivered, Kurtz et al (1990).

The association between an extensive intraductal component (EIC) and local recurrence is controversial in the literature. Some authors have confirmed the relationship (Bartelink et al 1988, Fourquet et al 1989, Lindley et al 1989, Paterson et al 1992), while others have not (Fisher et al 1986, Spitalier et al 1986, van Limbergen et al 1987).

The Joint Center for Radiotherapy Treatment reported a 10-year failure rate in the breast following conservative surgery and radiation therapy of 35% when an EIC was present, compared with a failure rate of only 8% when this EIC factor was not present, (Osteen et al 1987, Schnitt et al 1987).

Holland et al (1985,1990) serially sectioned mastectomy specimens from woman who initially had a limited excision and correlated the presence and extent of residual tumour cells with the original histology. They found that EIC positive tumours were much more likely to have a significant amount of residual tumour remaining in the mastectomy specimen than were EIC negative tumours: 44% *versus* 3%. Moreover, 33% of patients whose primary tumours were EIC(+) had prominent intraductal carcinoma 2 cm or greater from the edge of the primary tumour compared with 2% of EIC(-) tumours. At a distance of 4 cm from the original tumour the findings were 14% versus 1%, Holland (1990). We therefore deliver a higher boost dose to EIC(+) tumours, keeping in mind that the chosen target volume of the implant for EIC should be large.

A furthur interesting question is *"What is our treatment policy when for example more than three positive lymph nodes are found in the axillary dissection? "* A six-field irradiation technique is used in BCT when lymph nodes fixed to each other are found, or more than three axillary lymph nodes are tumour positive and/or the apex of the axilla is positive for tumour metastases. This technique consists of two tangential wedge fields encompassing the whole breast, an internal mammary chain field and a modified McWhirter (1955) field.

It is essential that all fields correctly match geometrically in order to avoid dose inhomogeneities and thus local recurrences or severe fibrosis at the match lines. Our Utrecht technique was therefore developed using combined beam angulation and asymmetrical collimator matching techniques, Lagendijk & Hofman (1992). The dose prescribed in the midline of the axilla as well as at 3 cm from the skin for the supraclavicular part is 20 x 235 cGy, using four fractions per week with photon beams from 6-10 MV linear accelerators. No boost is delivered to the lumpectomy area when the resection of the primary is complete and the apex of the axilla is tumour positive. This is because the prognosis of these patients is determined far more by the axillary staging. Furthermore, these patients are treated pending their hormonal status with either chemotherapy [CMF(Cyclophosphamide, Methotrexate, 5-Fluorouracil) or FEC(5-Fluorouracil, Epi-doxorubicin, Cyclophosphamide)] or Tamoxifen. If the axilla or the breast is macroscopically not free from tumour a boost dose is delivered to that area of 5-7 x 200 cGy given by five fractions per week.

Conclusions

Skin dose measurements in implanted breasts revealed a mean dose of 9.5 Gy. Out of a total of 442 measured points 42 points received a higher dose than 15 Gy. For 21/42 needles this dose could be lowered by re-positioning the needle. For the other 21/42 points the dose could only be lowered by adjusting the active source length. Therefore it is mandatory to have a well balanced array of source lengths in the caesium-137 microSelectron-LDR/MDR afterloading set to ensure a good cosmetic outcome in breast conserving therapy.

References

Bartelink H, Borger JH, van Dongen JA et al, *The impact of tumour size and histology on local control after breast-conserving therapy*, Radiotherapy & Oncology, **11**, 297-303, 1988.

Fisher ER, Sass R, Fisher B et al, *Pathologic findings from the National Surgical Adjuvant Breast Project (protocol 6): II relation of local breast recurrence to multicentricity* , Cancer, **57**, 1717-1724, 1986.

Fourquet A, Campana F, Zafrani B et al, *Prognostic factors of breast recurrence in the conservative management of early breast cancer: a 25-year follow-up*, Int. J. Radiation Oncology Biology & Physics, **17**, 719-725, 1989.

Habibollahi F, Mayles HM, Mayles WP et al, *Assessment of skin dose and its relation to cosmesis in the conservative treatment of early breast cancer*, Int. J. Radiation Oncology Biology & Physics, **14**, 291-296, 1988.

Holland R, Velig SHJ, Mravunac M & Hendriks JHCL, *Histologic multifocality of Tis, T1-2 breast carcinomas*, Cancer, **56**, 979-990, 1985.

Holland R, Connolly JL, Gelman R et al, *The presence of an extensive intraductal component following a limited excision correlates with prominent residual disease in the remainder of the breast*, Journal of Clinical Oncology, **8**, 113-118, 1990.

Kurtz JM, Jacquemier J, Amalric R et al, *Risk factors for breast recurrence in premenopausal and postmenopausal patients with ductal cancers treated by conservation therapy*, Cancer, **65**, 1867-1878, 1990.

Lagendijk JJW & Hofman P, *A standardized multifield irradiation technique for breast tumours using asymmetrical collimators and beam angulation*, Brit. J. Radiology, **65**, 56-62, 1992.

van Limbergen E, van den Bogaert W, van der Schueren E et al, *Tumour excision and radiotherapy as primary treatment of breast cancer: Analysis of patient and treatment parameters and local control*, Radiotherapy & Oncology, **8**, 1-9, 1987.

Lindley R, Bulman A, Parsons P et al, *Histologic features predictive of an increased risk of early local recurrence after treatment of breast cancer by local tumour excision and radical radiotherapy*, Surgery, **105**, 13-20, 1989.

McWhirter R, *Simple mastectomy and radiotherapy in treatment of breast cancer*, Brit. J. Radiology, **28**; 128, 1955.

Osteen RT, Connolly JL, Recht A et al, *Identification of patient at high risk for local recurrence after conservative surgery and radiation therapy for stage I or II breast cancer*, Archives Surgery, **122**, 1248-1252, 1987.

Paterson DA, Anderson TJ, Jack WJL et al, *Pathological features predictive of local recurrence after management by conservation of invasive breast cancer: importance of non-invasive carcinoma*, Radiotherapy & Oncology, **25**, 176-180, 1992.

Recht A, Connolly JL, Schnitt SJ et al, *Conservative surgery radiation therapy for early breast cancer: results, controversies and unsolved problems*, Seminars Oncology, **13**, 434-449, 1986.

Schnitt SJ, Connolly JL, Khettry U et al, *Pathologic findings on re-excision of the primary site in breast cancer patients considered for treatment by primary radiation therapy*, Cancer, **59**, 675-681, 1987.

Spitalier JM, Gambarelli J, Brandone H et al, *Breast conserving surgery with radiation therapy for operable mammary carcinoma: A 25-year experience*, World J. Surgery, **10**, 1014-1020, 1986.

26

Pulsed LDR Brachytherapy: Current Clinical Status

J.J. Mazeron, G. Boisserie, N. Gokarn & F. Baillet

Centre des Tumeurs,
Groupe Hospitalier Pitié-Salpêtrière,
47, Boulevard de l'Hôpital,
75013 Paris,
France.

Radiobiological Aspects of PDR Brachytherapy

In principle, an increase in dose rate would lead to an increase in cell kill, (Hall 1972). This effect should be greater for late reacting normal tissues than for tumour cells, otherwise a loss of therapeutic ratio would result whenever the dose rate is increased. As each pulse delivers a small dose and is followed by an interval which allows some repair, the increase in radiobiological effect should be small, (Fowler & Mount 1992). The main question is whether or not the increased effect is greater on late responding normal tissues than on tumour cell kill.

To reproduce the biological effects of LDR brachytherapy using PDR remote afterloading, Brenner & Hall (1991) and Fowler & Mount (1992) give the following four recommendations.

[1] Same total dose.
[2] Same dose rate: typically about 0.5 Gy/hour.
[3] Pulse length of 10 minutes or more
    (or a dose rate not exceeding 3 Gy/h during the pulse)
[4] Pulse repeated each hour: typically 0.5 Gy.

If these conditions are met, the biological effects of PDR radiation therapy should be equivalent to those of LDR radiation therapy for all tissues. These conclusions were made from calculations taking into account both cell repair

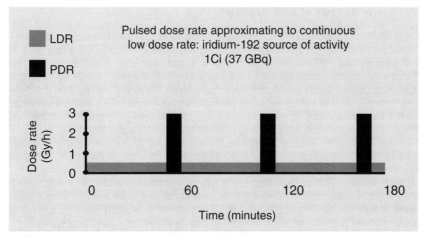

Figure 1. Illustration of the principle of pulsed brachytherapy. A continuous low dose rate of 0.5 Gy/h is replaced by a pulse of 0.5 Gy delivered in 10 minutes. As the single iridium-192 source decays with a half-life of 74 days, the pulse length is adjusted to maintain the dose per pulse to be precisely 0.5 Gy. Thus, the average dose rate is maintained and the overall treatment time for a given total dose remains fixed.

capacity estimated by α/β and the kinetics of repair estimated by $T_{1/2}$, for both tumours and late reacting normal tissues. The values of α/β for tumours and late reactions in human normal tissues have been estimated and are consistent with laboratory results using experimental animals, (Thames et al 1990). By contrast, because of a lack of clinical data, $T_{1/2}$ has been estimated from experimental data, (Turesson & Thames 1989, Thames et al 1990).

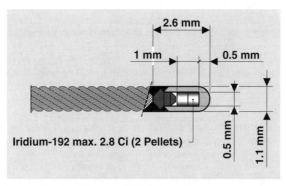

Figure 2. microSelectron-PDR iridium-192 stepping source.

Technical Aspects of PDR Brachytherapy

The microSelectron-PDR is a new generation low dose rate remote after-loading system which operates on a pulsed brachytherapy principle, Figure 1. It uses an iridium-192 stepping source of 1.1 mm diameter and 2.6 mm length, Figure 2. Source positions can be programmed in a maximum of 48 different locations within each of 18 different catheters. Treatment times can be pro-grammed from 0 to 999.9 seconds per position per pulse. The stepping source with its variable dwell time enables the isodoses to be optimised for individual patients, using what is effectively an infinitely variable source strength.

The single radioactive stepping source moves through all the implanted catheters during each pulse. A typical pulse length is 10 minutes per hour increasing to approximately 30 minutes three months later as the iridium-192 source decays. The pulsed treatment typically finishes exactly on the hour, so that nursing staff will know when they can enter the room without interrupting the irradiation.The microSelectron-PDR afterloading system has the following advantages (Table 1) when compared to previous systems, see also Table 2.

Table 1
Advantages of the microSelectron-PDR.

- Full radiation protection.
- No source preparation.
- No source inventory.
- Optimisation of the dose rate distribution.
- Only one source to replace every three months.
- All brachytherapy feasible with one machine:
    intracavitary, interstitial, intraoperative & intralumenal.

Table 2
Comparison of the microSelectron-PDR afterloading system with other systems.

Requirement	Manual afterloading	LDR remote afterloading system	PDR remote afterloading system
Primary storage room	Yes	Yes	No
Source inventory	Yes (for multiple sources, several times a week)	Yes (for multiple sources,several times a week)	No
Source calibration	Yes (for multiple sources, once a month)	Yes (for multiple sources,once a month)	For one source, four times a year
Source preparation	Yes (for multiple sources, for each treatment)	Yes (for multiple sources, for each treatment)	No
Source transportation	Yes	Yes	No
Secondary storage room	Yes	Yes	No
Shielded treatment room	Yes	Yes	Yes
Manual loading of sources	Yes	No	No
Manual removal of sources	Yes	No	No

The microSelectron-PDR has been designed for use with a 1 Ci iridium-192 source. This relatively high activity may require modifications for shielding in some of the existing brachytherapy rooms, which are currently suitable for LDR treatments. On the other hand, however, calculations made in the Hôpital Pitié-Salpêtrière showed that an elementary source with an activity of 0.25 Ci or less should be adequate for PDR treatments, even for the largest implants, if the dose rate required is 0.9 Gy/h or less, Table 3.

Table 3
Percentage of our patient series of 316 cases for whom PDR treatment meets the previously described conditions.

Source stock		Dose/pulse	Percentage of cases by tumour site		
No.	Activity (Ci)	(Gy)	Breast	Head & neck	Uterus
1	0.25	0.9	93		
1	0.25	0.6	84		
1	0.25	0.6-0.9	100		
1	0.107	0.9	59		
1	0.107	0.6	88		
1	0.107	0.6-0.9	88		
2	0.25 & 0.107	0.9	97		
2	0.25 & 0.107	0.6	100		
2	0.25 & 0.107	0.6-0.9	100		
1	0.107	0 4		79	55
1	0.045	0.4		96	88
2	0.107 & 0.045	0.4		100	100

Source Strength Study

In our attempt to determine what is the most convenient strength for the stepping source we reviewed the charts of the last 316 consecutive patients treated in the Hôpital Pitie-Salpêtrière by LDR irradiation for adenocarcinoma of the breast (177/316), squamous cell carcinoma in the head and neck region (42/316) and endometrial carcinoma (97/316). These estimates were made for three iridium-192 source strengths (0.25 Ci, 0.107 Ci which is the activity of a 0.25 Ci iridium-192 source after three months, and 0.045 Ci which is the activity of the same source after six months) and we made the following six assumptions.

[1] The geometry of the implant is not modified.
[2] The total dose on the 85% reference isodose is the same for both LDR and PDR treatments.
[3] Pulses are repeated each hour with a lower limit of some 10 minutes.
[4] 0.4 Gy pulses are delivered for endometrial carcinoma and cancers of the head & neck and pulses in the range from 0.6 Gy to 0.9 Gy for adenocarcinoma of the breast. This is according to conclusions in the recent literature on the effects of dose rates in LDR brachytherapy.
[5] Dwell positions are spaced by 0.5 cm.
[6] Dwell times are identical for a given PDR treatment and consequently treatments are not optimised.

We used the following formula:

$$10 \leq 60 . S . N . (K/K1) . (D/D1) \leq 60$$

where S is the spacing in cm between dwell positions, N is the total number of dwell positions, K is the linear reference kerma rate for iridium-192 wires [LDR treatments], K1 is the reference kerma rate for the iridium-192 stepping source [LDR treatments], D is the dose rate on the reference isodose [LDR treatments] in Gy/hour and D1 is the dose rate on the reference isodose (or dose per pulse, assuming that pulses are repeated each hour) [PDR treatments] in Gy/hour.

Table 3 shows the percentage of patients for whom PDR treatment meets these conditions (pulse duration 10-60 minutes) according to the tumour site, dose per pulse and activity of stepping source. It was from this data that we concluded that [1] the initial activity of the stepping source should be 0.25 Ci and [2] several stepping sources of different strengths should be kept in stock so that the dose rate can be optimised. In practice, a stepping source of 0.25 Ci should be ordered from the manufacturer every three months and retained for nine months in order to have at any time a choice of three stock activities.

Clinical Aspects of PDR Brachytherapy

When compared to existing LDR remote afterloading systems the microSelectron-PDR has two major advantages: only one source to be ordered every three months and the dose rate may be adjusted and the dose distribution optimised.

Dose rate has been shown to have a significant effect on survival of cells irradiated *in vitro* (Hall & Bedford 1964, Hall 1972). One randomised trial (Gerbaulet et al 1991) and two retrospective studies (Mazeron et al 1991a,b) have shown recently that in LDR brachytherapy, dose rate may have a statistically significant effect on tumour control and/or the probability of late side effects. With PDR remote afterloading systems for a given source strength, dose rate may be adjusted by modifying dwell times and/or pulse intervals. However, according to radiobiological recommendations cited above, to obtain a given mean dose rate it is preferable in most cases to repeat pulses each hour and to adjust for dwell times. Furthermore, if after the initiation of the treatment, the irradiation has to be delayed for a short period of time, dose rate corrections may be made to achieve the PDR irradiation in the planned overall treatment time.

In brachytherapy, dose distribution optimisation may be required in two practicular situations.

[1] With the PDR remote afterloading system a non-uniform dose pattern due to geometrical imperfections in the actual implant may be corrected by adjusting dwell times, Figures 3-6.

[2] A reference isodose may be shaped to treat an unusual tumour geometry. Isodose volumes can then be created flexibly by a combination of careful placement of the catheters and an adjustment of dwell times. On the other hand, dose distribution optimisation may lead to an increase in hyperdose sleeves (or else in volumes receiving a dose at least twice that of the reference dose) and

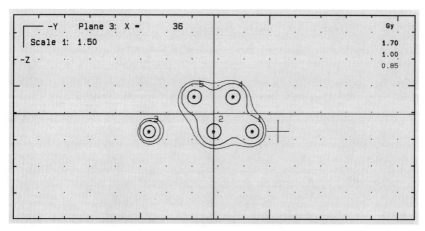

Figure 3. In this theoretical implant of five lines, the position of line 3 is not optimal. Isodose curves have been drawn following the rules of the Paris system and we can see a cold spot between lines 2,3 and 4. Inner isodose is 170%, central isodose is 100% and outer isodose is 85%.

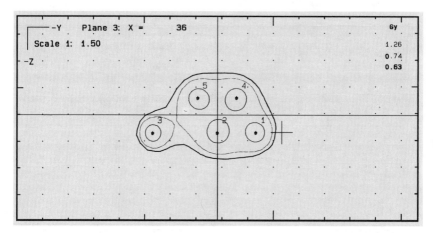

Figure 4. This is the same implant as in Figure 3. Isodose curves have been drawn following the rules of the Paris system but by choosing a reference isodose rate equal to 85 % of the minimal basal dose rate instead of 85 % of the mean basal dose rate (the overall treatment time is then longer than in **Figure 3**), we can see a hot spot between lines 1,2,4 and 5. Inner isodose is 170%, central isodose is 100% and outer isodose is 85%.

then to a decrease in both tumour control and late reacting normal tissue tolerance. Recent analysis of results obtained in Henri Mondor Hospital with LDR treatments of stage T1-2 of mobile tongue and floor of mouth showed that 15-20 mm intersource spacings may be associated with a lower local control and higher necrosis rate than 10-14 mm spacings, (Simon et al 1993).

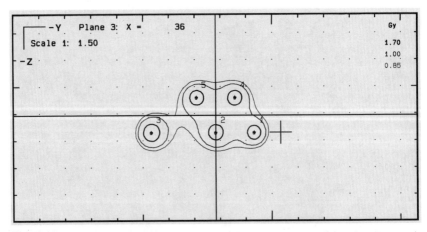

Figure 5. This is the same implant as in **Figure 3**. The distribution of dose has been opti-mised by increasing dwell times in line 3 (dwell times in line 3 have been multiplied by 1.5 and the overall treatment time is then the same as in **Figure 3**), homogeneity of the dose distribution in the target volume is acceptable. Inner isodose is 170%, central isodose is 100% and outer isodose is 85%.

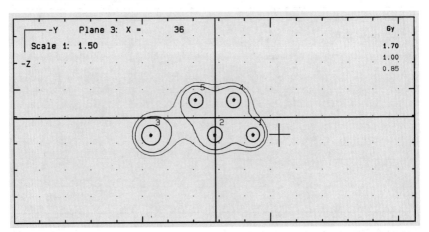

Figure 6. This is the same implant as in **Figure 3**. The distribution of dose has been opti-mised by increasing dwell times in line 3 (dwell times in line 3 have been multiplied by 1.8 and the overall treatment time is then the same as in **Figure 3**), homogeneity of the dose distribution in the target volume is satisfactory. Inner isodose is 170%, central isodose is 100% and outer isodose is 85%.

Conclusions

The microSelectron-PDR enables equivalent continuous low dose rate treatments to be given with all the advantages of a stepping source. The feasibility of clinical studies are just beginning. At the time writing (1992) about 20 patients have already been treated by PDR irradiation in phase I-II studies. No abnormal reaction of early reacting tissues have been reported. No information is available on either tumour control or late reacting tissue tolerance. Some animal experiments are concurrently being undertaken by Armour et al (1991). More data with sufficient follow-up are needed to observe late effects in both experimental and clinical trials. However, from a simple radiobiological point of view PDR Brachytherapy could be a potentially useful modality.

References

Armour E, Wang Z, Corry P & Martinez A, *Equivalence of continuous and pulse simulated low dose rate irradiation in 9L gliosarcoma cell at 37° and 41°C*, Int. J. Radiation Oncology Biology & Physics, **22**, 109-114, 1991.

Brenner DJ & Hall EJ, *Conditions for the equivalence of continuous to pulsed dose rate brachytherapy*, Int. J. Radiation Oncology Biology & Physics, **20**, 180-190, 1991.

Fowler JF & Mount M, *Pulsed brachytherapy: the conditions for no significant loss of therapeutic ratio compared with traditional low dose rate brachytherapy*, Int. J. Radiation Oncology Biology & Physics, **23**, 661-669, 1992.

Gerbaulet A, Haie-Meder C, Lambin P, Kramar A, Delapierre M, Scalliet P, Michel G, Prade M, L'Homme C & Chassagne D, *Etude randomisée comparant deux débits de dose en curiethérapie préopératoire des cancers utérins (311 cas)*, Bulletin Cancer Radiotherapy, **78**, 484-485, 1991.

Hall EJ & Bedford JS, *Dose rate: its effect on the survival of Hela cells irradiated with gamma rays*, Radiation Research, **22**, 305-315, 1964.

Hall EJ, *Radiation dose rate: a factor of importance in radiobiology and radiotherapy*, Brit. J. Radiology, **45**, 81-97, 1972.

Mazeron JJ, Simon JM, Crook JM, Calitchi E, Otmezguine Y, Le Bourgeois JP & Pierquin B, *Influence of dose rate on local control of breast carcinoma treated by external beam irradiation plus iridium-192 implant*, Int. J. Radiation Oncology Biology Physics, **21**, 1173-1177, 1991a.

Mazeron JJ, Simon JM, Le Péchoux C, Crook JM, Grimard L, Piedbois P, Le Bourgeois JP & Pierquin B, *Effect of dose rate on local control and complications in definitive irradiation of T1-2 squamous cell carcinomas of mobile tongue and floor of mouth with interstitial iridium-192*, Radiotherapy & Oncology, **21**, 39-47, 1991b.

Simon JM, Mazeron JJ, Pohar S, Le Péchoux C, Crook JM, Grimard L, Piedbois P, Le Bourgeois JP & Pierquin B, *Effect of intersource spacing on local control and complications in brachytherapy of mobile tongue and floor of mouth*, Radiotherapy & Oncology, **26**, 17-26, 1993.

Thames HD, Bentzen SM, Tureson I, Overgaard M & van den Bogaert W, *Time factors in radiotherapy: a review of human data*, Radiotherapy & Oncology, **19**, 219-235, 1990.

Turesson I & Thames HD, *Repair capacity and kinetics of human skin during fractionated radiotherapy: erythema, desquamation, and telangiectasia after 3 and 5 years follow-up*, Radiotherapy & Oncology, **15**, 169-188, 1989.

27

Pulsed Low Dose Rate Interstitial and Intracavitary Therapy The Clinical Experience at UCSF

P.S. Swift, K.K. Fu, T.L. Phillips, L.W. Roberts &
K.A. Weaver

University of San Francisco California,
Department of Radiation Oncology,
San Francisco,
CA 94143,
USA.

Introduction

The remote afterloading pulsed low dose rate microSelectron was developed to combine the radiobiological benefits of standard continuous low dose rate brachytherapy with the isodose optimisation and radiation safety features of the high dose rate remote afterloading units. Cell line studies of the biological equivalence of pulsed and continuous low dose rate regimens suggest that the pulsed treatment can safely be administered in the clinical setting as long as the dose administered per pulse is kept below 100 cGy and interval between pulses is less than 3-4 hours. (Brenner & Hall 1991, Fowler & Mount 1992, Hall & Brenner 1991, 1992). A clinical protocol was therefore established at UCSF to evaluate the relative acute toxicity of pulsed low dose rate brachytherapy.

Materials & Methods

All patients who are considered appropriate clinical candidates for standard afterloading brachytherapy procedures utilising caesium-137 or iridium-192 in a continuous low dose rate fashion regardless of site, histology, or prior radiation are eligible for this study. The brachytherapy portion of treatment was carried out using the pulsed low dose rate microSelectron with an initial source strength of 1.0 Curie iridium-192. The source was replaced at three month intervals (minimum strength 0.3 Curie). Isodose distributions were calculated using the UCSF developed brachytherapy software programme. The isodose line encompassing the target volume was selected by the attending physician as was the total brachytherapy dose delivered. When possible, treatment volume dose rates of between 40-80 cGy per hour were selected to approximate rates standardly used in continuous low dose rate procedures. A pulse was administered every hour in a 24 hour period until the prescribed dose was delivered.

For the purpose of this study, acute grade III or IV toxicities, defined as those toxicities requiring medical or surgical intervention, were recorded. Patients were seen in follow-up on a schedule that included visits at 1-2 weeks after the initial procedure, monthly afterwards to three months, then 2-3 months for the following year. Delayed toxicities and response were recorded at each follow-up.

Table 1
Treatment site distribution.

Site	No. of Cases
Cervix	23
Uterus	6
Vagina	3
Tongue	3
Oesophagus	2
Sarcoma	2
Rectum	2
Breast	1
Neck node	1
Nasopharynx	1

Results

Between 16 February 1992 and 22 September 1993, a total of 46 brachytherapy procedures were carried out in 44 patients using the pulsed low dose rate microSelectron at UCSF. Sites of disease are listed in Table 1, with a preponderance of gynaecological sites noted. 20 intracavitary procedures were performed as well as 17 perineal interstitial templates, seven interstitial catheters in other sites and two intralumenal placements for oesophageal malignancies. 33 patients had brachytherapy as a portion of their treatment for primary disease, and 11 for recurrent disease. 6/44 patients had received prior radiation to the implanted area. Six patients received concomitant chemotherapy, four concurrent hyperthermia, and five proceeded to post-radiation surgery as part of their planned course of treatment.

A total of 38 treatments were carried out using the desired dose rate of 40-80 cGy/hour (Table 2). In an additional eight treatments (Table 3), higher dose rates were deemed clinically appropriate: three vaginal ovoids for postoperative uterine carcinomas, one nasopharyngeal insertion, one oesophageal intralumenal placement, one perineal template and one tandem and ovoid insertion were treated at a more rapid dose rate due to advanced age of the patients in an attempt to minimise duration of hospital stay, one catheter placement for recurrent rectal cancer was treated with an accelerated rate due to time delays associated with technical difficulties.

Table 2
Dose rate distribution range: 45-130 cGy/hr.

Dose Rate (cGy/hour)	No. of Cases
40-80	38
80-100	5
>100	3

Table 3
Data for eight patients treated using
dose rates > 80 cGy/hr

Site	Stage	Procedure	PDR dose rate (cGy/hr)	PDR duration (hr)
Uterus	IIIa	Ovoids	100	15
Uterus	IVb	Ovoids	100	15
Rectum	Rec.	Catheters	83	24
Vagina	Rec.	Template	85	47
Cervix	T1aN1	Insertion	87	35
Uterus	Ib	Ovoids	125	48
Nasopharynx	T1N1	Intralumenal	130	4
Oesophagus	T3N0	Intralumenal	119	16

Total radiation doses ranged from 4000 to 10,000 cGy, with the brachytherapy doses to the prescribed region ranging from 500 to 6000 cGy. Status at last follow-up (mean follow-up of 11 months) was as follows: 29 with no evidence of disease, four dead with disease, eight alive with disease, four under treatment, one lost to follow-up.

4/44 acute or subacute complications requiring therapeutic intervention occurred (Table 4). In two of these cases, patients had received prior radiation.

The first was a woman with a vaginal recurrence of rectal cancer, developed a superficial skin infection requiring a prolonged course of oral antibiotics. Her combined total dose of radiation was 8630 cGy (4680 cGy with external beam in 1983 and 4000 cGy with brachytherapy in 1992).

The second, a patient with recurrent rectal cancer who had received a total dose of 8100 cGy (3600 cGy with external beam and 4500 cGy with brachytherapy) in conjunction with three separate abdominal pelvic surgical procedures, developed a partial small bowel obstruction requiring placement of an NG tube for relief. The patient was discharged after one week without further surgery, but died within one month with wide spread intraperitoneal and distant disease.

The third patient developed severe perineal pain which required oral narcotic therapy for six months, strating approximately one day after removal of the perineal template for stage II-B cervix cancer with markedly distorted anatomy. Her total dose was 7500.

The final case was a 78 year old female with stage II-B uterine adenocarcinoma receiving preoperative radiotherapy. During the night, she became markedly confused and removed her intrauterine instrument manually between pulses. She developed no significant sequela from the action.

Table 4
Patient data on acute complications requiring therapeutic intervention.

Site	Stage	Procedure	PDR dose rate (cGy/hr)	PDR dose (cGy)	Complication
Vagina	*Recurrence	Implant	80	4,500	Superficial skin infection requiring prolonged p.o. antibiotics
Rectum	*Recurrence	Implant	52	4,500	Partial SBO conservatively treated
Cervix	IIb	Implant	69	3,600	Perineal pain syndrome requiring narcotics
Uterus	IIb	Insertion	70	910	Patient confusion: patient removed applicator during night with no injury

*Patients with a history of prior irradiation at initial presentation

Four cases of delayed complications have been recorded (Table 5). One patient with oesophageal cancer developed stenosis after intralumenal brachytherapy, requiring repeat dilations and delayed oesophagetomy. At final pathology, a 3 cm ulcer was found with recurrent disease present within the ulcer. One case of soft tissue radionecrosis developed after an interstitial template and external beam therapy for squamous cell carcinoma of the oral tongue. The patient with perineal pain syndrome was previously described in the acute complications section. One patient with a recurrent extremity sarcoma developed delayed wound infection requiring oral antibiotics and aggressive skin care without grafting after a total dose of 10,000 cGy (4000 cGy from the current implant and 6000 cGy by external beam delivered three years previously).

Table 5
Cases of delayed complications.

Site	Stage	Procedure	PDR dose rate (cGy/hr)	PDR dose (cGy)	Total dose (cGy)	Complication
Oesophagus	T3N0	Intralumenal	50	2,000	7,000	Stenosis requiring two dilations, 3 cm. ulcer found to be recurrence at oesophagectomy
Tongue	T3N0	Catheters	50	2,500	7,540	2 mm. ulcer, soft tissue necrosis
Cervix	IIb	Implant	69	3,600	7,500	Perineal pain syndrome requiring narcotics
Sarcoma	Rec	Catheters	70	4,000	10,000*	Wound infection at one month with pronounced radiation erythema p.o. antibiotics and domeboro treatments

*Prior irradiation: 6000 cGy delivered three years before implant

Discussion

In our initial clinical study, there does not appear to be any significant increase in acute toxicity associated with the pulsed approach when compared with the standard continuous low dose rate approach previously used at our institution. It is essential to point out, however, that this is true under the conditions outlined, namely, hourly pulses of 40 cGy-100 cGy. Extrapolation of these conclusions to higher dose rates or to longer intervals cannot safely be made as indicated by radiobiologic data (Brenner & Hall 1991, Fowler & Mount 1992, Hall & Brenner 1991,1992). Further trials will need to be carried out to determine if more rapid dose rates are capable of providing comparable therapeutic ratios.

Pulsed low dose rate brachytherapy, using pulsed low dose rate microSelectron, offers the increased therapeutic ratio of low dose rate over high dose rate brachytherapy, combined with the optimisation advantage of the variable source dwell time programme. In addition, the relatively brief pulse duration ensures that sufficient time remains during the remainder of the hour for adequate nursing and medical attention to the patient with no radiation exposure to the medical staff.

References

Brenner DJ & Hall EJ, *Conditions for the equivalence of continuous to pulsed low dose rate brachytherapy*, Int. J. Radiation Oncology Biology & Physics, **20**, 181-190, 1990.

Fowler J & Mount M, *Pulsed brachytherapy: the conditions for no significant loss of therapeutic ratio compared with traditional low dose rate brachytherapy*, Int. J. Radiation Oncology Biology & Physics, **23**, 661-669, 1992.

Hall EJ & Brenner DJ, *The dose-rate effect revisited: radiobiological considerations of importance in radiotherapy*, Int. J. Radiation Oncology Biology & Physics, **21**, 1403-1414, 1992.

Hall EJ & Brenner DJ, *The dose-rate effect in interstitial brachytherapy: a controversy resolved, Brit. J. Radiology*, **65**, 242-247, 1992.

28

Continuous versus Pulsed LDR: Preliminary Analysis of Rat Rectal Toxicity

A. Martinez[1], J. White[1], E. Armour[1], A.R. Armin[2],
G. Edmundson[1] & P. Corry[1]

William Beaumont Hospital,
[1]Radiation Oncology Department,
[2]Anatomic Department,
3601 W. 13 Mile Road,
Royal Oak,
MI 48073-6769,
USA.

Introduction

A recent advance in the technology available for administering interstitial or intracavitary continuous low dose rate brachytherapy (CLDR) holds the potential for greatly improving this cancer treatment modality. The new method utilises a single radioactive source which is scanned throughout a treatment volume. As a result, individual cells are irradiated with discrete high dose rate pulses separated by intervals of time. This is in contrast to the traditional method where cells are irradiated continuously at a low dose rate. Although several technical advantages are gained with this new methodology, increased normal tissue toxicity could conceivably result because irradiation is applied in discrete pulses.

The current method of CLDR delivery uses many radioactive sources placed into catheters which have been surgically positioned into a tumour or an involved cavity (eg. cervix, vagina, uterus, rectum). These sources are left in place continuously in a fixed position until a prescribed total dose is delivered. The radioactive sources can be placed into the catheters that are in the tumour or cavity either manually or by a mechanical remote control afterloading apparatus. The result is that cells receive continuous irradiation at a low dose rate (0.3-0.9 Gy/h) over a period of time extending up to 80 hours or more.

The new method, which we will refer to as *pulse low dose rate irradiation* (PLDR), utilises catheters surgically placed into a tumour or involved cavity in a manner identical to the traditional CLDR method. In PLDR, a single radioactive source is used to irradiate the treatment volume in discrete pulses. At specific time intervals, the radioactive source is transported into each of the implanted catheters sequentially. During the irradiation period, the radioactive source is moved from position to position within the catheters until the treatment volume has received a predetermined fraction of the total radiation dose. This pulsing period is of the order of several minutes. After delivering the dose fraction, the source then returns to the afterloader's lead safe for a specified interval of time before the next dose fraction is delivered. This cycle is repeated many times over the course of a treatment. With PLDR, tumour cells receive periodic pulses of irradiation which alternate with intervals of no irradiation. The instantaneous dose rate to an individual cell during a pulse exposure may be greater than 100 times the overall average dose rate. The overall average dose rate (Gy/h) with the PLDR method will be the same as that used presently in clinical CLDR.

Advantages of PLDR

The new technique of PLDR, offers several advantages over conventional CLDR and these include:
[A] The distribution of radiation dose can be more easily controlled and tailored permitting the following improvements:
[1] More precise application of the prescribed dose to the treatment volume.
[2] Better reproducibility of treatment plans.
[3] Greater flexibility to change the dose distribution through the course of treatment if necessary (Edmundson 1990).
[B] Improved radiation safety for clinical and physics staff since there is only a single source.
[C] Elimination of the need to keep an inventory of numerous radioactive sources and of the resultant complex and time consuming manipulation of these sources by clinical and physics staff. This could possibly result in decreased costs.
[D] An overall simplification of the afterloading apparatus. For example, the mechanical components are fewer, and the number of sources is reduced from a few hundred to one. These simplifications could make this technology available to a greater number of clinical centres.

Treatment Parameters

Prior to implementation of PLDR appropriate treatment parameters which will result in predictable and acceptable normal tissue toxicities must be chosen. The first step in maintaining dose equivalence to CLDR will be maintaining overall average dose rate in the range used for the traditional modality. Another parameter, which is not applicable to CLDR but which will have a significant impact in PLDR is fractional dose per pulse. It has been well established in external beam irradiation that normal tissue toxicity is very sensitive to fraction size, (Thames et al 1990), and there is no reason why such relationships would not apply to brachytherapy. Although overall average dose rate may remain the same as in CLDR, maintaining a sufficiently small fraction pulse size will be necessary to prevent increased normal tissue toxicity.

For technical and clinical reasons such as instrument fatigue and nursing care of patients, it is necessary to maintain the spacing between pulses, and thus the dose per pulse, as large as possible, (Brenner & Hall 1991). The optimal application of PLDR will therefore utilise pulse dose fractions which are as large as possible without increasing normal tissue toxicity. This creates the dilemma referred to above for which obvious answers are not in the literature.

The *shoulder* region of an acute survival curve is believed to take its shape as the result of the target cell's ability to repair sublethal radiation injury. The linear quadratic model has been used extensively to analyse the effect of response curve shape in various systems. Those cells or tissues with a capacity to recover sublethal injury after larger acute doses of irradiation will have larger shoulder regions or higher α/β ratios. Although response of late occurring normal tissue injury cannot be measured in terms of cell survival curves, the concepts developed for survival curves are useful in analysing late normal tissue radiation toxicity. The linear quadratic model has thus been utilised to predict the role of dose rate and fraction size in normal tissue in the absence of survival curves. Late responding normal tissues generally have low α/β ratios and thus are more sensitive to radiation fraction size than most tumours. This does not mean that they have a lesser capacity to repair sublethal damage when fraction size is kept sufficiently small.

The dose rate effect varies with an individual tissue's capacity (both amount and rate) for repair of sublethal radiation damage. In general, tumour cells demonstrate less of a dose rate effect, (Fu et al 1975, Moulder et al 1990) especially in the region below 2 Gy/h, (Turesson 1990). This lack of dose rate sparing with tumour in the low dose rate range has been demonstrated in a mouse tumour system where no difference in survival was observed between 8 Gy/h and 0.40 Gy/h (Hill & Bush 1973). This means that in the clinical application of low dose rate irradiation there is a desirable increase in the ratio of normal tissue sparing relative to tumour (Glickman & Leith 1988, Hall 1988).

From studies performed with multifractionated external beam radiation, it is known that the parameters of total dose, dose per fraction, and overall treatment time determine the degree of normal tissue injury as well as tumour toxicity. All three parameters have an important role in the intensity of the acute response of normal tissues to irradiation. In contrast, it is well documented that the degree of late radiation damage in normal tissue depends more critically on the size of the dose per fraction (Fowler 1984). This has significant implications for the expected pattern of normal tissue response to PLDR. Since late normal tissue reactions depend more critically on dose per fraction, there is concern that PLDR will produce more extensive late toxicity. Assuring that normal tissue toxicity does not increase is vital because tumour toxicity is expected to not increase until much larger fractions are applied.

Studies Using Rat 9L Gliosarcoma Cells

Studies in our laboratory using rat 9L gliosarcoma cells have demonstrated biological equivalence between PLDR and CLDR for pulses smaller than the D_q of these cells (Armour et al 1992). Further studies using cultured human fibroblast cells are being conducted to establish the range of pulse parameters which yield biological equivalence in normal cells in vitro. However, the clonogenic cell's response in vitro cannot reliably predict the extent of late normal tissue toxicity in vivo. More importantly, in vitro studies cannot provide an assessment of a functional (ie. clinical) endpoint. It is thus necessary to develop another method for determining *in vivo* equivalence between the two techniques in terms of normal tissue toxicity. The normal tissue and animal model to be studied are important considerations. They must be good emulator of the human condition so that the information obtained will allow for conclusions that will be pertinent to the clinical setting.

Rectum as the Normal Tissue to be Studied

We have chosen the rectum as the normal tissue to be studied. Toxicity to the rectum can be observed following clinical brachytherapy of pelvic malignancies. Interstitial and intracavitary CLDR irradiation are used in the treatment of prostate, cervix, uterine and vaginal cancers. The proximity of the rectum to these organs places it at risk to suffer radiation injury. For instance, there is a 10%-18% risk of chronic rectal symptoms in patients who have been treated with a combination of external beam radiation and CLDR for cervical cancer (Hanks et al 1983, Montana & Fowler 1989). Some studies have shown that the frequency and severity of proctitis increased with cumulative rectal dose and volume treated (Esche et al 1987, Pourquier et al 1982). From the Perez (1984) review of complications in the cervical cancer patients traced at Washington University, the onset of rectal symptoms which required recurrent medical management, hospitalisation, or surgery occurred months to years after irradiation. Overall, approximately 80% of the rectosigmoid complications were observed within 30 months. Since it is the later rectal complications which cause patients the most morbidity and also may be impacted to a greater extent by the PLDR method, this proposed investigation will concentrate on late toxicities.

The response of the normal human rectum to external beam therapy has been well described in the literature (Fajardo 1982, Glinsky et al 1983). Clinical manifestations of injury to the large intestine occur at a rate proportional to the increase in total dose above 50-60 Gy during fractionated external beam irradiation. Histologically, there are also characteristic changes seen predominantly in the epithelium. The net result is that the epithelium cannot replace itself so that the mucosa which normally sloughs every 4-7 days in the rectum becomes denuded. With larger doses there are more severe changes which can lead to ulceration. The degree of epithelial recovery and mucosal healing during the acute period is variable depending on the dose received and the extent of damage (Berthong & Fajardo 1981).

Late radiation rectal complications occur six months to 10 years after completion of radiation treatment. Microscopically the mucosa is atrophied, the epithelium is flattened and there is mild atypia of cells. Progressive changes are seen in the blood vessel walls of hyalinisation and intimal fibrosis which can compromise the calibre of the vessel lumen. In the connective tissue, the initial edema is followed by prominent fibrosis. Stricture, a common late complication, can result from submucosal fibrosis. The results of the progressive vasculature and connective tissue changes are ischemia, ulceration and necrosis. When ulceration occurs, it is followed by scarring and frequently subsequent stenosis, (Berthong & Fajardo 1981).

The rat rectum has proven to be a useful model for analysing radiation injury to the human rectum. A number of studies have been performed using rats to assess the response of the rectum to external beam irradiation (Black et al 1980, Breiter & Trott 1986a,b). The rat rectum has been shown to demonstrate histological patterns and clinical syndromes similar to those described above in response to radiation injury. Specifically, epithelial changes are seen in the acute reaction and ulcer formation, necrosis, obliterative endarteritis and connective tissue fibrosis typify the late reaction (Black et al 1980). Therefore, the rat rectum provides a good model for quantifying radiation induced normal tissue toxicity.

Experimental Design & Methods: Introduction

Overall this investigation is designed to compare differences in rectal injury in rats for exposures consisting of CLDR or various fractionation schemes of PLDR. Our goal is to determine if there is greater functional and/or histological toxicity to the rectal wall of rats treated with intracavitary PLDR. Specifically, it is our intent to determine the upper limit of fraction size within the PLDR method that will produce late rectal injuries no worse than CLDR. To accomplish this we have developed and demonstrated the viability of a rectal intracavitary applicator system that will be utilised for both the PLDR and CLDR irradiation in rats. Fixed position low activity iridium-192 sources positioned in ribbons will be inserted into and sealed in the rectal applicator for LDR. A *specially modified microSelectron-HDR afterloader* with a single 1 Ci iridium-192 source will be used with the rectal applicator for PLDR.

All studies within this investigation will be performed in the female Wistar rat. This species was successfully used by others in assessing rectal injury in response to external beam irradiation. In those studies, the rectum of the female Wistar rat demonstrated functional and histological changes in a dose response fashion similar to what has been previously described in humans. This investigation will be accomplished in two steps.

[1] The first step is the experimental comparison of CLDR and five PLDR fractionation schedules.

[2] The second stage will be the comparison of CLDR and two selected schemes of PLDR when combined with a fractionated external beam treatment.

Experimentation will proceed directly into procedures designed to compare five pulsing schemes of PLDR with CLDR. These schemes will model present and proposed clinical situations in which brachytherapy is given as a single modality. Treatment in the CLDR and PDLR categories will proceed concurrently. Rats will either be irradiated continuously by placing iridium-192 sources into rectal applicators for CLDR or with pulsing schemes by connecting the specially modified microSelectron-HDR afterloading device to rectal applicators at defined intervals.

For PLDR a 1 Ci iridium-192 source will be transferred briefly into each rectal applicator to give a pulse of irradiation. After each PLDR pulse the rats will be returned to their cages. The average overall dose rate of the pulsed irradiation in PLDR will be the same as the dose rate during CLDR (0.75 Gy/h). All rats will receive identical anaesthesia, bowel cleansing procedures and placement of rectal applicators. Radiation will be performed in segments of 48 hours. The first 48 hours will be an irradiation period. The rectal applicator will be removed for the second 48 hours in which no irradiation is given. Another 48 hours of irradiation will follow the resting period. This process will continue until the entire prescribed dose is given. Doses up to 80 Gy will be completed within two irradiation segments. At the completion of treatment, rats will be returned to cages and fed normal rat chow throughout the follow-up period. All rats will be followed for 300 days with routine observation for changes in rectal function. At the end of 300 days or if a rat has signs of impending bowel destruction the rat will be sacrificed and its rectum prepared for histological examination.

Treatment of rats in each pulsing category will be rotated so that the accumulation of rats into all categories will be uniformly spread over the course of this phase of the project. Rats will be randomly selected and assigned to dose categories.

Concurrent with this CLDR *versus* PLDR phase of the project, we will also have 'sham treated' control rats, and rats which receive a single fraction of pulsed irradiation.

In the second experimental phase, rats will be irradiated with a course of external beam fractionated irradiation and then exposed to CLDR or PLDR. This scheme mimics a common clinical setting. The fractionated course will be combined with CLDR and two pulse size categories of PLDR. Upon the conclusion of the first phase, we will have preliminary results to guide us in deciding upon the appropriate pulse sizes to use in the second phase. LDR procedures will be identical to those for the first phase of this project. Functional and histological data will be accumulated over a relatively long time period.

Upon completion of the first phase, all histological samples from this section will be scored blindly. The functional and histological results from the different groups will be analysed and conclusions drawn about the equivalence or nonequivalence of different pulse size categories.

Experimental Design & Methods :

Preliminary Results for an Animal Model

Preliminary studies have been carried out in our laboratory to develop an animal model which can be used to study brachytherapy induced rectal toxicity. A system in which rat rectum is irradiated using an intracavitary applicator has been developed and demonstrated to be a viable experimental system.

A rectal applicator has been designed, which will allow loading of iridium-192 sources in ribbons by hand for CLDR, or with a specially modified microSelectron-HDR afterloading device for intermittent scanning of a single iridium-192 source for PLDR. The applicator is composed of a stainless steel tube surrounded by a nylon sleeve. The applicator diameter was chosen to distend the rectal wall without creating local trauma. The length of the applicator is sufficient to allow a 1-3 cm homogeneous irradiation region along the length of the applicator. The dose distribution in this region was measured by film densitometry and found to be homogeneous to ± 1.25%. For pulsed irradiation, the microSelectron transfer tube will be connected directly to the end of the applicator for short time periods (0.5-5.5 minutes) at appropriate intervals. Rats will be immobilised in a plastic confinement device during these short time intervals. Between pulses of irradiation, the rats will be detached from the afterloading transfer tube and returned to their cages.

A flexible rat restraint system has been developed. This system, however, preserves close to 75% of the rats normal activity. Animals in this flexible restraint are able to stretch, move about their cage, and eat and drink normally. Rats fed continuously and normally have a large amount of fecal storage within the bowel. The problems of obstruction and controlling the fecal flow have been approached by two methods. The first has been to reduce fecal flow and the second has been to perform bowel cleansing prior to placement of the rectal applicator.

Experimental Design & Methods: Applicator Control

A series of 28 rats has been treated using this protocol of bowel preps and two segments of 48 hour implantation/rest periods (96 hour irradiation simulation). Rats have been observed for any untoward side effects from the procedures with follow-up to 155 days. The rats had acceptable weight loss and stress during the procedure and regained weight quickly after completion of the sham irradiation. Of 28 rats entering a treatment schedule of two cycles of 48 hour implants, none have died during treatment or follow-up. During follow-up, these unirradiated animals have gained weight normally and we have had no observed functional abnormality.

In addition to the '2-cycle' series of rats described above, six rats have been implanted, without irradiation, using the 48 hour segmented procedure through 2 cycles (108 hour treatment simulation) with no observable toxicities. The amount of faeces observed on applicators when removed was very similar in these rats to that observed in the above series. The only faeces consisted of a layer of less than 1 mm which consistently was near the superior end. This consisted of approximately 25% coverage. This region is above the homogenous dose region which is approximately 1 cm from the superior end.

As part of the development of this animal model, we have developed a system to analyse the health state of the rats during the period of implantation. Rats are examined daily for the position of the catheter, fit of the restraint jacket, amount of abs, amount of liquid food eaten, and amount of stress.

Functional Follow-Up Results

Rats undergoing 2 or 2.5 cycles of 48 hour sham treatments as described above have not demonstrated any observable functional morbidity during follow-up compared to their 'no treatment' counterparts. No rats have experienced diarrhoea or bloody stool. As already stated, the sham treated rats gain weight identical to that of the untreated rats for up to five months which is presently the extent of our follow-up period. The range of completed follow-up days is 12-155. A total of 16 of the 34 rats in this phase have completed their assigned follow-up period. They have been sacrificed and their excised rectums have been placed in formalin awaiting histological evaluation.

Radiobiological Consequences of 48 Hour Segmenting of LDR

As stated above, the 48 hour intervals were selected as the appropriate exposure and gap lengths because the rats tolerated the treatment well and as has been observed with sacrificed animals, accumulate minimal feces around the applicator. In addition, the length of the irradiation and gap periods should result in insignificant radiobiological sparing due to the gap. Segmenting the low dose rate exposures into 48 hour segments should not have a significant effect on the ED50s (dose required to produce a designated response in 50% of the animals) for the late effect endpoints which are of interest.

Analysis has indicated that separation of two fractions of low dose rate irradiation does not change the effectiveness of the irradiation as long as the length of time during the irradiation segment is much longer (> 10 times) than the repair half-time. A further assumption is that proliferation is not a factor. Although the half-time for repair of late responding rectal injury is not known, estimates from other endpoints range from 0.1 to 3.5 hours, (Hill & Bush 1973, Hall 1988, Edmundson 1990). The 48 hour exposure time per fraction in these experiments is certainly much greater than even the longest reported half-times. The second factor which could play a role is mucosal turnover.

As indicated by published data, repopulation for the first few days after a large irradiation dose is very slow. Their study reported that no repopulation sparing was observed over a period of a week when two fractions of 12 Gy acute irradiation were given. The 48 hour LDR scheduling which gives 36 Gy per segment should suppress proliferation over the intervening 48 hours and thus repopulation should not be a factor.

An additional point is that any effect of splitting LDR doses should be very similar on both CLDR and PLDR. Any possible differences due to the segmented scheduling will be the same in both CLDR and PLDR and thus differences should remain constant for both single exposure or segmented low dose rate irradiation.

Summary of LDR Procedural Studies

The combination of flexible restraint, bowel cleansing, rectal applicator device and 48 hour segmented irradiation schedule has resulted in a procedure which can be used to successfully carry out the remainder of the research.

Acute External Beam Irradiation

A method for external beam irradiation of the rat rectum has been successfully established and implemented. An apparatus has been designed that secures the rat horizontally in the supine position under a lead shield, except for a 1 cm x 2 cm cut-out area which corresponds to an estimated 2 cm of rectum and allows transmission of the X-ray beam. To verify that the rectum is indeed localised in the 1 cm x 2 cm irradiation field, diagnostic films are taken pre-treatment with the radio-opaque rectal applicator in place. Once the position of the rectum within the radiation field is verified the rectal applicator is removed and the animal is treated. The dose rate is similar to that utilised clinically for external beam irradiation. 51 rats have been treated with acute doses between 12 Gy and 28 Gy using these techniques. This set of rats is near completion of follow-up. Acute toxicities to this point have been very similar to that observed by others. The radiation dose dependence of functional and histological results obtained by us will be compared to those previously published by others. This external beam irradiation technique which is reproducible has not only allowed for successful completion of the acute external beam phase, but will allow for the completion of the proposed combined treatment of external beam and brachytherapy part of this project.

Acknowledgements

The authors would like to thank the many members of the Radiation Research Laboratory for their assistance and support performing the experiments. We also like to thank Glenda Noble, C.P.S. for her secretarial support. This research has been supported by NIH grant RO1-CA 56620-01A1 and William Beaumont Research Institute Grant RI-92-24R.

References

Armour E, Wang Z, Corry P & Martinez A, *Equivalence of continuous and pulsed low dose rate irradiation in 9L gliosarcoma cells*, Int. J. Radiation Oncology Biology & Physics, **22**, 1992.

Berthong M & Fajardo L, *Radiation injury in surgical pathology. Part II. The alimentary tract*, Amer. J. Surgical Pathology, **5**, 153-178, 1981.

Black W, Gomez L. Yuhas J & Klingerman M, *Quantification of the late effects of X-irradiation on the large intestine*, Cancer, **45**, 444-451, 1980.

Breiter N & Trott KR, *Chronic radiation damage in the rectum of the rat after protracted fractionated irradiation*, Radiotherapy & Oncology, **7**, 155-163, 1986.

Breiter N & Trott KR, *The pathogenesis of the chronic radiation ulcer of the large bowel in rats*, British Journal of Cancer, **53**, 29-30, 1986.

Brenner DJ & Hall EJ, *Conditions for the equivalence of continuous to pulsed low dose rate brachytherapy*, Int. J. Radiation Oncology Biology & Physics, **20**, 181-190, 1991.

Edmundson G, *Geometry based optimization for stepping sources implants*, in:*Brachytherapy HDR and LDR*, Martinez AA, Orton CG & Mould RF (Eds) Nucletron:Columbia, 1990.

Esche B, Crook J & Horiot J-C, *Dosimetric methods in the optimisation of radiotherapy for carcinoma of the cervix*, Int. J. Radiation Oncology Biology & Physics, **13**, 1183-1192, 1987.

Fajardo LF, *Pathology of radiation injury*, 47-74, Masson Publishing:New York, 1982.

Fowler JF, *Review: Total doses in fractionated radiotherapy-implication of new radiobiological data*, Int. J. Radiation Oncology Biology & Physics, **46**, 103-120, 1984.

Fu K, Phillips T, Kane L & Smith V, *Tumour and normal tissue response to irradiation in vivo: variation with decreasing dose rates*, Radiology, **114**, 704-716, 1975.

Glickman A & Leith J, *Radiobiological considerations of brachytherapy*, Oncology, **2**, 25-32, 1988.

Glinsky NH et al, *The natural history of radiation induced proctosigmoiditis: an analysis of 88 patients*, Quarterly Journal of Medicine, **205**, 40-53, 1983.

Hall EJ, *Radiobiology for the radiologist*, 3rd edn, 113-125, Lippincott:Philadelphia, 1988.

Hanks G, Herring D & Kramer S, *Patterns of care outcome studies. Results of the national practice in cancer of the cervix*, Cancer, **51**, 959-967, 1983.

Hill RP & Bush RS, *The effect of continuous or fractionated irradiation of a murine sarcoma*, British Journal of Radiology, **46**, 167-174, 1973.

Montana G & Fowler W, *Carcinoma of the cervix. Analysis of bladder and rectal radiation dose and complications*, Int. J. Radiation Oncology Biology & Physics, **16**, 95-100, 1989.

Moulder JE, Fish BL & Wilson JF, *Tumour and normal tissue tolerance for fractionated low-dose-rate radiotherapy*, Int. J. Radiation Oncology Biology & Physics, **19**, 341-348, 1990.

Perez C et al, *Radiation therapy alone in the treatment of carcinoma of the uterine cervix. II. Analysis of complications*, Cancer, **54**, 235-246, 1984.

Pourquier H, Dubois JB & Delard R, *Cancer of the uterine cervix: dosimetric guidelines for prevention of late rectal and rectosigmoid complications as a results of radiotherapeutic treatments*, Int. J. Radiation Oncology Biology & Physics, **8**, 1887-1895, 1982.

Thames H et al, *Time dose factors in radiotherapy: a review of the human data*, Radiotherapy & Oncology, **19**, 219-235, 1990.

Turesson I, *Radiobiological aspects of continuous low dose rate irradiation and fractionated high dose rate irradiation*, Radiotherapy & Oncology, **19**, 1-16, 1990.

29

Safety Programmes for Remote Afterloading Brachytherapy: High Dose Rate and Pulsed Low Dose Rate

B.L. Speiser & J.A. Hicks

St. Joseph's Hospital and Medical Center,
Department of Radiation Oncology,
350 West Thomas Road,
Phoenix,
Arizona 85013,
USA.

Introduction

On April 20, 1993 the Nuclear Regulatory Commission released NRC Bulletin 93-01 titled "Release of Patients after Brachytherapy Treatment with Remote Afterloading Devices". The bulletin included a description of circumstances in which they outlined an overdose of radiation. The full report described an outpatient, undergoing treatment with a remote afterloading brachytherapy device, returned to a nursing home with a radioactive source remaining in her body (Indiana Regional Cancer Center).

The treatment had taken place on 16 November 1992 and the patient died on 21 November, 1992. The cause of death was listed in the official autopsy report as "acute radiation exposure and consequences thereof". The investigation had detailed numerous deficiencies in the safety program incorporated at that facility and as a result led to the issuance of Bulletin 93-01.

The purpose of this chapter is to describe safety features for remote afterloading brachytherapy devices that were instituted before the above described event, and continuing work in progress. The remote afterloading devices we used were the microSelectron-HDR and the microSelectron-PDR.

The descriptions will include: additional safety devices that have been incorporated into existing HDR and PDR afterloading devices, as well as, procedures developed to prevent misadministration of radiation with such devices.

Quality Assurance

Quality Assurance (QA) is divided up into [I] QA on the Treatment Unit, [II] QA on the Treatment Planning System, and [III] QA on the Patient Treatment Procedure (*after* Hicks & Ezzell 1992).

[1] QA on the Treatment Unit

Daily QA is performed every day a patient is to be treated. All monitors and interlocks are to be checked. These include the door interlock, emergency off buttons, treatment interrupt buttons, audio-visual monitors, and radiation room monitor. The treatment unit read out of time, date, and current source strength is to be checked for correctness. A test run has to be made which will demonstrate reproducibility of source positioning, accuracy of dwell time setting and normal termination of treatment. At the same time, the mechanical integrity of the applicator connections to the treatment can be checked. Finally, the availability of emergency response equipment is to be verified.

On a monthly basis, the radiographic markers should be tested to show alignment with the programmed source positions. The source activity should be checked to show agreement with decayed activity. The integrity of the applicators most often used should be checked for mechanical damage, ease of coupling, kinks or mechanical deformation. For new source installation, the head of the treatment unit (housing the source) is to be surveyed to establish exposure levels to the personnel working in the room. Areas adjacent to the treatment room should be surveyed as well, depending on local regulatory requirements. The source position is to be checked at this time, as well as the accuracy and linearity of the treatment times. The source and any devices used for constancy or decay verification are calibrated at this time.

[II] QA on the Planning System

With each change of software, a test plan is to be run to verify calculation accuracy. Enough parameters should be included in the test case to identify any problems. A test might consist of the dose at a number of distances for a single source, the dose at a number of distances for multiple sources. A check of reconstruction accuracy for each type or reconstruction to be used can be easily included in such test cases. Each type of planning system will have substantially different tools to accommodate easy planning. For each system, a suitable test should be designed to verify that errors in such features which would adversely affect treatment accuracy will be detected.

Check that paper documentation accurately reflects all pertinent dosimetry information input to the computer. Check that information transfer media, such as programming cards or magnetic disks, accurately transfer information to the treatment unit.

[III] QA on the Patient Treatment Procedure

Localising X-rays (orthogonal or semiorthogonal) are obtained with the applicator(s) in place and the appropriate dummy sources. The physician reviews the X-rays and indicates treatment positions. A self adhesive label is attached to the film which includes; patient's name, date, names of the radiation oncologists, and physicist. The procedure is identified as the number i.e. 1, 2, 3 (1st, 2nd, 3rd) of the total number to be performed. The dose in cGy is specified at a depth or distance in millimetres. Each catheter is listed for start and stop positions. If an offset is used, the length, ie. 985 mm instead of 995 mm if a 1 cm offset is used, is listed. Both the physician and physicist determine these points independently and sign the label if they are in agreement.

For each patient treated one must verify the agreement between the source activity used in the plan and the activity indicated by the treatment unit (if so configured) and manually calculated activity from decay. Some check of the accuracy of the reconstruction of the implant is to be performed. The treatment times should be checked before treatment by manual calculation, verifying input to the computerised calculation or by performing an independent computer calculation.

Verify that the transfer of times, treatment positions and catheters or applicators to the treatment unit is correct. The correct connection of catheters or other applicators to the treatment unit should be verified by a second person. After treatment the documentation of treatment from the treatment unit should be checked for normal termination and correct application.

Weekly a physicist, other than the original physicist, reviews the plan and treatment records to check for adequate documentation and accuracy.

Misadministration of Radiation

In 1992, a radioactive source from a remote high dose rate remote afterloader was lost (Indiana Regional Cancer Center). The source fractured from the cable and was left within catheters implanted in a patient. Sources involved in high dose rate have a maximum activity of 10 Ci and the normal range is 3 - 9 Ci.

Problem I: Applicator Identification

Catheters placed in this patient were not properly identified and/or labeled. This led to two separate problems: The first was that the transfer tubes or connecting tubes from the machine were connected to the wrong catheters. Secondly, when the error occurred, indicating that a treatment could no progress, the operator and/or physician involved identified the wrong catheter not being treated.

Solution

All catheters, needles, tubes or other apparatus must always be labeled.

Example 1: Endobronchial Catheters

When two or more catheters are placed into the patient, the catheters must be labeled as they are placed into the patient. The first catheter is labeled #1, the connector is placed on and then a dummy source is placed into the catheter which in turn has a label #1. This is repeated for catheter #2 and all subsequent catheters, so that the catheter and the dummy source numbers correspond. If one or more labels are dislodged, there are sufficient labels still present to allow the correct identification of the catheters. In a worst case scenario, where the dummies are removed and the labels fall off, the patient must be resimulated to make sure that the proper identification of catheters has occurred.

Example 2: Implant of Needles or Hollow Catheters

When these procedures are performed in the operating room, the recommendation is that at the time of simulation, the catheters are labeled and then the connecting tubes with the corresponding numbers are attached to those numbers. Those catheters should remain attached to the needles and/or catheters, so that once again there is redundant identification.

Problem II: Applicator Movement

The patient involved in the accident was implanted on one day and did not undergo simulation for several days thereafter. No check was performed to ensure that the catheters were still in the original location.

Solution

When performing high dose rate or pulsed low dose rate treatments on patients extending over a period of greater than two hours, it is mandatory that the catheters, needles or other apparatus are securely fastened before each treatment.

If there are to be fractionated treatments or in the event of pulsed low dose rate with 24 fractions or less per day, the catheters, needles or other apparatus must be checked on a regular basis or prior to treatment to ensure that they are secure and have not moved in position.

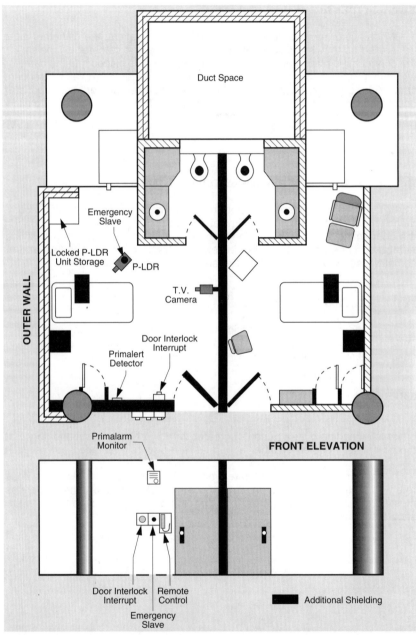

Figure 1. Floor plan of the pulsed low dose rate (P-LDR) microSelectron-PDR remote afterloading facility.

Problem III: Supervision of Treatment

Neither the physicist nor physician were present during the treatment. The physicist was out of the facility and the physician, while in the facility, was in his room and not directly supervising the treatment.

Solution

Remote afterloadings with HDR or pulsed LDR are still relatively new techniques and require a high level of training. In the above case, there was evidence of insufficient training for all members involved in the technique. The ideal solution is for a physicist and/or physician well trained in the procedure to be present from the beginning to end of treatment. For HDR treatments lasting a few minutes, this is not an undue burden and should be followed.

Conclusions

Radiation accidents such as the above should not occur if proper procedures are outlined and consistently followed.

Treatment Room Modifications and Equipment Connections for Pulsed Low Dose Rate & High Dose Rate Units

Installation

The microSelectron-PDR is installed in a modified hospital room. Modifications include: additional shielding greater than presently required to walls and to the door to ensure that personnel and patients outside of the treatment room do not receive greater than allowed levels of radiation (Figure 1). The room modifications also include cabling from within the room to allow control of the treatment device from a remote control located immediately outside of the room adjacent to the door (Figure 2) as seen on the schematic. This remote unit is a micro processor system that is connected via cabling to the master computer in the microSelectron-PDR and to the main control unit which is housed in the nursing area (Figure 3). Immediately adjacent to this master control unit is a TV screen which monitors the patient and treatment unit. Monitoring continues on a 24 hour basis until the patient is disconnected from the microSelectron-PDR.

At St. Joseph's Hospital and Medical Centre the microSelectron-HDR is installed in a linear accelerator room. Monitoring by TV and radiation detector is constant until the treatment is completed.

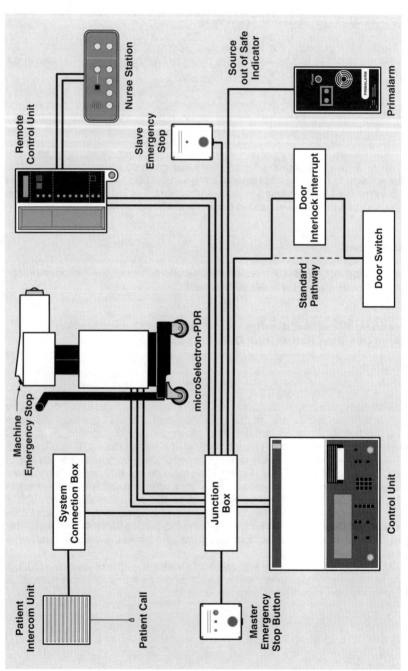

Figure 2. Schematic diagram of the microSelecron-PDR connections for emergency switches and interlocks

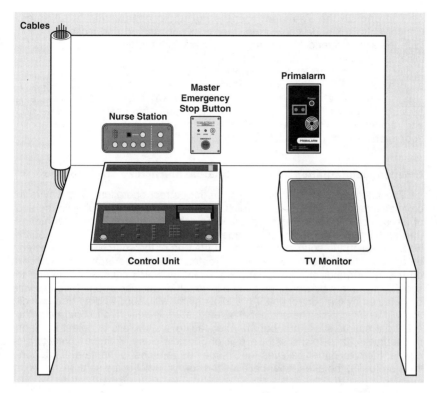

Figure 3. Schematic diagram of the microSelectron-PDR main nursing control area.

Safety Features

Door Interlock Interrupt (for Pulsed Low Dose Rate Unit)

An additional safety interlock has been tested. Its purpose is to ensure checking the room each time a treatment is started. The following steps show how this is done.

[1] Press the yellow button inside the room while the door is open
  The yellow button will light.
[2] Close the door (after leaving the room).
[3] Press the yellow button outside the room. The yellow button will light.
[4] The start button is now enabled and may be pushed at any time.

Any change in the order of steps 1,2 or 3 will require starting over. If the door is opened at any time, steps 1 2 and 3 must be repeated before the treatment can be resumed.

The door to the treatment room is not under observation at all times. Conceivably, someone could enter the room unobserved and close the door. With the simple interlock supplied by the manufacturer, the treatment could be initiated by pushing the start button outside the door or at the nursing station, subjecting the person inside to exposure. The additional interlocks require that a nurse has to go in the room any time the treatment needs to be restarted. Note that the treatment needs to be restarted any time the door has been opened. Requiring that the nurse has to go in the room enables the detection and removal of any person who may have entered. The circuitry for the above door interlock interrupt is detailed in Appendix I.

Independent Radiation Monitor & Audible Alarm for a Stuck Source

The afterloader checks in many ways for correct operation. One way is to correlate stepping motor pulses (which drive the source in and out) with the end of the source cable. The end of the source cable is detected by optical means (the opto-coupler pair). The afterloader expects to see the end of the source when returning the source to the safe. If the end of the source is not detected, an audible alarm is sounded and the treatment sequence is stopped with an error condition indicated. Normally any event by which causes the source to stick, or any event by which the source is cut off or detached from the cable will be detected by the control unit. An audible alarm will sound and an error condition will be indicated. The additional safety feature is designed to operate in the event the source sticks out, but the afterloading system fails to detect it. When the source returns to the safe, a pair of contacts close. If these contacts are closed, the afterloader believes the source has returned to the safe. If the contacts are open, the afterloader believes the source is not in the safe.

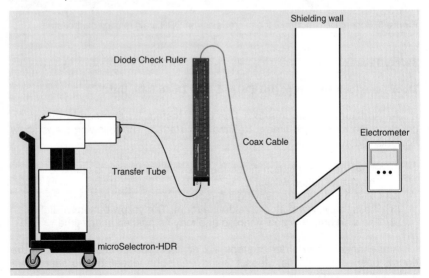

Figure 4. Connection of the active source check ruler to the exterior electrometer.

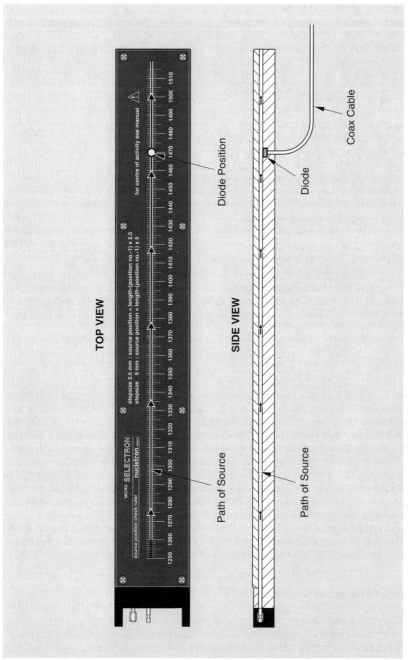

Figure 5. Top and side views of the source check ruler.

After a channel has been treated, the source returns to the safe before the next channel will be treated. Therefore, if a source falls out during a treatment, it will be pushed along by the cable until the last position in a channel is treated and remains in the catheter when the cable is retracted. If the afterloader detects the event it will sound an alarm. If it does detect this, the switch indicating the source return will be closed. This is the feature which will enable an audible alarm from the independent radiation monitor.

The Primalert remote radiation indicator will flash a red light whenever it detects radiation. The audible alarm switch in the Primalert is connected to the switch contacts in the afterloader, so an audible alarm will sound whenever there is radiation detected while the afterloader believes the source is in the safe. This provides a backup for failure of the afterloader system to detect a source remaining out. If the afterloader does detect it, it will sound an alarm. If the unit does not detect it, Primalert alarm will sound.

Check Ruler for Active Source

On a daily basis the Nucletron check ruler is used to check accuracy of source positioning. The Nucletron check ruler is attached to the treatment unit through a treatment transfer tube. The ruler consists of a scale and a rod which is moved by the check cable or source as it moves through the check ruler. One can verify the motion of the check sources or actual source by programming motion to a dwell position and checking the motion indicated by the displacement of the rod.

This technique works well, but it only indicates the motion of the end of the device. Also, when a treatment is programmed, the check source goes out further than the actual source. This means the physical motion of the actual source can only be checked in a special mode, not in an ordinary treatment. We have modified a check ruler to incorporate a diode radiation detector to indicate source position. The diode is a 1 mm square photodiode placed within a few millimeters from the source path. Its position corresponds to a fixed distance from the treatment head. The diode is connected via coax cable to an electrometer. As the source gets near the diode, the reading on the diode increases. The electrometer readings can be correlated to source position with an accuracy of 0.1 millimetre. We have found this accuracy sufficient to detect differences in lengths of transfer tubes, as well as the variation of path length with relaxation or change of curvature of the transfer tube. The design and testing of this device will be detailed in a separate publication.

An advantage of this method is that since it is sensitive to the radiation emitted by the source, it could detect a shift in the source position within the cable assembly as well as a change in activity greater than 10 %.

Quick Disconnect Umbilical

The quick disconnect umbilical was designed for two different purposes and is composed of two portions. The transfer tube portion is composed of eighteen transfer tubes with the tubes numbered 1-18. This section measures a total of

86 cm. The transfer tube machine interface is the standard connecting tube that is placed into the indexer of the head of the machine and locked in place with the locking ring. On the distal portion of this assembly, the tubes are fixed in place in the female portion of the umbilical compression locking mechanism. The second portion is composed of the male portion of the umbilical locking device which is mounted to a lucite plate. This portion measures 39 cm and the distal portion is the compression fitting for attachment to needles or catheters.

The tubes at their proximal end are once again numbered, and are fixed in place into the compression fitting. This attachment to the lucite plate can be rotated and the plate itself can be attached to the patient. The attachment to the patient takes the tension off the transfer tubes and helps prevent kinking of the tube, which in turn decreases the chance of source being stuck or a treatment not progressing as planned. The second purpose for the umbilical connection was as a quick disconnect for non radiation emergency situations. The disconnect is quite easily accomplished, such that the nurse could rapidly disconnect and remove the patient from the treatment machine and room any time that an emergency is felt to exist.

Appendix

Procedures for Use of Pulsed Low Dose Rate & Emergency Procedures.

Connection of Patient to the Treatment Unit

A. A physician, dosimetrist, or physicist and the nurse who is taking care of the patient, are to be involved for the connection.

B. The pulsed low dose rate sheet, listing the 18 channels, must be filled out showing the connections of the catheters to applicators and to the unit.

C. The transfer tube is connected to the patient's applicators and then connected to the machine per connection, and the locking ring rotated counterclockwise.

D. All connections are checked to make sure that they are in the fully seated position, both for transfer tube to patient applicator connection, and transfer tube to locking ring.

E. The patient is to be instructed in what is to be expected when the machine is operating, and how to notify the nurses for assistance.

F. The treatment unit is programmed by the physician, physicist, or dosimetrists.

G. The treatment parameters are printed out and checked against the planning computer calculations.

H. Treatment is to be initiated in the presence of the physician, physicist, or dosimetrist, who has entered the treatment parameters and checked them, as well as a nurse from the floor. The physician, physicist, or dosimetrist must remain through the first cycle or treatment to ascertain that the unit is functioning correctly.

Interruption & Continuation of Treatment

A. Treatment may be interrupted at any time of the follow means:
1. Opening of the patient door.
2. Pressing the "Interrupt" button on any console of the unit.
B. Following such an interruption, treatment will not be able to be continued until the "Start" button is pressed.
C. When the cause of the interruption has been resolved, and if the door to the patient's room has been opened, then the authorised personnel must first enter the patient's room and verify continued safe operation conditions. The door interlock sequence must be initiated.
1. Press the yellow button inside the room while the door is open. The yellow button will light.
2. Close the door (after exiting the room).
3. Press the yellow button outside the room. The yellow button will light.
4. The start button is now enabled and may be pushed.
D. The following represent possible causes of interruptions of the treatment. (All of the activities listed below should be performed during the non treatment interval, and if possible the only interruptions during the treatment interval should be restricted to emergencies or need for patient assistance).
1. Nursing care.
2. Physician care.
3. Delivery of meals.
4. Visitors (visitors will not be allowed in the room unless allowed by the authorized nurse at a time corresponding to the completion of the last pulse, and the visitor must be asked to leave the room by the same nursing personnel, who will then activate restart of the treatment.
E. When any individual is in the patient room, the door is to remain open.

Disconnection of the Patient from the Unit

A. There may be occasions when the patient must be disconnected from the treatment unit.
B. If a patient is to be reconnected to the unit, this must be supervised by the physician, physicist, dosimetrist, or nursing personnel trained to perform this procedure. The setup sheet will be followed to ensure that the connection is made properly.
C. The machine will not, under any circumstances, be allowed to resume treatment until the tubes are connected correctly.

Emergency Procedures (Non-Radiation Emergencies)

A. If the patient must be removed from the room in a non-radiation emergency, i.e:
1. Fire.
2. Medical (i.e. movement to ICU, etc.).

B. Rotate locking collar on machine clockwise, releasing all connecting tubes simultaneously.

C. Pull all connecting tubes out of the machine, thus disconnecting the patient completely from the treatment machine.

D. If more time is available, a second option consists of disconnection of the transfer tubes from the patient's applicators.

E. Any emergency procedure will include the termination of treatment and storage of the radioactive source in the treatment safe. If any problem is detected, an alarm will bleep. The radiation monitor will register no radiation, indicating that the radioactive source is properly stored.

F. Trained authorised nursing personnel will be able to clear the alarm and resume treatment in almost all cases. Where the treatment cannot be resumed, the physician on call must be notified.

Emergency Procedure Outline for Response to Various Alarm Events. (Radiation Emergencies)

A. microSelectron-PDR Sounds an Alarm and Stops Treating.
  1. If Primalert continues flashing, begin emergency procedures and send for physicist on call.
  2. If Primalert is not flashing, read error code on machine, check connections, locking ring, etc.

B. Primalert is Flashing and Audible Alarm is Sounding Treatment in Progress.
  Begin emergency procedures and send for physicist on call.

C. Primalert is Flashing and there is no Treatment in Progress.
  Begin emergency procedures and send for physicist on call.

Emergency Procedure

A. 1. Hit the emergency Stop button (located on the wall adjacent to the treatment room door or at the nursing station).
  2. Have a co-worker notify the physicist on call to come to the room.

B. 1. Turn on survey meter.
  2. Check battery.
  3. Turn to x1 range.
  4. Check meter for operation with check source.

C. 1. Open the door.
  2. Go into the room until you can see the patient.
  3. Measure the radiation exposure.

D. 1. If there is no radiation,
  2. Go to the patient and survey the patient and the microSelectron-PDR.
  3. If there is still no radiation, wait for the physicist and/or the medical director.

DO NOT RESTART THE TREATMENT.

E. 1. If there is radiation anywhere in the room, hit the emergency Stop on the head.
2. Rewind the source lever.
3. If there is still radiation,
4. Remove the applicators and place them in the storage pig if possible.
5. If not possible, let them hang from the microSelectron-PDR.

DON'T DISCONNECT ANYTHING

(Remember to keep your distance from the catheters or applicators and use tongs if applicable. Keep the microSelectron-PDR or the patient between you and the source if possible).

(Note that all PDR procedures will be of the types whose applicators are removable by nursing personnel. Any new procedures will not be initiated until all nursing personnel are inserviced and appropriate removal kit (if necessary) is provided).

F. Survey the patient.
1. If there is radiation present, the physicist and/or the physician will direct further action, including surgical intervention, if necessary. (Physician on call will respond within 15 minutes during normal operating hours of the department and within 1 hour of night and/or weekends).
2. If there is no radiation present, remove the patient from the room. Close the door and don't let anyone in.

Acknowledgement

Financial support provided by the Foundation for Cancer Research and Education, 300 West Clarendon Road, Suite 350, Phoenix, Arizona 85013.

References

Hicks JA, Ezzell GA, Abstract: *Calibration & quality assurance, 7th International Brachytherapy Working Conference,* Baltimore/Washington: September 6-8, 1992.

Loss of an iridium-192 source and therapy administration at Indiana Regional Cancer Center, Indiana, Pennsylvania on November 16, 1992, U.S. Nuclear Regulatory Commission NUREG-1480: February 1993.

NRC Bulletin 93-01, *Release of patients after brachytherapy treatment with remote after-loading devices,* April 1993.

30

Calibration & Quality Assurance

J. Hicks[1] & G.A. Ezzell[2]

[1]St. Joseph's Hospital,
Radiation Oncology,
350 W. Thomas Road,
Phoenix, AZ 85028,
USA.

[2]Harper Grace Hospital & Wayne State University,
Gerhenson Radiation Oncology Center,
3990 John R Street,
Detroit,MI 48201,
USA.

Introduction

Field calibrations of high dose rate (HDR) iridium-192 sources are both necessary and practically achievable. They are necessary because the manufacturer's source certifications state a precision of ± 10% and several groups have reported that the measured activities often vary from the certifications by more than 5%. The practicality and consistency of field calibrations in the United States have improved in the past two years primarily because of two developments. [1] Acceptance by the American Association of Physicists in Medicine (AAPM) of an interpolative technique for deriving a calibration factor (N_x) for iridium-192. [2] Commercial availability of re-entrant well chambers specifically designed for HDR iridium-192 calibrations. The first part of this chapter reviews these developments and their routine application in the clinic.

Iridium-192 Source Calibrations

In the United States, the fundamental calibration for iridium-192 remains an in-air measurement of air kerma or exposure at a reference distance from the source, with absorbed dose calculated using standard techniques. Conceptually it is very much like a cobalt-60 teletherapy calibration, but with two significant exceptions. [1] At this time it is not possible to obtain a direct N_x value for iridium-192 from the National Institute of Standards and Technology (NIST). [2] It is not possible with current instrumentation to calibrate the source at the treatment distance.

N_x Values

The reason for the Nx difficulty is that the energy spectrum of iridium-192 falls between the lower energy range suitable for NIST's free-air chamber and the higher energy range suitable for NIST's spherical graphite chambers. A recent publication by Goetsch et al (1991) proposed an interpolative technique which the AAPM has approved for use by Accredited Dosimetry Calibration Laboratories (ADCLs): at least two of which can now provide N_x factors for iridium-192. The method requires that the chamber, equipped with a build-up cap of at least 0.3 g/cm^2 thickness, be calibrated for caesium-137 and 250 kVp orthovoltage energies. The factor for iridium-192 is then obtained by interpolating between these two values and accounting for the attenuation correction which depends on the total wall thickness: typically about 1.008 for a cobalt-60 build-up cap.

Problem of Calibration at the Brachytherapy Treatment Distance

The second problem referred to above is that one cannot calibrate at the treatment distance because that distance is so small for brachytherapy. There are two aspects to the problem. [1] Small uncertainties in positioning lead to large uncertainties in the measurement. [2] The variance in energy fluence across the chamber creates large uncertainties in relating the reading to dose at a point. The solution is to measure at some reference distance further from the source so that the chamber becomes more point-like and positioning uncertainty becomes less critical. On the other hand, as the distance increases the signal to noise ratio decreases and room scatter increases.

Room Scatter

To evaluate room scatter one can use a simple model which assumes that the total reading is caused by primary radiation from the source, proportional to the inverse square of distance, plus a constant room scatter term. One can take readings at different distances and fit the results to the model to derive the primary and scatter components.

Reproducibility of In-Air Measurements

With the application of correction factors for room scatter, chamber size, transit exposure, and electrical leakage, it is possible to make in-air measurements with a calibration jig at a fixed reference distance of 10-20 cm and achieve a reproducibility about 1.5%.

Re-Entrant Well Ionisation Chambers

The complete process for an in-air calibration, including determining the scatter effects, is time consuming and unlikely (and unnecessary) to be repeated at each source change. One can use the results of a complete in-air calibration to derive a calibration factor for an alternative, quicker technique using simpler instruments. One example is a solid phantom calibration tool, in which the chamber and source positions are held to tight mechanical tolerances. Another example is a re-entrant well ionisation chamber, similar in concept to a dose calibrator used for nuclear medicine but designed for the higher current densities and potential recombination effects from HDR sources.

The reading from such a chamber depends significantly on the source position within it, so this must be controlled. At least three such chambers are available commercially with different design characteristics, but all show the basic advantages of this type of chamber: simplicity, speed, and reproducibility of 0.5% or better. An iridium-192 calibration factor may be obtained from ADCLs in the United States. For example, the calibration laboratory at the University of Wisconsin calibrates microSelectron-HDR sources using seven reference distances similar to the in-air technique described above. A recent study by Ezzell (1992) demonstrated that each of these three commercial systems works well for HDR iridium-192 calibrations and that they can also be used for LDR quality assurance tests.

The response constancy of such chambers may be checked using LDR caesium-137 sources, (the dynamic range is large enough to also permit QA checks of LDR sources), or using external beams from a cobalt-60 unit or a linear accelerator: which have the advantage of producing signal levels comparable to HDR sources.

QA of Routine Calibration Procedures

Quality assurance of routine calibration procedures is an important consideration. Errors of 5-10% may go undetected if the source certification is used as the sole check of the calibration. A simple solution is to perform duplicate measurements for each new source, using different chambers and apparatus. This needs not be tedious; measurements can be made with a well chamber with one electrometer, followed by measurements with a Farmer-type chamber in a solid jig with another electrometer, each taking only few minutes.

The broader issues of quality assurance for remote afterloading system can be separated into three parts. **[1] QA on the Treatment Unit. [2] QA on the Treatment Planning System. [3] QA on the Patient Treatment Procedure.** The quality assurance programme should test every aspect of performance which has an effect on accuracy of patient treatment and safety for both patient and operating personnel. The frequency of such QA should be governed by the importance of a particular function, its probability for failure and to a lesser extent, the ease with which its function can be tested. There is room for great variation in opinion on each of these points. One should not hesitate to modify a QA procedure when experience or protocol dictate the need. We submit the following outline which contains procedures currently used in our and other institutions.

[1] QA on the Treatment Unit

Quality assurance procedures on the treatment unit can be separated into daily, monthly, and procedures made with each source exchange.

Daily QA

Daily QA is performed every day a patient is to be treated. All monitors and interlocks are to be checked. These include the door interlocks, emergency off buttons, treatment interrupt buttons, audiovisual monitors and room radiation monitors. The ability to detect a missing or misconnected applicator or transfer tube should be tested, as well as other such functions. The treatment unit readout of time, date and current source strength is to be checked for correctness. A test run is to be made which will demonstrate reproducibility of source positioning, accuracy of dwell time setting and normal termination of treatment. At the same time, the mechanical integrity of the applicator connections to the treatment unit can be checked. Finally the availability of emergency response equipment is to be verified.The daily QA need only take five minutes when aided by an appropriate procedure sheet and check list such as is suggested in Table 1. Note that in the procedure used in Table 1, the source position is seen over closed-circuit TV with an appropriate lens for observation. Other methods such as a check ruler or autoradiography (Jones 1988) can be used. When a photodiode is positioned very close to the source path in a Nucletron HDR check ruler, it can provide sub-millimetre accuracy in determining reproducibility of source positioning by detecting the radiation intensity. Hicks has drilled a hole into the check ruler and positioned the active part of the diode about 4 mm from the source path. The diode is connected to an electrometer next to the control console with coaxial cable. The check ruler is light proofed with black tape. Figure 1 shows the response of the diode as a function of programmed source position. The sensitivity of the diode to source position on the slope is about 0.2 mm. Part of our daily QA is to programme the source position to be on each slope and in the centre position. The technologist writes the readings for each position on a prepared chart, Table 2.

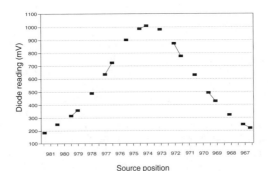

Source position

Figure 1. Relative diode reading as a function of source position for the positioning reproducibility check device described in the text.

There are no calculations to be made. Limits for each position have been tabulated previously for each possible day of treatment. If readings are beyond limits, a physicist must be consulted. We have found the technique sensitive enough to detect differences in transfer tube length and differences in curvature of the transfer tube. We have concluded a rigid and non-interchangeable transfer tube would be better for this test. Preliminary investigation suggests this technique could also be used to verify source activity.

Table 1
Daily check on the microSelectron-HDR iridium-192 unit.

Date: ___/___/___   Tech: _____

Procedures

1. Attach the check ruler to channel 1 using a red-ended interconnection cable. Put the ruler where it can easily be seen with the TV camera.

2. Program standard 99 for channel 1. This will program:
Positions	5, 9, 13, 17, 21
Length	995
Dwell times	at least 2 s (9-21), 20 s (5)

3. Run the program and observe the motion of the source cable. The end of the source should align with the marked distance indicators to within 1 mm (950, 960, 970, 980, 990 mm.)

4. While the source is dwelling at position 5, test the operation of the interrupt key, door interlock, and emergency stop. The source should return to position 5 (end at 990) after each restart.

5. Check the printout for the correct date, time, activity, program, and treatment information.

6. If any errors or malfunctions occur, save the printout and inform the physics staff before treating any patient.

_____ Date
_____ Time
_____ Activity on printout within 50 mCi of posted activity
_____ Program on control panel
_____ Program on printout
_____ Alignment with check ruler
_____ Interrupt key
_____ Door interlock
_____ Emergency stop
_____ Door light
_____ TVs
_____ Intercom
_____ X-ray set: line voltage adjust
_____ X-ray set: exposure at 70 kVp, 200 mA, 1/2 s
_____ CARM: Line voltage adjust
_____ CARM: 3 exposures at ABC Fluoro settings
_____ Paper supply in console printer
_____ Inspect routine interconnect cables for kinks, etc.
_____ Emergency cart stocked
_____ GM counter battery check and constancy check

Notes: _____

_____

Table 2
Daily diode check of position and output. Use standard 95 ....set length= 992

Dwell Position	➤ 7		9		11	
Day	Low	High	Low	High	Low	High
18-Sep-92						
27-Oct-92	389____641		1160____1282		344____572	
28-Oct-92	385____635		1150____1271		340____567	
29-Oct-92	381____629		1139____1259		337____561	
30-Oct-92	378____623		1128____1247		334____556	
31-Oct-92	374____618		1118____1235		331____551	
01-Nov-92	371____612		1107____1224		328____546	
02-Nov-92	367____606		1097____1212		325____541	
03-Nov-92	364____601		1087____1201		322____536	
04-Nov-92	361____595		1077____1190		319____531	
05-Nov-92	357____589		1067____1179		316____526	
06-Nov-92	354____584		1057____1168		313____521	
07-Nov-92	351____578		1047____1157		310____516	
08-Nov-92	347____573		1037____1146		307____511	
09-Nov-92	344____568		1027____1135		304____506	
10-Nov-92	341____562		1018____1125		301____502	
11-Nov-92	338____557		1008____1114		298____497	
12-Nov-92	335____552		999____1104		296____492	
13-Nov-92	331____547		990____1094		293____488	
14-Nov-92	328____542		980____1083		290____483	
15-Nov-92	325____537		971____1073		288____479	
16-Nov-92	322____532		962____1063		285____474	
17-Nov-92	319____527		953____1053		282____470	
18-Nov-92	316____522		944____1044		280____465	
19-Nov-92	313____517		935____1034		277____461	
20-Nov-92	310____512		927____1024		274____457	
21-Nov-92	307____507		918____1015		272____452	
22-Nov-92	305____503		910____1005		269____448	
23-Nov-92	302____498		901____996		267____444	
24-Nov-92	299____493		893____987		264____440	
25-Nov-92	296____489		884____977		262____436	
26-Nov-92	293____484		876____968		259____432	
27-Nov-92	291____480		868____959		257____428	
28-Nov-92	288____475		860____950		255____424	
29-Nov-92	285____471		852____941		252____420	

Instructions

..........................Program 10 seconds in dwell positions 7,9,11
(or recall Sstandard 95) set length = 992
..........................Use channel 1 and length will be the default 992
..........................Connect channel one to the length ruler with the diode
..........................Turn voltmeter and electrometer leave switch on zero insure that the
reading is zero
..........................Turn on unit (ie. start treatment)
..........................Write down numbers for each dwell position
(Note that 11 is first, 9 is second, 7 is last)
..........................If any reading is not between the low and high limit,
a physicist or physician must approve continuing.

Table 3
Monthly Quality Assurance Tests on microSelectron-HDR

Date: _____ Signature:_____

Activity Calibration Check (acceptance criterion 2%)
Source id: _____ Calibrated activity: _____Ci on ____/ ____/ ____

HDR-1000 chamber with Keithley 35617 electrometer (C, D, or E)
Run 6F catheter to bottom of chamber well
Settings: 0.25 cm step size, Length=995, Positions 15-23, 20 sec/position
Maximum reading expected in position 18-20

Position	23	22	21	20	19	18	17	16	15
Distance	940.0	942.5	945.0	947.5	950.0	952.5	955.0	957.5	960.0
nA Rdg									

T _____ P_____ Ctp _____ Time of Day _____ Decay to 0:00_____

Max nA rdg * Ctp * Decay * 0.1238= _____ Ci
Charted activity for this date = _____ Ci   Ratio:_____

Applicator Checks

_____ Bronchial catheters inspected, marks coincide with dummy
_____ Ring and tandem applicators and interconnect tubes inspected
_____ Vaginal cylinder applicators and interconnect tubes inspected
_____ Interstitial interconnect tubes inspected

Radiograph/autoradiograph of   Length
                                       Parameter   Deviation
Bronchial applicator with adaptor and Nucletron dummy   _____   _____
Interstitial applicator with HDR dummy pushed to end   _____   _____
Intrauterine tandem with special Nucletron dummy   _____   _____

[V film, 100 kVp, 600 mAs; HDR @ 0.1 to 0.3 s]

_____ Perform source positioning check per daily QA procedure
_____ Dummy position check (spec. mode 5) matches source position
_____ Date, time, and activity on printout correct
_____ Interrupt key
_____ Emergency off
_____ Door interlock
_____ Door light
_____ Door light (Primalert) with AC power off to Primalert
_____ GM counter battery check and constancy check
_____ Emergency cart stocked
_____ Error detected for indexer ring not latched
_____ Error detected for applicator not inserted
_____ Error detected for applicator obstructed

Monthly QA

On a monthly basis, the radiographic markers should be tested to show alignment with the programmed source positions. The source activity should be checked to show agreement with decayed activity. The integrity of the applicators most often used should be checked for mechanical damage, ease of coupling, kinks or mechanical deformation. Table 3 illustrates the procedure and check list for a monthly QA. Note that a well type chamber is used to check activity. Note also that the lengths of applicators which will not accommodate the maximum treatment distance are checked for consistency.

Table 4 gives explicit instructions for verification of accuracy of radiographic markers (dummies). The markers were made 'in house' and feature a collar which allows precise adjustment to match the real source position. The procedure illustrates the verification of both the dwell position and length specification.

Table 4
microSelectron-HDR monthly QA procedure verification of dummy positions and source repositioning accuracy.

1. Tape 4 catheters 2 cm apart on a sheet of XV-2 film
   Make sure the entire length of the catheter is taped down
2. Attach the couplers to the end of each catheter
3. Place dummies 1-4 in each catheter, making sure the stop collar on the dummies abuts the coupler on each catheter
   A. if the collar on a dummy does not abut, check the length of the dummy against the others, the amount of excess plastic beyond the last seed, and the length of the catheter
   B. Adjust the collar, trim excess plastic or discard the too short catheter, depending on the determination in part A
4. Radiograph the dummies using 80 kV, 200mAs. Then remove the dummies
5. Program the microSelectron-HDR to dwell 0.1 to 0.2 sec, depending on source activity, according to the following:

Catheter 1	1	5	9	13	17	21	25	29	33	37	41	45	48
Catheter 2	1	5	9	13	17	21	25	29	33	37	41	45	48
Catheter 3	1	5	9	13	17	21	25	29	33	37	41	45	48
Catheter 4	1	5	9	13	17	21	25	29	33	37	41	45	48

Length = 995 for all above
6. Run the program, exposing the film
7. Program the microSelectron-HDR for 0.3 secs, according to the following:.

Catheter 1	Dwell position	5 only	Length 985
Catheter 2	Dwell position	5 only	Length 945
Catheter 3	Dwell position	5 only	Length 895
Catheter 4	Dwell position	5 only	Length 885

8. Run the program, exposing the film
9. Develop the film. Record the maximum deviation from the dummy positions. If any dummy shows deviation greater than 2 mm, determine if the dummy is at fault by visual measurement against a dummy which is accurate. If the dummy is at fault, adjust the collar to correct the length. If it appears the deviation is due to the microSelectron-HDR unit, notify Nucletron immediately by telephone, and the physicist and the Director of Brachytherapy. The unit should not be used without approval of the physicist.

Source Change QA

In addition to the checks enumerated in the monthly QA schedule, at the time of a new source installation, the head of the treatment unit (housing the source) is to be surveyed to establish exposure levels to personnel working in the room. Areas adjacent to the treatment room should be surveyed with the source exposed as well, depending on local regulatory requirements. Again the source position, radiographic markers, all safety interlocks and system checks are to be verified. The accuracy and linearity of the treatment times are to be checked. The source activity is to be measured (calibration) and any devices used for constancy or decay verification should be calibrated at this time.

Tables 5 and 6 illustrate the survey and calibration as made at one of our institutions. Note the calibration is made with a well chamber as well as in a lucite phantom. For additional reference see Ezzell (1988), Löffler (1988) and Jones & Bidmead (1988).

[2] QA on the Planning System.

Quality assurance as applied to the planning system is primarily concerned with the accuracy with which source coordinates (or dwell positions) are represented with respect to the coordinates of dose prescription points and with the accuracy of the calculation of dose to these points. Typically a planning system is subject to intense scrutiny of its performance at the time when the planning system is being commissioned for clinical use. There are many features of the planning system which will be examined and each system may have significantly different features of interest. A user of a planning system will have to design tests to find errors in such systems that would adversely affect treatment accuracy. The QA procedure should be performed on each new version of software implemented.

The typical procedure is to run a test plan for each type of planning expected to be undertaken clinically. That is, if coordinate input is to be made by typing in coordinates, or orthogonal reconstruction, or by shift or variable angle methods, then the test should implement each of these data input methods.

The test set of data could be the films taken for each of the reconstruction techniques used of a test phantom containing dummy seeds. These films would be used to evaluate each set of software revision. The accuracy of reconstructing the coordinates of the dummy seeds is then determined. The calculation of dose to selected points by the planning system would then be compared with dose calculated manually (Killian et al 1988). The last part of the QA would check that paper documentation accurately reflects all pertinent dosimetry information input into the computer. If information is transferred to the treatment unit via programming cards or magnetic disks, the accuracy of this data transfer is to be checked.

Table 7 shows the part of the result of a test made on a phantom consisting of three radiographic markers each at 90° to each other. An orthogonal pair of radiographs was used to digitise the markers. These markers were in three straight lines with seeds one cm apart. This corresponded to dwell positions 1, 5, 9 etc. when a dwell separation of 2.5 mm is used. The reconstructed coordi-

Table 5
Radiation safety survey and source calibration for the microSelectron-HDR.

Date:___/___/___   Signature: _____ROC id#: _____

Source Receipt Survey

Meter: _____ Battery OK: _____Check source OK: _____
mR/hr @ 1 meter: _____ @ surface: _____

Mallinckrodt Diagnostica Data

S/N: _____Activity: _____Ci on: ___/___ /___ (M/D/Y)
Decay factor to ROC calibration date: _____

Safety Survey After Installation

Exposure rate near treatment unit with source retracted

	Right	Left	Above	Below	Front	Rear	
@ 1 m.							(mR/hr)
@ 10 cm							[<3]

Exposure rate outside treatment room with source exposed

Control Console	Door	Cobalt Unit	Electronics Lab

Source Calibration

HDR-1000 chamber (0.1250 Ci/nA using 0.4596 R/Ci hr at 1 metre)
Keithley 35617 EBS electrometer SN 43473 (E) (1.004 nA/Rdg)
Run 6F catheter into bottom of chamber well
Settings: 0.25 cm step size, Length 995; Positions 15-23; 20 sec/position
Maximum reading expected in position 18-20

Position	23	22	21	20	19	18	17	16	15
Distance	940.0	942.5	945.0	947.5	950.0	952.5	955.0	957.5	960.0
nA Rdg									

Temp: _____ Press: _____ Ctp: _____
Time of day: _____ Decay to 0:00 hr (>1.00) _____

Max nA Rdg * Ctp * Decay * [0.1250 * 1.004 * (0.4596/0.466)] = Activity

_____ * _____ * _____ * 0.1238 = | Ci |

      ROC result
---------------------------- = -------------------------------- = | |
Mall. Diag. * decay

nates of the ends of one of the markers were compared against actual lengths to determine accuracy. Similar comparisons are made with each of the three line markers.

Table 6
Secondary calibration check (acceptance criterion 2%).

Using PTW N 23333 SN A216 with Keithley 35617 (C or D)
Connect channels 1-4 to needles on lucite cube phantom, LENGTH=839
Temp: _____ Press: _____ Ctp: _____
65 s in each channel: _____ mean: _____ nC
5 s in each channel: _____ mean: _____ nC
leakage in s: _____scaled to 240 s: _____ nC
               Net= (65 s rdg) - (5 s rdg) - (240 s leakage): _____ nC

$$\text{Activity} = \frac{(\text{Net} * \text{Ctp})}{2.12} * (\text{Decay to 0:00 hr}) = \underline{\hspace{1cm}} \text{Ci} \quad (\text{HDR log \#2 pg 11})$$

(Well chamber result) / (Solid phantom result) = [   ]

Timer Linearity (acceptance criterion 2%)
Use channel 1 only; Length = 839
Net= [reading - 5 s reading]

Time set	Reading	Net	Net time	Net current	Ratio
5 s	nC	xxx	0 s	xxx nA	
6 s			1		
10 s			5		
15 s			10		= 1.000
25 s			20		
35 s			30		

_____ Interlocks (attach monthly sheet)
_____ Source/dummy positioning films (attach monthly sheet)
_____ Source inventory form updated
_____ New activity and decay table in calculation and daily QA books
_____ New activity entered in microSelectron-HDR treatment unit
_____ New activity posted on treatment unit console
_____ New activity entered in Nucletron Planning System

       Customizing file names: _____

_____Treatment times updated for ongoing patients

       Patient names: _____

Table 7
HDR planning system test.

Patient Name	QA Test	Activity in Curie	4.481

			Coordinates		
			X	Y	Z
Test Point	A		23.3	11.6	52

Cath	1				
Dwell	1	5	9	21	
Time	50	50	50	50	
X	23.5	23.5	23.4	23.3	
Y	6.6	-3.6	-13.7	-44.2	
Z	52.1	52.2	52.3	52.6	
Dist	5.0	15.2	25.3	55.8	
Angle	87.7	89.2	89.8	90.0	
Anisot	1.00	1.00	1.00	1.00	
Meisb	1.015	1.018	1.018	1.001	
Dose	1124.6	122.2	44.1	8.9	

Test Point	A	Dose	1280 cGy
	Manually Calculated Dose		1299.9 cGy
	Difference in percent		1.5

Distance from dwell position 1 to 21

From computer coordinates	50.8
From measurement	50.0
Difference in mm	0.8
Difference in percent	1.6

Test Point	B		23.3	-8.6	47
Cath	1				
Dwell	1	5	9	21	
Time	50	50	50	50	
X	23.5	23.5	23.4	23.3	
Y	6.6	-3.6	-13.7	-44.2	
Z	52.1	52.2	52.3	52.6	
Dist	16.0	7.2	7.4	36.0	
Angle	18.5	46.1	-46.1	-8.9	
Anisot	1.00	1.00	1.00	1.00	
Meisb	1.018	1.016	1.016	1.015	
Dose	109.9	541.3	521.1	21.7	

Test Point	B	Dose	1185 cGy
	Manually calculated dose		1194.0 cGy

Doses to points A and B from the planning system were compared with doses manually calculated using Meisberger coefficients (Meisberger et al 1968). However, one must be careful to use the appropriate anistropic correction if the planning system corrects for anisotropy. Table 8 is an example of a form documenting the QA on the software version tested.

Table 8
Planning system QA sheet.

Software Version _____   Date _____

Evaluator _____

_____ Lengths OK (within 2 mm or 2%)
_____ Dose calculation OK (within 2%)
_____ Optimization OK
_____ Paper documentation adequate
_____ Accurate transfer to Treatment Unit

"Bugs" noted

_____
_____
_____
_____
_____
_____
_____
_____

Suggestions for software changes

_____
_____
_____
_____
_____
_____

[3] QA for Patient Treatments

For each patient treated one must verify the agreement between the source activity used in the plan and the activity indicated by the treatment unit (if so configured) and manually calculated activity from decay. Some check of the accuracy of the reconstruction of the implant is to be performed. The lengths of a straight line segment of radiographic markers used for localisation can be used for this purpose by determining the length calculated from reconstructed coordinates.

Other errors of reconstruction may be difficult to determine, so an independent check of input data by a second person is important.

The treatment times should be checked before treatment by manual calculation, verifying input to the computerised calculation or by independent computer calculation. Table 9 illustrates part of the QA made at the time of the planning.

A single point check of dose is illustrated. Two dose points are defined 10 cm on opposite sides of the implant volume. The average of these doses is multiplied by 100 and divided by the source activity and total implant time in seconds. This value is called the K factor which varies with volume and extension of the

Table 9
HDR brachytherapy dosimetry sheet.

Patient name _____

Current activity Iridium-192 _____ Curie

Proc.# _____

Catheter	Time	Active positions	Date _____
_____	____	_____	
_____	____	_____	
_____	____	_____	
_____	____	_____	
_____	____	_____	

Reconstruction: Orthog. X-rays   CT   Semi-orthog. (NPS)

Reconstruction check   _____ Dummies *versus* positions
Activity check   _____ (manual calculation of decay)

Dosimetry by: _____

Checked by: _____   K= _____

Prescription dose   _____

Physician signature _____

K= Avg of dose in cGy at 0,0,100 and 0,0,-100 from computer
(perpendicular to plane of implant)
divided by activity in Ci and divided by total time (in sec)

K= Avg ∗ 100/Act/Time

K=   1.05 - 1.20 for pulmonary
(- for elongation, + for Z extension)

K=   1.10 - 1.20 for vaginal cylinder
(ie. short single catheter)

K=   .95 - 1.1 for long oesophagus
(ie. long single catheter)

implanted volume. Experience has shown that this value falls within a small range for each type of implant. It can be used for a check against gross errors in dosimetry but will not substitute for a careful examination of dwell times in various catheters and the examination of the isodose lines around each catheter. At the time of patient treatment, the transfer of times, dwell positions, and catheters or applicators to the treatment unit should be checked and the treatment record tape initialled. The correct connection of the catheters or applicators to the treatment unit should be verified by a second person. After treatment, the documentation of treatment from the treatment unit should be checked for normal termination.

QA General Commentary

Finally, three points about quality assurance deserve emphasis. **[1]** Experience has shown the value of systematising quality assurance procedures. Each QA process should have its own checklist developed to both guide and document. **[2]** This is a warning about **[1]**. There is a tendency for the generation of QA documentation to become an end in itself, impairing the real function, which is the uncluttered, sceptical review of the process under consideration. **[3]** Everyone involved in HDR brachytherapy treatment should also be involved in quality assurance. Useful and appropriate tasks can be found for therapists, dosimetrists, physicians, and physicists. No procedure is so complicated that its critical components cannot be explained to a colleague, and the act of explanation will often open the mind, uncovering the error which was camouflaged by the underbrush of expectation.

References

Ezzell GA, *Evaluation of calibration techniques for the microSelectron-HDR*, in:Brachytherapy 2, Mould RF (Ed), 61-69, Nucletron:Leersum, 1989.

Ezzell GA, *Use of new re-entrant ionisation chambers for brachytherapy calibrations and quality control*, Medical Physics, **19**, 776, 1992.

Goetsch SJ, Attix FH, Dewerd LA & Thomadsen BR, *A new re-entrant ionisation chamber for the calibration of iridium-192 high dose rate sources*, Int. J. Radiation Oncology Biology & Physics, **24**, 167-170, 1992.

Goetsch SJ, Attix FH , *Pearson DW & Thomadsen BR, Calibration of iridium-192 high dose rate afterloading systems*, Medical Physics, **18**, 462-467, 1991.

Jones CH, Bidmead AM & Margareth A, *Calibration of the microSelectron-HDR System*, in:Brachytherapy 2, Mould RF (Ed), 75-82, Nucletron:Leersum, 1989.

Jones CH, *microSelectron-HDR localisation techniques*,in:Brachytherapy 2, Mould RF (Ed), 83-87, Nucletron:Leersum, 1989.

Killian H, Baier K, Löffler E, Sussenbach K & Dorner KA, *Comparison of different planning algorithms used in interstitial radiotherapy with iridium-192 wires*, in:Brachytherapy 2, Mould RF (Ed), 92-100, Nucletron:Leersum, 1989.

Löffler E, *Source calibration of iridium-192 wires: part of a quality assurance program*, in:Brachytherap 2, Mould RF (Ed), 70-74, Nucletron:Leersum:, 1989

Meisberger LL, Keller RJ & Shalek RJ, *The effective attenuation in water of the gamma rays of gold-198, iridium-192, caesium-137, radium-226 & cobalt-60*, Radiology, **90**, 953-957, 1968.

Slessinger ED & Grigsby PW, *Verification studies of 3-dimensional brachytherapy source reconstruction techniques*, in:Brachytherapy 2, Mould RF (Ed), 130-135, Nucletron:Leersum, 1989.

31

Evaluation & Optimisation of Interstitial Brachytherapy Dose Distributions

H. Meertens, J. Borger, M. Steggerda & A. Blom

The Netherlands Cancer Institute,
Antoni van Leeuwenhoek Huis,
Plesmanlaan 121,
1066 CX Amsterdam,
The Netherlands.

Introduction

Advances in technology over the past decade have initiated a process of redefinition of planning and evaluation of brachytherapy. The traditional approaches such as the Manchester, Quimby and Paris systems are largely related to idealised implants tailored to specific dimensions of a target volume. The new approaches involve conformal positioning of a source configuration for which the treatment isodose contour is adapted to the shape of the target volume which is defined by 3-dimensional imaging.

Table 1
Areas in treatment planning in which a high level of sophistication has been achieved.

- Viewing of target volume & other relevant anatomical structures.
- Calculation of 3-dimensional dose distributions.
- Display & evaluation of dose distributions.
- Use of dose-volume histograms.

Computer hardware and software is now available to obtain a high level of sophistication, for instance in treatment planning, Table 1. In addition, new afterloading equipment became available allowing a large variety in source placement in the catheters.

LDR, PDR & HDR Brachytherapy

For LDR brachytherapy there is a tendency to apply seeds of different strengths and a non-uniform spacing within one implant instead of seeds of equal strengths and a uniform spacing, or wires with a uniform strength per unit length. The development of pulsed dose rate (PDR) techniques is very promising and it can be expected that LDR simulated brachytherapy by means of PDR can make the use of non-uniform source distributions with afterloading techniques feasible for basically LDR applications. For HDR brachytherapy with a stepping source afterloading device, the use of a wide variation of source positions inside the catheters and of different source strengths (dwell times) for each position is already clinical practice.

Criteria for a Good Implant

As a result of the introduction of these new technologies, the criteria for a good interstitial implant have to be (re)established. A good implant aims for a balance between good coverage of the target volume, a high dose uniformity inside the target volume, a small number of catheters and a steep dose fall-off outside the target volume. Although some adaptation of the dose distribution is possible after the source catheters have been positioned, it is of utmost importance that the implantation of these catheters is performed as good as possible in relation to the target volume. The catheters are usually placed near the edge of the target volume for a volume implant and in a plane for a planar implant. The second step, in the case of afterloading, is the determination of the position of the sources in the catheters and their strengths and dwell times. The catheters are then loaded with sources.

Optimal Loading

How we can determine which loading is optimal for a given target volume and catheter configuration? Whenever possible, dose evaluation should involve an inspection of 3-dimensional images of the target volume with an overlay of isodose contours calculated from accurately registered source locations. In addition to evaluating the coverage of the target volume and minimum dose within the target volume, it is useful to examine the complete dose distribution within this volume or alternatively, the volume distribution as a function of dose: dose-volume histograms. Since the dose rate variations are typical characteristics of interstitial implants, it would be appropriate to examine the relative homogeneity, defined as the amount of target volume receiving a range of dose rates. The significance of dose-volume evaluation is increasingly being recognised.

Implant Quality Indices

Several authors (Anderson 1986, van der Laarse 1992, Paul et al 1991, Saw & Suntharalingam 1988, 1990 & Wu et al 1988) have introduced a number

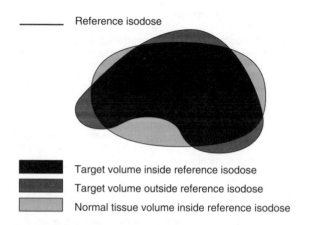

——— Reference isodose

■ Target volume inside reference isodose
■ Target volume outside reference isodose
□ Normal tissue volume inside reference isodose

Figure 1. Target and normal tissue volumes in relation to the reference isodose surface.

of indices to quantify the quality of an implant. The division of the target volume and the normal tissue volume by a reference isodose surface into several parts that might be relevant for the outcome of the treatment is shown schematically in Figure 1. Table 2 summarises the proposed indices that are related to the homogeneity of the dose distribution resulting from a given source configuration or as it exists inside the target volume. Table 3 shows the dosimetric parameters that have been used in the clinical example of a stereotactic brain implant that is given in this chapter. It is not yet clear what is the clinical significance of these various indices and to what extent they are correlated.

Table 2
Indices related to the uniformity of the dose distribution.

Index	Reference	Relates dose distribution with:
Uniformity	Anderson (1986)	Reference dose
Relative dose homogeneity	Saw et al (1988)	Target volume
Dose non-uniformity ratio	Saw et al (1988)	-
Dose homogeneity	Wu et al (1988)	Treatment volume
Volume gradient ratio	van der Laarse (1992)	-

Conformal Planning

Conformation therapy can be defined as a procedure of high precision irradiation of a 3-dimensional target volume where the dose distribution conforms as closely as possible to the shape of the target volume. Conformal planning may involve an iterative adjustment of sources and inspection of the 3-dimensional dose distribution or it may involve an iterative adjustment of sources and inspection of an objective function by computer. For the latter procedure, however, criteria for optimisation are needed. Dose points at the surface of the target volume and inside this volume, together with some of the indices mentioned previously might be useful for this purpose.

Stereotactic Brain Implant

The various aspects mentioned previously will be illustrated for the optimisation of the source loading of a stereotactic brain implant, prepared for a treatment with a microSelectron-HDR. After fixation of the Leksell stereotactic frame to the skull of the patient, a series of CT images are made: typically 30 slices with a 3 mm position increment. The images are transferred to a 3-dimensional treatment planning system (Scandiplan) and the target volume is delineated. Then the desired placement of the catheters for the implant, in relation to the target volume, is determined. We use various templates and for this discussion templates B and C have been used for treatment planning. Both templates are meant for seven parallel placed catheters (source strings), six on a circle and one central. The diameters of the circles are 1.5 cm and 2.0 cm respectively for the templates B and C.

Table 3
Dosimetric parameters for the description of the quality of a brachytherapy application.

Coverage Index (CI)
Fraction of the target volume receiving a dose equal to or greater than the reference dose.

External Volume Index (EI)
Amount of normal tissue volume that receives a dose equal to or greater that the reference dose. The volume is expressed as a percentage of the target volume.

Relative Dose Homogeneity Index (HI)
Fraction of the target volume receiving a dose in the range of 1.0 to 1.5 times the reference dose.

Overdose Volume Index (OI)
Fraction of the target volume receiving a dose more then 2.0 times the reference dose.

Sum Index (SI)
Weighted sum of the coverage index, external index and relative dose homogeneity index.

Four alternative plans a, b, c and d have been studied using the indices mentioned in Table 3 and Table 4 gives the major characteristics of these four plans. The diameter of the template circle determines the position the catheters (source) to the target volume in the direction perpendicular to the catheters. For the plans b, c and d (template C) the sources are near the edge of the target volume. For plans a, b and c the source positions in the direction of the catheter lengths were just inside the outline of the target volume. For plan d these latter sources were extended to 0.8 cm outside the target volume to follow the Paris system but note that plan d is not fully in line with the Paris system. Such an extended catheter placement would also result in more physical trauma of the normal brain tissue and is therefore not desirable.

Table 4
Description of four different treatment plans.
(Source spacing in string of 10 mm)

Plan	Template	Dwell times	Comments
a	B	Equal	Sources well inside target volume
b	C	Equal	Sources near edge of the target volume
c	C	Different	Interactive optimisation
d	C	Equal	Extended strings:Paris system

The source spacing within each catheter was about 10 mm. For plan c the dwell times for the various source positions were different. A manual optimisation has been performed. Regions of underdosage of the target volume and overdosage of the normal tissue volume were determined from an analysis of the dose distribution. The strengths of sources near these regions were adjusted in line with the findings from the dose evaluation.

Figure 2 gives the results of the CI, EI, OI and HI indices for plan c. For a comparison of the four alternative plans a-d the coverage index has been taken as 90% for all plans. From Figure 2 we see that this results in a reference dose of 30 Gy with EI= 40%, OI=12% and HI=60%.

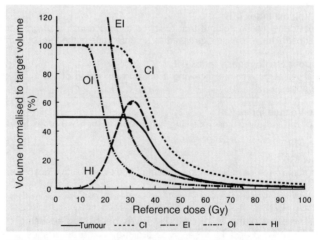

Figure 2. Variation of the coverage index (CI), external volume index (EI), relative dose homogeneity index (HI) and overdose volume index (OI) as a function of the reference dose for plan c of a brain implant. The dots show the value of the various indices for a 30 Gy reference dose. The integral dose volume histogram of the tumour (outline of the enhancement ring) is also given.

In order to find an overall figure of merit, the values of the CI, EI and HI indices can be added, resulting in the sum index SI= (CI - EI + HI) :the minus sign is because a low EI value is desired. For a particular plan the dose at maximum SI value would give the best reference dose, while absolute SI values could be used to compare different plans. Instead of an equal weight, different weighting factors could be introduced in the equation for SI.

Table 5
EI, HI, OI and SI values of four different treatment plans
for a CI value of 90%, where SI=(CI-EI+HI)

Plan	EI (%)	HI (%)	OI (%)	SI (%)
a	41	30	20	80
b	50	65	10	105
c	40	60	12	110
d	64	68	8	94

The results for the four plans are shown in Table 5. The external index (EI) has the lowest (best) value for plan c as a result of the manual optimisation. The highest (worst) value for EI was found for plan d, which was not surprising because the sources extended outside the target volume into the normal brain tissue. The homogeneity index (HI) was, however, the best for plan d, also due to the extended source positions and worst for plan a as a result of the concentration of the sources near the centre of the target volume (template B, diameter 3.0 cm). For the overdose figure a similar results was found: good for plan d, bad for plan a. Using the sum index one could conclude that plan c was the best.

Although new data on target volume coverage, irradiation of normal tissue and dose homogeneity became available for this particular type of implant using these various indices, it is still very difficult to combine these data and to deduce the optimal source distribution.

Conclusions

It can be concluded that the current interest in dose evaluation is no longer in the use of approximation methods which are only valid for idealised implants, but is directed towards identifying the dose surface that just encompasses the 3-dimensional target volume, provided that the catheters have been placed adequately inside the target volume. To facilitate optimisation procedures, new parameters for the judgement of the quality of interstitial implants have been suggested. The clinical impact of the conformal approach has to be established in the near future. The departure from classical systems, for instance by introducing new implant quality indices, has to be made with great care to avoid unwanted effects.

References

Anderson LL, *A "natural" volume-dose histogram for brachytherapy*, Medical Physics, **13**, 898-903, 1986.

Laarse van der R, *Private communication*, 1992.

Paul JM, Philip PC, Brandenburg RW & Khan FR, *Histograms in brachytherapy*, Endocurietherapy/Hyperthermia Oncology, **7**, 13-26, 1991.

Saw CB & Suntharalingam N, *Reference dose rates for single-plane and double-plane iridium-192 implants*, Medical Physics, **15**, 391-396, 1988.

Saw CB & Suntharalingam N, *Quantitative assessment of interstitial implants*, Int. J. Radiation Oncology Biology & Physics, **20**, 135-139, 1990.

Wu A, Ulin K & Sternick ES, *A dose homogeneity index for evaluating 192Ir interstitial breast implants*, Medical Physics, **15**, 104-107, 1988.

32

Three-Dimensional Brachytherapy Treatment Planning at New York Medical College

B.S. Hilaris[1], M. Tenner[2], C. Moorthy[1], M. High[2], L. Shih[1], D. Silvern[1], D. Mastoras[1] & L. Stabile[1]

[1]Department of Radiation Medicine,
[2]Department of Radiology,
New York Medical College,
Valhalla,
New York 10596,
USA.

Introduction

The objective of clinical optimisation of brachytherapy is to determine the best possible target dose likely to control the tumour, while limiting the radiation effects on surrounding normal tissue. Physical optimisation of brachytherapy begins with the target dose specified by the clinician and it involves several steps that are necessary to determine the number, position, strength and spacing of sources. A customised template can be fabricated in suitable cases in order to facilitate and increase the accuracy of interstitial brachytherapy.

The widespread use of computers and computer graphics combined with extensive utilisation of computed tomography and magnetic resonance imaging can be credited for the current popularity of 3-dimensional treatment planning.

In the light of growing clinical evidence that improved local control increases the possibility of long-term survival, 3-dimensional treatment planning provides radiation therapy with the tools necessary to improve local control and therefore also cure rates. The investigation of 3-dimensional treatment planning and delivery currently focuses on external radiation therapy (Photon Treatment Planning Collaborative Working Group 1991, Lichter et al 1992), while 3-dimensional brachytherapy planning is still in its infancy.

Potential Benefits of 3-Dimensional Brachytherapy Planning

3-dimensional treatment planning depends heavily on dose calculations and volume displays. Most of the benefits are therefore related to the ability to delineate and localise more accurately volumes of anatomical structures, to compute dose-volume histograms, to quantitate the dose to target area and to adjoining normal tissues and to display all this information in real time to verify the treatment, modify it when appropriate and monitor the response when applicable.

3-Dimensional Brachytherapy Research at New York Medical College

A 3-dimensional brachytherapy optimisation planning program was initiated at New York Medical College in 1990 for the treatment of patients with prostate, gynaecological, head & neck and non-small cell lung cancers (High et al 1991). A 3-dimensional brachytherapy dose distribution system is linked to 3-dimensional anatomy to study the feasibility of dose optimisation. The current status of this investigative protocol is as follows.

Defining Structures of Interest for 3-Dimensional Display

Imaging. The patient is scanned using cross-sectional imaging machines such as CT or MR. Between 70 and 100 serial axial CT scans, 2 to 5 mm apart, are obtained. The patient is positioned in an immobilisation device with external markers placed on the skin corresponding to relevant anatomical landmarks. This is to help form a coordinate system when the scan is later utilised in the brachytherapy planning system, Figure 1.

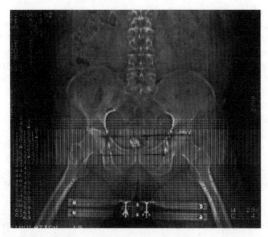

Figure 1. The patient is scanned in the treatment position. A total of 70-100 CT cross-sections are obtained to provide data for both target and normal tissues. Contiguous slices with thicknesses in the range of 2 mm for the target and 5-10 mm for normal tissue are usually adequate.

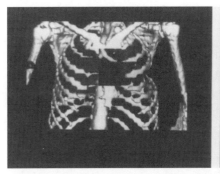

Figure 2. Typical 3-dimensional digital images obtained from CT scans. The range of the data to be displayed can be chosen by the user. For instance on the **left** only bone and lung are displayed, whereas on the **right** the lung, trachea and bronchi are visualised.

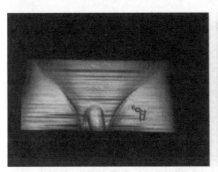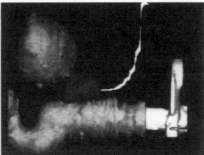

Figure 3. 3-dimensional graphic display of CT digital images of pelvic anatomy. On the **left** is seen the contour of the patient's skin surface. On the **right** the internal organs are displayed including the bladder, prostate, urethra and rectum with a template.

Definition of Structures. Once the cross-sectional images are obtained they are loaded into the ISG system (ISG Technologies Inc, Toronto, Canada) using magnetic tape. Target volumes and critical organs are outlined on each relevant slice. Automatic contouring has the potential to speed the process. However, this is very effective only for drawing the skin surface and internal structures with densities substantially different than soft tissue such as bone and lung. This approach does not work very well for structures with water-like densities and for target volumes. Manual slice by slice contouring is currently employed utilising either a digitiser pad or track ball. This user interactive approach is laborious and burdened by the inherent variability and differences between users.

3-Dimensional Anatomy Display. The operator of the ISG system reconstructs and displays the 3-dimensional anatomy with the target and critical organs outlined, Figures 2 and 3. In addition the operator measures and reports the target volume to the physicist.

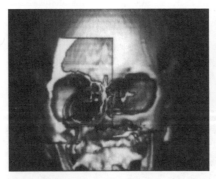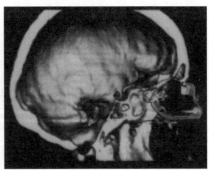

Figure 4. Frontal and lateral view of bony anatomy and a paranasal tumour with superimposed iodine-125 isodose line distributions. The inner line represents the 100% dose and the outer line the 50% dose.

Establishing Implant Design Aims & Constraints

The physicist discusses with the clinician the planned minimum dose to the target volume, the allowable dose range within this target and the maximum recommended dose to the whole or to a part of the critical organs. The required total activity for the specified target volume is calculated using a reference table and the number of sources is determined based on the activity per source provided by the manufacturer.

The physicist determines the position of the needles within the target volume (approximately 75% in the periphery and 25% in the centre) using uniform spacing, taking into consideration anatomical constraints and assuming that the needles are perpendicular to the template utilised at CT simulation. The number and position of the sources within each needle, spaced 0.5-1.5 cm apart is based on the cephalocaudal dimensions measured in the 3-dimensional volume.

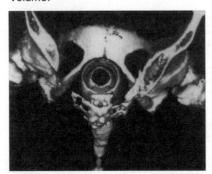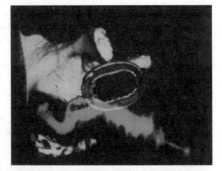

Figure 5. Frontal and lateral view of pelvic anatomy, bones, vagina with HDR applicator and rectum with probe. In this example the inner line represents the 100% dose and the outer line the 50% dose obtained with the Nucletron optimisation treatment planning system. Cutting through selected anatomical regions permits a better evaluation of the dose distribution in the vagina and rectum.

Designing of Possible Plans/Isodose Distributions

The source coordinates are entered into the Multidata Planning System for interstitial brachytherapy and the Nucletron Brachytherapy Planning System for iridium-192 high dose rate brachytherapy. The Nucletron system provides a preliminary optimised plan which is then loaded into the Multidata system. An initial slice by slice isodose distribution is generated by the treatment planning system. The generated isodose contours are magnified to match the 3-dimensional anatomy display. They are subsequently superimposed onto the 3-dimensional anatomy and inspected to determine whether the entire tumour is adequately encompassed by the specified isodose surface and that the dose to critical organs does not exceed the upper limits of the specified tolerance dose, Figures 4-6.

Optimisation of the dose distribution is achieved by repeated adjustments of source position, strength and number, until the desired configuration is reached. At this time the final isodose distribution is registered.

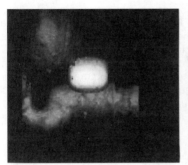 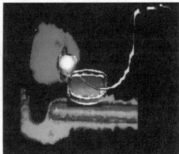

Figure 6. Lateral display of a palladium-103 prostatic implant dose distribution. On the **left** the 100% isodose surface completely covers the prostate (the light gray area). On the **right** a cut through the middle of the gland demonstrates the 100% and the 50% isodose distributions. The target area receives 100% of the dose while the anterior rectal wall receives approximately 50% of the dose.

Figure 7. Two examples of reformatted individual coronal images of the same patient's anatomy, with the superimposed dose distribution. Such displays are helpful in the evaluation of the treatment plan.

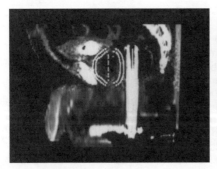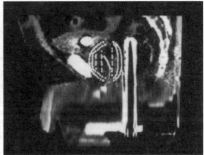

Figure 8. Examples of reformatted sagittal images of the same patient. They are used to evaluate the treatment plan.

Plan Evaluation & Implementation

The evaluation of a dose distribution on reconstructed coronal, Figure 7, sagittal, Figure 8, or transverse planes, Figure 9, is a valuable tool for the evaluation of 3-dimensional distributions. The system, however, has a 3-dimensional display with real time viewing capabilities. This latter capability enables the radiation oncologist to view the target volume or normal tissue volume with the superimposed isodose surfaces. The anatomical structures can be studied either individually or as several together. This feature is extremely useful for determining proper coverage of the tumour target volume and for accurate sparing of critical structures, especially if they are situated in close proximity to each other.

Future Directions

More sophisticated techniques are currently being tested to improve the accuracy and reproducibility of target definition (Chaney & Pizer 1992), to incorporate cumulative dose volume frequency distributions [ie. dose-volume his-

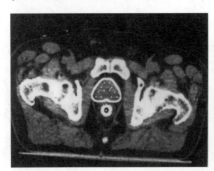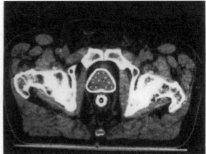

Figure 9. Examples of transverse planes of the same patient which are used for additional plan evaluation..

tograms], (Drzymala et al 1991, Hilaris et al 1988), and to develop biological models for tumour control, (Schultheiss et al 1983, Gotein 1992) and normal tissue complication probability, (Lyman & Wolbarst 1987, Kutcher et al 1991). The final and most exciting step of our programme is the development of *computerised brachyrobotics* which will guide the brachytherapy source(s) through a sensor device to the treatment target within the patient's anatomy and thus allow the accurate implementation of the optimised 3-dimensional brachytherapy plan.

References

Chaney EL & Pizer SM, *Defining anatomical structures from medical images*, Seminars in Radiation Oncology, **2**, 215-225, 1992.

Drzymala RE, Mohan R, Brewster L et al, *Dose-volume histograms*, Int. J. Radiation Oncology Biology & Physics, **21**, 71-78, 1991.

Gotein M, *The comparison of treatment plans*, Seminars in Radiation Oncology, **2**, 246-256, 1992.

High M, Shih L, Silvern D & Hilaris BS, 3-D *brachytherapy treatment planning*, in:*Proceedings of Prostate cancer in the 90's, advances in diagnosis and treatment*, Department of Radiation Medicine, New York Medical College:Valhalla, 1991.

Hilaris BS, Nori D & Anderson LL (Eds), *Interstitial brachytherapy planning and evaluation*, in: *Atlas of Brachytherapy*, 70-95, Macmillan:New York, 1988.

Kutcher GH, Burman C, Brewster L et al, *Histogram reduction method for calculating complication probabilities for three-dimensional treatment planning evaluations*, Int. J. Radiation Oncology Biology & Physics, **21**, 137-146, 1991

Lichter AS, Sandler HM, Robertson JM et al, *Clinical experience with three-dimensional treatment planning*, Seminars in Radiation Oncology, **2**, 257-266, 1992.

Lyman JT & Wolbarst AB, *Optimisation of radiation therapy, III: A method of assessive complication probabilities from dose-volume histograms*, Int. J. Radiation Oncology Biology & Physics, **13**, 103-109, 1987.

Photon Treatment Planning Collaborative Working Group, State-of-the-art of external photon beam radiation treatment planning, Int. J. Radiation Oncology Biology & Physics, **21**, 9-23, 1991.

Schultheiss TE, Orton CG & Peck RA, *Models in radiotherapy, volume effects*, Medical Physics, **10**, 410-415, 1983

33

Volume Optimisation: an American Viewpoint

G.K. Edmundson

William Beaumont Hospital,
3601 W. 13 Mile Road,
Royal Oak,
MI 48072,
USA.

Introduction

There are two basic types of dwell time optimisation available in the Nucletron Planning System. The first, dose point optimisation, depends on the establishment of points to which dose is prescribed. The second is Geometric Optimisation (GO) in which no points are used. The geometric relationships among the dwell positions themselves are used to determine dwell times, Figure 1.

The proper functioning of GO is dependent upon assumptions which, we have found, are not identical in Europe and the USA. This has limited the usefulness of GO and has had interesting side effects upon it's development.

Modern interstitial brachytherapy in Europe is closely associated with the Paris system in which continuous wires of iridium-192 are placed, often with large inter-wire spacings. In contrast, American experience has been based upon the work of Ulrich Henschke in which sources consist of iridium-192 ribbons. These are nylon tubes containing short (3 mm) pieces of iridium-192 wire, conventionally spaced at 1.0 cm. These composite *point sources* are placed close together, in the range 10-15 mm between catheters.

In this system the implant consists of large numbers of point sources, spaced at approximately the same distance in all three dimensions. An important, but often unstated assumption of the Paris system is that sources should ideally be continuous. The equivalent, and even less often stated assumption of American practice is that sources should be equally spaced in all three dimensions.

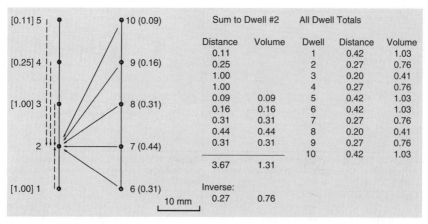

Figure 1. GO in a nutshell.

These assumptions are of course mutually exclusive. When workers on both sides of the Atlantic attempted cross-migration of their respective systems and assumptions to the realm of optimised implantation with stepping sources, confusion arose. GO is clearly a product of the American approach and falters when forced into a continuous source context.

History of GO

The first working computer programme to implement Geometric Optimisation was written in 1987, as an attempt to cope with what was then our new capability to build iodine-125 ribbons of variable spacing. It was a two-dimensional programme in that it accounted only for inter-catheter distances in the central plane. A relative weight was determined for each catheter which could then be implemented as different time in situ, or different spacing within that ribbon. The algorithm worked well but proved difficult to incorporate into any of the planning systems we had available.

In early 1989 we were contemplating the prospect of using HDR as a substitute for intra-operative electron beam therapy. A method was needed for fast, if crude, optimisation of volume implants of perhaps low quality. The old code was reviewed, extended to three-dimensions and tested in the new context.

The new method worked very well for completely regular implants, but over-compensated for implants where catheters converged, Figures 2 and 4. The problem, we reasoned, was that the dose contributions of each source assumed unit time for each source. This assumption was true prior to optimisation but not true afterwards. The most obvious solution was to iterate: repeat the process again after optimisation and continue this process until the dwell times no longer changed. This appeared to the American investigators to work well and the first clinical implementation was written by Ezzell of Harper Hospital, Detroit, to be used in his Theraplan system, Figure 6.

When the method was tested in the Nucletron NPS planning system by van der Laarse, he found that the iterated results were always worse than the initial

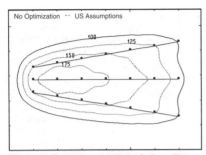

Figure 2. Two plane implant of six catheters with deviation. Calculation is midway between planes.

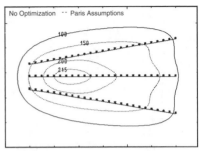

Figure 3. Same implant with 2.5 mm step size. Note that dose variation is larger than the USA case.

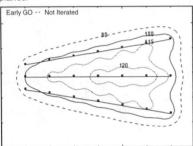

Figure 4. Without iteration the target line does not encompass the catheters. The hot spot moves beyond the centre: over-optimisation

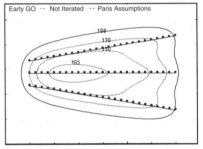

Figure 5. With a short step size the implant is under-optimised.

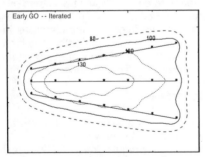

Figure 6. With iteration the target line now encompasses entire volume.

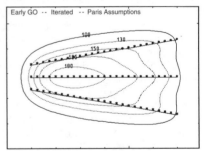

Figure 7. With iteration, even less optimisation is obtained.

calculation. This result was very surprising to us in the USA as we had two different programmes running very successfully.

We did not realise at the time that he was using example cases with large inter-catheter spacing and a very small (2.5 mm) step size, Figures 3, 5 and 7. As an alternative to iteration, van der Laarse proposed limiting the contribution that could be counted from a single dwell position.

In discussions between van der Laarse, Luthman and myself we worked out various schemes. One was to electively not count contribution from the same catheter. This became the *volume* method adopted in NPS. It had the benefit of filling in cold spots between catheters, a useful but sometimes dangerous attribute.

Another limitation on contribution was to limit the contribution from a single 'other' dwell position by setting the distance of any very close dwell to a user selected minimum. This became the *minimum* distance parameter used in NPS. It prevents two nearby dwell positions for annihilating one another. In practice, the default value of 2.5 mm assigned in NPS is sufficient for most clinical cases. Further refinements were added to the final release code in NPS which result in faster calculation. Our current in-house implementation at William Beaumont Hospital requires approximately 20-30 milliseconds to optimise an implant of 90 dwell positions.

Using GO

It has been our experience that GO may be used for almost all implant situations, without help from the dose point method, if dwell positions are spaced no closer than 1.0 cm along each catheter, Figures 8 and 9. If a user must place dwell positions close together in the catheters, combine GO with the dose point method, or to begin with, use a point method. A prime clinical example of this is an implant in the base of tongue. There, catheters diverge much as shown in Figures 8 and 9, and a critical dose region exists at the dorsum of the tongue, analogous to the right-hand end in the illustrations.

It is most important that a full dose be delivered to this surface. If dwell positions are chosen too close together the implant will be under-optimised. This is somewhat masked in the illustrations, which are normalised to the minimum dose in the implanted volume, ie. standard American practice. If the same distributions were normalised according to Paris points, ie. dose minima in the central plane, Figure 8 would remain unchanged but Figure 9 would have dose reduced by about 35%.

The one instance where GO can be dangerous is where you have a small number of catheters and attempt to use the volume method, Figure 10. In this type of case, the algorithm will attempt to produce a uniform distribution midway between the catheters with the result that the local doses near the divergent ends of the catheters are extremely high. This may be appropriate at times but requires very careful consultation between the physician and physicist. Using the distance method instead is likely to produce a more appropriate result, Figure 11.

It is especially dangerous to use volume optimisation where one of the catheters is shortened, Figure 12. In this situation there are no nearby restraining points at the superior end, with the result shown. This type of error will usually be obvious by the extremely large dwell times generated at one end. It is always important, however, to calculate proper distributions prior to treatment. Once again, using the distance method, Figure 13, will produce the desired result.

In Figure 1, two catheters are shown, 15 mm apart, with dwell positions numbered. The numbers in brackets are the inverse square distances to dwell #2. Relative time in dwell #2 is determined by summing the inverse square dis-

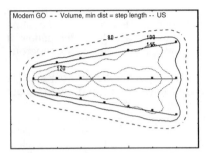

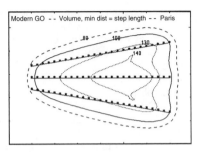

Figure 8. Our current method with the minimum distance set at 10 mm.

Figure 9. Our current method using Paris system assumptions and a minimum distance of 2.5 mm.

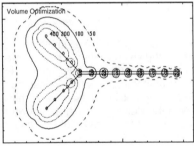

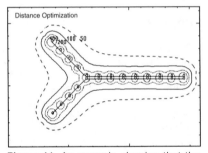

Figure 10. Volume optimisation on a catheter implant gives an equal dose between catheters.

Figure 11. An example showing that the distance method produces excellent results.

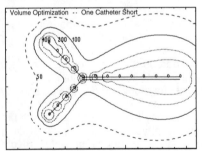

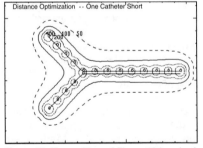

Figure 12. This illustrations shows a most dangerous situation: one catheter short with volume optimisation.This illustrations shows a most dangerous situation: one catheter short with volume optimisation.

Figure 13. The problem of Figure 12 is solved by using the distance method.

tances of all dwells (distance method) or dwells in the other catheter only (volume method), then taking the inverse of the sum. This procedure is performed once for each dwell position. The totals shown are the relative dwell times for each dwell position.

34

The Stepping Source Dosimetry System as an Extension of the Paris System

R. van der Laarse

Nucletron Research BV,
Waardgelder 1,
3905 TH Veenendaal,
The Netherlands

Introduction

During recent years there has been a significant increase in the use of high dose rate (HDR) brachytherapy with a single source which steps along the lengths of the catheters.

Although in HDR brachytherapy, low dose rate (LDR) dosimetry systems (Meredith 1967, Glasser et al. 1967, Shalek and Stovall 1969, Dutreix et al. 1982) may be applied if one corrects for dose rate effects (Hall & Brenner 1992), HDR stepping source brachytherapy offers the additional possibility of adapting individual dwell times in order to cover the target volume with as homogeneous a dose distribution as possible. To obtain this, treatment planning software to optimise the dwell times in the dwell positions along the catheters is indispensible (Edmundson 1990, van der Laarse & de Boer 1990, van der Laarse et al 1991).

The Paris Dosimetry System (PDS) is designed for implants performed with wires of equal linear activity (Dutreix et al. 1982,1987). It is based on parallel catheters in a single-plane implant or a double-plane implant, afterloaded with iridium-192 wires or with regularly spaced pellets of equal activity (Marinello et al. 1985, Paul et al. 1989). For a given target volume, the Paris system specifies the spacing between the active lengths in the catheters. It gives rules how to implant a target volume $V = L \times W \times T$ as a function of L, W and T, with L the length, W the width and T the thickness of the target volume.

The Paris Dosimetry System was developed as an LDR system using iridium-192 wires or strings with equidistant caesium-137 pellets. It can easily be adapted to HDR by applying equidistant dwell positions with equal dwell times.

The Stepping Source Dosimetry System SSDS is a system to optimise implants with needles or flexible catheters with an HDR source stepping through them. Because the HDR stepping source implants are so much like the iridium-192 wire implants, the SSDS is developed as an extension of the PDS. The main difference is the use of increased dwell times at the longitudinal ends of the implant to keep the active dwell positions inside the target volume. It also reduces the dwell times in the central part of the implant to increase the dose homogeneity across the target. This chapter discusses the differences between the two dosimetry systems.

The Paris Dosimetry System

The Paris System uses the following parameters, see Figure 1.

[1] S is the spacing between the catheters.

[2] In a single-plane implant the lateral margin m_l is the lateral distance between the reference isodose line and the outer catheters in the central transversal and longitudinal plane.

[3] In multi-plane implants the safety margin m_s is the distance between the reference isodose line and the outer catheters in the central transversal plane.

The PDS implantation rules can be approximated as follows.

[1] The spacing S varies between 8 - 15 mm for short implants (L $\leq$ 3 cm, AL $\leq$ 4 cm) and 15 - 22 mm for long implants (L $\geq$ 7 cm, AL $\geq$ 10 cm).

[2] For a target thickness T $\leq$ 12 mm single plane implants are used, with S $\approx$ T / 0.6, which gives $m_l \approx$ 0.35 x S.

[3] For T $\geq$ 12 mm double plane implants are used. A double plane implant with a catheter pattern in triangles must conform to S $\approx$ T / 1.3, which gives $m_s \approx$ 0.2 x S. For a double plane implant in squares S $\approx$ T / 1.57, which gives $m_s \approx$ 0.27 x S.

[4] The active lengths in the catheters for single and double plane implants are given by AL $\approx$ L / 0.7 for iridium wires but by AL $\approx$ L / 0.8 for iridium pellets spaced 5 mm apart. The active lengths extend outside the target to correct for the bending of the reference isodose surface in between the catheter ends.

Basal dose points are defined in the central transversal plane through the implant and are located midway between the catheters where the dose rate is lowest, see again Figure 1. The basal dose BD is the mean dose in these dose points. The reference dose RD is taken as 85% of the basal dose. It defines an isodose surface extending 0.5 cm from the outer catheters, Figure 2. This isodose surface will encompass the target volume T x W x L if forementioned rules are followed.

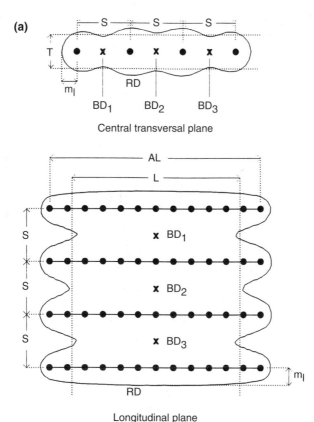

Figure 1. Definitions of the parameters of the Paris Dosimetry System for a **(a)** single-plane implant, **(b)** double-plane implant in a triangular pattern and **(c)** double-plane implant in a square pattern.

● : dwell position in the plane of dose distribution.
o : dwell position either behind or in front of the plane of dose distribution.
x : basal dose point, midway between the surrounding catheters.
S : spacing between the catheters.
T : thickness of the target volume.
L : length of the target volume.
AL : active length of the catheter.
$BD = (BD_1+BD_2+BD_3)/3$: basal dose, defined as the average dose in the basal dose points in the central transversal plane.
RD : reference isodose line, defined as 85 % of BD.
m_l : lateral margin between the reference isodose line and the outer catheters in a single plane implant.
$m_s = (m_1+m_2+m_3+m_4+m_5)/5$ **(Figure 1b)** or $(m_1+m_2+m_3+m_4+m_5+m_6)/6$ **(Figure 1c)**: safety margin, defined as the average margin between the reference isodose line and the outer catheters.

(b)

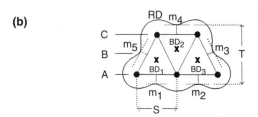

Central transversal plane

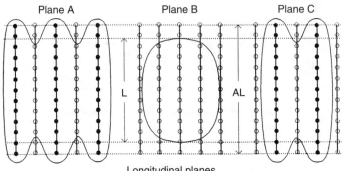

Longitudinal planes

(c)

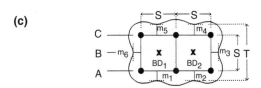

Central transversal plane

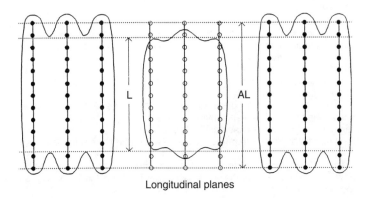

Longitudinal planes

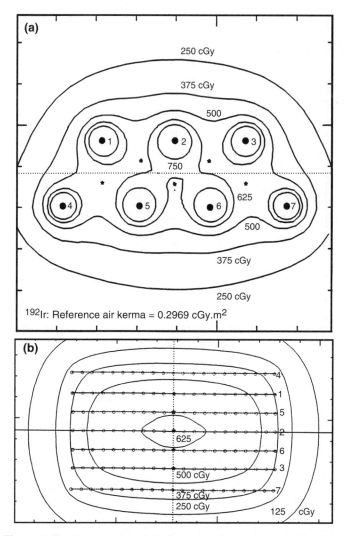

Figure 2. Double-plane breast implant according to the Paris Dosimetry System. The dwell positions are equally spaced at 0.5 cm and are equally weighted. The reference dose RD is defined as 85 % of the average dose in the basal dose points in the central transversal plane. RD = 500 cGy.

● : dwell position in the plane of dose distribution.
o : dwell position either behind or in front of the plane of dose distribution.
* : basal dose point, midway between the surrounding catheters.
(a) Central transversal plane.
············ indicates the central longitudinal plane.
(b) Central longitudinal plane.
············ indicates the central transversal plane.

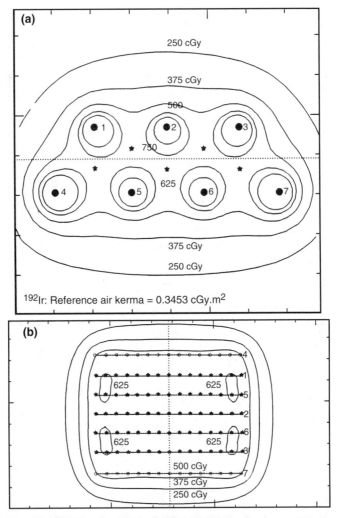

Figure 3. Double-plane breast implant optimised according to the Stepping Source Dosimetry System. Active length of the catheters is 7 cm. The dwell positions are equally spaced at 0.5 cm. The optimisation aims at the same dose in all dose points midway between the catheters. The reference dose RD is defined as 85 % of the mean dose in all dose points. RD = 500 cGy.

● : dwell position in the plane of dose distribution.
o : dwell position either behind or in front of the plane of dose distribution.
★ : basal dose point, midway between the surrounding catheters.
(a) Central transversal plane.
·········· indicates the central longitudinal plane.
(b). Central longitudinal plane.
·········· indicates the central transversal plane.

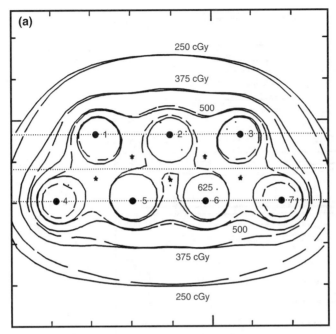

Figure 4a. Dose distribution in the central plane of the PDS implant and the SSDS implant of **Figures 2 and 3**.
———— : Dose distribution optimised according to SSDS to the same dose in all dose points. Active length of the catheters is 7 cm. The reference dose RD is defined as 85 % of the mean dose in all dose points. RD = 500 cGy.
---------- : Dose distribution according to the Paris System. The reference dose RD is defined as 85 % of the mean dose in the basal dose points in the central transversal plane. RD = 500 cGy.
·············· : Longitudinal planes of **Figure 4b**.
Both reference isodose lines coincide except around the outer catheters where the Paris RD isodose line bends inwards to the implant. The SSDS dose distribution is more homogeneous than the Paris one.

The Stepping Source Dosimetry System

SSDS uses the same implant rules as the Paris Dosimetry System, except that the active lengths in the catheters remains within 0.5 cm from the reference isodose surface. Thus AL ≈ L - 1.0 cm. The dwell positions in the catheters are again taken equidistant.

In SSDS dose points are defined between the catheters along the active lengths, thus through the whole target volume, Figure 3. The dwell times are optimised such, that practically the same dose is obtained in all dose points. The Reference Dose RD is taken as 85% of the mean dose in all dose points.

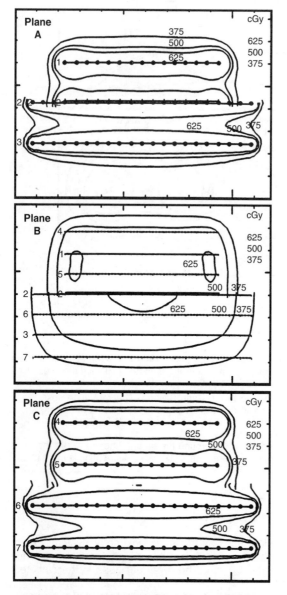

Figure 4b. Comparison of the dose distributions in longitudinal planes of the Paris implant of **Figure 2** and the SSDS implant of **Figure 3**. The upper part of each dose distribution is given by the SSDS implant, the lower part by the Paris implant. Note the more regular shape of the 500 cGy RD isodose line of the SSDS implant as compared to the Paris implant.

Plane A: the plane through catheters 1, 2 and 3 in **Figure 4a**.

Plane B: the central longitudinal plane.

Plane C: the plane through catheters 4,5,6 and 7 in **Figure 4a**.

SSDS is an HDR system and cannot be used in LDR applications. It is, however, suitable for pulsed dose rate applications (Hall & Brenner 1992, Fowler & Mount 1992). In the following section the differences between SSDS and PDS dose distributions are presented.

Differences between SSDS and PDS

[1] Active Lengths in Catheters

In a PDS implant the active wires or pellets must extend outside the target volume in order to compensate for the dose fall-off at the ends of the implanted wires or catheters. For example, the extension for a target length of 7 cm, treated with a double plane implant, is 1.5 cm at either end, see Figure 2b.

In an optimised HDR stepping source implant the dwell times are such that the same dose is obtained in all dose points midway between the catheters over the whole length of the implant. This results in increased dwell times at the outer parts of the implant, see Figure 3b. Contrarily to the Paris-type implant, all dwell positions are now located inside the target volume. The RD isodose surface is encompassing the implant at a distance of 0.5 cm from the active dwell positions in the outer catheters.

[2] Target Volume & Treated Volume

In a Paris implant the reference isodose dips deeply between the catheters at the outer ends of the implant, due to the linear source strength of the wire or the equal source strength of the pellets, Figure 4b. Therefore, implants according to the Paris system extend the active lengths outside the target. This results in an appreciable volume outside the target, receiving a dose equal or higher than the reference dose.

In an SSDS implant the increased dwell times at the outer ends of the catheters flatten the reference isodose surface in that area. As a result the outer active dwell positions should stay inside the target volume at 0.5 cm from the target surface, see again Figure 4b.

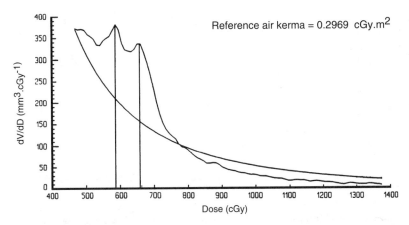

Figure 5. Differential volume-dose histogram of the Paris implant of Figure 2. The curve underlying the histogram is given by a point source in the centre of the implant, indicating the influence of the inverse square law on the histogram. The peak at 660 cGy is caused by the volumes between the inner catheters 1,2,5 , 2,5,6 and 2,3,6; the peak at 580 cGy is caused by the volumes between the outer catheters 1,4,5 and 3,6,7.

[3] Dose Homogeneity over the Target Volume

In both implant systems the dose is quite uniform along the catheters in the central part of the implant. In the Paris system the inner catheters have the same strength as the outer ones, resulting in a higher dose in the central part, Figure 2. The differential volume dose histogram shows a peak at two dose values, each peak corresponding to a large volume, Figure 5. The volume found at the lower dose is the volume between the outer catheters 1, 4, 5 and between 3, 6, 7. The volume found at the higher dose corresponds to the volume between catheters 1, 2, 5; 2, 5, 6 and 2, 3, 6 in Figure 2a.

In SSDS the optimisation of the dwell times of the stepping source leads to the same dose in all dose points in the inner regions but also in the outer regions of the implant. As is clearly seen in the differential volume-dose histogram, Figure 6, a single large peak now appears, corresponding to a much larger volume under the peak dose. This is due to the optimisation process which aims at the same dose in all dose points placed between the catheters and results in a large volume with that dose, see Figure 3.

[4] Reference Dose

In PDS and SSDS the Reference Dose RD is the prescribed dose value on an isodose surface encompassing the target volume. In the Paris system the RD is based on the mean value of the basal dose points in the central plane only. In SSDS the RD is based on the mean dose over all dose points in the implant. As the dwell times are optimised to obtain the same dose in all dose points, the mean dose over all dose points is practically equal to the mean dose over the dose points in the central plane only. This explains why the reference isodoses of both systems practically coincide in the central plane, except around the outer catheters.

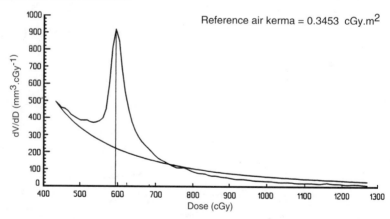

Figure 6. Differential volume-dose histogram of the SSDS implant of Figure 3. The curve underlying the histogram is given by a point source in the centre of the implant, indicating the influence of the inverse square law on the histogram. The large volume under the peak dose of 590 cGy corresponds to the volumes around the dose points between the catheters, which are optimised to the same dose. Note that 85 % of 590 cGy is 501.5 cGy, very close to the reference dose of 500 cGy in Figure 3; the difference being caused by the voxel size of the histogram.

This is demonstrated in Figure 4a by catheters 4 and 7. In SSDS the outer catheters 4 and 7 are more weighted than the inner catheters, in order to compensate for the lack of dose from surrounding catheters. This prevents the inward bending of the 500 cGy reference isodose line around the catheters 4 and 7, as occurring in the Paris System .

In the volume-dose histogram of the SSDS implant, see Figure 6, the dose under the peak, thus the dose with maximum volume-dose gradient dV/dD, is equal to the mean dose in all dose points. So the reference dose is also equal to 85 % of the peak dose in the differential volume-dose histogram.

[5] Dose Distribution

The difference between the dose distribution according to the Paris Dosimetry System and according to SSDS is presented in Figure 4. The reference dose RD of the Paris-type implant is taken as 85 per cent of the mean dose in the dose points in the central plane only, the reference dose RD of the SSDS-type implant is taken as 85% of the mean dose in all dose points over the implant. The Reference Dose RD is in both cases 500 cGy. The dotted lines in Figure 4a are the isodose lines obtained with the Paris Dosimetry System. The solid lines are the isodose lines obtained by SSDS, thus optimised to the same dose in the dose points placed midway between the catheters along the whole length of the implant

Figure 4b compares the dose distribution of SSDS and the Paris system in the planes through needles 1,2,3; through needles 4,5,6,7 and in the longitudinal mid-plane. The upper half of the dose distribution of each plane is given by the SSDS implant, the lower half by the Paris-type implant. It is clearly shown that the SSDS implant gives a more homogeneous dose coverage of the target volume than the Paris implant. The RD isodose line extends in the transversal planes 0.5 cm outwards, in the longitudinal planes to at least 0.25 cm outwards.

Future Developments

A stepping source dose distribution obtained by geometrical optimisation (Edmundson 1990) has a homogeneity over the target, which lies between the one obtained with optimisation on rows of dose points and the one according to the Paris system. Preliminary results show that by taking the active length in each catheters equal to the corresponding target dimension, thus AL ≈ L, the reference isodose surface again encloses the target volume completely.

Conclusions

A given target volume, implanted according to the Paris Dosimetry System, can be treated with the dwell positions remaining all inside the target volume. This is achieved by optimising the dwell times to the same dose in dose points situated in rows, with each row midway between the surrounding catheters.

The mean dose in these dose points equals the dose value under the peak in the differential volume dose histogram. Thus, the reference dose may be defined as 85% of the mean dose or as 85% of the histogram peak dose.

The optimised dose distribution is considerably more homogeneous than the unoptimised one. There are no high dose cuffs extending out of the target volume as in the Paris System.

References

Dutreix A, Marinello G & Wambersie A, *Dosimétrie du Système de Paris*, in:*Dosimêtrie en Curietherapie*, Masson:Paris, 109-138, 1982.

Dutreix A & Marinello G, *The Paris System*, in:*Modern Brachytherapy*; Pierquin B, Wilson JF & Chassagne D (Eds), Masson :New York, 25-42, 1987

Edmundson GK, *Geometry based optimisation for stepping source implants*, in: *Brachytherapy HDR and LDR*, Martinez AA, Orton CG & Mould RF (Eds), Nucletron: Columbia, 184-192, 1990.

Fowler J & Mount M, *Pulsed brachytherapy: the conditions for no significant loss of therapeutic ratio compared with traditional low dose rate brachytherapy*. Int. J. Radiation Oncology Biology & Physics., **23**, 661-669, 1992.

Glasser O, Quimby EH, Taylor LS, Weatherwax JL & Morgan RH, *Physical foundations of radiology*, 3rd edn, Chapter 13, Harper & Row:New York, 1967.

Hall EJ & Brenner DJ, *The dose-rate effect in interstitial brachytherapy: a controversy resolved*, Brit.J.Radiology, **65**, 242-247, 1992.

Marinello G, Valero M, Leung S & Pierquin B, *Comparative dosimetry between iridium wires and seed ribbons*, Int. J. Radiation Oncology Biology & Physics, **11**, 1733-1739, 1985

Meredith WJ (Ed), *Radiation dosage, the Manchester system*, 2nd edn, Livingstone:Edinburgh, 1967.

Paul JM, Philip PC, Brandenburg RW & Koch RF; *Comparison between continuous and discrete sources in the Paris system of implants*. Medical Physics, **16**, 414-424, 1989.

Shalek RJ & Stovall M (Eds), *Dosimetry in implant therapy*, in: Attix FH & Tochilin E (Eds): Radiation dosimetry, 743-807, Academic Press:New York, 1969.

van der Laarse R & de Boer RW, *Computerized high dose rate brachytherapy treatment planning*, in: *Brachytherapy HDR and LDR*, Martinez AA, Orton CG & Mould RF (Eds), 169-183, Nucletron:Columbia, 1990.

van der Laarse R, Edmundson GK, Luthmann RW & Prins TPE, *Optimisation of HDR brachytherapy dose distributions*. Activity Journal, **5**, 94-101, 1991.

35

Introduction to HDR Brachytherapy Optimisation*

R. van der Laarse & T.P.E. Prins

Nucletron Research B.V.,
Waardgelder 1,
3905 TH Veenendaal,
The Netherlands.

This chapter was presented as a poster at the 7th International Brachytherapy Working Conference, Baltimore, Washington, USA, September 1992.

Introduction

Optimisation in high dose rate (HDR) brachytherapy aims to optimise the dose distribution of implants with rigid catheters or needles by adjusting the dwell time of the stepping source in each dwell position.

There are two approaches to optimise such a stepping source implant: (1) "Optimisation on distance" is made in a single plane implant where an isodose surface with a given dose is required at a given distance from the catheters. (2) "Optimisation on volume" is made in a multi-plane, volume implant, aiming at a homogeneous dose distribution in the volume between the catheters. In *Display 1* the various steps of the optimisation of an HDR stepping source implant are stated.

Part 1

Displays 2 to 9 present in a pictorial way the optimisation on dose points and the geometric optimisation.

First the optimisation on distance around a single straight catheter is discussed. The appearance of negative dwell times when the dose points are at a distance much larger than the step size, is explained in *Displays 2 and 3*. The wildly varying positive and negative dwell times in a straight catheter with step size 2.5 mm when optimising to the same dose in points at 1 cm distance is given in *Display 4*. The backbone of the SSDS optimisation is the concept of the dwell time gradient restriction: the restriction of the difference in dwell times between successive dwell times, as presented in *Display 5*.

The central problem of the optimisation on volume is that there are never enough dose points for proper optimisation. This is assessed in *Display 6*, where two dose points are situated between 3 dwell positions. The same clinically bad result is obtained if two rows of dose points are placed between three parallel catheters. Optimisation on dose points midway between the catheters in a two-plane breast implant leads again to an clinically unacceptable result, see *Display 7*. It shows that optimising on three dose points between five catheters gives more than one possible mathematical solution. The one selected here minimizes the sum of the squares of the source strengths (dwell times). It is better than the solution with only catheter active, but is still clinically unacceptable.

One solution to this problem of the insufficient number of dose points to optimise a volume implant, is the geometric optimisation, see *Display 8*. This is an optimisation procedure based on the implant geometry. In this approach the dwell positions themselves are used as dose points. *Display 9* uses geometric optimisation to get the relative dwell times (often called the dwell weights) and two dose points to define the reference dose.

Part 2

Displays 10 to 18 present the mathematical background of the Stepping Source Dosimetry System. An overview of the two branches, optimisation with and without dose points, is given in *Display 10*. When no dose points are available for optimisation, the geometric optimisation may be used for distance optimisation and for volume optimisation. Optimisation on dose points often leads to an enormous number of equations and variables, as each dose point generates an equation and each dwell position is an variable in that equation. (see Display 11.) This problem is solved by the polynomial optimisation appoach. Finally, *Display 10* shows how for volume implants the polynomial approach on a restricted set of dose points, together with geometric optimisation on volume, leads to a clinically good solution. This combination of polynomial and geometrical optimisation is called "polynomial optimisation on volume".

Display 11 shows that each dose point leads to an equation, with the dwell times t_i as the unknown variables and the dose D_i as then prescribed value. In the example shown here, only the inverse square law has been applied. Note that the dwell time gradient restriction is implemented as an additional set of equations, each neighbouring pair of dwell positions leads to such an equation. In the chi-squared function w_k is usually taken equal to 1, so the only parameter here is v: the importance of the dwell time gradient equations in the total set of equations. *Display 12* indicates that for large implants the corresponding large number of equations and unknowns make a practical implementation of this approach impossible.

The concept of dwell time gradient restriction leads to smooth behaviour of the dwell time along the catheter, see *Display 13*. Due to this smooth behaviour, the change of relative dwell time along the catheter as a function of the distance to the first dwell position, can be approximated by a polynomial function of a much lesser degree than the number of dwell positions. The coefficients a$_j$ in the polynomial approximation of the dwell time along the catheter are called parameters. *Display 14* gives the implementation of this parameterisation in the chi-squared function. By taking the derative of chi-squared to each parameter, a set of equations is generated with a square matrix of coefficients, *Display 15*. The dimension of this matrix is equal to the number of parameters, consequently it is much smaller than the non-parameterised rectangular matrix of coefficients as given in Display 12.

Display 16 presents the simple mathematics of geometric optimisation on distance and on volume. In volume implants geometric optimisation is often not strong enough to fill in the lower dose regions at the outer ends of the active parts of the catheters. Therefore geometric optimisation has been blended with dose point optimisation to fully optimise a volume implant, see *Display 17*. This so called polynomial optimisation on volume is based on the following two steps. Step 1: Perform geometric optimisation. Determine the sum of the dwell times for each catheter (R$_i$ for catheter I) and for the whole implant (R^{geo}). R$_i$ / R^{geo} is now the ratio of the total dwell time in catheter I and the total dwell time in the implant. Step 2: Incorporate this ratio into the chi-squared expression for polynomial optimisation as an additional constraint, similar to the one for dwell time gradient restriction. Parameterise again as presented in *Displays 13 and 14*.

Results of polynomial optimisation on volume are given in Chapter 36 on *Comparing the Stepping Source Dosimetry System and the Paris System, using Volume - Dose Histograms of Breast Implants*. Display 18 represents a fully optimised dose distribution around a two plane breast implant. Note that the reference isodose line (85% of the dose in the dose points) runs completely around the implant. Thus all active dwell positions are now contained within the target volume.

Part 1

Highlighting the Optimisation Approaches of SSDS.

- Dose Point Optimisation
- Negative Dwell Time
- Dwell Time Gradient Restriction
- Minimising the Sum of the Squares of the Dwell Times
- Geometric Optimisation
- Geometric Optimisation merged in Dose Point Optimisation

Part 2

Mathematical Background of the Optimisation Routines.

- Dose Point Optimisation
- Dwell Time Gradient Restriction
- Parameterisation of the Dwell Times
- Geometric Optimisation
- Geometric Optimisation merged in Dose Point Optimisation

Acknowledgements

Important aspects of SSDS were contributed by R.W. de Boer, Amsterdam, The Netherlands, G.K. Edmundson, Detroit, USA, D.A. Ingham, Exeter, UK, R.L. Luthmann, Jacksonville, Florida, USA and R. Sloboda, Edmonton, Canada.

Display 1

Optimisation on Dose Points at Border of Target Volume
Positive Dwell times

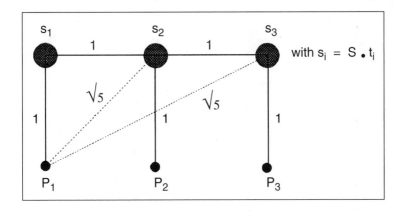

with $s_i = S \cdot t_i$

Optimize the source strengths s_i to dose 10 in P_1, P_2 and P_3.

$$P_1 : D_1 = \frac{s_1}{1^2} + \frac{s_2}{\sqrt{2}^2} + \frac{s_3}{\sqrt{5}^2} = 10$$

$$P_2 : D_2 = \frac{s_1}{\sqrt{2}^2} + \frac{s_2}{1^2} + \frac{s_3}{\sqrt{2}^2} = 10$$

$$P_3 : D_3 = \frac{s_1}{\sqrt{5}^2} + \frac{s_2}{\sqrt{2}^2} + \frac{s_3}{1^2} = 10$$

$$\left. \begin{array}{l} \\ \\ \\ \end{array} \right]$$

$s_1 = 7.1$
$s_2 = 2.9$
$s_1 = 7.1$

S : Dose rate at distance 1 from the point source
s_i : Strength of source i, defined here as S x dwell time t_i
P_i: Dose point i
D_i: Prescribed dose in dose point i

Optimisation on Dose Points at Border of Target Volume
Negative Dwell time

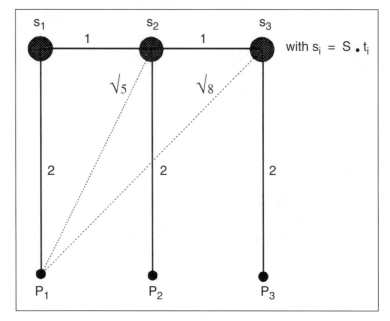

Optimize the source strengths s_i to dose 10 in P_1, P_2 and P_3.

$$P_1 : D_1 = \frac{s_1}{2^2} + \frac{s_2}{\sqrt{5}^2} + \frac{s_3}{\sqrt{8}^2} = 10$$

$$P_2 : D_2 = \frac{s_1}{\sqrt{5}^2} + \frac{s_2}{2^2} + \frac{s_3}{\sqrt{5}^2} = 10$$

$$P_3 : D_3 = \frac{s_1}{\sqrt{8}^2} + \frac{s_2}{\sqrt{5}^2} + \frac{s_3}{2^2} = 10$$

$s_1 = 36.4$
$s_2 = 18.2$
$s_1 = 36.4$

S : Dose rate at distance 1 from the point source
s_i : Strength of source i, defined here as S x dwell time t_i
P_i: Dose point i
D_i: Prescribed dose in dose point i

Display 3

Optimisation on Dose Points at Border of Target Volume
The Dwell Time Gradient Restriction

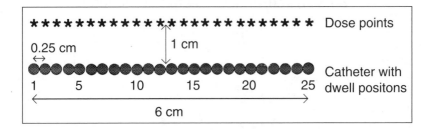

No Dwell Time Gradient Restriction

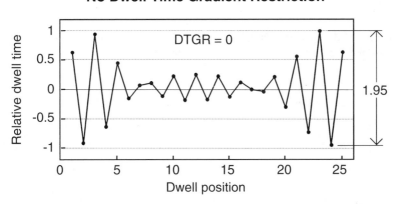

Optimized relative dwell times when there is no dwell time gradient restriction (DTGR) imposed on dwell times of adjacent dwell positions. The maximum difference of successive dwell times is nearly 2, the limit value.

Optimisation on Dose Points at Border of Target Volume

Small Dwell Time Gradient Restriction

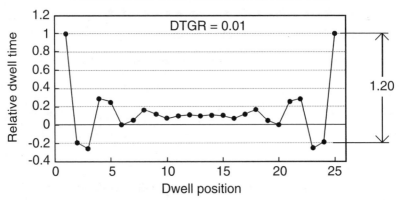

Optimized relative dwell times with a small DTGR of 0.01. The maximum difference of successive dwell times is reduced to 1.2.

Sufficient Dwell Time Gradient Restriction

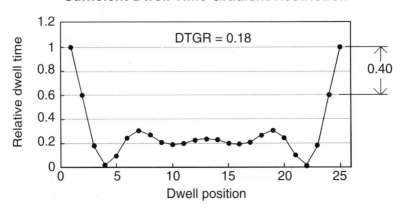

Optimized relative dwell times with a DTGR of 0.18. The maximum difference of successive dwell times is 0.4. All dwell times are positive zero, so this represents the best possible fit of an isodose line through the dose points.

Display 5

Optimisation on Dose Points between Dwell Positions
Minimize sum of squares of source strengths

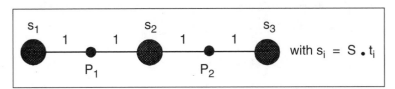

with $s_i = S \cdot t_i$

Optimize the source strengths s_i to dose 10 in P_1, P_2.

$$P_1 : D_1 = \frac{s_1}{1^2} + \frac{s_2}{1^2} + \frac{s_3}{3^2} = 10$$

$$P_2 : D_2 = \frac{s_1}{3^2} + \frac{s_2}{1^2} + \frac{s_3}{1^2} = 10$$

Infinite number of solutions

Minimize $\sum_{i=1}^{3} s_i^2$ to get unique solution

s_1	s_2	s_3	$\sum_{i=1}^{3} s_i^2$
0	10	0	100
1	8.89	1	81.2
.	.	.	.
.	.	.	.
.	.	.	.
3	6.67	3	62.4
3.4_3	6.22	3.4_3	61.6
4	5.56	4	62.9

Clinically bad:
Center of implant hot

S :   Dose rate at distance 1 from the point source
s_i :   Strength of source i, defined here as S x dwell time t_i
P_i :   Dose point i
D_i :   Prescribed dose in dose point i

Display 6

Optimisation on Dose Points between Dwell Positions
Minimize sum of squares of source strengths

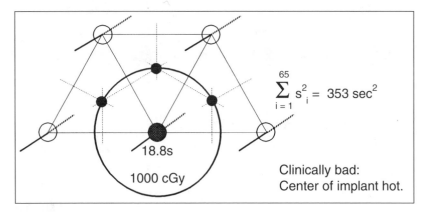

$$\sum_{i=1}^{65} s^2_i = 353 \ \text{sec}^2$$

18.8s

1000 cGy

Clinically bad:
Center of implant hot.

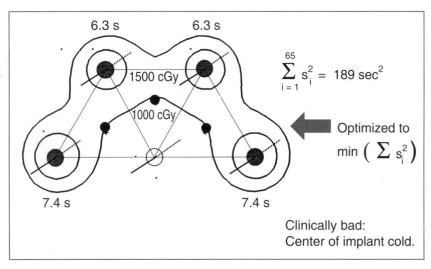

6.3 s   6.3 s

1500 cGy

1000 cGy

7.4 s   7.4 s

$$\sum_{i=1}^{65} s^2_i = 189 \ \text{sec}^2$$

Optimized to

$$\min \left(\sum_i s^2_i \right)$$

Clinically bad:
Center of implant cold.

Implant of 5 catheters, each dwell positions 1-13, step length 0.5 cm.
Reference Air Kerma Rate is 4.0682 cGy.h^{-1}.m^2, i.e. 10 Ci ^{192}Ir.

● : Active source dwell position
○ : Inactive source dwell position
● : Dose points, midway between catheters along 6 cm active length

Display 7

Optimisation based on Implant Geometry
Use Source Positions as Dose Points

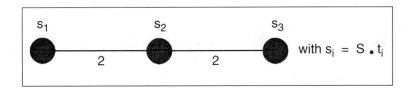

with $s_i = S \cdot t_i$

Optimize the source strengths based on the implant geometry.

Start with equal source strengths: $s_1 = s_2 = s_3 = s$

Dose in outer source positions : $D_1 = D_3 = \dfrac{s}{2^2} + \dfrac{s}{4^2} = \dfrac{15}{16} s$

Dose in center source position : $D_2 = 2 \dfrac{s}{2^2} = \dfrac{1}{2} s$

Relative source strengths:

$$s_1 : s_2 : s_3 = \dfrac{1}{D_1} : \dfrac{1}{D_2} : \dfrac{1}{D_3} = \dfrac{16}{5} : 2 : \dfrac{16}{5}$$

Set largest relative source strength to 1:

$$s_1 : s_2 : s_3 : = 1 : 0.625 : 1$$ ⬅ Clinically good

S : Dose rate at distance 1 from the point source
s_i : Strength of source i, defined here as S x dwell time t_i

Display 8

Optimisation on Dose Points between Dwell Positions
Geometric Optimisation merged in Dose Point Optimisation

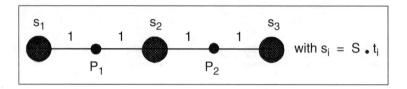

Optimize the source strengths s_i to dose 10 in P_1 and P_2.

Geometrical optimisation:

$$s_1 : s_2 : s_3 : = 1 : 0.625 : 1 \qquad (1)$$

Dose point optimisation:

$$\left.\begin{array}{l} P_1 : D_1 = \dfrac{s_1}{1^2} + \dfrac{s_2}{1^2} + \dfrac{s_3}{3^2} = 10 \\[4mm] P_2 : D_2 = \dfrac{s_1}{3^2} + \dfrac{s_2}{1^2} + \dfrac{s_3}{1^2} = 10 \end{array}\right] \qquad (2)$$

Substitution of (1) in (2) gives:

$$
\begin{aligned}
s_1 &= 5.76 \\
s_2 &= 3.60 \qquad \Longleftarrow \quad \text{Clinically good} \\
s_3 &= 5.76
\end{aligned}
$$

S : Dose rate at distance 1 from the point source
s_i : Strength of source i, defined here as S x dwell time t_i

Optimisation Approaches in HDR Brachytherapy
The Stepping Source Dosimetry System SSDS

Optimising on distance is done on single plane implants where a isodose surface is required at a given distance from the catheters.

Optimising on volume is done on multi plane, volume, implants aiming at a homogeneous dose distribution in the target volume.

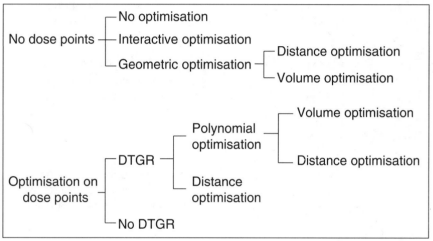

DTGR: Dwell Time Gradient Restriction

No dose points
(I) Interactive optimisation: manually changing dwell times and visually evluating the resulting dose distributions.
(II) Geometrical optimisation: dwell positions are also used as dose points. Optimisation on distance is obtained by taking all dwell positions into account, optimisation on volume uses only the dwell positions in the other catheters.

Optimizing on dose points
(I) Without the dwell time gradient restriction DTGR negative dwell times may result.
(II) With DTGR: solving the equations results in optimisation on distance.
    Polynomal optimisation approximates the dwell times along a catheter as a function of the distance to the first dwell position in that catheter. When the total time of each catheter obtained by geometric optimisation, is added as an additional constraint to the polynomal optimisation, a dose distribution optimised on a volume results.

Display 10

Optimisation of Dwell Times to Prescribed Doses
with Dwell Time Gradient Restriction

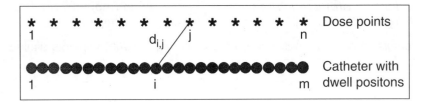

$$D_1 = \frac{S \bullet t_i}{d^2_{1,1}} + \cdots + \frac{S \bullet t_m}{d^2_{m,1}} + \varepsilon_1$$ $$\vdots$$ $$D_1 = \frac{S \bullet t_i}{d^2_{1,n}} + \cdots + \frac{S \bullet t_m}{d^2_{m,n}} + \varepsilon_n$$	Equations representing the prescribed doses in the dose points 1 to n.
$$O = -t_1 + t_2 + \delta_1$$ $$\vdots$$ $$O = -t_{m-1} + t_m + \delta_{m-1}$$	Equations representing the dwell time gradient restriction between successive source positions 1 - m.
$$\chi^2 = \sum_{k=1}^{n} w_k \bullet \varepsilon^2_k + \sum_{k=1}^{m-1} v \bullet \delta^2_i$$	Chi-squared function to be minimized of the weigthed squares of the differences between prescribed and actual doses.

D_k : Prescribed dose in dose point k.

S : Source strength, defined here as "dose rate at unit distance".

$d_{i,k}$: Distance between source i and dose point k.

t_i : Dwell time in source position i.

ε_k : Difference between prescribed and actual dose in dose point k.

w_k : Importance of the prescribed dose in dose point k, that is, the weight of equation k in the total set of equations.

δ_i : Difference between dwell time i and dwell time i+1.

v : Importance of the dwell time gradient restriction, that is, the weight of each equation representing the dwell time gradient in the total set of equations.

Optimisation of Dwell Times to Prescribed Doses with Dwell Time Gradient Restriction - Singular Value Decomposition Method -

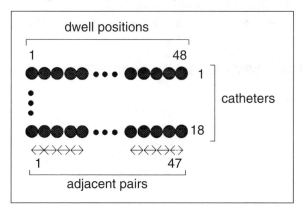

dwell positions

1   48

catheters

18

adjacent pairs

1   47

Number of equations with 300 dose points:

300 + adjacent pairs = 300 + 18 x 47 = 1146 equations.

Number of dwell times (unknowns):

number of dwell positions = 18 x 48 = 864 unknowns.

Method to solve these equations:

Singular Value Decomposition Method.

# of equations > # of unknowns.
Minimize sum of squares of dwell times.
# of equations = # of unknowns.
Algebric solution.
# of equations < # of unknowns.
Least squares solution.

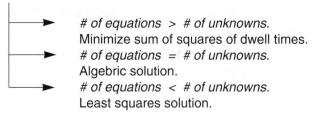

Set to solve: $A \vec{x} = \vec{b}$ with $A = \begin{pmatrix} a_{1,1} & \bullet\bullet\bullet & a_{1,864} \\ \vdots & & \vdots \\ a_{1146,1} & \bullet\bullet\bullet & a_{1146,864} \end{pmatrix}$

Display 12

Parameterisation of the Dwell Times in χ^2
Sufficient Dwell Time Gradient Restriction

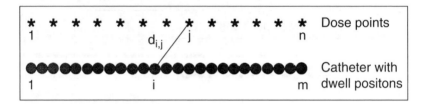

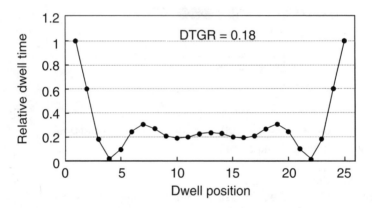

Curve of dwell time t versus distance x to first dwell position is smooth due to dwell time gradient restriction DTGR.

Approximate t(x) with polynominals P (x) to the degree p with p < m:

$$t(x) = \sum_{j=1}^{p} a_j \cdot P_j(x) \ ,$$

Suitable value for degree: $p = 2\sqrt{m} - 1$, thus 48 dwell times in a catheter may be approximated by p = 13.

m: Number of source dwell positions.

n : Number of dose points.

p : Number of parameters.

a_j: j^{th} parameter.

p_j: j^{th} polynomial.

Polynomial Optimisation
Parameterisation of the Dwell Times in χ^2

Sufficient Dwell Time Gradient Restriction

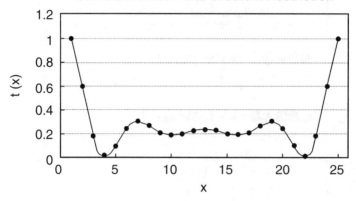

$$\chi^2 = \sum_{k=1}^{n} w_k^2 \cdot \left(D_k - S = \sum_{i=1}^{m} \frac{t_i}{d_{i,k}^2} \right)^2 + \sum_{i=1}^{m-1} v^2 \cdot \left(-t_i + t_{i+1} \right)^2$$

Parameterize t: $t(x) = \sum_{j=1}^{p} a_j \cdot P_j(x)$,

with x the distance along catheter to first dwell position.
Substitute in χ^2 : $t_i = t(x_i)$
Solve normal equations for a_j : $\dfrac{\delta \chi^2}{\delta a_j} = 0$ (j = 1,..., p)

Obtain dwell times by back substitution : $t_j = \sum_{j=1}^{p} a_j \cdot P_j(x_i)$,

m: Number of source dwell positions.
n : Number of dose points.
p : Number of parameters. Suitable value $p = 2\sqrt{m} - 1$.
a_j : j^{th} parameter.
P_j : j^{th} polynomial.

Display 14

Parameterisation of the Dwell Times in χ^2
Limits of microSelectron-HDR

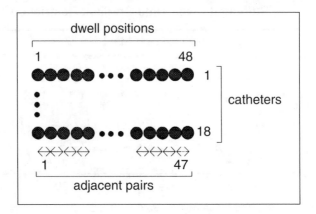

Parameterize 18 catheters, each with 48 dwell positions.
Optimal results: $p = 18 \times (2\sqrt{48} - 1) = 18 \times 13 = 234$.

Set to solve: $A \vec{x} = \vec{b}$ with $A = \begin{pmatrix} a_{1,1} & \bullet\bullet\bullet & a_{1,234} \\ \vdots & & \vdots \\ a_{234,1} & \bullet\bullet\bullet & a_{234,234} \end{pmatrix}$.

A less precise approximation with 7 parameters per catheter, instead of 13, still results in a dose distribution which is practically equal to the one with 13 parameters.
Number of parameters: $18 \times 7 = 126$

Set to solve: $A \vec{x} = \vec{b}$ with $A = \begin{pmatrix} a_{1,1} & \bullet\bullet\bullet & a_{1,126} \\ \vdots & & \vdots \\ a_{126,1} & \bullet\bullet\bullet & a_{126,126} \end{pmatrix}$,

which is easily done.

Display 15

Geometric Optimisation

Geometric Optimisation.
Relative dwell time in a dwell position equals the inverse of the dose contribution from other dwell positions.

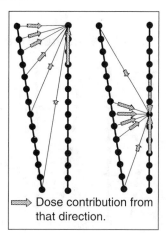

Optimisation on Distance.
Take the dose contributions of dwell positions in all catheters into account. Influence of dose contributions from distant catheters is small.

Optimisation on Volume.
Take only the dose contributions of dwell positions in other catheters into account. Influence of dose contributions from distant catheters is large.

$\Longrightarrow$ Dose contribution from that direction.

Dose in dwell position i delivered by the other dwell positions:

$$D_i = \sum_{\substack{j=1 \\ j \neq 1}}^{m} \frac{t_j}{d_{i,j}^2} \, \phi\left(d_{i,j} \right)$$

with t_j the dwell time in dwell position j and $\phi\left(d_{i,j} \right)$ the function for tissue absorption and scatter.

Set all dwell times t_j to 1. Disregard tissue absorption and scatter.

$$D_i = \sum_{\substack{j=1 \\ j \neq 1}}^{m} \frac{t_j}{d_{i,j}^2}$$

Take the relative dwell time t_i equal to $\dfrac{1}{D1}$:

$$t_1 : t_2 : \ldots : t_m = \sum_{\substack{j=1 \\ j \neq 1}}^{m} \frac{1}{d_{i,j}^2} : \sum_{\substack{j=1 \\ j \neq 2}}^{m} \frac{1}{d_{2,j}^2} : \ldots : \sum_{\substack{j=1 \\ j \neq m}}^{m} \frac{1}{d_{m,j}^2}$$

Display 16

Geometric Optimisation incorparated in Polynomial Optimisation

Parameterisation of the Dwell Times in χ^2

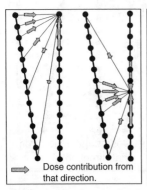

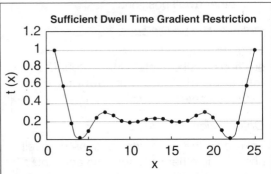

Sufficient Dwell Time Gradient Restriction

Dose contribution from that direction.

Step 1: Geometric Optimisation

$$\tau_1 : \tau_2 : \ldots : \tau_m = \sum_{\substack{j=1 \\ j \neq 1}}^{m} \frac{1}{d_{1,j}^2} : \sum_{\substack{j=1 \\ j \neq 2}}^{m} \frac{1}{d_{2,j}^2} : \ldots : \sum_{\substack{j=1 \\ j \neq m}}^{m} \frac{1}{d_{m,j}^2}$$

Step 2: Incorporate Geometric Optimisation in Polynomial Optimisation.
Parameterize t, solve normal equations and substitute back.

$$\chi^2 = \sum_{k=1}^{n} w_k^2 \bullet \left(D_k - S = \sum_{i=1}^{m} \frac{t_i}{d_{i,k}^2} \right)^2 + \sum_{i=1}^{m-1} v^2 \bullet \left(-t_i + t_{i+1} \right)^2 +$$

$$+ u^2 \bullet \sum_{l=1}^{c} \left(R_l^{geo} \bullet \sum_{i=1}^{l_m} t_i - \sum_{i=l_1}^{l_m} t_i \right)^2 \quad \text{with} \quad R_l^{geo} = \sum_{i=l_1}^{l_m} \tau_i / \sum_{i=1}^{m} \tau_i$$

c   : Number of catheters.
m   : Number of source dwell positions.
n   : Number of dose points.
l1   : First dwell position in catheter l.
lm   : Last dwell position in catheter l.
p   : Number of parameters. Suitable value $p = 2 \sqrt{m} - 1$.
R_l^{geo} : Ratio of total dwell time in catheter l and total dwell time in implant, after geometric optimisation.

Display 17

Bi-plane Breast Implant optimised according to SSDS

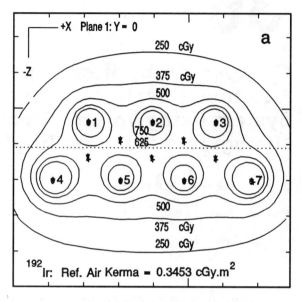

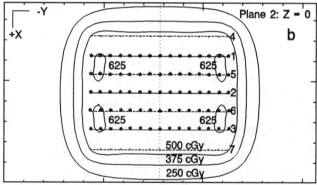

Active lengths of catheters is 7 cm. The dwell positions are equally spaced at 0.5 cm. The dwell times are optimised to the same dose in all dose points indicated by *.

Reference Dose RD is defined as 0.85 x best-fit dose over all dose points. RD = 500cGy.

a. Central transversal plane. ····· indicates central longitudal plane.
b. Central longitudal plane. ⋮ indicates central transversal plane.

Display 18

36

Comparing the Stepping Source Dosimetry System and the Paris System Using Volume-Dose Histograms of Breast Implants*

R. van der Laarse & T.P.E. Prins

Nucletron Research B.V.,
Waardgelder 1,
3905 TH Veenendaal,
The Netherlands.

* This chapter was presented as a poster at the 7th International Brachytherapy Working Conference, Baltimore, Washington, USA, September 1992.

Introduction

This chapter compares the Stepping Source Dosimetry System (SSDS) for high dose rate brachytherapy with the Paris Dosimetry System (PDS) for low dose rate brachytherapy.

SSDS follows the Paris rules for implantation. However, it places dose points midway between the catheters not only in the central plane but all along the catheters. The dwell times in the catheters are optimised such, that the same dose is delivered to these dose points. Consequently, the dwell times in the outer ends of the catheters of an implant are increased substantially. This results in the outer active dwell positions now being all inside the target volume, contrarily to the active wires in the Paris System, which extend outside the target.volume. The dose homogeneity over the target volume is also much better in the SSDS approach, because the same dose is obtained in the volume between the catheters up to their outer ends.

To assess the quality of the dose distributions obtained with these brachytherapy dosimetry systems, different types of volume-dose histograms (VDHs) are introduced.

Display 1 discusses the differences between the dose distributions of a SSDS implant and a PDS one. These differences will be highlighted in *Displays 2 to 9*. *Display 2* gives the contents of the second part. The use of VDHs to compare the dose distributions of both systems is in *Displays 10 to 18*.

The comparison of the SSDS and the Paris System starts in *Display 3*. The corresponding dose distributions in the transverse central plane are given in *Display 4*. Note that SSDS gives a more homogeneous dose distribution in the center of the implant. And also that the 500 cGy reference isodose line cGy runs more squarely around the implant. *Display 5* is an overlay of *Displays* 3 and 4. Note that in SSDS the 500 cGy isodose line keeps its 5 mm distance from the outer catheters, while in PDS the reference isodose line bends inwards to the outer catheters. This is discussed in *Display 6*.

The differences between the dose distributions in a series of longitudinal planes through the implant is given in *Displays 7, 8 and 9*. *Display 7* shows that the hot spot in the center of the PDS implant moves to the outer ends of the SSDS implant. This moves the 500 cGy reference isodose line outwards, so it runs now completely outside the catheters. *Display 8* compares the dose distributions in three longitudinal planes. In the upper half of each picture the SSDS distribution is given and in the lower half that for PDS. This is discussed in *display 9*.

The introduction of volume dose histograms (VDH) starts in *Display 10*, where the influence of distance on the quotient dV/dD, the change of volume V with change of dose D, is presented. The relation between dV/dD versus D is given. To distinguish between the histograms of dV/dD versus D, and V versus D, the terminology of differential volume-dose histogram and cumulated volume-dose histogram is introduced. In *display 11* the actual differential volume dose histogram of an 1iridium-192 point source is given. It coincides practically with that of an ideal point source with no tissue scattering and absorption.

In *Display 12* the "natural" volume-dose histogram for a point source is obtained by changing the dose axis from D to $D^{-3/2}$ (noted as u) and the axis dV/dD to $dV/dD^{-3/2}$, noted as dV/du. This histogram gives a horizontal line for a point source, as is derived mathematically.

Display 13 gives the dose distribution for a PDS implant. The differential volume - dose histogram is given in *Display 14*. The concept of the Volume Gradient Ratio (VGR) is introduced. The higher the VGR value is, the more volume is around the peak dose and the less volume outside it. To remove the influence of the inverse square law, VGR is based on the difference between the actual implant histogram and the corresponding point source histogram. So for a single point source, VDG will be equal to 1. The two peaks in this histogram originate from the large volume with a higher dose in the center of the Paris implant with about 660 cGy and the large volume between the outer triangular intersections of the catheters with about 590 cGy.

The "Natural" VDH of the same Paris-type implant is given in *Display 15*. The shape of the histogram is explained. The concept of the Uniformity Index UI is introduced. Note that the reference dose (here called target dose TD) is part of UI. Thus the value of UI depends on the selected TD value. Basically, UI scores how well the dose distribution of the implant covers the target volume.

Displays 16, 17 and *18* repeats *Display 13, 14 and 15* but now for an SSDS optimised implant for the same target volume. Note that the SSDS implant is about 3 cm shorter than the PDS one in Display 13. Due to the same dose in the volumina between the catheters, a single peak in the histograms now occur. VGR increases from 1.32 for a Paris-type implant to 2.02 for an SSDS-type implant. The lesser increase in Uniformity Index between the two "natural" volume-dose histograms, from 1.62 to 1.89 is due to the fact that the reference iso-dose value is part of this index. An index, similar to the Uniformity Index but with LD, instead of TD, is the Quality Index. This index behaves similar to the Volume Gradient Ratio, as both are independent of the reference dose and score the dose distribution given by the implant, irrespective of whether or not the implant covers the target volume.

Part 1

Highlighting the differences between the dose distribution of a Paris-type breast implant and an SSDS implant.

- Paris Dosimetry System
  - Active wires of equal linear activity or catheters containing pellets of equal activity. In HDR stepping source brachytherapy: equidistant dwell positions with equal dwell times.
  - Basal Dose defined midway between the catheters in central transversal plane only.
  - Reference Dose defined as 85% of the mean dose in the basal dose points.
  - Active lengths extend outside target volume.

- Stepping Source Dosimetry System
  - Equidistant dwell positions with optimised dwell times.
  - Dose points defined midways between the catheters along their active lenghts.
  - Dwell times in equidistant dwell positions are optimised to the prescribed dose in these dose points.
  - Active dwell positions remain inside target volume.

Display 1

Part 2

Using Volume- Dose Histograms to compare breast implants according to the Paris Dosimetry and SSDS.

- Differential Volume-Dose Histogram
  - Point source
  - Implant according to Paris System
  - Implant according to SSDS
  - Volume-Gradient Ratio

- "Natural" Volume-Dose Histogram
  - Point source
  - Implant according to Paris System
  - Implant according to SSDS
  - Uniformity Index
  - Quality Index

Acknowledgements

Important aspects of SSDS were contributed by R.W. de Boer, Amsterdam, The Netherlands, G.K. Edmundson, Detroit, USA, D.A. Ingham, Exeter, UK, R.L. Luthmann, Jacksonville, Florida, USA and R. Sloboda, Edmonton, Canada.

Important contributions on volume-dose histograms were received from D.A. Ingham, Exeter, UK, C. Koedooder, Amsterdam, The Netherlands, R.L. Luthmann, Jacksonville, Florida, USA, A. van 't Riet, Deventer, The Netherlands and R. Sloboda, Edmonton, Canada.

Display 2

Comparison of SSDS and the Paris System

In SSDS the dwell times of the source stepping through the implant are optimised to the same dose in dose points placed through the whole target volume. The Paris Dosimetry System is designed for implants with active wires of equal linear activity or with catheters containing equidistant pellets of equal activity.

In SSDS and in the Paris Dosimetry System the reference dose RD is the prescribed dose value on an isodose surface encompassing the target volume.

In an unoptimised implant the active wires or pellets must extend outside the target volume in order to compensate for the dose fall-off at the ends of the implanted wires or catheters. This extension for a target length of 7 cm treated with a two plane implant is for example 1.25 cm at either end, see figures below.

One approach to treat a given target volume with an unoptimised HDR stepping source implant is to rigorously apply the implantation rules of the Paris Dosimetry System.

The difference between the dose distribution according to the Paris Dosimetry System and according to SSDS is presented.

Display 3

Bi-Plane Breast Implant according to Paris System

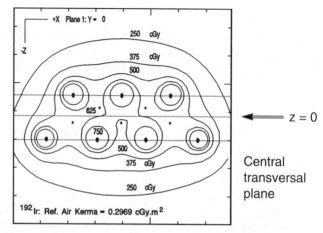

Active length of catheters is 10 cm. Dwell step is 0.5 cm. Dwell times are equal. Reference Dose RD is 0.85 x mean dose in basal dose points in central tranversal plane. RD = 500cGY. ····· indicate longitudal planes.

Bi-Plane Breast Implant optimised according to SSDS

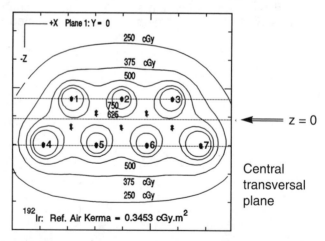

Active length of catheters is 7 cm. Dwell step is 0.5 cm. Dwell times are optimised to same dose in dose points. Reference Dose is 0.85 x best-fit dose over dose points. RD = 500cGY. ····· indicate longitudal planes.

Display 4

Central Transversal Planes of both Systems superimposed

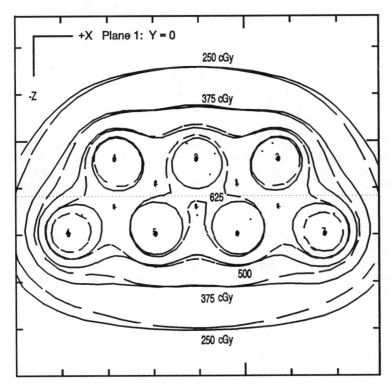

Dose distribution in the central transversal plane of the unoptimised and the optimised breast implant.
Both reference isodose lines coincide except around the outer catheters whwere the Paris RD iso line bends inwards to the implant.
The SSDS dose distribution is more homogeneous than the Paris one.

——— : Dose distribution optimised according to SSDS to the same dose in all dose points. Active length of the catheters is 7 cm.
Reference dose RD is defined as 0.85 x best-fit dose over all dose points. RD = 500 cGY.

- - - - - : Dose distribution according to the Paris System. Reference dose RD is defined as 0.85 x mean dose in dose points * in the central transversal plane. RD = 500 cGy.

·········· : Central longitudal plane.

Display 5

Comparison of SSDS and the Paris System Dose
Distribution in Central Transversal Plane

The dotted lines in *Display 5* are the isodose lines obtained with the Paris Dosimetry System. The solid lines are the isodose lines obtained by SSDS, thus optimised to the same dose in the dose points placed midway between the catheters along the whole length of the implant.

In both implant systems the dose is quite uniform along the catheters in the central part of the implant. In the Paris system the inner catheters have the same strength as the outer ones, resulting in a higher dose in the inner part. In SSDS the inner catheters are reduced in strength in order to obtain the same dose in the areas between the inner and outer catheters.

The reference dose RD of the Paris-type implant is taken as 85% of the mean dose in the dose points in the central plane only, the reference dose RD of the SSDS-type implant is taken as 85% of the mean dose in all points over the implant. The Reference Dose RD is in both cases 500 cGy.

It is clearly visible that in SSDS the outer catheters 4 and 7 are more weighted than the inner catheters in order to compensate for the lack of dose from surrounding catheters. This explains the deviation between the 500 cGy reference isodose line of the Paris System and of SSDS around the catheters 4 and 7.

Display 6

Bi-Plane Breast Implant according to Paris System

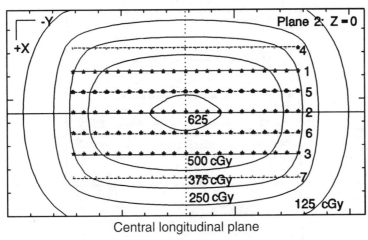

Central longitudinal plane

Active length of catheters is 10 cm. Dwell step is 0.5 cm. Dwell times are equal. Reference Dose RD is 0.85 x mean dose in basal dose points in central tranversal plane. RD = 500cGY.

Bi-Plane Breast Implant optimised according to SSDS

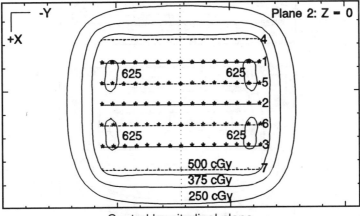

Central longitudinal plane

Active length of catheters is 7 cm. Dwell step is 0.5 cm. Dwell times are optimised to same dose in dose points. Reference Dose is 0.85 x best-fit dose over dose points. RD = 500cGY.

Display 7

Longitudinal Planes of both Systems compared

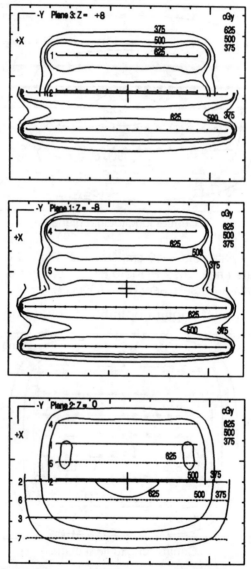

Comparison of the dose distributions in longitudinal planes of the Paris-type and the SSDS implant. Plane Z = 0 is central longitudinal plane; plane Z = -8 is the plane through needles 4,5,6 and 7; plane Z = +8 is the plane through needles 1, 2 and 3. The upper part of each dose distribution is given by the SSDS implant, the lower part by the Paris implant.

Display 8

Comparison of SSDS and the Paris System Dose Distribution in Longitudinal Planes

Display 8 at the left compares the dose distribution of SSDS and the Paris system in the planes through needles 1,2,3; through needles 4,5,6,7, and in the longitudinal mid-plane as indicated by the horizontal dotted line. The upper half of the dose distribution of each plane is given by the SSDS implant, the lower half by the Paris-type implant.

In an optimised HDR stepping source implant the dwell times are such that the same dose is obtained in all dose points midway between the catheters over the whole length of the implant. This results in increased dwell times at the outer parts of the implant. Contrarily to the unoptimised case, all dwell positions are now located inside the target volume.

It is clearly shown that the SSDS implant gives a more homogeneous dose coverage of the target volume than the Paris implant. The RD isodose line extends in the transversal planes 0.5 cm outwards, in the longitudinal planes to at least 0.25 cm outwards.

Display 9

Dose Distribution around Point Source
Approximation of the volume-dose gradient dV/dD

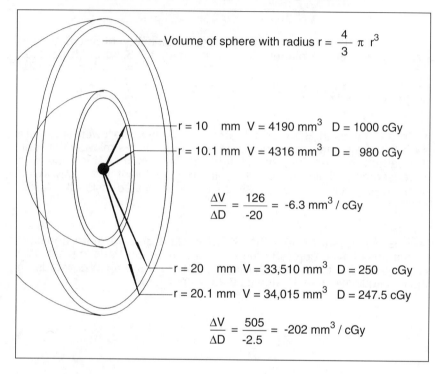

Volume of sphere with radius $r = \dfrac{4}{3} \pi \, r^3$

$r = 10$ mm $V = 4190$ mm^3 $D = 1000$ cGy

$r = 10.1$ mm $V = 4316$ mm^3 $D = 980$ cGy

$$\frac{\Delta V}{\Delta D} = \frac{126}{-20} = -6.3 \text{ mm}^3 / \text{cGy}$$

$r = 20$ mm $V = 33,510$ mm^3 $D = 250$ cGy

$r = 20.1$ mm $V = 34,015$ mm^3 $D = 247.5$ cGy

$$\frac{\Delta V}{\Delta D} = \frac{505}{-2.5} = -202 \text{ mm}^3 / \text{cGy}$$

Using $D(r) = \dfrac{S}{r^2}$ it is easily derived that

$$\frac{dV}{dD} = -2\pi \bullet S^{3/2} \bullet D^{-5/2}$$

Approximation of the volume-dose gradient dV/dD around an ideal point source which gives 1000 cGy at 10 mm distance.
dV/dD is approximated for D = 1000 cGy and D = 250 cGy.
Tissue attenuation and scattering is disregarded.

Display 10

Differential Volume-Dose Histogram of ^{192}Ir Piont Source

Differential volume - dose histogram

^{192}Ir point source, 1000 cGy at 1 cm in tissue

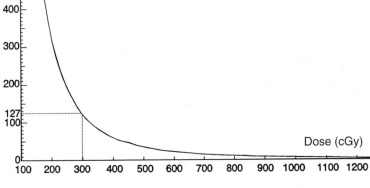

The differential volume - dose histogram of an ^{192}Ir point source coincides practically with that of an ideal point source, which is given by

$$\frac{dV}{dD} = -2\pi \bullet S^{3/2} \bullet D^{-5/2}. \quad \text{For S = 1000 cGy at 10 mm}$$

and D = 300 cGy, $\dfrac{dV}{dD} = 127$ mm^3. cGy^{-1}, see graph.

Differential volume dose histogram of an ^{192}Ir point source which delivers 1000 cGy at 1 cm in soft tissue.
The dotted line relates the 300 cGy dose with the theorectical value 127 mm^3. cGy^{-1}.

"Natural" Volume-Dose Histogram of ^{192}Ir Piont Source

"Natural" volume - dose histogram

^{192}Ir point source, 1000 cGy at 1 cm in tissue

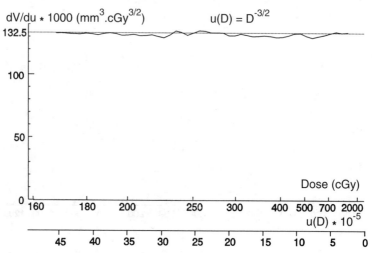

The differential volume - dose histogram of an ^{192}Ir point source coincides practically with that of an ideal point source, which is given by

$$\frac{dV}{dD} = -2\pi \bullet S^{3/2} \bullet D^{-5/2}.$$

Define $u(D) = -D^{-3/2} +$ const., then $\quad \dfrac{dV}{du} = \dfrac{dV}{dD} \bullet \dfrac{dD}{du} = -\dfrac{4}{3}\pi \bullet S^{3/2}$

"Natural" volume dose histogram of an ^{192}Ir point source which delivers 1000cGy at 1 cm in tissue. The - signs of dV/du and u are disregarded.

——— indicates the actual histogram

············ indicates the theoretical value $-\dfrac{4}{3}\pi \bullet S^{3/2}$

Display 12

Bi-Plane Breast Implant according to Paris System

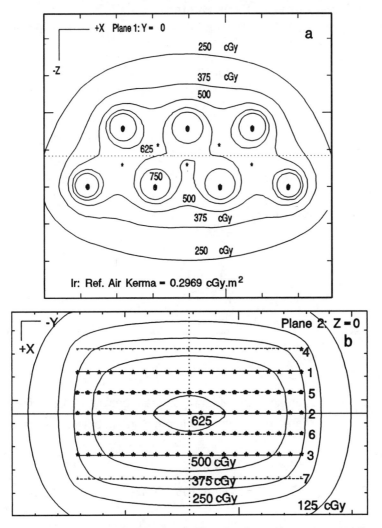

Active lengths of catheters is 10 cm. The dwell positions are equally spaced at 0.5 cm and are equally weighted. Reference dose RD is defined as 0.85 x mean dose in basal dose points ∗ in the central transversal plane. RD = 500cGy.

a. Central transversal plane. ····· indicates central longitudinal plane.
b. Central longitudinal plane. ⋮ indicates central transversal plane.

Differential Volume - Dose Histogram of Bi-Plane Breast Implant according to Paris System
Scoring of dose distribution with Volume - Gradient Ratio

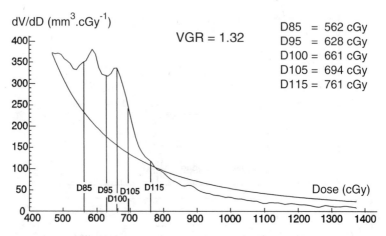

Volume   Gradient   Ratio
Bi-plane breast implant, not optimised
Ref. Air Kerma = 0.2969 cGy.m^3

$$VR\ (D1\text{-}D2)\ =\ \frac{\text{area under implant histogram between D1 and D2}}{\text{area under point source histogram between D1 and D2}}$$

$$VGR = \frac{VR\ (D95\text{ - }D105)}{\sqrt{VR\ (D85\text{ - }D95) \times VR\ (D105\text{ - }D115)}} = \frac{2.03}{\sqrt{1.74 \times 1.35}} = 1.32$$

The area under the implant histogram between doses D1 and D2 is the volume in the inplant between the isodose surfaces D1 and D2, so VR is the ratio of the volume between isodose surfaces D1 and D2 of the implant and the point source.

"Natural" Volume-Dose Histogram of Bi-Plane Breast Implant according to Paris System

"Natural" volume dose histogram
Bi-plane breast implant, not optimised
Ref. Air Kerma = 0.2969 cGy.m^2

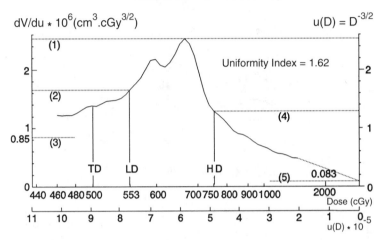

"Natural" volume - dose histogram of the unoptimised bi-plane implant Line (1), the value of the highest peak, represents dV/du due to the volumes around the three rows of dose points in the centre of the implant; the lower peak represents dV/du due to the volumes around the two outer rows of dose points.

Line (3) represents the theoretical limit, $(4/3) \pi (nS)^{3/2}$ of dV/du at a large distance from the implant, with n number of dwell positions and $S = D(r) / r^2$ the source strength of the ideal point source. Line (2) lies midway between lines (1) and (3) and defines the so called "Low Dose". Line (5) represents the theoretical limit $(4/3) p nS^{3/2}$ of dV/du for very high dose values. Line (4) lies midway between line (1) and (5) and defines the so called "High Dose".

The Uniformity Index UI is defined as $\quad UI = \dfrac{V(TD - HD)}{u(TD) - u(HD)} * \dfrac{U(TD)}{V(TD)}$

with V(TD - HD) the volume between doses TD and HD, and V(TD) the volume with doses higher than TD.

Display 15

Bi-Plane Breast Implant optimised according to SSDS

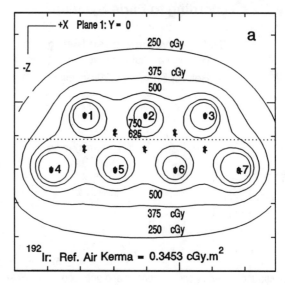

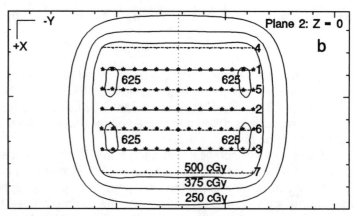

Active lengths of catheters is 7 cm. The dwell positions are equally spaced at 0.5 cm. The dwell times are optimised to the same dose in all dose points indicated by *.

Reference Dose RD is defined as 0.85 x best-fit dose over all dose points. RD = 500cGy.

a. Central transversal plane. ····· indicates central longitudinal plane.

b. Central longitudinal plane. ⋮ indicates central transversal plane.

Differential Volume - Dose Histogram of Bi-Plane Breast Implant optimised according to SSDS
Scoring of Dose Distribution with Volume - Gradient Ratio

Volume   Gradient   Ratio

Bi-plane breast implant, optimised according to SSDS

Ref. Air Kerma = 0.3453 cGy.m^2

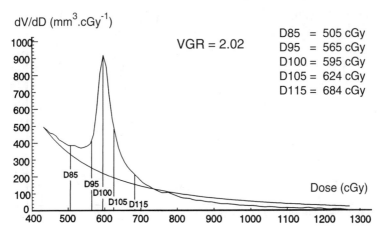

VGR = 2.02

D85 = 505 cGy
D95 = 565 cGy
D100 = 595 cGy
D105 = 624 cGy
D115 = 684 cGy

$$VR\ (D1\text{-}D2)\ =\ \frac{\text{area under implant histogram between D1 and D2}}{\text{area under point source histogram between D1 and D2}}$$

$$VGR = \frac{VR\ (\ D95 - D105)}{\sqrt{VR\ (\ D85 - D95)\ x\ VR\ (\ D105 - D115)}} = \frac{3.14}{\sqrt{1.32\ x\ 1.82}} = 2.02$$

The area under the implant histogram between doses D1 and D2 is the volume in the inplant between the isodose surfaces D1 and D2, so VR is the ratio of the volumina between isodose surfaces D1 and D2 of the implant and the point source.

Display 17

"Natural" Volume-Dose Histogram of Bi-Plane Breast Implant optimised according to SSDS
Uniformity Index versus Quality Index

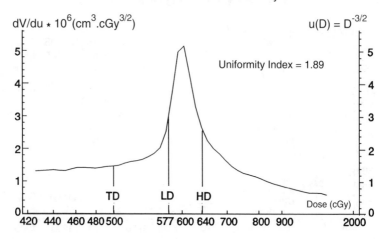

"Natural" volume dose histogram
Bi-plane breast implant, optimised
Ref. Air Kerma = 0.3453 cGy.m^2

$dV/du * 10^6 (cm^3.cGy^{3/2})$ $u(D) = D^{-3/2}$

Uniformity Index = 1.89

"Natural" volume - dose histogram of the unoptimised bi-plane implant. Note the relatively small change in the Uniformity Index UI compared to the unoptimised case, 1.89 versus 1.62.
This is due to the different definition of TD in the optimised and in the unoptimised implant.

By replacing TD with LD in the definition for UI, an implant quality index QI is obtained, a Figure of Merit irrespective whether the implant covers the target or not.

$$QI = \frac{V(LD - HD)}{u(LD) - u(HD)} * \frac{U(LD)}{V(LD)} \qquad QI = \frac{V(LD - HD)}{LD^{-3/2} - HD^{-3/2}} * \frac{LD^{-3/2}}{V(LD)}$$

Display 18

37

New Radionuclides for Brachytherapy

J.J. Battista[1] & D.L.D. Mason[2]

[1] London Regional Cancer Centre,
790, Commissioners Road East,
London,
Ontario,
Canada N6A 4L6.

[2] Toronto-Bayview Regional
Cancer Centre,
2075, Bayview Avenue,
Toronto,
Ontario,
Canada M4N 3M5.

Introduction

Irène Curie and Fréderic Joliot discovered artificial radioactivity on New Year's Eve in 1933 (Sullivan & Brucer 1979). Since that time, the development of the nuclear reactor and of particle accelerators has allowed the production of approximately 2500 isotopes of which only 300 have half-lives of between 10 days and 100 years. Of these 300, approximately 10 are radioactive isotopes which have applications in clinical brachytherapy. Specialists involved in brachytherapy have therefore been very selective in their choice of radionuclides for insertion or implantation into cancer patients. Table 1 summarises the physical properties of radioactive isotopes which determine their clinical usefulness for brachytherapy applications.

In this chapter we have restricted our attention to those radionuclides which emit photons in the form of X and gamma-rays. The energy of these emissions determines the penetration of the radiation within tissue (μ) and through radiation shielding (TVL). A low energy emission is less penetrating in tissue, but eases the radiation protection requirements. The photon energy also affects the differential absorption of radiation in tissue (f_{tissue}) particularly in high atomic number tissues such as bone.

As the energy is decreased the photoelectric effect becomes more prevalent, giving rise to localised dose enhancements in bone. Photon energy also affects the linear energy transfer (LET) of the charged particles set in motion by

X and gamma interactions within the patient. LET influences the biological effect (RBE) of the radiation per unit dose. Generally speaking, this enhanced radiobiological effect is only of concern for the low energy photon emitters, ie. of energies <100 keV, such as iodine-125.

A second important property of radionuclides is the half-life. This largely determines whether the source can be used in permanent or temporary brachytherapy implants and also has relevance to the shelf-life and ongoing costs of the clinical use of the source.

Thirdly, the specific activity (activity per unit mass) of the source determines the lower limit for source size and the maximum dose rate at which the radiation can be delivered.

Finally, the density and atomic number of the materials used in the brachytherapy source and its encapsulation will determine whether these sources can be easily localised in the patient by radiographic techniques. In combination with the energy emitted, the density and atomic number also influence the isotropy of the dose distribution in the vicinity of a brachytherapy source such as a seed or a miniature stepping source.

The practical difficulty is therefore in producing a radionuclide for brachytherapy when many of the requirements are in direct conflict with each other. For example a higher photon energy improves tissue penetration but complicates radiation shielding requirements which can make ancillary equipment necessary and escalate the capital costs, eg. remote afterloaders and shielded patient rooms.

Conversely very low energy photons are differentially absorbed in various tissues of different atomic number. The increased LET of low energy sources impacts on the RBE and makes it difficult to plan treatments only on the basis of experience with low LET photon emitters such as caesium-137.

In the British Institute of Radiology report *Radionuclides in brachytherapy: radium and after* edited by Trott (1987), it is concluded that the *ideal radionuclide* should emit photons with energies of approximately *200 keV and have a half-life of a few days for permanent implants and a much longer half-life (ie. years) for temporary implants.* This recommendation on optimal energy was based on a compromise of the various factors listed in Table 1.

Table 1
Radionuclide physical properties and factors of relevance
for determining clinical usefulness in brachytherapy.

Physical property	Factor of relevance for brachytherapy
Photon energies	
μ (water)	Dose homogeneity
TVL (lead)	Radiation protection
f_{tissue}	Bone damage
LET	Radiobiology (RBE)
Half-life	Temporary or permanent implants
Specific activity	Dose rate
Density & atomic number	Radiographic visibility & dose isotropy

In this chapter we now review the newer brachytherapy radionuclide sources of palladium-103, samarium-145, americium-241 and ytterbium-169 and summarise their basic physical and radiobiological characteristics. They have only been described for brachytherapy applications during the past five years and may offer advantages over the traditional sources such as caesium-137, gold-198, iridium-192 and iodine-125, just as these in former times offered advantages over radium-226 and radon-222.

Palladium-103

Palladium-103 has been studied at Yale University and at the Memorial Sloan-Kettering Cancer Center (Meigooni et al 1990, Chiu-Tsao & Anderson 1991) and introduced as a commercial product by the Theragenics Corporation of Norcross, Georgia, USA. Table 2 summarises the major characteristics of this radionuclide. Although the maximum specific activity is not reported, small sources with sufficient activities have been manufactured for LDR brachytherapy.

Table 2
Characteristics of palladium-103.

• Atomic number	46
• Photon energy range	20-497 keV
• Mean photon energy	21 keV
• Half-life	17 days
• TVL (Lead)	0.03 mm
• Maximum specific activity	Unknown
• Aim in brachytherapy use	Improved radiobiology *versus* iodine-125

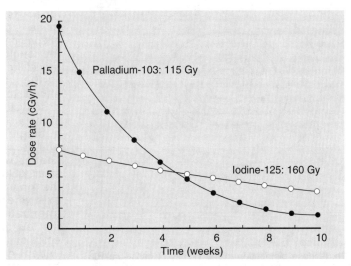

Figure 1. Dose rate changes with time for comparable bioeffective dose delivered by palladium-103 and iodine-125, adapted from Meigooni et al (1990).

The main motivation underlying the development of palladium-103 seeds is the radiobiological effect. As seen in Figure 1, the short half-life of palladium-103 (17 days) *versus* that of iodine-125 (60 days) allows a greater initial dose rate in the delivery of the total dose. This *front loading* of the dose is believed to be advantageous in the control of rapidly proliferating tumour cells. Based on the TDF model of Orton (1974), a palladium-103 implant delivering an overall dose of 115 Gy is as effective radiobiologically as a dose of 160 Gy delivered using the radionuclide iodine-125 because the palladium-103 dose is delivered at a greater initial dose rate.

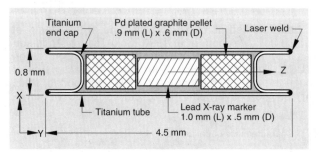

Figure 2a. Schematic of palladium-103 seeds. (Reproduced with permission of Theragenics Corporation).

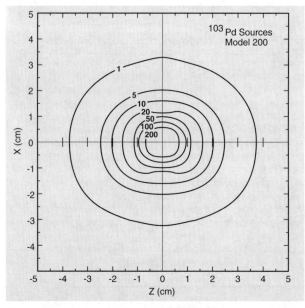

Figure 2b. Isodose distribution in the vicinity of palladium-103 seed (Model 200), adapted from Meigooni et al (1990), data normalised to 100% at 1.0 cm along transverse axis.

A schematic diagram of a palladium-103 seed is shown in Figure 2A and consists of two graphite pellets which are coated with radioactive palladium and separated by a lead marker to enhance radiographic visibility when the seeds are implanted in patients. The end caps of the seed are designed to minimise photon absorption along the longitudinal axis of the seed. Figure 2B shows the isodose distribution in the vicinity of a single seed and is oval in shape with a small kink along the longitudinal axis where the attenuation of the low energy emissions is still evident despite the effort at shaping the end caps.

Samarium-145

Table 3 summarises the major characteristics of samarium-145: the maximum achievable specific activity is estimated from the data of Fairchild et al (1987). The motivation in developing samarium-145 was to improve on brachytherapy relevant factors of iodine-125. In addition to the aim given in Table 3 it is noted that the photon energy emitted allows sensitisation of biological cells to radiation damage with the addition of the compound iodinated deoxyuridine (IUdR). This enhancement of the radiation effect is caused by selective k-absorption of the samarium-145 photons by the iodinated DNA structure (see also section on Americium-241).

Table 3
Characteristics of samarium-145.

● Atomic number	62
● Photon energy range	38.2-61.4 keV
● Mean photon energy	41 keV
● Half-life	340 days
● TVL (Lead)	0.2 mm
● Maximum specific activity	73 GBq.mm^{-3}
● Aim in brachytherapy use	Improved dose distribution and shelf-life *versus* iodine-125, and IUdR sensitisation

Figure 3A shows the energy spectrum of samarium-145 and Figure 3B shows the tissue variation of relative dose rate with distance from the source of the four radionuclides iodine-125, samarium-145, cobalt-60 and iridium-192. The relative dose shown has been *boosted* for inverse square law attenuation from a point source and indicates the reduced tissue attenuation of the samarium-145 photons when compared with those of iodine-125. Samarium-145 was activated at the Brookhaven National Laboratory in the USA and to our knowledge has not been produced commercially for widespread clinical use.

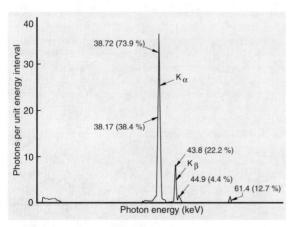

Figure 3a. Photon energy spectrum from titanium encapsulated samarium-145 source measured with a Si(Li) detector, adapted from Fairchild et al (1987).

Americium-241

Table 4 summarises the major characteristics of americium-241, a radionuclide source which was developed at Yale University (Nath & Gray 1987) with the intention that it would be suitable to use in the treatment of gynaecological cancers (Nath et al 1988). The motivation underlying this intention was to improve the ease of *in vivo* shielding from that which could be obtained with caesium-137. Using such a lower energy radionuclide it is possible to reduce the shielding requirements for equipment and also for external shielding and to develop new applicators containing internal shielding.

Table 4
Characteristics of americium-241.

• Atomic number	95
• Photon energy range	13.9-59.5 keV
• Mean photon energy	60 keV
• Half-life	432 years
• TVL (Lead)	0.42 mm
• Maximum specific activity	0.34 GBq.$^{mm-3}$
• Aim in brachytherapy use	Alternative to caesium-137 for cancers of the cervix & endometrium. IUdR sensitisation.

A further benefit which can be obtained by using americium-241 is that it has a photon energy which is very suitable for IUdR sensitisation (Mitchell et al 1986, Nath et al 1987). The IUdR compound substitutes for thymidine in the DNA structure and thus concentrates in rapidly proliferating cells.

Iodine, when tagged onto the DNA structure can preferentially absorb photons which have an energy above its k-absorption edge at 33.7 keV. This photoelectric absorption yields a cascade of characteristic x-rays and Auger electrons of higher LET. This creates significant and localised radiation damage to the DNA structure. Thus by labelling tumour cells with IUdR and irradiating them with americium-241, there is enhancement in the cell kill per unit dose, as evidenced in Figure 4A. For higher energy irradiations, Figure 4B, the enhancement due to IUdR persists but it is less than the gain in cell kill achieved with lower incident photon energy.

The likely clinical use of this therapeutic advantage is in the treatment of rapidly growing tumours which would preferentially incorporate the drug as the cell synthesises DNA, by comparison with the normal host cells which are less or non-proliferating: for example brain tumours (Leibel & Phillips 1992).

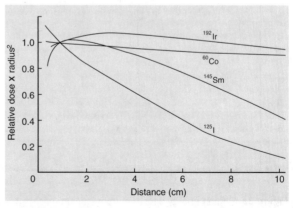

Figure 3b. Radial dose function for samarium-145 seed, adapted from Fairchild et al (1987).

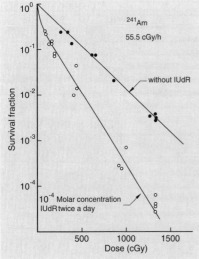
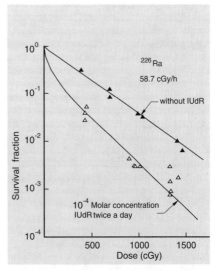

Figure 4a. Survival curves for IUdR treated (open circles) and untreated (closed circles) Chinese hamster cells irradiated by americium-241 photons at a dose rate of 55.5 cGy/h, adapted from Nath et al (1987).

Figure 4b. Survival curves for IUdR treated (open triangles) and untreated (closed triangles) Chinese hamster cells irradiated by radium-226 photons at a dose rate of 58.7 cGy/h, adapted from Nath et al (1987).

Ytterbium-169

The characteristics of ytterbium-169 are listed in Table 5, (Mason et al 1992), and the energy spectrum of this radionuclide is shown in Figure 5, as was measured in our laboratories with a high purity germanium detector.

Table 5
Characteristics of ytterbium-169.

● Atomic number	70
● Photon energy range	49.8-307 keV
● Mean photon energy	93 keV
● Half-life	32 days
● TVL (Lead)	3.3 mm
● Maximum specific activity	350 GBq.mm^{-3}
● Aim in brachytherapy use	Improved dose distribution *versus* iodine-125 & palladium-103.
	Improved radiobiology *versus* iodine-125.
	Possibly IUdR sensitisation.

The main motivation underlying the development of this source was to improve on the isodose distributions available with either iodine-125 or palladium-103 seeds. Ytterbium-169 has a half-life of 32 days which also improves the initial dose rate which can be achieved in permanent implants compared to iodine-125. However, it offers no advantage over palladium-103 in this respect as that radionuclide has a half-life of 17 days, Table 2.

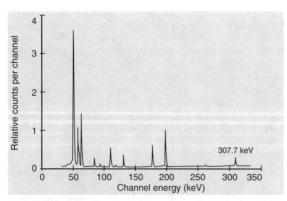

Figure 5. Photon spectrum for ytterbium-169 obtained with an HPGe spectrometer.

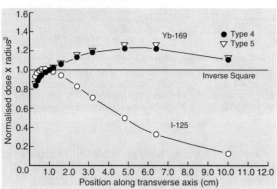

Figure 6. Radial dose function for ytterbium-169 seed (Amersham Type 4 and 5) and iodine-125 seed.

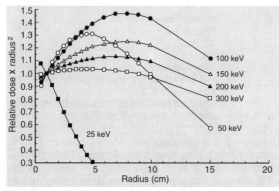

Figure 7. Radial dose function for various monoenergetic photon point sources: results of Monte Carlo calculations.

A second motivation was to provide a replacement for iridium-192 as a source for both conventional low dose rate (LDR) and high dose rate (HDR) treatments, as the reduction in energy should greatly simplify the design and cost of remote afterloading equipment. In addition, there may be cost savings in the reduced shielding requirements for hospital brachytherapy rooms.

The penetrating characteristics of ytterbium-169 photons are shown in Figure 6 in terms of the radial dose function along the transverse axis of the seed. This is compared with data for iodine-125. The greater photon energy offered by ytterbium-169 makes the radiation more penetrating through tissue. In addition the photon energy spectrum favours multiple Compton scattering which *tops up* the dose at a distance of approximately 5 cm distance from the seed. This effect is observed only with this intermediate energy range and is not observed with low energy sources such as iodine-125 and palladium-103, or for higher energy sources such as iridium-192, (see Figure 7).

Brachytherapy from Radium to Optimization

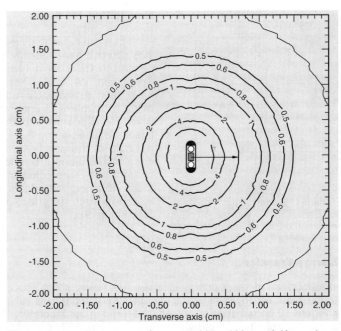

Figure 8a. Isodose curves for a ytterbium-169 seed (Amersham Type 2). Normalised to 1.00 at 1.0 cm along transverse direction.

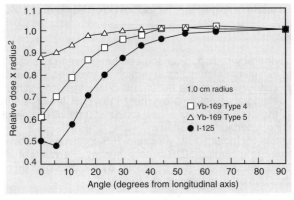

Figure 8b. Radial dose function for ytterbium-169 (Amersham Type 4 and 5) and iodine-125.

The clinical significance of this effect is probably minimal, however, since the inverse square law effect is dominant and such subtleties in scattered dose can generally be offset by optimal seed spacing. The dose distribution for ytterbium-169 is shown in Figure 8A and polar plots in Figure 8B show the improved dose distribution isotropy which can be achieved with ytterbium-169 seeds.

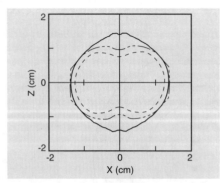

Figure 9. 50 cGy/hr isodose curves for three types of iodine-125 seed (Best Industries, Model 2300 Series): 100 U sources: 50 cGy/h isodose curves.(U: Unit of source strength (air kerma) μGy.m^2.hr^{-1}.

New Iodine-125 Seeds

It must be noted that new iodine-125 sources have recently become available from Best Industries, Springfield, VA, USA. These seeds have been considerably redesigned using a double-wall encapsulation which increases the photon energy fluence emitted along the longitudinal axis of the seed. As a result, dose distributions are much more uniform and more competitive with those obtained with higher energy isotopes such as ytterbium-169, (see Figure 9).

Linear Energy Transfer

The development of lower energy isotopes has raised some concerns with respect to the linear energy transfer (LET) of the charged particles set in motion in tissue. Figure 10 shows survival curves measured in our laboratory for ytterbium-169 and for cobalt-60. It is evident that ytterbium-169 is a medium-LET radiation and increases the cell kill per unit dose. We conclude that the RBE for ytterbium-169 relative to cobalt-60 is 1.2 ± 0.2 for the clinical dose rate range of 10-50 cGy/h: a value similar to that for iodine-125, (Plume et al 1993).

Conclusions

New brachytherapy radionuclide sources have been developed in the past five years that exhibit characteristics approaching ideal requirements. Each new source design encourages unique dosimetric challenges and stimulates market competition, yielding a steady improvement in overall brachytherapy practice. An example is the development of a new iodine source when challenged by the dose uniformity of ytterbium-169 seeds.

As a substitute for iridium-192, ytterbium-169 continues to show promise for temporary implants including HDR brachytherapy. Permanent implants with ytterbium-169 are feasible but may be stalled by the pressure on reducing recommended radiation protection limits still further.

Acknowledgements

The authors acknowledge the collaboration of Amersham International in funding the development of ytterbium-169 seeds and would also like to thank the developers of palladium-103, samarium-145 and americium-241 for permission to use their published data. We are also grateful to Mrs. Susan Davidson for her patience in the production of this manuscript.

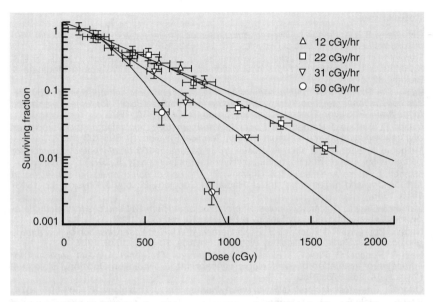

Figure 10a. Survival curves for Chinese hamster cells irradiated with cobalt-60, adapted from Plume et al (1993).

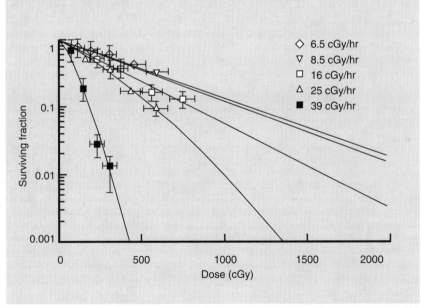

Figure 10b. Survival curves for Chinese hamster cells irradiated with ytterbium-169, adapted from Plume et al (1993).

References

Chiu-Tsao S & Anderson L, *Thermoluminescent dosimetry for 103Pd seeds (model 200) in solid water phantom*, Medical Physics, **18**, 449-452, 1991.

Fairchild R, Kalef-Ezra J, Packer S, Wielopolski L, Laster B, Robertson J, Mausner L & Kanellitsas C, *Samarium-145:a new brachytherapy source*, Physics in Medicine & Biology, **32**, 847-858, 1987.

Leibel S & Phillips T, *A randomised phase III study of conventional radiation therapy versus conventional radiation therapy and bromodeoxyuridine (BUdR) for tumors metastatic to the brain*, Radiation Therapy Oncology Group (RTOG), USA, 1992.

Mason D, Battista J, Barnett R & Porter A, *Ytterbium-169: Calculated physical properties of a new radiation source for brachytherapy*, Medical Physics, **19**, 695-703, 1992.

Meigooni A, Sabnis S & Nath R, *Dosimetry of palladium-103 brachytherapy sources for permanent implants*, Endo-curietherapy/Hyperthermia Oncology, **6**, 107-117, 1990.

Mitchell J, Russo A, Kinsella T & Glatstein E, *The use of non-hypoxic cell sensitizers in radiobiology and radiotherapy*, Int. J. Radiation Oncology Biology & Physics, **12**, 1513-1518, 1986.

Nath R & Gray L, *Dosimetry studies on prototype americium-241 sources for brachytherapy*, Int. J. Radiation Oncology Biology & Physics, **13**, 897-905, 1987.

Nath R, Bongiorni P & Rockwell S, *Enhancement of IUdR radiosensitisation by low energy photons*, Int. J. Radiation Oncology Biology & Physics, **13**, 1071-1079, 1987.

Nath R, Peschel R, Park C & Fisher J, *Development of an americium-241 applicator for intracavitary irradiation of gynecologic cancers*, Int. J. Radiation Oncology Biology & Physics, **14**, 969-978, 1988.

Orton C, *Time-dose factors (TDFs) in brachytherapy*, Brit. J. Radiology, **47**, 603-607, 1974.

Plume C, Daly S, Porter A, Barnett R & Battista J, *The relative biological effectiveness of ytterbium-169 for low dose rate irradiation of cultured mammalian cells*, Int. J. Radiation Oncology Biology & Physics, **25**, 835-840, 1993.

Sullivan W & Brucer M, *Trilinear Chart of the Nuclides*, Mallinckrodt Nuclear:St. Louis, 1979.

Trott NG (Ed), *Radionuclides in brachytherapy: radium and after*, The British Institute of Radiology: London, 1987.

38

Dose Rates of the Future

J.J. Battermann

Department of Radiotherapy,
University Hospital Utrecht,
P.O. Box 85500,
3508 GA Utrecht,
The Netherlands.

Introduction

Following the discovery of radium in 1898, brachytherapy was first applied to treat benign surface lesions, although by 1903 the interstitial use of radium had been suggested by Alexander Graham Bell in the USA and by Strebel (who proposed an afterloading technique) of Munich. The initial surface applications are generally credited to Danlos in Paris, but the first successful brachytherapy treatment of cancer was in St. Petersburg by two dermatologists, Goldberg & London, in 1903, (Mould 1993). Intracavitary brachytherapy for gynaecological tumours soon followed and at the end of the first decade of the 20th century was as well established as surface brachytherapy.

Table 1
Dose rate definitions of ICRU Report No.38 (1985).

Dose rate	cGy/h	cGy/min
Low (LDR & PDR)	< 200	< 4
Medium (MDR)	200-1200	4-20
High (HDR)	> 1200	> 20

From these early days, radium tubes and needles were widely used and various 'systems' were developed at major centres such as the Institute Curie in

Paris, the Radiumhemmet in Stockholm and the Christie Hospital in Manchester, and these (Paris, Stockholm, Manchester) were in routine practice in many centres by the end of the 1930s. These classical systems were all low dose rate (LDR) applications although Paris and Stockholm used different dose-fractionation schemes for cancer of the cervix and Manchester (Paterson & Parker) developed a system not only for intracavitary cancer of the cervix applications but also for surface mould brachytherapy and for interstitial brachytherapy in single and double planes. Today, though, higher dose rates are practical, see Table 1, than during the first 50 years of brachytherapy and with remote afterloading technology the spectrum of choice for the brachytherapist has changed out of all recognition from even 30 years ago. The introduction of artificially production radioactive isotopes has also given a new dimension to brachytherapy applications and miniature iridium-192 source design technology has revolutionised the design of remote afterloading equipment compared to the 1970s when the Cathetron with its cobalt-60 pellet sources was developed for high dose rate (HDR) applications. These new iridium-192 stepping sources have initiated new applications using pulsed dose rate (PDR) brachytherapy which may in the future replace a large number of what are now considered to be conventional LDR remote afterloading intracavitary and interstitial techiques as well as for new intralumenal applications.

Radiobiology

From a radiobiological point of view a dose rate of about 50 cGy/h remains ideal (Fowler 1990) and has biological effects comparable to those for conventional 2 Gy fractions delivered by external irradiation with an optimum balance between early (tumour) and late effects. In general LDR practice a dose rate of 40-100 cGy/h is the aim and it was stated by Pierquin et al (1973) that there are no dose rate effects between these dose rate values. However others, including Mazeron et al (1989) and Stout & Hunter (1989) have reported a serious increase in late complications.

Table 2
Dose rate corrections, after Stout & Hunter (1989), expressed as a percentage reduction to the prescribed dose at point A for the two clinical trials.
ICT: Intracavitary trial, stage I and IIa, 1980-1988.
W3ST: Wedge-3 Selectron-LDR/MDR trial,
stage Ib (bulky), IIb and III, 1983-1988.

Findings	ICT	W3ST
Significantly increased morbidity	0 6	
No significant difference in mordibity or primary failure when compared to radium	12.5	9 17
Significantly increased primary failure	19	

These different outcomes may be explained by differences in dose (boost versus full dose brachytherapy), treatment volume, site and total number of patients (Hall & Brenner 1991). Mazeron et al (1989) did find a dose rate effect in head and neck applications, although the number of patients in their series and the small differences in effect only were demonstrated with dose rates smaller than 50 cGy/h and larger than 50 cGy/h.

In the series of gynaecological applications from The Christie Hospital in Manchester, it was shown that a 17% reduction in total dose was necessary to avoid serious late damage, Table 2. This series faced brachytherapists with the problems of changing from one technique (manually preloaded sources) to another (remote afterloading) with a considerable difference in dose rate.

Although we should try to keep the complication rate as low as possible with any technique, we also should not forget that when changing to a new technique an underdose finally results in recurrences that are encountered relatively late and consequently often not receptive to further management. Alternatively, an overdose results in complications that are encountered more quickly and therefore still have treatment possibilities.

In radiobiology the 'four Rs' are well recognised: **Repair** of sublethal damage takes place in the range 30 minutes to several hours, **Redistribution** in fast proliferating tissues within a few days and **Repopulation** in several weeks. **Reoxygenation** is of importance, especially in tumours, and although not well known, takes probably a few days (Steel 1986). Reduction of the dose rate will result in a longer time period to deliver a certain dose, hence a number of these radiobiological processes will influence the radiation reaction during a continuous irradiation with LDR.

According to the total treatment times in LDR brachytherapy, repair is the most important factor. Redistribution is thought to be of limited importance, since the total application time should be long enough to result in an accumulation of cells in the more sensitive phases of the cycle. Redistribution is probably only of relevance in permanent implants using radionuclides with a relatively long half-life such as iodine-125 with 59.6 days. Alternatively some recent laboratory work indicates that the effect of synchronisation holds for much longer than a cell cycle, thus also influencing further irradiations and combinations of brachytherapy and external beam therapy (Williams et al 1991).

Reoxygenation is more effective in LDR than in HDR, especially in patients who receive brachytherapy alone. This is because hypoxic cells will suffer more damage with LDR than with fractionated HDR treatment and oxygenated tumour cells suffer more damage than oxygenated normal cells with HDR than with LDR (Joslin 1992).

Why Choose an Alternative to LDR?

The question now arises in the 1990s as to why should we consider other dose rate regimes than traditional LDR? The main reason is logistical since fractionated HDR therapy can be applied to several patients a day in contrast to the one machine devoted to only one patient situation with remote afterloading LDR. It is clear that HDR is of advantage in centres with a large population of uterine cervix cancer patients. This is especially true of the major centres in developing countries. Furthermore, HDR can be given on an outpatient basis.

Although fractionated HDR treatment for cervix cancer is widely accepted, other applications and tumour sites are still not totally clear. However, especially for palliative indications HDR can be of further advantage in minimising hospitalisation and number of external irradiation sessions. Two such examples are intralumenal brachytherapy for cancers of the lung and oesophagus.

HDR Brachytherapy for Cervix Cancer

For a long period of time HDR systems have been in use for gynaecological applications. To obtain similar results with HDR in terms of tumour control and incidence of late side effects as with LDR brachytherapy, the total brachytherapy dose should be fractionated over 4-10 sessions. The smaller the number of fractions, the higher the risk of late complications.

In an extensive worldwide survey of follow-up data after LDR and HDR brachytherapy for cervix cancer, Orton et al (1991) showed comparable data for both dose rates, both for tumour control and incidence of complications. If any difference should exist, this study found that the probability of a better outcome was in favour of HDR: with a slightly better local control rate in stage III, Table 3.

Table 3
5-year survival rates for HDR *versus* LDR, after Orton & Somnay (1992).
Tests for a statistical difference gave a P-value of 0.45 for all stages
and a P-value of 0.005 for stage III.

Disease stage	5-year survival rate (%)	
	HDR	LDR
All stages	60.8	59.0
Stage III	47.2	42.6

The mean number of HDR fractions in this Orton et al (1991) survey was 4.8 and the dose per fraction 7.45 Gy. Only the Horiot et al (1988) series demonstrated a better survival for a combined stages patient group after LDR treatment. However, the incidence of complications was also higher in the Horiot et al (1988) series: 27.59% moderate and severe complications (Crook et al 1987).

In the Orton et al (1991) survey there was a relationship between fraction dose (and hence number of fractions) and the complication rate (7.6% *versus* 10.5% for point A doses less than and greater than 7 Gy). A lower complication rate after HDR can be explained by the short treatment times which allow a better positioning of the sources and more packing around the sources. The dose fall-off gradient advantage of a brachytherapy dose distribution can be fully exploited with the short treatment times required for HDR gynaecological applications.

Palliation

Although intralumenal brachytherapy is not a new concept and was in use for oesophageal cancer at least as early as 1913, (Mould 1992,1993), the microSelectron-HDR gave a new stimulus to the application of brachytherapy, with the advantage of full radiation protection and a very short treatment time because of its 10 Ci iridium-192 stepping source. Thus especially for palliative purposes HDR intralumenal therapy is now widely accepted both for bronchial cancer (Stout et al 1990) and for oesophageal cancer (Flores 1990).

Speiser et al (1990) studied the side effects of this treatment modality and came to the conclusion that the complication rate can be reduced by lowering the dose. The palliative intention of most treatments and the acknowledged poor prognosis of these tumours does not allow any study in depth of the incidence of late effects. A furthur (palliative) application of HDR brachytherapy is as a boost to increase the total tumour dose to a primary site for tumours other than those of the bronchus and oesophagus.

microSelectron-HDR Iridium-192 Stepping Source

The single iridium-192 stepping source enables an optimised dose distribution to be achieved, both for a single 'linear source' intention or for a 'multilinear source' arrangement. The advantages of a single stepping source for implants are obvious: short treatments on an outpatient basis at relatively low cost without any source preparation.

Some authors already use a single fraction of HDR brachytherapy, such as Jacobs (1992) for breast cancer and Bertermann & Brix (1990) for cancers of the prostate: two fractions. When the brachytherapy is given as a boost, in general the LDR dose is relatively low level in the range 15-30 Gy and the application of HDR with an appropriate fractional dose in the range 5-12.5 Gy will probably not result in severe damage. On the other hand it will be difficult to visualise differences with LDR in terms of local control or complications. However, especially for higher doses, the use of a single fraction of HDR brachytherapy will result in serious sequelae. The radiobiological principles are similar in external beam therapy as in brachytherapy. For a reduction, particularly of late, side effects, many fractions are mandatory as was shown in the Orton et al (1991) overview for cervix cancer.

Pulsed Brachytherapy

With the introduction of a pulsed variable dose rate machine the use of many fractions a day will be possible. As shown from a theoretical point of view by Brenner & Hall (1991) a pulsed dose rate (PDR) treatment course with intervals of between 30 minutes and two hours will result in a similar biological effectiveness to that of a continuous LDR irradiation. Although the PDR concept seems to be the *egg of Columbus*, there are still some problems to overcome. For logistical reasons the intervals between fractions should be as long as possible: preferably four hours or greater. However, from a radiobiological point of view the interval should be less than one hour or two hours at the most. Since in many countries and states it will not be allowed to irradiate patients without full safety guarantee, including the presence of a qualified expert (radiation oncologist/radiation physicist), treatment during the night and weekend may have to be avoided. Furthermore, it will be unrealistic to disconnect a patient from the machine when the interval is one hour and the treatment time per fraction 15-30 minutes.

Finally, for radiation safety reasons, a source strength of 1-2 Ci iridium-192 is advocated for a PDR machine, rather than a 10 Ci source which is used with the microSelectron-HDR. Hence the PDR machine will be a specially dedicated replacement for an LDR remote afterloading machine but will not be satisfactory for HDR purposes.

Fractionated HDR Treatment

The disadvantage of PDR as mentioned above, bring us back to the topic of a 10 Ci iridium-192 HDR source and fractionated HDR treatments. A true advantage of PDR or fractionated HDR is the fact that patients are no longer confined to their shielded room with the doors closed for many days, in spite of the remote afterloading techniques and the interruptions by medical staff and visitors. Therefore we should work out treatment schedules using HDR brachytherapy with 2-5 fractions a day and intervals of 2-6 hours delivered in an overall treatment time similar to an LDR irradiation.

Especially for boost doses of 15-30 Gy, such a fractionated HDR regime will possibly result in a similar local control rate and complication rate to that obtained with LDR continuous irradiation. Brachytherapy as sole method for early breast cancer using the microSelectron-HDR, is already advocated by Kuske et al (1992). They used a total dose of 32 Gy in two fractions per day of 4 Gy over a total period of four days. The implant was performed peroperatively and the preliminary results showed no wound dehiscence. Also, in other respects the results were similar to continuous LDR. However, late side effects have not yet been assessed.

Only the future will tell us whether a fractionated regimen using 2-5 fractions per day with intervals of 2-6 hours will give similar results to those obtained with a PDR protocol and with an LDR continuous irradiation protocol.

Conclusions

In conclusion, LDR continuous brachytherapy will keep its place within the spectrum of cancer treatment modalities. However, for financial and logistical reasons, including radiation safety, a fractionated brachytherapy course giving an equivalent total dose according to the linear quadratic model in a similar overall treatment time with fraction intervals of several hours, applied during working hours, will probably have good prospects in the future.

References

Bertermann H & Brix F, *Ultrasonically guided interstitial high dose brachytherapy with iridium-192: technique and preliminary results in locally confined prostate cancer*, in: *Brachytherapy HDR and LDR*, Martinez AA, Orton CG & Mould RF (Eds), 281-304, Nucletron:Columbia, 1990.

Brenner DJ & Hall EJ, *Conditions for the equivalence of continuous to pulsed low dose rate brachytherapy*, Int. J. Radiation Oncology Biology & Physics, **20**, 181-190, 1991.

Crook JM, Esche BA, Chaplain G, Insturiz J, Sentenac I & Horiot J-C, *Dose volume analysis and the prevention of radiation sequelae in cervical cancer*, Radiotherapy & Oncology, **8**, 321-332, 1987.

Flores AD, *A review of radiotherapy of cancer of the oesophagus and cardia*, Activity Selectron Brachytherapy Journal, **4**, 5-9, 1990.

Fowler JF, *The radiobiology of brachytherapy*, in: *Brachytherapy HDR and LDR*, Martinez AA, Orton CG & Mould RF (Eds), 121-138, Nucletron:Columbia, 1990.

Hall EJ & Brenner DJ, *The dose rate effect revisited: radiobiological considerations of importance in radiotherapy*, Int. J. Radiation Oncology Biology & Physics, **21**, 1403-1414, 1991.

Horiot J-C, Pigneux J, Pourquirer H, Schraub S, Achille E, Keiling R, Combes P, Rozan R, Vrousos C & Daly N, *Radiotherapy alone in carcinoma of the intact uterine cervix according to G.H. Guidelines: a French cooperative study of 1383 cases*, Int. J. Radiation Oncology Biology Physics, **14**, 605-611, 1988.

Jacobs H, *HDR afterloading experience in breast conservation therapy*, Activity Selectron Brachytherapy Journal, **6**, 14-18, 1992.

Joslin CA, *The future of brachytherapy*, in: *International Brachytherapy*, Mould RF (Ed), 145-150, Nucletron:Veenendaal, 1992.

Kuske RR, Bolton JS, McKinnon W, Sardi A, Scroggins T, Hawkins R & Wilenzick RM, *Brachytherapy as sole methode for early breast cancer*, in: *International Brachytherapy*, Mould RF (Ed), 80, Nucletron:Veenendaal, 1992.

Mazeron JJ, Simon JM, Le Pechoux C, Piedbois, Le Bourgeois JP & Pierguin B, *Effect of dose rate on local control and complications in definitive irradiation of T 1-2 squamous cell carcinomas of mobile tongue and floor of mouth with iridium-192*, Radiotherapy & Oncology, **21**, 39-47, 1991.

Mould RF, *Oesophageal applicators before remote afterloading*, Activity Selectron Brachytherapy Journal, **6**, 44-46, 1992.

Mould RF, *A century of X-rays and radioactivity in medicine with emphasis on photographic records of the early years*, Institute of Physics Publishing:Bristol & Philadelphia, 1993.

Orton CG, Seyedsadr M & Somnay A, *Comparison of high and low dose rate remote afterloading for cervix cancer and the importance of fractionation*, Int. J. Radiation Oncology Biology & Physics, **21**, 1425-1434, 1991.

Orton CG & Somnay A, *Results of an international review on patterns of care in cancer of the cervix*, in: *International Brachytherapy*, Mould RF (Ed), **59**, Nucletron:Veenendaal, 1992.

Pierquin B, Chassagne D, Baillet F & Paine CH, *Clinical observations on the time factor in interstitial radiotherapy using iridium-192*, Clinical Radiology, **24**, 506-509, 1973.

Speiser B & Spratling L, *High dose rate remote afterloading brachytherapy in the control of endobronchial carcinoma*, Activity Selectron Brachytherapy Journal Supplement, 1, 7-**15**, 1990.

Steel GG, Down JD, Peacock JH & Stephens TC, *Dose rate effects and the repair of radiation damage*, Radiotherapy & Oncology, **5**, 321-331, 1986.

Stout R & Hunter RD, *Clinical trials of changing dose-rate in intracavitary low dose-rate therapy*, in: *Brachytherapy 2*, Mould RF (Ed), 219-222, Nucletron:Leersum, 1989.

Stout R, Burt PA, Barber PV, O'Driscoll BR & Notley HM, *HDR brachytherapy for palliation and cure in bronchial carcinoma: the Manchester experience using a single dose technique*, Activity Selectron Brachytherapy Journal Supplement,1, 48-50, 1990.

Williams JR, Yong-gang Zhang & Dillehay LE, *Sensitisation processes in human tumour cells during protracted irradiation: possible exploitation in the clinic*, Int. J. Radiation Oncology Biology & Physics, **21**, Supplement 1, 176, 1991.

39

Intraoperative Brachytherapy: Rationale & Future Directions

D. Nori

Booth Memorial Medical Center,
Flushing,
New York 11355,
USA.

Introduction

Loco-regional control of solid tumours may be accomplished with surgery, radiation or chemotherapy, alone or in combination. Great strides have been made in the treatment of pelvic, head & neck and extremity tumours with the use of surgery and radiation. In contrast, typical abdominal malignancies such as pancreatic and gastric carcinomas remain a persistent problem, as do locally advanced tumours in any location. Complete surgical resection is possible in many cases and palliative bypass is a frequent option, although the majority of patients succumb to disease.

Although many promising pilot studies have been published, adjuvant chemotherapy regimens alone have not demonstrated an ability to contribute significantly to local control or survival in many sites. The potential impact of local control on cure of disease in other common sites such as lung, oropharynx, prostate and bladder has been reviewed by the NCI and from that estimation, fully 10%-15% of all diagnosed patients may be cured through improvements in local control alone.

Because radiation therapy can achieve local control and in many cases improve survival it has made it an integral part of treatment in tumours of the head and neck, chest, pelvis and extremities. A key factor is the ability to provide cancerocidal doses to the tumour bed and regional nodes with acceptable morbidity. For example, a course of treatment for primary cervical carcinoma will entail external beam therapy to 4500 cGy with a brachytherapy boost to deliver a dose to point A of 4000 cGy for total of 8500 cGy.

That such high doses can be tolerated and that cure can be achieved with reasonable predictability is not only a result of many years of meticulous analysis of host/tumour characteristics and dosimetry, but also the inherent radiation tolerance of the local pelvic structures. Perhaps most important is the presence of a readily accessible cavity for the delivery of brachytherapy. Treatment of cervical carcinoma stands as a clear example of dose enhancement contributing to increased local control and survival.

In contrast, intracranial, thoracic, upper abdominal and pelvic tumours pose a vexing problem to the radiation oncologist. The central and peripheral nervous structures, lung, kidneys, liver, small and large bowel and bladder each have dose limiting tolerances which, if exceeded, may contribute significant additional toxicity. Precision high dose radiotherapy utilising CT based treatment planning typically can deliver in excess of 5000 cGy to the tumour bed. However, higher doses may be associated with sharply increased morbidity. Results with adjuvant and radical external radiation schemes have fallen short of providing complete local control at these levels. Essentially, it may not be possible to provide an adequate tumouricidal dose to such critical locations via external beam therapy alone.

Recognition of these constraints has stimulated great interest and creativity in methods of dose delivery to the target site. The concept of the intraoperative boost to directly enhance tumour dose has taken a number of forms. The most promising of these include intraoperative electron beam therapy (IOEBT), permanent interstitial implantation and temporary interstitial techniques utilising afterloaded high or low dose rate sources. Each method has its own advantages and limitations.

Howard University and the Mayo Clinic pioneered the use of IOEBT in the USA. IOEBT allows treatment of larger volumes than are possible with interstitial implantation and poses virtually no risk to operating room personnel. Pelvic malignancies including otherwise unresectable rectal carcinomas have been treated with notable success in these trials.

Although IOEBT has been used primarily on locally advanced disease in the USA, Abe & Takahashi (1981,1988) in Japan have gained considerable experience in the adjuvant and definitive treatment of primary gastric carcinoma. In a single institution study they have improved the results of surgical resection alone by the addition of a 2800-4000 cGy boost via IOEBT to the tumour bed, achieving 80% survival for stage II disease and 20% survival in advanced tumours which were otherwise uniformly fatal. At the Mayo Clinic more than 90% three-year actuarial local control has been achieved in a series of locally advanced pelvic tumours. However, this important technique has a number of limitations including those listed in Table 1.

Interstitial implantation of brain, lung, and pancreatic tumours coupled with external beam treatment has shown impressive local control and in selected patients increased survival. The advent of CT and ultrasound based planning techniques have made pre-planning and implementation more accurate in for example, intracranial and prostate lesions. The technique works well in such areas but there are some disadvantages including those in Table 2.

Table 1
Limitations of IOEBT.

- Dosimetric complexity, especially in areas of field overlap,
- Technical and logistical difficulty.
- Only one single high dose rate fraction is possible, minimising advantages of fractionated or low dose rate treatment.
- Severe late effects: ureteral stenosis and PNS damage, although manageable, are observed in long-term survivors in a dose dependant fashion when IOEBT is used as a single modality or in combination with external beam irradiation, as shown in animal and human data.

Table 2
Disadvantages of interstitial brachytherapy combined with external beam irradiation for tumours such as those of brain, lung and pancreas.

- Size limitation: no more than a 4 cm x 5 cm area may be effectively implanted.
- A corollary of the above size limitation disadvantage is that an interstitial implantation cannot effectively treat broad areas of partially resected tumours such as is typical in thoracic or abdomino-pelvic sites with adherence or direct invasion of unresectable structures.
- Personnel exposure to radioactive sources in the operating room. Although this is minimal in the hands of experienced teams using low energy radionuclides.

Table 3
Advantages of intraoperative brachytherapy boost therapy.

- Catheter flexibility allows conformation to the tumour bed.
- Accurate dosimetry can be determined postoperativly.
- Dose rate can be high or low and single or hyperfractionated regimens may be used.
- May be combined with a permanent interstitial implant to enhance deep coverage when invasive tumour is not adequately included within the catheter isodose.
- Operating room personnel is protected from any exposure.

A third approach to the problem of intraoperative boost relies on afterloading catheter or needle techniques. These are now frequently used in IOBRT (intra-operative brachytherapy) of sarcomas and high grade gliomas. Experience gained in treatment of extremity, head and neck and pelvic sites demonstrate many advantages, including those in Table 3.

The major disadvantage of this technique is size limitation, unlike IOEBT fields which can be matched to increase coverage, the maximum area which may be effectively implanted with catheters is 10 cm x 10 cm. However the majority of clinical situations will typically fall within this constraint.

Our experience in intraoperative brachytherapy in extremity sarcoma is described in this chapter. The same technique can also be applied in the treatment of lung, head and neck and other sites.

Soft Tissue Sarcoma

Soft tissue sarcomas account for less than 1% of all neoplasms in adults. The American Cancer Society estimates that in the United States in 1992 a total of 5600 people will develop this tumour and that 3000 will die due to the sarcoma, Table 4. The most frequent sites of appearance of soft tissues sarcomas are the extremities. These tumours are the most aggressive, spreading extensively along anatomical structures.

Table 4
Improvement in cure rates with enhanced local control.

Malignancy	New cases/year	No. of local-regional failures	Additional no. of cures if local disease is controlled
Uterine cervix	16,000	3,680	2,700
Oropharynx	18,700	5,050	2,200
Colorectum	120,000	36,000	17,600
Ovarian	18,000	7,200	2,000
Lung	102,000	20,400	7,200
Prostate	75,000	9,750	3,600
Bladder	38,500	11,935	3,000
Soft tissue sarcoma	4,250	1,275	900
All malignancies	392,450	95,290	38,000

Complex surgical procedures such as forequarter amputation and hemipelvectomy were designed to adequately treat the clinically evaluable tumour and its micro-extensions. In the early 1950s en bloc muscle bundle resection was popularised as an alternate to amputation with function preserving considerations. Unacceptable local tumour recurrences resulted in re-evaluation of the existing surgical techniques and has identified need for adjuvant treatments. Thus many surgeons recognised the limitations of surgery and sought the additional use of radiation and chemotherapy. Because of the nature of origin of these tumours in connective tissue, earlier reports suggested that sarcomas might be radiation resistant.

Treatment of these tumours by radiation alone demonstrated that a significant number can be locally controlled and tumour sterilisation can be observed in many patients. Many other reports appeared in the literature indicating successful use of radiation therapy as a means of controlling invisible microscopic residual tumour after resection.

At Memorial Sloan-Kettering Cancer Center we have investigated the feasibility of using intraoperative tumour bed brachytherapy after resection to increase local control and to maximise function preservation. The technique of combined surgery and brachytherapy has undergone several phases with advances in understanding surgical principles and radiation treatment planning. The most commonly used afterloading brachytherapy techniques were pioneered and popularised by Henschke & Hilaris, (Henschke et al 1963).

These techniques were successfully by Ellis (1975a,b) in Oxford in the treatment of soft tissue sarcoma, who favoured intraoperative brachytherapy in place of pre-operative or postoperative external radiation in the treatment of extremity sarcomas. He suggested 'implanting radioactive sources in the bed of the operation field at the time of surgery'. By this method, the cells inadvertently left behind by the surgeon may be subjected to a very large dose of radiation. This precise administration of radiation therapy at depth in the tumour bed also avoided much of the damage to adjacent normal tissues which was sometimes not possible with standard external beam radiotherapy.

Shiu et al (1984) reported the experience of treating 33 patients who had locally advanced soft tissue sarcomas of the upper and lower limb, using function saving excision and an afterloading removable iridium-192 tumour bed implant. The majority of these patients had been advised to undergo amputation because of the large size and deeply infiltrative tumours as evidenced by the CT scans. More than 50% had involvement of adjacent neurovascular bundle, bone or joint. In many instances the surgeon could resect only the grossly visible tumour, leaving behind microscopic or macroscopic fragments of sarcoma. The extent of surgical resection in these patients was dictated mainly by the anatomical disposition of the sarcoma, whether it was present within a single muscle compartment of the limb, or extended through muscular septa to involve a major blood vessel, nerve or bone; or arose in an inter-compartmental area such as the antecubital or popliteal space.

Following resection of the sarcoma, the brachytherapy oncologist marked out the tumour bed using small metal clips for radiological identification. The brachytherapy treatment field generally extended several centimetres beyond the actual or the suspected confines of the tumour.

The dimensions of the area to be implanted (width and length) were measured using a caliper and were then recorded. A variable margin of not less than 2 cm was added to these dimensions to ensure a satisfactory dose distribution.

The number of afterloading catheters required to be placed in the treatment area, in order to deliver 1000 cGy/day was determined by the use of a nomogram developed by Anderson et al (1985) at MSKCC. The prescribed number of plastic catheters are then inserted percutaneously through 17 gauge hollow needles, to be secured by chromic catgut sutures covering the entire extent of the target area. Afterloading catheters are individually secured to the skin by means of a threaded stainless steel button fixed to the catheter by crimping and anchoring to the underlying skin by silk sutures. A plastic hemispherical bead cushioned the button on the skin protecting it from undue pressure.

Postoperative AP and lateral radiographs with radio-opaque markers in the lumen of the catheters provide information for computerised dosimetry calculations. In almost all cases a single plane array of catheters is sufficient for delivery of the prescribed dose at depth. The total treatment time is calculated from the prescribed dose and maximum dose rate for which a continuous contour was evident in the region of interest. Separate determination of radiation doses are made for other points of interest such as skin, bone and neurovascular bundle.

A minimal peripheral tumour dose of 4500 cGy over 4-5 days was found to be adequate in almost all cases. Radiobiologically, the prescribed dose of 4500 cGy over 4-5 days is considered equivalent to 5500-6000 cGy of conventional external beam radiation. The sources are loaded usually five days after surgery to permit initiation of wound healing.

Following completion of the prescribed radiation, the sources and catheters are removed and the patient is discharged the same or the next day. If the patient has high grade tumour, adjuvant chemotherapy is offered using Doxorubicin with or without other drugs.

Initial Pilot Study Results

The results of treatment in the first 33 patients were encouraging. The follow-up in these patients ranged from 19 months to seven years with a median of 36 months. 17/33 patients had previously untreated tumours but none of the 17 developed local tumour recurrence after combined surgical excision and brachytherapy.

63% local control was observed in the previously treated group. The fact that more than half of the patients had been advised to undergo amputation because of deeply invasive tumours, leaves little doubt about the efficacy of this combined limb preserving surgery and perioperative brachytherapy.

Delayed wound healing was noted in 6/33 patients and 4/6 required repair with skin draft or rotation skin flaps. Many of these complications were encountered during the earlier part of the experience, often associated with inadequate soft tissue closure of the surgical incision. The function of the limb after treatment was carefully assessed. In all, 80% of patients in the study enjoyed good to excellent preservation of limb function.

Results of Conservative Resection & Brachytherapy in the Treatment of Popliteal & Antecubital Soft Tissue Sarcomas

Sarcomas in the antecubital and popliteal space pose additional difficulty in treatment due to proximity of major blood vessels, nerves and joints. The tumour either directly invades one or more of these vital structures or lies so close that microscopic involvement is likely. Successful surgical eradication necessitates an amputation. A multimodality treatment programme consisting of limb sparing resection and tumour bed irradiation using brachytherapy has yielded satisfactory preservation of limb function in 10 patients reported from our institution. These results are superior to those of 14 patients with similar tumours treated earlier by surgery alone.

Prevention of Wound Complications
Following Surgery & Brachytherapy

In our earlier experience, loading of the radioactive sources into the catheters on the first through to the fifth postoperative day resulted in a 48% overall incidence of moderate and severe wound complications. Our previous animal experiments would suggest that delay of application of radiation to one week after surgery is accompanied by significant improvement in wound breaking strength, new H3 hydroxyproline accumulation and improved force tension curves.

As part of our ongoing prospective randomised trial of the effects of brachytherapy on local control, a change was made. The catheters were loaded five or more days postoperatively. Wound complications were then reviewed in 50 patients following this single change in brachytherapy delivery. Of the 21 patients receiving brachytherapy, 14% had significant wound complications, 10% of 29 unirradiated patients had wound complications of similar severity. This decrease in morbidity from 48% to 14% suggested that the timing of radioactive source loading in the postoperative period is a major factor in radiation induced wound healing delay.

Tolerance Limits of Major Neurovascular Structures to Brachytherapy in the Treatment of Sarcomas

While there is debate in the literature concerning the tolerance of neurovascular structures to external beam radiation, the tolerance of these tissues to interstitial radiation has never been clearly studied. To evaluate the dose of radiation and its effect on early and late toxicity of neurovascular structures, we have undertaken a review of 299 patients treated during the period 1975-1987 for extremity sarcomas and who underwent limb sparing and tumour bed iridium-192 interstitial implantation. 45/299 (15%) of this group were found to have locally advanced tumours involving major neurovascular structures.

Of this patient series a total of 64% presented with tumours measuring 10 cm or greater and 68% had high grade lesions. Wide local excision of these tumours entailed meticulous dissection of the associated neurovascular bundle which in most cases was intimately involved with the lesion. 11% had evidence of gross residual disease on these structure and an additional 58% had microscopic residual disease at or close to the margins of resection.

Eight patients in this group had previous radiation to the treated field and 13 patients received postoperative radiation. With a median follow-up of four years the five-year actuarial disease free survival rate was 69% and the five-year actuarial freedom from in-field failure rate was 79%.

84% of the patients maintained long-term preservation of limb function without the need for amputation. Four patients (9%) ultimately developed evidence of radiation neuritis 6-20 months post-therapy. All four patients received additional radiation with cumulative doses exceeding 9000 cGy to the neurovascular bundle. This experience suggests that the cumulative dose to neurovascular structures should be below 9000 cGy in order to avoid undue toxicity.

Brachytherapy in the Treatment of Recurrent Extremity Sarcomas After Surgery & Irradiation

Treatment of recurrent extremity sarcoma following surgery and radiation is a challenging problem for Surgical and Radiation Oncologists. The management options are either amputation, disarticulation, hemipelvectomy or forequarter amputation. In a selected group of patients with recurrent sarcoma we have investigated the role of brachytherapy and function preserving surgery in recurrent extremity sarcoma.

For the period 1979-1988 a total of 40 patients who have received a full dose of prior external radiation were treated with salvage brachytherapy and conservative resection. The median follow-up after treatment was 11-120 months with a median follow-up of 36 months. The actuarial local control at five years is 70%. Five patients developed complications requiring surgical intervention. Five patients developed local failures and an additional two patients had both local and distant failure. All of the local recurrences occurred in the group of patients who had more than three prior recurrences.

This review suggests that brachytherapy can be used as an effective form of re-treatment in selected patients with recurrent extremity sarcoma following previous surgery and irradiation.

Brachytherapy in the treatment of extremity sarcomas offers several theoretical and practical advantages over conventional external beam radiation. There may be a theoretical advantage to radiation given during the immediate perioperative period before the healing process traps the tumour cells in scar tissue which may be less well oxygenated, rendering them more resistant to radiation. The placement of afterloading catheters directly into the tumour bed can deliver an effective dose to the target volume with maximal sparing of adjacent normal tissues. Joint attendance of the brachytherapy oncologist and the surgeon at the time of the operation will alow the most accurate delineation of the tumour bed and the most optimal soft tissue closure. The most important practical advantage of this approach is that the treatment is completed within five days and does not substantially prolong the hospital stay and the patients can be spared the long course of external beam radiation of several times a week for six weeks.

In view of the effectiveness of well planned single plane afterloading brachytherapy in the control of locally advanced tumours, including those with microscopic or macroscopic residual tumour after surgical resection and its effectiveness in controlling recurrent tumours after prior surgery and radiation, we conducted a prospective randomised trial of resection plus brachytherapy versus resection alone.

A preliminary analysis of the results shows that for high grade tumours a statistically significant increase in local control is obtained in patients who underwent surgery plus brachytherapy (P=0.03). The trend in low grade sarcoma is not obvious. In this study, of the 206 eligible patients, 117 were entered and 52 were randomised to the brachytherapy arm and 65 to the non-brachytherapy arm. Many of the patients treated for high grade sarcomas also received adjuvant chemotherapy, but this was equally distributed between the two groups of patients treated with and without brachytherapy.

Prospective Randomised Trial of Adjuvant Brachytherapy

After the initial experiences in which we saw a promising improvement of results but also morbidity, we felt the need to address two questions. The first was whether this method of treatment could offer benefit to all patients with soft tissue sarcoma of the limb. The second was to assess how much of the wound healing problem was related to the surgical procedure as opposed to the radiation treatment and how to decrease the overall risk of wound complications.

In 1982 we began a prospective randomised trial of tumour bed brachytherapy after resection of soft tissue sarcoma of the limb and superficial trunk in adult patients. We included the trunk lesions because these tumours shared a common histological composition and clinical behaviour. In this trial, all patients were eligible to enter as long as they underwent excision of the grossly visible tumour. Included were patients whose tumour excision margin showed microscopic evidence of sarcoma.

The design stratified patients according to histological grade of the tumour (high or low), maximum tumour diameter (greater or less than 5 cm), depth in relation to the superficial fascia, proximal versus distal site if in an extremity, and whether the tumour was a primary or locally recurrent lesion. Patients who had previously received chemotherapy or radiation therapy were excluded.

A standardised temporary implant of iridium-192 was used. The prescribed dose according to the New York System of dosimetry was 4500 cGy over 4-5 days with loading of the sources on the fifth or sixth day after surgery. Patients who had high grade tumours were encouraged to receive postoperative adjuvant chemotherapy that included Doxorubicin if they had adequate cardiac function.

A preliminary report of the trial has been published. At a median follow-up of 16 months, 2/52 recurred locally in the brachytherapy group, as compared with 9/65 in the group with no brachytherapy, suggesting a trend toward benefit due to brachytherapy (P=0.06: not significant). However, when only patients treated for high grade tumours were considered a significant difference in local control was found. 0/41 tumours treated by brachytherapy failed locally, as compared with 5/47 in the group not treated by brachytherapy (P=0.03). The resection margin of 17 patients showed tumour. 9/17 of these patients received brachytherapy with one observed local recurrence and 8/17 did not receive brachytherapy, with one local recurrence and one recurrence with metastasis. No survival benefit was observed.

Analysis of the salutary effect of brachytherapy on local control showed no association with sex, age, adjuvant chemotherapy, microscopic margin of resection or presentation of tumour as primary or recurrent. Since publication of this preliminary report, additional patients were entered into the trial. Further follow-up of this larger patient population has confirmed the statistically significant benefit of brachytherapy on local control, due mainly to its effect on high grade lesions. These observations thus uphold our conviction that adjuvant tumour bed brachytherapy combined with function saving, but macroscopically complete resection, is a highly effective method of management of high grade soft tissue sarcomas. The results are quite competitive with those reported from centres experienced in the use of external radiation therapy for soft tissue sarcomas. The number of low grade tumours in our study is still too small for conclusions to be drawn, and the study is ongoing for this lesion subgroup.

The superior results in limb salvage, functional preservation and local control achieved with this approach associated with its other practical advantages of short treatment time highlights brachytherapy as one of the most desired treatment options in the management of extremity sarcomas.

The Brachytherapy Treatment Option

Technique

The basic of the sealed end temporary implant technique is recommended, depending on the location of the tumour. The surgical treatment consists of an end block resection of the sarcoma and the involved tissue around it, including all previous incisions and biopsy paths. The entire specimen is excised in one block without cutting through the tumour if possible.

The main aim of resection is not only to remove all tumour but also to maintain normal function, when the tumour abuts on a major artery, vein, nerve, bone or joint, the structure is carefully dissected off and preserved if technically feasible.

Target Volume

After the surgical removal of the tumour, the overlying skin and soft tissues collapse onto the underlying structures. This composite slab of tissue forms the tumour bed treatment target, it can be flat or uneven. Usually a single plane implant is found satisfactory.

A margin of 2-5 cm beyond the boundaries of gross or suspected tumour must be added. The extent of the margin is normally larger along muscles, nerves, and vessels than transverse to those structures. The dimensions of the area to be implanted are measured with a ruler and are recorded.

The number of afterloading tubes that must be placed in the target area in order to deliver 1000 cGy/day is determined using the planar implant nomogram of the New York-Memorial system of dosimetry, (Anderson et al 1985). The tubes are inserted through normal skin after surgical resection but before completion of any reconstruction and wound closure. To ensure a proper implant the points of needle insertion are marked on the skin with a sterile pen.

Parallel stainless steel needles are spaced uniformly and embedded in the depth of the operative field. The closed end of each afterloading nylon tube (in the sealed end technique) is threaded through the needle until it emerges from the opposite end of the needle. The needle is then withdrawn while holding the plastic tube in place until the needle is out of the skin. This process is repeated for the total planned number of afterloading tubes. Each tube is secured in proper position in the tumour bed with #2 or #3 absorbable suture material.

Metallic clips are placed near each blind end of the nylon tube for later identification of this end on the localisation radiographs. The afterloading tubes are individually secured to the skin by means of a stainless steel button that is threaded over the tube, fixed to it by crimping and anchored to the underlying skin by silk sutures. A plastic hemispherical bead cushions the button on the skin protecting it from undue pressure.

Wound Closure

Because of the use of radiation, wound closure requires extra planning and care to avoid undue tension predisposing to wound breakdown. To diminish further the wound complications, the loading of iridium-192 ribbons is delayed until 4-5 days after surgery. Prior to loading, AP and lateral radiographs with radioopaque markers in the lumens of the plastic tubes provide the information necessary for computerised dosimetry calculations and dose rate determination.

Target Dose

The post-implantation physical evaluation of the implant involves calculating the dose distribution in multiple planes that are approximately perpendicular to the ribbons and selecting the highest dose rate for which the isodose contour is continuous. By dividing the prescribed dose by this treatment dose rate the treatment time is determined. The recommended dose for tumour bed implants is 4500-5000 cGy delivered in 3-5 days. External radiation should be given if all gross tumour was not resected and in such a case the implant boost dose is 2500-3000 cGy supplemented by 4000-4500 cGy delivered using external beam radiotherapy.

Special Situations

In implants of the leg, or generally in areas with minimum tissue between the skin and the implant plan, it is important that all drainage tubes are positioned superficially to the nylon tubes. This is so that they artificially increase the distance between the skin and the radioactive plane. Furthermore, these drainage tubes should lie within the field of irradiation so that tumour recurrences along their track can be avoided. Separate determinations of radiation dose are made with a diode probe or other sensitive radiation detector permitting isodose contours to be drawn directly on the skin.

These measurements are correlated with computer determinations for points of interest such as skin, major vessels and bone. If the projected dose to the normal tissues is more than 4000 cGy over an area of more than 25 cm2 then the target dose should be proportionally decreased until the preceding tolerance doses are met.

Occasionally, in removing a soft tissue sarcoma, a large skin defect is created. When direct wound closure cannot be achieved without tension in such a large skin defect, a pedicoled or myocutaneous flap can be utilised to ensure uncomplicated healing. Routine nursing and medical care is provided as usual, but prolonged exposure of staff should be avoided by the sharing of nursing duties and the use of portable lead shields. Upon completion of the planned duration of treatment, the afterloading nylon tubes and the iridium-192 seeds are removed. The puncture sites on the skin require no special care and most of the patients are discharged the following day from the hospital.

Intraoperative HDR Brachytherapy: Case History

Mr HK is a 56 year old white male with a history of smoking who developed a non-productive cough. Work-up, including chest X-ray, CT, bronchoscopy and bone scan revealed non-metastatic non-small cell lung carcinoma. At surgery, however, tumour was found to be adherent to the lateral chest wall. Intraoperative radiotherapy consultation was obtained. Inspection of the lesion demonstrated a deep component and so a combined brachytherapy procedure was performed. The tumour bed was sewn through with four iodine-125 Vicryl sutures to deliver a total dose of 16,000 cGy and afterloading catheters were placed at the site of resection with margin coverage. The patient was brought to the department the next day where dosimetry and optimisation were performed.

He received a single fraction of 1000 cGy using HDR, without delay in wound healing nor increase in length of stay, Figure 1. This was followed by a full course of external beam irradiation. At his most recent follow-up there was no evidence of disease and he was without any complaint. A phase I study to explore the feasibility of HDR intraoperative brachytherapy technique is currently on-going at our centre.

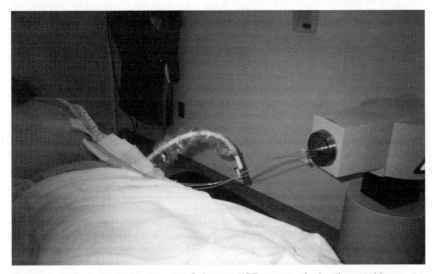

Figure 1. Patient attached to the microSelectron-HDR remote afterloading machine.

This case illustrates how intraoperative brachytherapy may be easily integrated into the daily practice of the surgical and radiation teams. With initial attention paid to catheter placement, dosimetric and optimisation considerations may be deferred from the hectic pace of the operating room to the less hurried atmosphere of the Radiation Department.

Conclusions

Local control with function preservation is a key consideration of cancer management. Achievement of this elusive goal would provide increased quality of life in most patients and increase survival in some who are at present destined to fail from local disease. In lesions with direct invasion of unresectable structures, negative margins are infrequently obtained. In cases such as these, the additional area coverage necessary limits the use of permanent interstitial techniques, as the presence of immobile critical structures and/or poor access as in chest wall tumours may limit the utility of IOEBT.

It should be noted that although risks of severe late effects exist, the high rate of local control provided by IOEBT has substantially improved quality of life in these patients in comparison with radical surgery or tumour progression. However, with the ready availability and current large installed base of HDR afterloading machines, a technique is now available to institutions who otherwise would be limited in their ability to provide intraoperative boost techniques of any kind. In the case of such machines with stepping source capability, commercially available optimisation software can maximise dose homogeneity in the case of difficult or complex geometry.

The study progress in IOEBT and permanent interstitial techniques has been hampered by the limitations placed by geometry, dose, expense dose and exposure. These compromises render them less than ideal. In contrast, the inherent advantages of afterloading techniques, including conformational control, dose rate flexibility, fractionation, dosimetry optimisation, low cost, and minimal exposure can place in the hands of community radiation oncologist a technique that may add to quality of life, increase local control and improve the results of treatment in many patients otherwise destined to fail locally.

References

(Those marked * are referred to in the text. The remaining references are for further reading.)

*Abe M & Takahashi M, *Intraoperative radiotherapy: the Japanese experience*, Int. J. Radiation Oncology Biology & Physics, **7**, 863, 1981.

*Abe M, Takahashi M & Ono K et al, *Japan gastric trials in intraoperative radiation therapy*, Int. J. Radiation Oncology Biology & Physics, **15**, 1431, 1988.

*American Cancer Society, *Cancer facts and figures*, 1992.

*Anderson LL, Hilaris BS & Wagner LK, *A nomograph for planar implant planning*, Endocurietherapy/Hyperthermia Oncology, **1**, 9, 1985.

Bowden L & Booher RJ, *The principles and techniques of resection of soft parts for sarcomas*, Surgery, **44**, 963, 1958.

Calvo FA, Azinovic I, Escude MDL, *Intraoperative radiotherapy in cancer management*, Applied Radiology, **21**, 15-23, 1992.

Cullinan S, Moertel C, Fleming T et al, *A randomised comparison of 5-FU alone (F) and 5-FU plus mitomycin C (FAM) in gastric and pancreatic cancer*, Proc. Amer. Society Clinical Oncology, **3**, 137, 1984.

Devereux DF, Kent H & Brennan M, *Time dependent effects of Adriamycin and X-ray therapy on wound healing in the rate*, Cancer, **45**, 2805, 1980.

Dobelbower RR, Merrick HW, Ahuta RK & Skeel RT, *Iodine-125 interstitial implant, precision high dose external beam therapy and 5fu for unresectable adenocarcinoma of the pancreas and extrahepatic biliary tree*, Cancer, **58**, 2185-2195, 1986.

*Ellis F, *Connective tissue sarcomata*, in:*Handbook of Interstitial Brachyhterapy*, Hilaris BS (Ed), 263-276, Publishing Sciences Group:Acton, 1975.

*Ellis F, *Tumor-bed implantation at the time of surgery*, in:*Afterloading: Twenty Years of Experience*, 1955-1975, Hilaris BS (Ed), 263-273, Memorial Sloan-Kettering Cancer Center:New York, 1975.

Gastrointestinal Tumour Study Group, *Treatment of locally unresectable carcinoma of the pancreas: Comparison of combined-modality therapy (chemotherapy plus radiotherapy) to chemotherapy alone*, JNCI, **80**, 751, 1988.

Greenblatt D, Nori D, Tankenbaum A, Brenner H, Anderson LL & Hilaris BS, *Brachytherapy techniques utilising iodine-125 seeds*, Endocurietherapy/Hyperthermia Oncology, **3**, 73-80, 1987.

Gunderson LL, Shipley WU, Suit HD, et al, *Intraoperative irradiation: A pilot study combining external-beam photons with "boost" dose intraoperative electrons*, Cancer, **49**, 2259, 1981.

Gunderson LL & Sosin H, *Adenocarcinoma of the stomach: Areas of failure in a reoperation series (second or symptomatic looks): Clinicopathologic correlation and implications for adjuvant therapy*, Int. J. Radiation Oncology Biology & Physics, **8**, 1, 1982.

Gunderson LL, Tepper JE, Biggs PJ et al, *Intraoperative and external beam irradiation*, Curr. Probl. Cancer, **7**, 11, 1983.

Gunderson LL, Martin JK, Earle JB et al, *Intraoperative and external beam irradiation and resection: Mayo pilot experience*, Mayo Clinic Proceedings, **59**, 691, 1984.

Gunderson LL, Martin JK, Beart RW et al, *Intraoperative and external beam irradiation plus 5IU for locally advanced colorectal cancer*, Annals Surgery, **27**, 52, 1988.

Gunderson LL, Martin JK, Beart RW, Nagorney DM, Fieck JM, Wieand HS, Martinez A, O'Connell MJ, Martenson JA & McIlrath DC, *Intraoperative and external beam irradiation for locally advanced colorectal cancer*, Annals of Surgery, **207**, 1988.

Gunderson LL, Nagorney DM, MvIlrath DC et al, *External beam and intraoperative irradiation of soft tissue sarcomas*, Int. J. Radiation Oncology Biology & Physics, **15**, 184, 1988.

Gutin PH, Prados MD, Phillips TL et al, *External irradiation followed by an interstitial high activity iodine-125 implant "boost" in the initial treatment of malignant gliomas: NCOG Study 6G-82 2*, Int. J. Radiation Oncology Biology & Physics, 1991.

Hall EJ & Lam YM, *The renaissance in low dose-rate interstitial implants: radiobiological considerations*, Frontiers Radiation Therapy Oncology, **12**, 21, 1978.

Hanks GE, *Intraoperative radiation therapy of pancreatic carcinoma. A report of RTOG 8505*, Int. J. Radiation Oncology Biology & Physics, **21**, 1145-1149, 1991.

Henschke UK, *Interstitial implantation in the treatment of primary bronchogenic carcinoma*, Amer. J. Roentgenology, **79**, 981-989, 1958.

*Henschke UK, Hilaris BS & Mahan GD, *Afterloading in interstitial and intracavitary radiation therapy*, Amer. J. Roentgenology, **90**, 386, 1963.

Hilaris BS, Shiu MH, Nori D, Batata MA, Hopfan S & Anderson LL, Hajdu SI & Turnbull AD, *Perioperative brachytherapy and surgery in soft tissue sarcomas*, in:*Brachytherapy Oncology*, Hilaris BS (Ed), 11-17, Memorial Sloan-Kettering Cancer Center:New York, 1982.

Hilaris BS, Nori D, Beattie EJ Jr. & Martine N, *Value of perioperative brachytherapy in the management of non-oat cell carcinoma of the lung*, Int. J. Radiation Oncology Biology & Physics, **9**, 1161-1166, 1983.

Hilaris BS & Nori D, *Brachytherapy Oncology: concepts and techniques*, in: *International Trends in General Thoracic Surgery*, McKenna RJ & Murphy GP (Eds), **1**, 207-216, 1985

Hilaris BS, Shiu MH, Nori D, Anderson LL & Manolatos S, *Limb-sparing therapy for locally advanced soft tissue sarcomas*, Endocurietherapy/Hyperthermia Oncology, **1**, 17-21, 1985.

Hilaris BS, Nori D & Martini N, *Results of radiation therapy in stage I and II unresectable non-small cell lung cancer*, Endocurietherapy/Hyperthermia Oncology, **2**, 15-21, 1986.

Hilaris BS, Nori D & Anderson LL, *New approaches to brachytherapy*, in:*Principles and practice of oncology*, De Vita , Hellman & Rosenberg (Eds), 1986.

Hilaris BS & Nori D, *Brachytherapy oncology: concepts and techniques*, in:*Fundamentals of Surgical Oncology*, McKenna RJ & Murphy GP (Eds), 335-344, McMillan:New York, 1986.

Hilaris BS & Nori D, *The role of external radiation and brachytherapy in unresectable non-small cell lung cancer*, Surgical Clinics of North America, **67**, 1061-1071, 1987.

Hilaris BS, Nori D & Anderson LL, *Clinical applications in cancer of the lung*, in:*Atlas of Brachytherapy*, Hilaris BS, Nori D & Anderson LL (Eds), McMillan:New York, 1988.

Kalser MH & Ellenberg SS, *for Gastrointestinal Tumour Study Group, Pancreatic cancer: adjuvant combined radiation and chemotherapy following curative resection*, Archiver Surgery, **120**, 899, 1985.

Kinsella TJ, Sindelar WF, Glatstein EJ & Rosenberg SA, *Preliminary results of a phase III study of adjuvant radiotherapy in resectable adult retroperitoneal soft tissue sarcomas: High dose external beam radiotherapy (HEBT) versus intraoperative and low dose external beam radiotherapy (IORT+ LEBT)*, Proc. Amer. Society Clinical Oncology, **6**, 136, 1987.

Lindberg RD, Martin RG et al, *Conservative surgery and postoperative radiation therapy in 300 adults with soft tissue sarcoma*, Cancer, **47**, 2269, 1981.

Lindberg RD, *Role of radiotherapy in soft tissue sarcomas*, Baker LH (Ed), Nishoff:Boston, 1983.

Manolatos S, Hilaris BS, Nori D, Linares L, Shiu MH, Anderson LL & Brennan M, *Intraoperative brachytherapy in the management of locally advanced pancreatic cancer: identification of prognostic factors*, in:*Proceedings of the American Endocurietherapy Society Annual Meeting*, **2**, 217, 1986.

Marchese M, Nori D, Anderson LL & Hilaris BS, *A versatile permanent planar implant technique utilising iodine-125 seed embedded in Gelfoam*, Int. J. Radiation Oncology Biology & Physics, **194**, 747-751, 1981.

McNeer GP, Cantin J, Chu F et al, *Effectiveness of radiation therapy in the management of sarcoma of soft somatic tissues*, Cancer, **22**, 391, 1968.

Nori D, Sundaresan A, Bains M & Hilaris BS, *Bronchogenic carcinoma with invasion of the spine: treatment with combined surgery and perioperative brachytherapy*, J. Amer. Medical Association, **248**, 2491-2492, 1982.

Nori D & Hilaris BS, *Brachytherapy in lung, prostate and soft tissue sarcomas*, in: Proceedings of the Endocurietherapy Research Foundation Meeting, Los Angeles, 115-**130**, 1984.

Nori D, Hilaris BS, Chadha M, Bains M, Jain S, Hopfan S & Anderson LL, *Clinical applications of a remote afterloader*, Endocurietherapy/Hyperthermia Oncology, **1**, 1193-2000, 1985.

Nori D, Hilaris BS & Martini N, *Intraluminal irradiation in bronchogenic carcinoma*, Surgical Clinics of North America, **67**, 1093-1102, 1987.

Nori D, Bains M, Hilaris BS, Harrison L, Fass D, Peretz T, Donath D & Fuks Z, *New intraoperative brachytherapy techniques for positive or close surgical margins*, Journal of Surgical Oncology, **42**, 54-59, 1989.

Nori D, *Role of brachytherapy in the treatment of soft tissue sarcomas of the extremities, techniques and results*, Presidential Address, 12th Annual Meeting of the American Endocurietherapy Society, 1989.

Nori D, Shupak K, Shiu MH & Brennan MF, *Role of brachytherapy in recurrent extremity sarcoma in patients treated with prior surgery and irradiation*, Int. J. Radiation Oncology Biology & Physics, **20**, 1229-1233, 1991.

Ormsby MV, Hilaris BS, Nori D & Brennan MF, *Wound complications of adjuvant radiation therapy in patients with soft-tissue sarcomas*, Annals of Surgery, **210**, 93-99, 1989.

Powers BE, Gillette EL, McChesney SL & Withrow SJ, *Bone necrosis and tumour induction following experimental intraoperative irradiation*, Int. J. Radiation Oncology Biology & Physics, **15**, 204, 1988.

Powers BE, Gillette EL, McChesney Gillette SL, LeCouteur RA & Withrow SJ, *Muscle injury following experimental intraoperative irradiation*, Int. J. Oncology Biology & Physics, **20**, 463-471, 1991.

Rostock P, *Indikations stelling und dan erertoig sarkomen*, Fort. Schr. Therapie, **4**, 241, 1928.

Shaw EG, Gunderson LL, Martin JK, Beart RW, Nagorney DM & Podratz KC, *Peripheral nerve and ureteral tolerance to intraoperative radiation therapy: clinical and dose-response analysis*, Radiotherapy & Oncology, **18**, 247-255, 1990.

*Shiu MH, Turnbull AD, Nori D et al, *Control of locally advanced extremity soft tissue sarcoma by function-saving resection and brachytherapy*, Cancer, **53**, 1385, 1984.

Shiu MH, Collin C, Hilaris BS, Nori D, Manolatos S, Anderson LL, Hajdu SI, Lane JM, Hopfan S & Brenman MF, *Limb preservation and tumour control in the treatment of popliteal and antecubital soft tissue sarcomas*, Cancer, **576**, 1632-1639, 1986.

Shiu MH & Brennan MF, *Surgical Management of Soft Tissue Sarcoma*, Shiu MH & Brennan MF (Eds), 1989.

Suit HD, Poppe KH, Mankin HJ et al, *Preoperative radiation therapy for sarcoma of the soft tissue*, Cancer, **47**, 2269, 1981.

Suit HD, *Radiation therapy in cancer. Principles and practice of oncology*, Lippincott:Philadelphia, 1057-1060, 1982.

Tepper JE, Noyes D, Krall JM, Sause WT, Wolkov HB, Dobelbower RR, Thomson J, Owens MJ & Hanks GE, *Intraoperative radiation therapy of pancreatic carcinoma: a report of RTOG 8505*, Int. J. Radiation Oncology Biology, **21**, 1145-1149, 1991.

Zelefsky MJ, Nori D, Shiu MH & Brennan MF, *Limb salvage in soft tissue sarcomas involving neurovascular structures using combined surgical resection and brachytherapy*, Int. J. Radiation Oncology Biology & Physics, **19**, 913, 1990.

40

Clinical Trials in Brachytherapy

A.T. Porter

Department of Radiation Oncology,
The Detroit Medical Center,
Wayne State University School of Medicine,
Detroit,
Michigan 48201,
USA.

Introduction

Brachytherapy is the oldest mode of delivering radiation for therapeutic applications. After the discovery of radium by Marie Curie in 1898, brachytherapeutic applications in the treatment of cancer of the cervix were first performed by Cleaves in New York and by Döderlein in Tubingen. Within a decade of these first brachytherapy applications, two schools of dose fractionation had evolved. One was the Stockholm system pioneered by Forsell, which utilised a treatment regimen in which several 10-12 hour applications of intracavitary radium were delivered to treat the tumour over several weeks. The second school developed almost simultaneously in Paris under Regaud and Coutard and involved the use of a single uninterrupted insertion lasting 120 hours, (Pierquin et al 1987).

The first retrospective clinical evaluation was reported by Heyman in 1914, who evaluated nearly 2000 cases treated by either of the then current techniques, Stockholm or Paris. Heyman reported no differences in outcome as measured by the endpoints of survival and local control. He also made the statement which has certainly stood the test of time regards clinical trial methodology: "Report all cases, even those not treated".

The 1950s through to the 1970s witnessed a substantial decline in the use of interstitial and intracavitary applications of radiation that paralleled changes that occurred within the technology available to radiation oncologists and to the education and training available to new practitioners.

The 1950s and 1960s saw the development of cobalt-60 and linear accelerator megavoltage therapy units, and the very real problems associated with the poor depth dose characteristics of the earlier orthovoltage units were considered to be no longer clinically relevant. A further contributing factor underscoring the reduction of interest in brachytherapy was the reduction in the expertise in the surgical skills required for effective and successful therapy. In some part, this was due to the fact that many early radiation oncologists entered this specialty from a background of being surgeons and gynecologists. It was only later that radiation therapy became the major speciality that supported the therapeutic applications of gamma rays and X-rays.

The development of the clinical trial as a form of medical evaluation procedure had a different evolution, being derived from the development of multiple pharmacological agents during and after the second world war and the recognition by medical specialists of the differing efficacies and side effects that required comparative examination and evaluation. It was logical that within the oncological context, clinical trial methodology followed the introduction of chemotherapeutic drugs and the development of the relatively new discipline of medical oncology. The rapid development of this field, as well as the growth within the pharmaceutical industry devoted to the production of novel anti-neoplastic agents, led to the attainment of a degree of formalism in clinical trial methods which has become to all intents and purposes 'de rigueur" in the assessment of any new oncological procedure, as well as determining for many previously well established procedures their place within the armamentarium of the spectrum of therapies.

Thus brachytherapy, the oldest radiotherapeutic modality and the first non-surgical oncological therapy, has been challenged due to the paucity of modern day clinical trial data support. This chapter will evaluate the needs and some of the requirements necessary for the design of state of the art clinical trials.

Clinical Trial Formalism

There are now several well recognised types of trials or investigations which can be divided into those listed in Table 1.

Table 1
Types of trials or investigations.

Pre-clinical
These include animal toxicology, biodistribution & teratogenicity.

Clinical
These include the classic three-phase model. [Phase 1] Dose escalation with a toxicity endpoint. [Phase 2] Efficacy studies at defined dose levels. [Phase 3] Randomised studies *versus* the current standard therapy.

Although much very useful information can be gleaned from phase 1 and 2 studies, it is the randomised studies that are the 'gold standard' in terms of identifying the appropriate place for these therapies. In reality, whilst most current phase 3 trials evaluate medically better understood concepts of survival, local control and complications. The newer concepts of cost and quality will also be subject to evaluation as cost benefit and cost utility methodologies become available.

Are Trials Needed in Brachytherapy?

Over the past 30 years there have been over 300 reports detailing techniques, results and outcomes in literally hundreds of thousands of patients treated with brachytherapy. With this large data set it is possible to draw several conclusions about these techniques.

As treatment for primary gynecological cancers of the cervix and uterus, the results of radiotherapy using brachytherapy have yielded similar results as is seen from the surgical literature. However, over the last 10 years there has been a steady increase in the proportion of cases treated surgically as compared to radiotherapeutically, (Pettersson 1989, Zola et al 1989).

The use of interstitial implantation of tumours of the **tongue** have demonstrated for comparable disease stages, outcomes in terms of survival and local control which are similar to that achieved with surgery but with organ preservation and conservation of function, (Gallery et al 1984, Baris et al 1985, Housset et al 1987, Puthawala et al 1988).

A further example suggesting the need for carefully controlled clinical trials is suggested by the dose escalation experience in **bulky prostate cancer** using brachtherapy. It has been demonstrated that it is possible to increase the histologically negative rate from 20-30% to 70-80% in patients with stage C disease. However, the price may be a substantially increased toxicity secondary to the effects of the increase in dose to the anterior rectal wall, (Porter & Forman 1993). This experience is now being repeated using external beam conformal therapy techniques. Thus there is a clear need to develop trials to affirm the place of brachytherapy in modern day oncological practice.

Table 2
Main factors to consider when designing clinical trials.

[1] The Clinical Question
[2] The Clinical Material
[3] The Design of the Study
[4] Statistical Analysis & Quality Assurance Considerations
[5] Endpoints

Design of Clinical Trials

Maybe investigators have been jaundiced by their experience in developing and conducting clinical investigations. In general, these experiences have been the result of poorly designed studies with inappropriate questions, endpoints, statistical considerations, or even clinical relevance: all of which prejudice the outcome or success of the study. There are several main factors to consider when designing clinical trials, Table 2, each of which will now be considered in separate sections.

The Clinical Question

The appropriateness of the question to be asked in the study is of paramount importance in determining the feasibility of the study and the design and analytical methodology to be employed. There are two main pitfalls associated with the development of tenable hypotheses, Table 3.

Table 3
The two main pitfalls when considering the 'clinical question' in the design of clinical trials.

[1] The choice of a clinically inappropriate question within the current clinical environment.

[2] The choice of an unacceptable question in terms of patient and/or physician acceptance.

In terms of choosing questions which are inappropriate to the current clinical environment, pertaining clinical realities may be described in terms of several examples. Consider the case of **stage I endometrial cancer** in which a proposal is submitted to evaluate the role of multifraction HDR therapy by randomising suitable patients to receive either a single fraction of HDR therapy or five fractions of smaller fraction size. Whilst it true that this study has substantial merit, in terms of elucidating local control and potential complications of two much debated regimens, unfortunately, the question most pressing to gynecological oncologists is whether or not intracavitary brachytherapy is needed at all to prevent vault recurrences in this group of patients. Therefore a more appropriate question, taking cognisance of the clinical milieu, would be a randomisation to immediate brachytherapy versus expectant management in this group of patients.

A second illustrative example can be drawn from the brachytherapy experience in **bladder cancer** in which there has been a long tradition in Europe. In fact, some of the best results in terms of local control have been reported by van der Werf Messing et al (1983) and Parsons & Million (1990). However, interest in evaluating these results in the USA by the conduct of a clinical trial utilising an iridium-192 afterloaded implant in patients with stage T3 (<5cm diameter) tumours was poorly received by the treating community as the 'in vogue' science in bladder cancer on this side of the Atlantic was the use of chemotherapy combined with radiation. Thus, all current trials conducted in the USA at the present time employ chemo-radiation in their design, (Porter 1990).

A second important consideration is to design studies which are acceptable to both physicians and patients alike in terms of the ability to accept randomisation. In several instances, good questions that are clinically pertinent have been impossible to answer because of the refusal of patients to be randomised generically, studies which have a 'No Treatment' arm are conceptually difficult to perform and may be more acceptable with a delayed or expectant therapy arm. When two quite different modalities of therapy represent the treatment arms, this can be difficult. The intergroup study, RTOG 5794 which recently closed, is a case in point. This study planned to evaluate the choice of a radical prostatectomy or radical radiotherapy in the treatment of **localised prostate cancer**. Even through the question was and remains valid, (Porter et al 1993), few patients were accessed to the study which had to be terminated early without meeting its accrual goals.

The Clinical Material

A further consideration in the design of studies, especially randomised trials, is that of the selection of a population of patients which are accessible to the trialists and represent a disease incidence that is frequent enough to allow rapid accrual to the study. Thus studies involving **prostate** or even **breast cancer** are eminently feasible, whilst studies in lymphomas or small cell lung cancer are more difficult. However, there have been three recently completed phase 3 brachytherapy studies in **sarcoma of the breast** and in **anaplastic brain tumours** which met their accrual goals.

Statistical Analysis & Quality Assurance Considerations

The statistical section in clinical randomised studies is often a neglected area but is of critical importance in the overall outcome of a study. The most difficult factor is determining the patient accrual numbers needed to meet the clinical objectives of the trial. This requires a knowledge or a good 'guesstimate' of the differences in outcome that are anticipated between the two arms of the study.

Outcome may refer to different endpoints such as survival, local control or complications, once the perceived differences are provided and the rigor of detection (power of a statistical test & statistical significance) are set, and with a recognition of when the differences are expected to occur. Then, tables will provide the numbers of patients required, (Peto 1978).

In brachytherapy, one of the most difficult factors to control is that of quality assurance. The much touted euphemism that 'Brachytherapy is an artform and not a science' may be partially true, as in many cases the skill of the operating physician determines the overall outcome of the procedure. This can be seen from the fact that several brachytherapists have reported steep learning curves, especially as regards complication rates. Martinez et al (1985) and Porter (1991) reported severe complication rates of between 15% and 20% with their early series of patients treated with temporary irdium-192 **prostate** implants. Both authors have demonstrated halving of this rate with technique refinement and improvement in expertise levels.

It is therefore quite difficult at the present time to countenance randomised multicentre trials in some of the more difficult implant situations. The recent experience with the radiation therapy oncology group trial in **breast cancer**, in which the evaluation of a brachytherapy boost was compared to an electron boost, was compromised by the high rate of major violations of the prescription specification in the brachytherapy treatment arm. It is thus important to consider randomised trial in situations in which the brachytherapy applications are relatively simple and well specified such as in gynecological applications, or in the use of linear sources in the treatment of **oesophageal or bronchial lesions**. The RTOG is currently completing a phase I/II study to evaluate the addition of an endoesophageal boost, in addition to chemo-radiation in **oesophageal cancer**.

Endpoints

The endpoints chosen in the trial are important. Much work has centred around the use of the more traditional end point such as survival, local control and complications. These measurements are of undoubted value, but in considering brachytherapy trials, there are other important end points worth considering. For example, the use of cosmetic scoring for techniques used in **breast** cancer (Clarke et al 1983), functional scoring in **paediatric** brachytherapy, and symptom relief in palliative situations, such as bronchial and biliary relief. The addition of quality adjusted measurements will also be importance in the future.

Conclusions

Brachytherapy has a distinguished past and still represents the optimum way, in selected situations. to deliver radiation with the ability to deliver a close to optimal relative integral dose. New techniques, including dose optimisation with sophisticated treatment planning and computerised afterloading systems, have revolutionised this field in the last decade. There is, however, an area that now needs more attention and that is the systematic and careful analysis and integration of this modality into current clinical practice by the execution of carefully designed and conducted clinical trials.

References

Baris G, Visser AG & Vanandel JG, *The treatment of squamous cell carcinoma of the nasal vestibule with interstitial iridium implantation*, Radiotherapy & Oncology, 4, 121-125. 2985.

Clarke D, Martinez A & Cox RS, *Analysis of cosmetic results and complications of patients in stage I and stage II breast cancer treated by biopsy and irradiation*, Int. J. Radiation Oncology Biology & Physics, **9**, 1807-1813, 1983.

Gallery CD, Spiro RH & Strong EW, *Changing trends in the management of squamous carcinoma of the tongue*, American J. Surgery, **148**, 449-454. 1984.

Housset MN, Baillet F, Dessard-Diana B, Martin D & Miglianico L, *A retrospective study of three treatment techniques with T1 and T2 base of tongue lesions. Surgery plus postoperative radiation, external radiation plus interstitial implantation, and external radiation alone*, Int. J. Radiation Oncology Biology & Physics, **13**, 511-516, 1987.

Martinez A, Edmundson JD, Cox RS, Gunderson LL & Howes AE, *A combination of external beam irradiation and multiple site perineal applicator for the treatment of locally advanced or recurrent prostatic perineum and gynaecological malignancies*, Int. J. Radiation Oncology Biology & Physics, **11**, 391-398, 1985.

Parsons JT & Million RR, *The role of radiation therapy alone or as an adjunct to surgery in bladder carcinoma*, Seminars in Oncology, **17**, 566-583, 1990.

Peto R, *Clinical trial methodology*, Biomedicine, **28**, 24-36, 1978.

Pettersson F (Ed), *Annual report on the results of treatment in gynaecological cancer*, **20**, FIGO:Stockholm, 1988.

Pierquin B, Wilson JF & Chassagne D, *Modern brachytherapy, Masson:New York*, 1987.

Porter AT, *Radiotherapy combined with chemotherapy in the treatment of muscle invasive bladder carcinoma*, Seminars in Oncology, **17**, 583-589, 1990.

Porter AT, *Brachytherapy in the treatment of prostatic tumours, in:Brachytherapy of prostatic cancer*, Bruggmoser G, Sommerkamp H & Mould RF (Eds), 179-185, Nucletron:Veenendaal, 1991.

Porter AT & Forman JD, *Prostate brachytherapy: an overview*, Cancer, **71**, 953-958, 1993.

Porter AT, Kaczor JG & Forman JD, *Perspectives on the role of radiotherapy in organ confined and locally advanced prostate cancer*, European Urology, **24**, 39-43, 1993.

Puthawala AA, Syed NA, Eades DL, Gillin L & Gates TC, *Limited external beam and interstitial iridium-192 irradiation in the treatment of carcinoma of the base of tongue: 10-year experience*, Int. J. Radiation Oncology Biology & Physics, **14**, 839-848. 1988.

van der Werf Messing BHP, Menon RS & Hop WCJ, *Carcinoma of the urinary bladder. Category T3 NX M0 treated by the combination of radium implant and external irradiation: second report*, Int. [J. Radiation Oncology Biology & Physics, **9**, 177-180, 1983.

Zola P, Volpe T, Castelli G, Sismondi P, Nicolucci A, Parazzini F & Liberati A, *Is the published literature a reliable guide for deciding between alternative treatments for patients with early cervical cancer?* Int. J. Radiation Oncology Biology & Physics, **16**, 785-797, 1989.

41

The Future of Brachytherapy

C.A.F. Joslin

Regional Radiotherapy Centre,
Cookridge Hospital,
Leeds LS16 6QB,
United Kingdom.

Introduction

Had one expressed an opinion about the future for brachytherapy 20 years ago I very much doubt that the rapid expansion in the applications to which brachytherapy is now applied could have been foreseen. If any one cause is to be identified it has to be the major technological developments that have taken place and this is likely to remain the major factor for the future. Among the other various factors which can be expected to play a role in the future is the development of new radionuclides, particularly in relation to the specific activity of the nuclide and its effect on the physical size of the radiation source.

Size will also interrelate with the strength of source necessary to provide the required dose rate at a specified distance from the source. While the inverse square law effect is the major reason for the fall-off in dose rate with distance for high energy gamma irradiation, new radionuclides with an emphasis on low energy gamma or particulate energies offer certain possible advantages in terms of improved dosimetry control within a restricted volume.

Safety, not only in relation to better quality control, reliability and reproducibility of treatment, is expected to remain paramount and to affect technological developments, making it safer to use certain types of radionuclide. For example, the tenth-value-thickness (TVT) in lead for iridium-192 gamma rays is 50% of that for cobalt-60 gamma rays, Table 1.

Battista & Mason in **Chapter 37** present interesting information on some of the new radionuclides available for brachytherapy: palladium-103, samarium-145, ytterbium-169 and americium-241. Ytterbium-169 is particularly of potential value, either in permanent implants or for fractionated HDR brachytherapy. This dual application is principally because of the short half-life (32 days) and a high specific activity (350 GBq/mm^3) of this radionuclide.

Our understanding of the effect of irradiation on living tissues is scientifically, still largely based on studies of tissue cultures and animal systems. The clinical situation remains mainly based on empirical data from clinical observations. Various studies have provided for a better understanding of dose effect but have unfortunately often failed to provide a basis for improved tumour control rates designed on radiobiological principles, although extensive efforts have been made to overcome the radioresistance of hypoxic cells. The effects of hypoxia can be largely overcome by delivering a very high dose of irradiation. However, this can only be safely achieved by restricting the treatment volume and brachytherapy is one way of achieving this.

The clinical objectives of treatment are also now becoming closely allied to the patient's view point and the present and future mission is Quality Management, that is 'freedom from doubt' for the patient and for the staff providing the treatment. These concepts are going to greatly affect the way we practice radiotherapy and in particular brachytherapy.

Technological Developments

Figure 1 provides an outline of the component parts of a modern brachytherapy machine. It illustrates an extremely sophisticated facility designed to deliver within certain restricted limits, an optimised dose distribution to a given target volume. By using such advanced technology it is becoming increasingly possible to reach almost any organ within the human body by using appropriate small diameter flexible source carriers. The range of treatment applicators available to facilitate the positioning of the radioactive source(s) continues to increase in number and complexity: each being claimed by its designer to offer some from of specific advantage!

The control and placement of individual source carriers can now be facilitated using either CT X-ray or ultrasound control. This provides for 'real time' treatment planning in a three-dimensional sense, designed to deliver treatment to a specific target volume: for treatment planning by either brachytherapy alone or combined with teletherapy. Various systems are being developed such as Nucletron's PLATO and that of Multidata which is described by Hilaris et al in **Chapter 32**, in which three-dimensional surfaces are superimposed on three-dimensional anatomy. The clinician is then able to relate geographical information to tailored dosimetry in order to provide fast and reliable dose optimisation.

One particular advantage related to future developments will be to produce methods of rapid selection and assessment of the most appropriate isoeffect envelope to cover a particular geographical target volume while a patient is anaesthetised. Such systems will need to be able to cope with either standard template, modified template or 'free-hand' implants.

Table 1
Variation of TVT with radionuclide: NCRP data.

Radionuclide	Gamma-ray energy (MeV)	TVT (mm)		
		Concrete density 2.35 g cm^{-3}	Steel	Lead
Gold-198	0.41	135	- -	11
Iridium-192	0.13-1.06	147	43	20
Caesium-137	0.66	157	53	21
Cobalt-60	1.17, 1.33	206	69	40
Radium	0.047-2.4	234	74	55

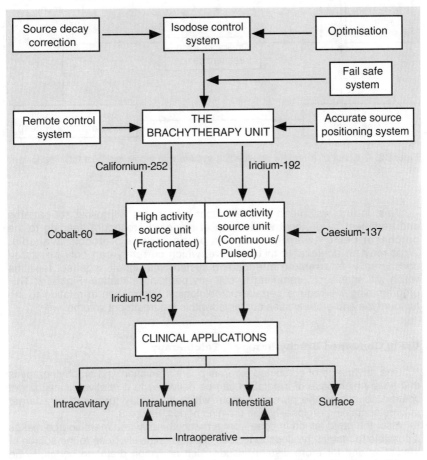

Figure 1. Schematic diagram illustrating current remote afterloading brachytherapy technology.

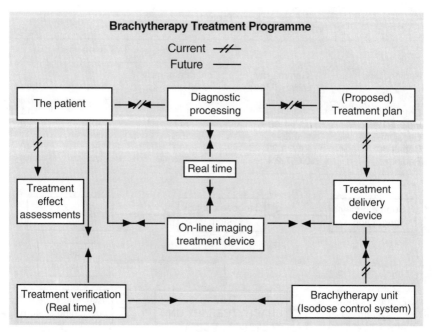

Figure 2. Concept of a remote afterloading system with inbuilt isoeffect facilities for any situation.

This, in turn, will mean that treatment procedures will follow set patterns and treatment by protocol will be part of standard procedure, leading to the purchaser being aware of the costs of the various protocols available. What may be achievable in the future, which currently can only be stated conceptually, is a remote afterloading system with inbuilt isoeffect facilities which will enable programming to suit any particular situation, Figure 2. This programming will require certain radiobiological information in relation to the tumour type and other tissues contained within the treatment volume.

Use of Combined Brachytherapy & Teletherapy

One advantage of combined external beam irradiation and brachytherapy is that a very high dose of irradiation can be delivered to a relatively small target volume containing the primary tumour which itself may form part of a larger volume containing regional lymph draining nodes, Figure 3.

Also, the rapid fall-off in dose from a brachytherapy treatment source makes it possible to restrict the dose to tissues situated relatively close to the source of irradiation and for more distant tissues such as lymph drainage nodes, to be irradiated in a homogeneous manner by external beam irradiation.

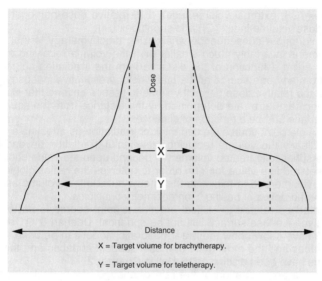

Distance

X = Target volume for brachytherapy.

Y = Target volume for teletherapy.

Figure 3. Schematic diagram illustrating target volume for brachytherapy and teletherapy.

This in turn leads to a lower risk of late reacting tissue damage to normal tissue structures within the much larger target volume covered by external beam irradiation. These existing therapeutic advantages will be further enhanced by planning treatment to be contained within radiobiological rather than within isodose envelopes. To make this possible will require additional knowledge and a better understanding of the dose volume limitations for a particular tissue effect within an irradiated volume. To a certain extent this type of information is already available for some tissues but more tissue specific data is required.

Dose-Volume Histograms

The concept and related understanding of dose-volume histograms is going to be increasingly important in order to determine the order of the dose limit required to maximise acute radiobiological effects to a specified tumour tissue within specified isodose surfaces and, in turn, minimise late reacting normal tissue effects both inside and outside a specified isodose surface.

The application of dose-volume histograms will bring into focus the need to define a critical effective unit volume for an irradiated tissue relative to the total irradiated volume of the same tissue, that is, a volume ratio. The critical volume may be defined as that volume which under irradiated conditions, such a 'hot spot' cannot be exceeded without affecting the eventual outcome, for example, morbid effects: or alternatively a 'cold spot' affecting the chance of 'cure'. This will then put meaningful limits on to 'cold or hot' spots in terms of limiting or critical volumes.

Meertens et al in **Chapter 31** discuss these problems and define dosimetric parameters for the description of the quality of a brachytherapy application: coverage index (CI), external volume index (EI), relative dose homogeneity index (HI), overdose voluime index (OI) and sum index (SI).

One unfortunate consequence when using brachytherapy is that the treatment volume is invariably much smaller than the volume receiving meaningful irradiation, being a function of the distance from the irradiation source. As the distance from any one source and a meaningful prescriptive isodose surface is increased, the relative dose per unit volume to tissues beyond that isodose surface will decrease at a rate determined by the distance from the source to that isodose surface and be a function of distance.

For a single point source we can think of irradiation as affecting a volume of $(4/3)\pi.r^3$. Clearly the volume receiving meaningful irradiation beyond the contour of the spherically treated volume will depend upon the value chosen for 'r'. What is required is a value for 'r' in order to optimise the radiobiological effects within that volume and to minimise the effects outside that volume as opposed to the current practice of basing 'r' on dosimetry principles.

For distances related to clinical practice a point source is not practicable and any given isodose surface will not be spherical. Deehan & O'Donaghue in **Chapter 3** have shown how the linear-quadratic model can be used to plot isoeffect surfaces and the movement of these isoeffect surfaces and the possible implications have been discussed by Hall in **Chapter 2**.

Figure 4 is an illustration of the rate of change of isoeffect with distance, which I produced several years ago when comparing the rate of fall-off in biological effect with distance from a Cathetron HDR cobalt-60 source and from an LDR radium source. I draw attention to the different relationships in order to illustrate the potential advantages and disadvantages. These concepts will further add to complexities of radiobiological optimisation not only in terms of acute reacting tissues but also of late reacting tissues.

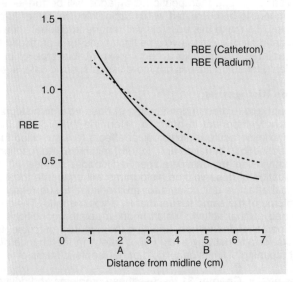

Figure 4. Radiobiological effectiveness with Cathetron HDR irradiation and with radium LDR irradiation.

A method of reducing the inverse square law effect would be to use a radionuclide with a restricted absorption range at which distance complete absorption is achieved. This raises the problem of finding a suitable nuclide, but clearly, particulate irradiation should be more appropiate than photon irradiation. Unfortunately, particulate irradiation and rapid absorption within an appropriate short distance brings with it dose collative problems when using more than one source of irradiation. The current issue is, therefore, one of source energies and idealising implant geometry.

Dose Rate

The quantities of radium used for conventional brachytherapy was, for many years dependent upon the strength of an individual source coupled with the size of a source which could be safely handled by manual means. While the source size for a given strength was dependent on the specific activity of the nuclide, the strength of the source used determined the dose rate at which treatment was delivered. While dose rate is absolute in terms of cGy/minute, the terms low, medium or high dose rate (LDR,MDR,HDR) are, however, relative terms: see **Chapter 38** by Battermann.

Table 2
Advantages of HDR compared with LDR radium for gynaecological brachytherapy.

The **patient advantages** include the following.
(1) Not being confined to bed for hours or days during irradiation with the consequent indignity of bed pans etc.
(2) No indwelling catheters or vaginal packing.
(3) Not being labelled "radiation risk zone" to relatives, visitors and staff.
(4) Day case treatments are possible.

A **possible disadvantage** is having several anaesthetics.

The **clinical advantages** include the following.
(1) Anatomical relationships not altering during treatment.
(2) The position of the source applicators is easily maintained during treatment.
(3) Patient preparation for treatment is simple.
(4) No specialised nursing.
(5) A relatively high throughput of patients on each machine.

The **physical advantages** include the following.
(1) Short treatment times.
(2) Similar irradiation procedures to external beam irradiation.
(3) Optimisation of dose distribution being relatively straightforward.

LDR therapy by convention ranges from about 10 cGy/hour to 100 cGy/hour and these are the rates that have been used since the early years of the 20th century. The advent of afterloading machines has allowed experimentation with rates other than 10-100 cGy/hour. In particular, efforts have been made to reduce treatment times which in turn reduces the imposition on patients. One example introduced in the 1950s was to increase dose rates with consequent reduction in treatment times compared to that for radium treatment times. This was particularly relevant for gynaecological brachytherapy where treatment was reduced to about 20 hours. In the 1960s treatment times were reduced to only a few minutes with further patient advantages, Table 2.

However, radiobiological differences in the effectiveness were quickly identi-fied and due to the increase in source activity it was found that a small amount of radium applied for a long time did not equate with a large amount of radium applied for a short time. That is, the product of source strength and time (mil-ligram-hours) did not serve a useful purpose in terms of describing radiobiologi-cal effects.

Fowler has claimed that dose rate of 50 cGy/hour is radiobiologically similar to conventional 2 Gy fractions delivered by external irradiation to provide an optimum balance between early and late tumour damage. Also, Dale has shown that the total dose delivered using HDR treatment should be reduced for a given number of fractions in order to maintain an effect which is equivalent to LDR for a particular α/β ratio.

As an example, for an α/β ratio of 10 Gy the HDR regime equivalent to an LDR regime delivering 40 Gy in 48 hours is 27.9 Gy given in three fractions. However, for late reacting tissues (α/β = 3.0 Gy) the dose required would need to be 23.7 Gy. The situation in terms of radiobiological effects is clearly extremely complicated and the future is likely to see the generation of a number of mathematical models supported by an increasing 'bank' of clinically produced radiobiological data. These are but an indication of what I see as some of the physical/technological/radiobiological problems for the future.

Oxygen Effect

No radiobiological discussion seems complete without consideration of the radiobiological situation under differing oxic conditions. A case for using contin-uous LDR therapy for overcoming the effects of hypoxia have been expressed on many occasions. This has been claimed as one of the major advantages of LDR irradiation. Alternatively, fractionated therapy can be shown to produce more radiation damage to oxygenated tumour cells and depending upon biolog-ical factors for tumour and surrounding normal tissues can produce a differen-tially therapeutic advantage in terms of tumour cell damage. The possibilities of combining HDR fractionated therapy concomitantly with LDR continuous irradia-tion needs to be considered. An alternative to using combined LDR and HDR would be to replace the LDR treatment with continuous infusion of a cytotoxic drug, but still retain the HDR.

The combination of brachytherapy with hyperthermia is already being used in clinical practice for treating some types of tumour. These studies are continu-ing and while it may be argued that if the results of such combined therapies had been of major impact, such treatment would now be firmly established, it is still possible that there may be some advantages yet to be identified for treating certain types of tumours.

Intraoperative Therapy

One major problem following surgical excision of a primary tumour is local recurrence. A considerable amount of effort is given to providing post-operative radiotherapy as a form of supportive or adjuvant treatment. In general, external beam irradiation is used and with it are the problems of restricting treatment to an ill defined target volume.

Intraoperative placing of interstitial catheters (see **Chapter 39** by Nori) to allow treatment to be delivered specifically to the region of the tumour bed has already much to commend it. However this form of therapy has a major problem of practicability. One aspect of this overall problem is the removal of the interstitial catheters following treatment. Where this is not practical, the development of biologically inert materials will be important. An alternative approach will be to produce biodegradable materials which can be used for the manufacture of catheter material.

Conclusion

Progress may often start with an idea which is then dependent upon technical and scientific developments before it can be put into practice. Brachytherapy is a good example of a radiotherapy technique which started with the introduction of radium into hospital practice, only to be overtaken by external beam developments, but it has more recently undergone a renaissance and looks set to continue its impact on cancer therapy, either alone or in combination with other modalities, well into the 21st. century.

Author Index

Subject Index

A

C

E

H

I

N

Nasal vestibule,cancer
    Complications 108
    Survival & local control rates 108
    Treatment techniques 107
Nasopharynx,cancer
    Applicator,silicone,Rotterdam 126
    Complications 115,128,129
    Epidemiology 122
    External beam treatment 122
    Moulded applicator,Paris System 107
    in Rottterdam,microSelectron-HDR 121-131
    Survival & local control rates 115,122-131
    Treatment technique 115
Neutron therapy,prostate,cancer 221
NPS (Nucletron Planning System)
    Bladder,cancer 234
    see Optimisation
    Pulsed dose rate (PDR) brachytherapy optimisation 250-252
    Stepping source dosimetry as an extension of the Paris System 319-330
    Three-dimensional planning,optimisation 311
NSD model, radiobiology 21,34

O

Oesophagus,cancer
    Chemotherapy 207,214
    Clinical staging 201
    Clinical trials 208,210,213
    External beam radiotherapy 201
    HDR brachytherapy
        Clinical trial,external beam radiotherapy & HDR brachytherapy 205
        Experience in P.R. China 204
        with External beam radiotherapy 203
        microSelectron-HDR 205
        as Only method of treatment 203
    Incidence,China 200

P

Q

R

S

T

U

Units of radiation measurement
Curie 1
Gamma-röntgen 1
Milicuries destroyed 1
Milligram-hours 1,7
Röntgen 1
Strength/intensity/activity 1
Threshold erythema dose 1
Uterus,*see* Endometrium

V

Volume-dose histograms,*see* Dose-volume histograms

W

Well chambers,re-entrant 285,287
Wertheim hysterectomy 68,70

Y

Ytterbium-169
Half-life,photon energy & TVL 379
Isodose curves,seed 381
IUdR sensitisation 379
Photon energy spectrum 380